KU-578-469

+4

H208

Reference, truth and reality

University of
BRISTOL
Department of Philosophy
9 Woodland Road, Bristol BS8 1TB

Reference, truth and reality

Essays on the philosophy of language

Edited by **Mark Platts**

Routledge & Kegan Paul

London, Boston and Henley

First published in 1980
by Routledge & Kegan Paul Ltd
39 Store Street, London WC1E 7DD,
Broadway House, Newtown Road,
Henley-on-Thames, Oxon RG9 1EN and
9 Park Street, Boston, Mass. 02108, USA

Set in IBM Press Roman by
Hope Services, Abingdon
and printed in Great Britain by
Redwood Burn Ltd, Trowbridge & Esher

© *Routledge & Kegan Paul 1980*
No part of this book may be reproduced in
any form without permission from the
publisher, except for the quotation of brief
passages in criticism

British Library Cataloguing in Publication Data

Reference, truth and reality.
  1. Languages – Philosophy
  I. Title II. Platts, Mark
  401   *P106*   *79-42859*

  ISBN 0 7100 0405 2
  ISBN 0 7100 0406 0 Pbk

Contents

Contents

Notes on contributors

Tyler Burge is a member of the Department of Philosophy in the University of California at Los Angeles.

Donald Davidson is a member of the Department of Philosophy in the University of Chicago.

Gareth Evans is Wilde Reader in Mental Philosophy in the University of Oxford.

Hartry Field is a member of the School of Philosophy in the University of Southern California.

John McDowell is a Fellow of University College, Oxford.

Colin McGinn is a member of the Department of Philosophy in University College, London.

Christopher Peacocke is a Fellow of New College, Oxford.

Mark Platts is a member of the Department of Philosophy in Birkbeck College, London.

Barry Taylor is a member of the Department of Philosophy in the University of Melbourne.

David Wiggins is Professor of Philosophy at Bedford College, London.

1 Introduction

Mark Platts

That the meaning of a sentence can be given by stating its truth-conditions is not a novel doctrine; as an explicitly held doctrine, it is at least as old as the work of Frege. Of late, however, it has been an object of renewed interest among philosophers of language and logic. An evident stimulus to this interest has been the work of Donald Davidson. Davidson's main contributions to date have been, schematically, of three kinds: to have emphasized the import for the understanding of the truth-conditions doctrine of Tarski's seminal work upon the concept of truth in formalized languages; to have initiated exploration of the ways in which Tarski's approach might be adapted to figure in the *empirical* construction of theories of meaning for natural languages; and to have put forward specific truth-theoretic proposals for handling various natural language constructions of logical, or more general philosophical, importance.

There has also been another, more recently influential, source of interest in the truth-theoretic conception of meaning, stemming primarily from the work of Michael Dummett. This focuses upon the *metaphysical* content which apparently is built into Davidson's account (as well as others' accounts) of the truth-conditions theory of meaning, a content reasonably labelled *realistic*. Specifically, Dummett has raised a worry as to whether the picture of the relation between language and the world apparently involved in the truth-theoretic account of meaning can mesh adequately with speakers' understanding, *manifestable* understanding, of their language.

This volume is a collection of papers, most published here for the first time, directed to issues raised by (though not only statable in terms of) the realistic truth-theoretic conception of meaning. They might be called working papers, since few, if any, of the contributors would think of themselves as having settled the issues they discuss; the hope, rather, is to have advanced understanding of the forms of the issues and of their possible solutions, to have settled a little of the blinding dust that has come to surround them. This introduction is no more than a sketch of one framework in which the contributions might be seen — although not necessarily the framework in which the contributors themselves would wish their efforts to be seen.

1

Mark Platts

The point and form of a theory of meaning

What is the aim of a theory of meaning? And what form, if any, does that aim either impose upon or invite for such a theory?

A theory of meaning for a language should be able to tell us the meanings of the words and sentences which comprise that language. The appearance of anodyne progress here is perhaps misleading since the notion of *the meaning* of a word or sentence is in part given content by the idea that it is the subject matter of a theory *of* meaning, and the proper conception of this is what we are trying to crystallize.

Still, resisting immediate immersion in this circle, we might begin by taking over from Frege the thought that it is the sentence, not the word, that is the primary unit of linguistic meaning; for it is the sentence, not the word, that can be used to perform complete linguistic actions, and it is the linguistic actions of speakers of a given language which constitute our starting-point in the construction of a theory of meaning for that language. The meaning of a word is then seen simply as its systematic contribution to the meanings of sentences in which it can figure.

That rationale for treating the sentence as primary, however, serves to remind that talk of the meanings of linguistic expressions is a theoretical abstraction from the data of linguistic usage. The character of a theory of meaning for a language, and so the specific account to be given of the notion of the meaning of some expression in that language, is constrained by the role of that theory in understanding the linguistic behaviour of speakers of that language. (This point about the inevitably theoretical character of any worthwhile analysis of the notion of meaning is distinct from that made two paragraphs back about the theoretical character of that notion itself.) So we are naturally led to ask: what is involved in understanding linguistic behaviour?

Suppose a native speaker of some alien tongue emits a string of noises; and suppose further — the point at which relevant theory first enters — that we take that native to be performing some intentional linguistic action. What we have to do is to make sense of that action as part of making sense of that speaker; and what that involves is redescribing that action, if possible, in such a way as to make that action, that performance, intelligible to ourselves in view of all we know and believe about the speaker.

Such a redescription will issue from an overall theory of linguistic behaviour, one component of which — the *theory of force* for the linguistic community under study — will have *at least* the following structure. There will be a *speech-act* component which (tentatively) identifies the mode of utterance — asserting, commanding, questioning, etc. There will be a *syntactic* component which serves to identify (tentatively) the

2

sentences uttered and their grammatical moods — indicative, imperative, interrogative, etc. And there will be what we might call a *monistic transformational* component, which pairs the sentence uttered, whatever its mood, with some sentence of the language under study of some one mood, that mood being antecedently fixed for all sentences that could be uttered. If the sentence uttered by the native is of this antecedently fixed mood, this transformational component will presumably operate as an identity function.

The idea behind this third, monistic transformational, component of the theory of force is this. Within the theory of meaning (which has yet to enter the scene but which will soon do so) there must be, in Dummett's terminology, some one key concept which has application in the derivation of the meaning of each and every sentence in the language — the doctrine of semantic monism. For only in this way will uniform word-definitions be possible. Any word can occur in any grammatical type of sentence — indicative, imperative, etc.; the meaning of a word is its systematic contribution to the meanings of sentences in which it can figure; but if one semantic concept figured in the derivations of the meanings of, say, indicative sentences while another, distinct, concept figured in the derivations of the meanings of, say, imperative sentences, then every word would require at least two dictionary entries — one to account for its contribution to the meanings of those indicative sentences in which it can figure, another to account for its, *ex hypothesi*, different (because different *kind of*) contribution to the meanings of those imperative sentences in which it can figure. But uniform word meanings can be given, so there must be one key concept which figures in the derivation of the meaning of any sentence, whatever its mood, the thesis of semantic monism. The rationale behind the third component of the theory of force, the monistic transformational component, is that it clears the ground for the application of the key concept within the theory of meaning. (Which is not yet to argue that this is the only way in which the need for semantic monism can be accommodated.)

Nearly all theories of meaning have concentrated upon the indicative mood (and the assertoric mode), suggesting that that should be the antecedently fixed mood of the output of the monistic transformational component. A minimal rationale for this is found by considering, first, the syntactic and semantic completeness of the indicative as compared with the imperative (e.g. the lack of *tense* in the imperative mood) and, second, the communicative completeness of the indicative as compared with the interrogative (e.g. the oddity of a language with resources primarily suited only to the asking of questions with none primarily suited to answering them[1]). Many philosophers have entertained stronger theses about the primacy of either the indicative mood or the assertoric mode. No case for such a thesis has yet been made good with clear sense attached to the notion of primacy in view of the seemingly obvious

3

Mark Platts

possibility that the only linguistic actions performed within a given
linguistic community might be, say, commands or might be performed
using only imperative sentences. (A quite distinct, and far more plausible, primacy thesis is that of belief over, say, desires and uncertainties.)
Still, perhaps tradition and the minimal rationale together give us
sufficient reason for expecting the indicative mood to be the output
of the monistic transformational component of the theory of force.

The theory of meaning or sense now enters the picture.[2] (I do *not*
mean to suggest that we could have all the pre-theory-of-meaning elements *fixed* before we go on to construct a theory of meaning; the
ordered separation of the components of the theory of linguistic behaviour in this exposition does not reflect any clear epistemological ordering.) The native speaker's emission of noise, tentatively identified as an
intentional linguistic action, has also now been tentatively identified by
the speech-act component of the theory of force as an utterance in a
specific mode; the mood (or moods) of the sentence (or sentences)
uttered has (or have) been tentatively identified by the syntactic component of the theory of force; and the monistic transformational
component of that theory has, tentatively, been made to yield for each
sentence of the native language uttered a paired sentence of that same
language in the indicative mood. This yield is the input to the theory of
meaning, a theory whose output is for each input sentence a sentence
of our own language which interprets, purports to give the meaning of,
that input sentence.

The end result of applying such an overall theory of linguistic behaviour, the combined theories of force and meaning, is a redescription of
the original performance by the native speaker; we can move from a
description of the form 'He uttered the noises . . .' to one like, say, 'He
asserted that it was raining', 'He ordered us to make it true that the
door is shut', and so on.

Thus the role of the theory of meaning within a theory of linguistic
behaviour is given. But nothing has yet been said about when that overall theory is a *good* theory; so nothing has yet been said about when the
component theory of meaning is acceptable. To fill this lacuna we now
have to introduce the connection — or, better, the diverse and complex
connections — between the redescriptions of linguistic actions delivered
by the theory of linguistic behaviour and the propositional attitudes
ascribed to speakers. Centrally, on the basis of someone's asserting that
p we can generally take it that he believes that p and that he intended
to say that p; on the basis of someone's commanding that q we can
generally take it that he desires that q and that he intended to order
that q; and so on. (This is, of course, far too simple a picture of the
connections: irony, sarcasm, deceit, insincerity, metaphor and conversational implicatures all complicate the picture, as do the ways in which
propositional attitude ascriptions themselves connect — for example,

4

the ways in which belief-ascriptions are tacit in most, if not all, desire-ascriptions. This is one area desperately in need of detailed, non-simplistic exploration.)

Such propositional attitude-ascriptions, together with the view that the native has then and there expressed such and such an attitude, can be plausible or implausible in countless ways in the light of all else we believe about the speaker. But the general point is simply stated: it can be no part of understanding a speaker's linguistic actions, and so no part of understanding the speaker himself, to attribute to that speaker propositional attitudes which it is unintelligible that he should have, or to attribute to him expressions of propositional attitudes which it is unintelligible that he should have issued — unintelligible, that is, in the light of all we believe about the speaker's circumstances.

The aim thus becomes that of finding a theory of linguistic behaviour which, in the light of all we believe about the speaker, issues, for each of his linguistic actions, in plausible propositional attitude-ascriptions to him, and which makes his having expressed those attitudes in his actions in the contexts in which those actions were in fact performed intelligible. To this end, any part of the theory of linguistic behaviour can be modified, even, if need be, back to the point of denying (or asserting) that some emission of noise by him was an intentional linguistic action. A theory of meaning for a language is thus seen to be an acceptable theory of meaning only if, in interaction with the other components of the theory of linguistic behaviour, it issues in plausible redescriptions of all of the linguistic actions performed by speakers of that language — plausible in view of the propositional attitudes consequently ascribed and of the propositional attitude expressions consequently attributed.[3]

The aim and role of the theory of meaning is thus described; but as regards the form of such a theory little progress has apparently been made. The output of the theory of meaning will be a potential interpretation in our language of each indicative sentence of the language under study. Two further lines of thought suggest a more detailed picture. One is this: the indicative sentences of any natural language being potentially infinite in number, but the sentence components (words and 'unstructured' phrases) being finite in number, our theory of meaning should yield an interpretation for each indicative sentence in the language under study via assignment of appropriate semantic properties to the finite stock of sentential components and modes of structural combination. A second, independent thought with much the same formal conclusion is this: the capacity of finite native speakers to understand a potential infinity of novel utterances — utterances of sentences that they have never before heard uttered — will be comprehensible only if an account of what it is they understand reveals it as deriving from some finite stock of meaning-determining rules and axioms. (Note that this is distinct from claiming that their capacity is comprehensible only if the account of how it is that they understand it reveals it as deriving from some finite stock of meaning-determining rules and axioms, and that that is distinct again from the claim that their capacity is comprehensible only if the account of how it is that they understand it reveals them as deriving it from some finite stock of meaning-determining rules and axioms. The threat of pseudo-explanation is ever present here.)

The more detailed formal picture of the theory of meaning so suggested is this. Suppose, in accordance with semantic monism, that there is some key concept ϕ such that the meaning of any indicative sentence in the language under study is given by stating, in our language, its ϕ-conditions. Then what is required is that possession of ϕ-conditions by sentences is seen to be derivable from the possession of ϕ-bearing properties by their parts together with the ϕ-import of the modes of structural combination of those parts. Thus we shall have an assignment within a finite set of axioms of ϕ-bearing properties to each of the primitive sentence components in the language, together with a finite set of rules giving the ϕ-import of each of the possible modes of structural combination in the language. These axioms and rules should be such as logically to yield a statement of the ϕ-conditions for any indicative sentence in the language under study. (This will almost certainly require that in the statement of the ϕ-conditions of sentences, schematically of the form '... is ϕ if, and only if, ...', the 'if, and only if' is read as creating an extensional context.[4])

What, then, should ϕ be? At this point we might well be tempted by a simple-seeming answer. The deliverances of our theory of meaning will be of the form

(M) s is ϕ if, and only if, p

where s is replaced by a structural description of an indicative sentence of the language under study and p by a sentence of our language which, if the theory of meaning is indeed a *good* theory of meaning (in the sense just explained), gives the meaning of s, interprets it. The thought now is that an immediately acceptable candidate for *is ϕ* will be *is true*; for if such an M-sentence is true, it will remain true if for *is ϕ* we substitute *is true*.

Entertaining this thought, we shall be struck by the parallels between the picture of the form of a theory of meaning to which we have just been led and Tarski's finitely axiomatized formal account of the definition of a truth-predicate for a formalized language. The conclusion will then be that a characterization of a truth-predicate in the style of Tarski is, in virtue of its form, fitted to be a theory of meaning. But whereas Tarski constrained such a characterization by the condition of translation, that p be a translation of s, we aim to obtain that condition as yielded by adopting the distinct condition that the Tarski-form theory be an acceptable theory of meaning by being part of a good overall theory of linguistic behaviour — one that enables us to make sense of the users of the language employed in the behaviour under scrutiny.

Understanding and reality

According to P. F. Strawson, to hold that the meaning of a sentence can be given by stating its truth-conditions is to hold true 'a generally harmless and salutary thing'.[5] Even if freed of condescension, this remark is importantly not beyond dispute.

The notion of truth entered the view of understanding language use just sketched rather late in the day. We had come to the thought that the deliverances of the theory of meaning should be of the form of

(M) s is ϕ if, and only if, p.

The tempting additional thought then encountered was this: if such an M-sentence is true, then it will remain true if we substitute *is true* for *is ϕ*. Hence the final connection of meaning with truth-conditions: a characterization of a truth-predicate for a language is fitted to be a theory of meaning for that language.

But, really, that connection is not so readily forged. It is important to be clear about the exact points at which and exact ways in which the argument for their putative connection becomes problematic.

One thought might be this: all we are entitled to conclude from the argument given is that M-sentences will remain true under the substitution of *is true* for *is ϕ*; from that, however, it does not immediately follow that they will still give the meanings of the sentences designated on their left-hand sides (LHSs). Of course, given the antecedent stipulations designed to ensure that the M-sentences are yielded by a *good* theory of meaning, the sentence used on the right-hand side (RHS) of an M-sentence will still, after the substitution of *is true* for *is ϕ*, interpret the sentence designated on the LHS; but it does not obviously follow that after such a substitution the M-sentence will, as it were, give the meaning of the designated sentence *as* the meaning of that sentence. Whether that is so or not will depend upon the capacity of M-sentences after substitution to meet any further controls there might be upon the notion of meaning.

This line of thought is importantly mistaken; seeing the mistake also brings important problems for a realistic truth-conditions semantics to light. The mistake is a critical misconception of the powers of the deliverances of a theory of meaning of the general form described — with or without the substitution of *is true* for *is ϕ*. If, as previously suggested, the 'if, and only if' in M-sentences is extensional, then it will not be by virtue of what M-sentences say — whatever ϕ is — that we know that their RHSs do indeed interpret the sentences designated on their LHSs, can indeed be used to redescribe linguistic actions performed by the use of the sentences there designated; for an M-sentence of which this is true will be no truer than one derived from it by substituting another sentence with the same truth-value for that used on the RHS. Such force as there is in the line of thought under examination about the deliverances of the theory of meaning not giving the meaning *as* the meaning does not come to bear by virtue of the move from *is ϕ* to *is true*; it arises earlier, already applying as soon as we move to the idea that the filling between the designated and interpreting sentence is of the form '. . . is ϕ if, and only if, . . .'.[6]

The general question thus raised is this: what more must someone know who knows the truth stated by an M-sentence (whatever ϕ is to be) for him to know that that sentence gives the meaning of the sentence designated on its LHS? Whatever answer we give to that question — perhaps in terms of additional knowledge that the M-sentence is a logical consequence of a theory of sense adequate by the preceding standards — we shall then have to consider another question: does the substitution of *is true* for *is ϕ* make that answer problematic?

Those questions merit detailed examination;[7] but there is a more general question, which has those questions as more specific components, that leads to a distinct substantial issue. Are there any further controls upon the notion of meaning which make employment of '. . . is true if, and only if, . . .' as the filling between designated sentence and interpreting sentence unacceptable?

One obvious area to be explored is the territory common to the notions of meaning and understanding. This territory is at least as difficult to map as the notion of understanding is to grasp. One feature of it will not much delay us: this is that it is a necessary condition of the acceptability of an overall theory of linguistic behaviour, and so of the acceptability of its components including the theory of meaning, that explicit propositional knowledge of that overall theory would equip one to be a competent user of the language concerned, would suffice for understanding it. This feature is neither unimportant nor unproblematic, raising as it does the questions touched upon two paragraphs back; but it need not now delay us since it concerns a sufficiency condition which it is doubtful, to say the least, that anyone who now speaks a natural language actually meets.

More realistically pressing is the matter of quite how an ordinary speaker's competence, his understanding of his language, should be seen to connect with the theory of meaning;[8] if we can become clear on that, we shall then be able to see whether this connection would be distorted, or broken, by the proposed use of '. . . is true if, and only if, . . .' in the deliverances of the theory of meaning.

Any discussion of this issue must be controlled by two considerations. The first of these, a brute empirical fact, is the unreflective character of natural language use. People simply say things without, in general, working out what it is they are to say and how it is to be said; others, and they themselves, just understand what was said without, in general, working out what has been said and how it was said. Ordinary linguistic competence is shown by appropriate (unreflectively appropriate) verbal behaviour and by appropriate (unreflectively appropriate) response, verbal or non-verbal, to the behaviour of others. The other controlling consideration is a philosophical *desideratum*: any propositional knowledge attributed to speakers must be manifestable by them if that attribution is to have defensible content.

The overwhelming bulk of natural linguistic activity involves the use of complete sentences. Given the two controlling considerations just adduced, this suggests that attribution to native speakers of propositional knowledge of any of the axioms of the theory of meaning specifying the meanings of sub-sentential components or of propositional knowledge of any of the rules of that theory determining the semantic import of different modes of combination of sub-sentential components will be problematic at best.[9] Such attribution is in obvious enough danger either of falsifying the unreflective nature of language use or of being an attribution without content. Still, at the sentential level, at the level of the M-sentences delivered by the theory of meaning, the prospects seem brighter. It is part of a speaker's competence that he can understand the utterances of others speaking the same language; an explicit manifestation of that competence is his ability to report others' sayings, to say things like 'He said that it was raining', 'He asserted that Britain is a one-party state', and so on. Such manifestations of understanding seem to be manifestations of knowledge of the literal meaning of what was said; they might thus also be taken as manifestations of knowledge of the M-sentences delivered by the theory of meaning. So, for example, when the theory of meaning works with *is true* in the place schematically occupied by *is φ* in M-sentences, we might take such successful reports of sayings as manifestations of the knowledge that the sentence uttered is true if, and only if, it was raining, or whatever. And so we can hold, apparently in consistency with our two controlling considerations, that native speakers at least have propositional knowledge of the M-sentences of the theory of meaning.

This argument is not unproblematic, nor does it have only unproblematic consequences. One worry arises from the fact that, in general, reports of others' sayings aim at capturing the gist of what was said, its import, not its literal meaning; it might not seem obvious that such gist-reporting capacities presuppose, and can therefore count as manifestations of, knowledge of the literal meanings of the sentences uttered. Knowledge of speech is not knowledge of language. Thus we might be led back to the thought that the notion of sentence meaning itself is a theoretical one. (Important in this context is the remarkably large number of successful speech-acts — successful in getting over what the speaker is trying to say — that involve ungrammatical and incomplete sentences.) Against this, it might be thought that the capacity to report the gist of an indefinite number of utterances would be mysterious unless it was based upon a capacity to hear them as having their literal meanings, where those literal meanings are systematically determined by repeatable meanings of sentence-parts and of their modes of structural combination. I am unclear whether this rejoinder is an invitation to pseudo-explanation or not. I am also unclear whether acceptance of this invitation will commit us to accepting a further invitation to attribute knowledge of the axioms and rules of the theory of meaning to competent speakers. And I am also unclear quite how to forge the move from knowledge of the literal meanings of sentences uttered, assuming such there to be, to knowledge of the deliverances of the theory of meaning, the M-sentences. Certainly, if *is* ϕ in those deliverances were a highly theoretical notion, the move would be problematic.

Let us pass over those anxieties for the moment, tentatively accepting that speakers do have propositional knowledge of the M-sentences of the theory of meaning for their language. With this claim about native speakers' understanding before us, we can return to the question of whether employment of '. . . is true if, and only if, . . .' as the filling in the deliverances of the theory of meaning is problematic.

Employing that construction, the deliverances of the theory of meaning will be of the form

(T) s is true if, and only if, p.

And relying upon the preceding argument, we shall attribute propositional knowledge of such T-sentences to ordinary speakers of the language under examination. But this carries consequences that threaten Strawson's 'generally harmless and salutary thing to say'.

Consider a well-known example of Dummett's, 'A city will never be built here'. This is a sentence of English which competent English-speakers understand, know the meaning of; it is also a complete indicative sentence of English utterances of which can be reported by those who understand English. A truth-conditions theorist of English will thus attribute to English-speakers propositional knowledge of a T-sentence along *something* like the following lines:

(T_n) 'A city will never be built here' is true if, and only if, a city will never be built here.[10]

We attribute, then, propositional knowledge of (T_n) to competent English-speakers. But the truth-conditions there given, knowledge of which is attributed to the competent English-speaker in virtue of his understanding of the sentence designated in (T_n), are such that they could not, even in principle, be recognized by any speaker as obtaining.[11] Roughly, anyone who claimed to have recognized the obtaining of this sentence's truth-conditions would thereby merely show that he did not understand that sentence. So a person's knowledge of these truth-conditions could not be manifested by his recognizing their obtaining together with his exhibition of that recognition. How, then, could that knowledge be made manifest?

Our original thought suggests this answer: by the reporting of uses of that sentence, by saying things like 'He said that a city will never be built here'. But now we might wonder whether *that*, just saying that, can manifest knowledge of the truth-conditions of the sentence; and if this wonder grows to a doubt, we shall be led to think that any knowledge of the theory of meaning for a language attributed to speakers of the language must, to have defensible content, be manifestable in some way other than by 'successful' reporting. But there seems to be no other way for such recognition-transcendent sentences.

There is a crucial point here. The only reason so far adduced for holding that speakers do know the T-sentences of the theory of meaning for their language is their capacity to report others' sayings; we could hardly accept that that is reason for such attribution, and then go on to deny that that capacity does manifest that knowledge. The same will be true for any other evidential reason for attributing such knowledge to speakers. The main anti-realist thought, I take it, is not that we have evidence that speakers know the deliverances of the theory of meaning for such recognition-transcendent sentences, but that it is essential to the point of such a theory of meaning that they know its deliverances. Here, the whole conception of those deliverances as governing rules that ground ordinary linguistic behaviour, rather than as specifications that serve (with other things) to describe that behaviour, becomes central. But however erroneous the anti-realist conception of the deliverances of the theory of meaning may be, realists should not be too hasty in cheerily concluding that speakers simply do not (always? ever?) have propositional knowledge of the deliverances of the theory of meaning: for, first, the entitlement of that theory to be considered still a theory of meaning would then become unclear, and, second, the point of the sufficiency condition — that the theory of linguistic behaviour be such that explicit propositional knowledge of it would ensure understanding — would then become utterly opaque. What is the point of a sufficiency condition which it is in principle impossible for *us* to fulfil? What a theory of 'meaning' would then be doing is utterly mysterious.

Let us be quite clear upon the issues in this argument. We assume, first, the impossibility of someone's manifesting his knowledge of (T_n) by his recognizing (and by his expressing his recognizing) the obtaining

of the truth-conditions there specified. We assume, second, that successful reporting of utterances of 'A city will never be built here' is inadequate as manifestation of knowledge of (T_n). We take it, third, that
there is no other way available to speakers of manifesting that knowledge. Fourth, we assume that speakers do indeed understand the sentence 'A city will never be built here'. And, finally, we have accepted
the claim that a competent speaker's understanding of his language is in
part propositional knowledge of the deliverances of the theory of meaning — not, now, on evidential grounds but because of the aim or point
of a theory of meaning. Given all that, we shall be led to reject the
employment of '. . . is true if, and only if, . . .' as the filling in the
deliverances of the theory of meaning, at pain of being led to making
knowledge attributions that lack defensible content.

Realism in truth-conditional semantics is the doctrine that the truth-
conditions of sentences, conditions which determine their meanings, can
transcend speakers' capacities to recognize those conditions as obtaining. What we have before us is a comprehensive argument against such a
realism. There are at least as many ways of defending realism against
that argument as there are premises in that argument which are not
required by realism and which can reasonably be questioned; and there
are at least as many forms of anti-realism prompted by that argument as
there are premises in that argument which are required by realism and
which can reasonably be denied.

Rather than pursue those issues here, I shall close this discussion of
realism in semantics by briefly sketching the final realist position. It is
useful, I think, to keep in mind the *comprehensive* character of the
anti-realist argument just presented. Since any term can occur in a
recognition-transcendent sentence, the argument earlier sketched for
semantic monism precludes the possibility of still employing a realist
truth-conditions theory of meaning for non-transcendent sentences
while relying upon some other kind of semantics for recognition-
transcendent sentences. There are, however, more modest anti-realisms
than this, anti-realisms about particular kinds or areas of discourse —
e.g. discourses on morals, or aesthetics, or secondary qualities, or
witches. (Although such modest anti-realisms will need careful formulation if they are not to imply, in conjunction with the doctrine of
semantic monism, the more comprehensive anti-realism.) Our understanding of the varieties of debates between the realist and the anti-
realist may be improved through reflection upon these more parochial
anti-realisms.[12]

There are two basic claims involved in a realist view of a given area
of discourse, together with further encrustations of theory. The first
claim is that the area of discourse (or 'thought') concerned is descriptive or assertoric. This amounts to the claim that the proper semantic
treatment of that area of discourse will be the same as that appropriate

to certain other specifiable segments of discourse, the paradigmatically descriptive segments — *whatever that treatment is.* Here, we seem already to be committed to various logical constraints — for example, we shall avoid assenting, at the same time, to each of a pair of sentences of the forms '*p*' and '~*p*'.

That first basic claim is a claim about language. The second claim is about reality to the effect that the world is such that it is how a number of non-negative sentences in this area of discourse claim it is. Given the first, language, claim, this second, reality, claim licenses *use* of the discourse under consideration without revision in our understanding of the descriptive character of that discourse.

To these two basic claims further layers of theory may be added. One is an identification of the appropriate form of semantics for descriptive discourses as truth-theoretic semantics. The difficult question of how much comes built into this layer has already been touched upon. Another addition is a claim about the applicability of the notion of truth within that discourse to the effect that it is recognition-transcendent, the claim that there can be (or are) truths in this kind of discourse the obtaining of which it is in principle impossible for speakers to recognize. This last claim is no inevitable component in a realistic truth-conditions treatment of *every* kind of discourse; it enters only in certain problematic areas. (Which is not to say that the consequences of its there entering may not be language-wide.) Even then, it becomes problematic only granted many further assumptions about the general nature of a theory of meaning and about the specific form and point of a truth-conditions theory of meaning. Some of these assumptions have been touched upon in the preceding; all need careful articulation and examination before we can be confident that 'harmful' is not the correct tag to apply to the doctrines usually encapsulated in the slogan that the meaning of a sentence can be given by stating its truth-conditions.

Semantic structure

The general constraint so far imposed upon any truth-conditions theory of meaning, determined by its role within a comprehensive theory of linguistic behaviour, is that its deliverances, statements of the putative truth-conditions of indicative sentences of the language under study, should, in combination with a theory of force, redescribe linguistic actions performed by speakers of that language in such a way as to license plausible propositional attitude-ascriptions and plausible propositional attitude expression ascriptions to those speakers.

In general, the deliverances of the theory that we shall need will be

13

interpretations of complete indicative sentences; only in general, since it is at least arguable that treatment of utterances of some interrogative sentences within a monistic theory — notably, *who, which, what* and *how* sentences — will require that we have interpretations of open sentences. Still, the general circumstance might be thought to threaten a large-scale indeterminacy or arbitrariness in the assignment of semantic structure *within* sentences, a large-scale arbitrariness about the employment of particular axioms assigning semantic properties to sub-sentential components or of particular rules assigning semantic import to structural configurations. Doubtless a difference in the treatment accorded to any one expression will require difference in treatments accorded to others; but might there not be different ways of effecting this trade-off all compatible with the general propositional attitude constraint put down?

This threat seems heightened by the unreflective character of language use: for while we have seen argument that natural language use can manifest speakers' knowledge of the M-sentences delivered by the semantic theory of their language, it remains quite unclear what in natural language use could manifest knowledge of any of the elements of the semantic theory yielding those M-sentences. And, of course, if any of the preceding doubts about the argument for speakers' manifestable knowledge of the M-sentences yielded by the theory of meaning are taken to have much force, the threat of indeterminacy will appear all the greater.

It is difficult to know how real an issue this is. It is perhaps best approached by examination of specific proposals for the semantic treatment of various supposed sentential components and by examination of assessments of those proposals. Most of the papers in this volume present such proposals, and many of the contributors theorize to some degree about modes of assessment of their own, and comparable, proposals. I shall not attempt here to draw any general morals for this matter from their discussions. Instead, I shall sketch one line of thought that may issue in an additional constraint, or additional constraints, upon assignments of sub-sentential semantic structures.[13]

In the homophonic case — say, where we as competent English-speakers are reflecting upon the semantics of English in English — we have, as native speakers, an immense advantage: years of access to the data of usage upon which any semantic theory must be based. But a danger accompanies this advantage, a danger to which we as reflective theorists are particularly prone: that of hiding from ourselves the (unnatural) theorizing we are engaged upon, with the consequent danger of being led to attribute to native speakers (ourselves as native speakers) some intuitive knowledge of the semantics of our language over and above that knowledge, if any, which they (we) ordinarily manifest. We may thus think, for example, that we naturally have some direct insight into the axioms for sub-sentential components and into the rules governing the semantic import of different modes of combination of such components. Thinking that, we shall then quickly be led into thinking – to modify a remark of John McDowell's in a different, though related, context – of our theory of meaning as fitting the pretheoretical facts from the axioms downward rather than from the theorems upward.[14] But that is an error that can be avoided without loss of the advantage our years of native linguistic exchange give us. The question is how to put that advantage to work.

Knowledge of the theoretical structure that yields M-sentences for a given set of sentences in a language is not necessary for competence in the usage of those sentences. Still, knowledge of that theoretical structure should, at least in the context of various other pieces of knowledge, suffice for competence in the usage of those sentences, for understanding of them. However, if this sufficiency condition were the only constraint upon the theory of meaning additional to the propositional attitude constraint already imposed, a new, though connected, worry would emerge: how are the theoretical structures relied upon in the theory of meaning, the structures that generate the M-sentences, to connect with *actual* speakers' knowledge or competence? Is there no connection here which might be relied upon at least to reduce any indeterminacy in the assignment of semantic structure, assuming such indeterminacy to have weathered both the propositional attitude constraint and the sufficiency constraint?

A suggestive idea is the following: that we want as close a fit as possible between the manifest competence of the ordinary speaker and that competence that would be manifested by one whose competence was grounded in his explicit knowledge of the theory of meaning, one who had that competence *because of* his knowledge of the theory (as if, so to speak, the latter was the *idealization* of the ordinary speaker[15]). Suppose we were to entertain this thought alongside the observation – but *observation* – that ordinary speakers who have been taught competence in the usage of some set of sentences $S_1, S_2, \ldots, S_n$ are generally then able, without any further instruction, to use some other set of sentences $S'_1, S'_2, \ldots, S'_n$. (It is in the making of such observations that our natural advantage is put to respectable work.) Then we shall conclude that a theory of meaning satisfying both the sufficiency condition and the new *desideratum* of fit between the (sufficiency-based) idealized speaker and actual speakers should employ in the derivation of M-sentences for $S_1, S_2, \ldots, S_n$ resources which also suffice to yield M-sentences (satisfying the propositional attitude constraint) for $S'_1, S'_2, \ldots, S'_n$.

To be clearer upon quite how this structural constraint enters the picture we need first to see that the requirement of fit between the idealized speaker and the ordinary speaker is the requirement that they

15

be *functionally isomorphic*. The relevant kind of difference produced in a person by linguistic training is neither psychological nor physical but functional: one who has learnt a language has a functional capacity he would otherwise have lacked. The same functional capacity can receive in different speakers, and in some one speaker through time, differing physical (say, neurophysiological) realizations. And even if, as in the case of the idealized speaker, a psychological difference is produced in a person as a result of language acquisition, such a difference is irrelevant from the functional standpoint. What is required of a theory of linguistic behaviour is that it describe such linguistic functional capacities; the theory of meaning plays a role in such a description, a role abstracting from the irrelevant and varying physical facts and the (usually non-existent) psychological facts. The requirement of fit as the requirement of functional isomorphism is simply a reflection of this standpoint from which the theory of meaning can be seen.

But if we reflect further upon that standpoint, and upon how it leads to adoption of the structural constraint, we come to see that the idealized speaker, along with his irrelevant psychology, can drop harmlessly out of the picture. The kinds of observations the structural constraint starts from are guides to the functional capacities of ordinary speakers and to functional isomorphisms between speakers. If, having been instructed in the usage of $S_1, S_2, \ldots, S_n$, a speaker can then understand, without further instruction, $S'_1, S'_2, \ldots, S'_n$, then whatever physical differences that initial instruction produced, they realize a functional capacity that also enables him to understand the untaught sentences $S'_1, S'_2, \ldots, S'_n$. Suppose we also observe that this unaided progression from $S_1, S_2, \ldots, S_n$ to $S'_1, S'_2, \ldots, S'_n$ occurs throughout the linguistic community.[16] Then the rationale for the structural constraint is that the theoretical resources employed in the theory of meaning relied upon as part of the description of the functional capacity induced by instruction in the usage of $S_1, S_2, \ldots, S_n$ should also suffice for description of the, *ex hypothesi*, consequent functional capacity to understand $S'_1, S'_2, \ldots, S'_n$; for the latter functional capacity is at least, so to speak, part of the former functional capacity.[17]

Whether there is anything here that amounts to functional explanation rather than to mere description of functional capacities is a further, somewhat obscure, question. And I am certainly not saying that the assumptions involved in this argument are either unproblematic or as well articulated as they might be. Nor am I saying that there is clearly a real threat of indeterminacy which adoption of some such structural constraint would at least reduce. But I do think it clear that something like the kind of observation the working of this constraint relies upon is tacitly invoked in many discussions of the semantic structures of particular segments of discourse; and I think that something along these lines might be one further way of giving content to the notion of detection, rather than assignment, of semantic structures.

Notes

1 The cautious phrasing here stems from the complexities of mood–mode relations.
2 I shall call it the theory of meaning; but it may well be the case that consideration of our pre-theoretical grasp, if any there be, upon the notion of meaning, and upon its connections with a notion of knowing the meaning, will invite the usage of the more evidently theoretical term 'sense' at this point, with the pre-theoretical notion of meaning perhaps then being constructed from the notion of sense *plus*.
3 Deep issues are involved in the shift to talk of communities of language-speakers and so to talk of *languages*, but these cannot now delay us.
4 Cp. Christopher Peacocke, 'Necessity and Truth-Theories', *Journal of Philosophical Logic* (1978).
5 P. F. Strawson, 'Meaning and Truth', in *Logico-Linguistic Papers* (London, Methuen, 1971), at pp. 188–9.
6 In this paragraph I am even more heavily indebted to discussions with John McDowell than elsewhere in this introduction.
7 Any plausible answers to these questions will require reliance upon intensional constructions in what we say *about* the theory of meaning; but it is not clear that we shall have to have such constructions *in* our theory in order to answer them.
8 Of course, the preceding idea of explicit propositional knowledge of the whole of the theory of linguistic behaviour is one bad answer to the question raised here. Why it is bad, and why we can claim that the sufficiency condition is never realized, should become clear from the ensuing remarks.
9 Hence the caution in the parenthetical remark on pp. 5–6.
10 This will not be quite right since 'here' is an indexical expression and the future tense an indexical construction, and such expressions and constructions require modification of the general constraint that the sentence used on the RHS of a T-sentence interprets (or translates) that designated on the LHS. It is also arguable that for sentences containing indexical constructions semantic vocabulary will occur on the RHS of the appropriate T-sentence; this may force modification, on grounds distinct from those now being considered and from those previously touched upon, of the view of knowledge and understanding just sketched. The example is also unfortunate because of crucial vagaries of 'never'. Compare, for example, 'Mark Platts will never forget his first Derby winner', 'Wittgenstein's work will never be forgotten', and 'The world will

never end'. Read the 'never' in Dummett's example like that in this last case and the example should not then mislead. I retain the example because of its familiarity.

11 Sentences of the form of (T_n) could, of course, be understood in some other way — the phrase 'is true' could be read differently — so that this consequence did not follow. It is realism *about truth* that produces this consequence. Hence there is the possibility of a theory of meaning of the same form as our truth-theoretic conception which does not have a realist metaphysics built into it. (This explains my double use of 'apparently' in the second paragraph of this introduction.)

12 The lines taken in such parochial realist debates and in the general realist debate just sketched stand in complex logical relations to each other, if any such relations there be. The issues involved in the two kinds of debate look to be quite different.

13 A line of thought first suggested to me by Martin Davies. I leave him to expound views on this matter that can reasonably be attributed to him.

14 In 'Physicalism and primitive denotation: Field on Tarski' (see Chapter 6 below, at p. 123).

15 Which is not to say that the idealized speaker would be better off.

16 Dolts who fail, unaided, to make this progression complicate this picture in important ways.

17 I have profited from discussions with Dorothy Edgington about the role of functional considerations in semantics.

2   Truth and use*

Colin McGinn

According to Michael Dummett, a truth-conditions theory of sense for a class of sentences is equivalent to realism in respect of their subject matter.[1] Realism is the thesis that truth (falsity) is an epistemically unconstrained property of a sentence; there is nothing in the concept of truth (falsity) to exclude the possibility that a sentence be unknowably true (false). This property of truth reflects the realist conviction, embodied in our customary linguistic practices, that the world, or a given sector of it, is determinately constituted, quite independently of any limitations on our capacity to come to know truths concerning it. Since, for the realist, truth-value may thus transcend our power to determine truth-value, as the world may transcend our power to discover its constitution, the principle of bivalence is regarded as generally assertible, whether or not we are equipped to determine, even in principle, *what* truth-value a sentence has. If it could be shown that there is some intrinsic difficulty in such a radically non-epistemic notion of truth, then realism, as a piece of commonsense metaphysics, would be undermined: the world, or some sector of it, could no longer be conceived in a realist way, as independent of our knowledge-acquiring capacities, but must rather be seen as somehow constituted or constrained by our cognitive activities, after the pattern, perhaps, of the intuitionists' conception of mathematical reality.[2] Now Dummett claims to have an argument showing that there is indeed an intrinsic difficulty in the idea of conditions for truth being possibly knowledge-transcendent.[3] The argument issues from an alleged failure of such a notion of truth-conditions to meet certain requirements, compulsory on any putative central semantic concept, deriving from the general theory of meaning. If Dummett's argument were sound, we should be compelled to repudiate realism with respect to any class of sentences, or sector of reality, for which those general requirements on the notion of truth, construed as the central concept of a theory of meaning, could not be met. My main purpose in this paper is to avert such wholesale metaphysical revision

*The first draft of this paper was written in the spring of 1976; since then I have had the benefit of reading other people's work on the subject and the comments of several friends.

by contending, against Dummett, that the requirements in question can be satisfied, though not in quite the way he envisages.

Imagine that we have a materially adequate formal theory of truth, in the style of Tarski, for a given natural language L, i.e. a finitely axiomatized theory entailing an infinity of theorems of the familiar disquotational form 's is true iff p'. If that theory is to serve as a theory of meaning for L, and if speakers are acknowledged to know what sentences of L mean, then there must be a sense in which the theory states, or serves to state, what speakers of L know in knowing what sentences of L mean. Since the theorems of the theory purport to state, or to be usable to state, what sentences of L mean, we must say that they state what speakers of L, *qua* speakers, know. In short, a semantic theory is a description of linguistic knowledge, or it is nothing. Now the complex state of implicit propositional knowledge thus described must relate suitably to the capacity, possessed by any speaker of L, to *employ* the language, to engage in those linguistic activities that comprise operating with a language. That is, it must be possible, if the theory is to be acceptable, to connect the propositional knowledge ascribed by the theory to what it is that a speaker is empowered to *do* with language by dint of knowing what the theory (better, its theorems) states. We must, in other words, be able, as theorists, to relate the ascribed semantic knowledge to some specific practical capacity, or capacities, to *use* the language. This demand that the connexion between knowledge of truth-conditions and linguistic use be articulated is warrantable in two ways. The demand can be justified by the general requirement that ascription of a propositional attitude, in this case an item of knowledge, to someone must be accompanied by some account of the difference possession of that state makes to the person's behavioural dispositions: we need to be told something about what would count as a manifestation of the disposition such a propositional attitude produces or consists in; and it is a reasonable expectation that specifically semantic knowledge will manifest itself in the use to which a speaker puts his language. But there is also a special, and more important, reason for insisting that the connexion be made out. In addition to the obvious fact that mastery of a language is essentially a practical capacity, it must be observed that language is precisely an instrument of *communication*. Plainly, if language is to fulfil its communicative function, sense must be a publicly accessible commodity. But then semantic knowledge must, of necessity, be manifestable in, and recoverable from, observable features of linguistic use (I here telescope a familiar line of argument). If, therefore, the semantic knowledge attributed by a theory of meaning to a speaker were not such as to be relatable adequately to linguistic use, then that theory would be, *ipso facto*, unacceptable; it could not possibly serve as a theoretical representation of linguistic understanding. What Dummett claims is that a theory of meaning framed in terms

of a realistic notion of truth precisely fails to forge the required connexion.

It is clear that we cannot, in general, equate knowledge of truth-
conditions with a capacity simply to *state* those conditions. If the
speaker used the same sentence to do this the account would be patently
circular; and if he moved to a different part of the language to state a
non-homophonic verbal equivalent, then the question would arise in
what his knowledge of the truth-conditions of *that* sentence consists,
with the attendant threat of a circle or a regress. Dummett now suggests
that knowledge of truth-conditions be identified, or correlated, with a
certain sort of *recognitional* capacity, viz. a capacity to recognize, or
come to know, the truth-value of sentences. Understanding a sentence
thus consists in an ability to determine its truth-value in some canonical
way, and acquiring mastery of a language consists in acquiring such
capacities with respect to its sentences. In fact, such a capacity is both
executive and recognitional: it consists in a disposition, when prompted,
to undertake a procedure which, in a finite time, terminates in a recognition, signalled by some overt gesture, that the sentence's truth condition is fulfilled or not fulfilled, as the case may be. It is because
(actual) possession of such an effective decision procedure for truth-
value is a practical capacity that it provides the needed link between
knowledge of sense and use. Trouble sets in, according to Dummett,
when we inquire with what generality this account can be applied. For,
if truth is a possibly recognition-transcendent property of a sentence,
what can the realist offer about knowing the truth conditions of sentences whose truth-value we are *not* equipped to determine? Obviously,
in the case of undecidable sentences, alleged grasp of transcendent
truth-conditions cannot be associated with possession of an effective
method for deciding truth-value. We are thus left, for such sentences,
with no account of how knowledge of their truth-conditions may be
manifested: lacking that, Dummett concludes, a realist theory cannot
represent sense as determining, and determined by, use. But if truth and
use fall thus apart the sense of a sentence cannot consist in its having
truth-conditions subject to bivalence. It follows that the semantic content of a sentence cannot represent conditions as they might obtain in
some recognition-transcendent reality; and so realism is false. A theory
of meaning cannot therefore be built around a transcendent central
concept, because that involves violation of the requirement that meaning be manifestable in use. We must, accordingly, assign only such conditions to sentences as determining their sense as are comprehensible
by our actual recognitional capacities − e.g. verification conditions −
and face the anti-realist consequences.

The foregoing is, as I understand it, the essence of Dummett's argument against realism. Before mounting a case against it I shall make two
observations, leading to a restatement of the argument.

The first is that the argument as we have it seems implicitly to assume that recognitional capacities are constant across a given linguistic community. But it is evident that speakers of what appears a common language may, and certainly could, differ, more or less extremely, in their powers of truth-value recognition. Thus, for example, sentences concerning certain regions of space and time might be decidable for one speaker and undecidable for another, depending upon how well equipped they were to inspect the region in question. Two reactions to such a situation seem possible. On the one hand, we could elect to restrict the theory of meaning to sub-groups of speakers (possibly one-membered) equivalent in their power to determine truth-value, so that a realistic theory, committed to the assertion of bivalence, for the class of sentences in question would be applicable to the (sub-)language of some groups in the community and inapplicable to that of other groups. This seems an unattractive suggestion, for at least three reasons. First, it denies an evident publicity in the semantics of the language. Second, the act of assertion would have no uniform significance in the community, an assertion being interpretable as a claim to truth or to justification, according as the asserted sentence was or was not decidable by the speaker. Third, the variation across speakers in respect of their entitlement to assert bivalence for a class of sentences would seem to deprive Dummett of any chance to derive general metaphysical conclusions from the form taken by a proper theory of meaning. On the other hand, one might prefer to assimilate the case to the phenomenon, remarked by Putnam, of the division of linguistic labour.[4] As speakers of a common language may diverge in their capacity to apply natural kind terms correctly, so we may envisage speakers differing in their ability to determine the truth-value of other types of sentence. On such a view, it is not the individual speaker to whom we should look for a manifestation of his semantic knowledge; rather, we should require, for sense to be manifest, only that there should exist, within the community, *some* speaker whose powers of recognition match the truth-conditions of the sentences in question. A truth-conditions theory of sense for a language would, then, connect with use only for the community as a whole, the individual speaker relying upon the recognitional capacities of his co-speakers, and no variability of semantic properties need be acknowledged. However, though this appears the better line to take, it is less than fully satisfactory, since it involves crediting speakers with conceptions of states of affairs of a kind not available to them during the course of their linguistic training and not such as to be manifestable in *their* actual linguistic practice; and this seems already to concede something to the realist.

The second observation concerns what it is for a sentence's truth-conditions to be recognition-transcendent. It is not, I think, necessary for transcendence of truth-conditions that a sentence's truth-value be undecidable; so an anti-realist critique might be in order for a class of sentences whose truth-value could be effectively settled. The reason is that it seems possible for a class of sentences to admit only of *indirect* verification, i.e. via the (direct) verification of other sentences, not in the given class, and inference. For such a class, a speaker's knowledge of truth-conditions does not correlate directly with some specific recognitional capacity. A direct method of determining truth-value, as Dummett explains this notion, reflects the semantically significant syntactic structure of the sentence whose truth-value is to be determined; and he requires, of the realist, not only that some decision procedure be available to the speaker, but further that the ascribed semantic knowledge be mappable on to a capacity to conduct a *direct* decision procedure.[5] Thus a direct verification of a quantified sentence would involve checking each element in the domain quantified over to determine whether it satisfies the appended predicate; an indirect method might be an induction, mathematical or empirical. It is open, then, that a class of sentences should be decidable indirectly but not directly; and for such a class a truth-conditions theory would, as before, traffic in conceptions that fail to correlate adequately with a manifesting recognitional capacity. Thus, suppose one's memory of a certain past interval of space–time were infallible and complete (or the gaps could be filled by inference): then any past-tense sentence concerning that interval would be decidable, but indirectly so. Or consider some fragment of number theory all of whose universally quantified sentences were decidable by mathematical induction, but none of them by direct inspection owing to the infinity of the domain. Or again, suppose there were a type of sentient creature whose mental states and events were invariably accompanied by some distinctive behavioural manifestation; although we could reliably determine the truth-value of any mental attribution to that creature, the state of affairs in virtue of which such a sentence was true would, according to a realist view of other minds, be itself inaccessible to our powers of recognition.[6] In each of these cases, it appears that the realist is unable to supply an appropriate recognitional capacity and so, by Dummett's argument, cannot relate semantic knowledge to linguistic use.

Let me now offer, by way of preparation for what is to come, the following gloss on Dummett's position. Think of the total theory of language mastery as a tripartite structure. It comprises (i) a theory of *sense*, (ii) a theory of *force*, and (iii) a theory of *understanding*. The theory of sense consists of a recursive specification of truth-conditions for the sentences of the object-language; it represents what it is a speaker knows in knowing the meaning of sentences. The theory of force embeds the propositions of the theory of sense in attributions, made upon the basis of linguistic behaviour, of specific contents to whole utterances; it identifies the kind of speech act being performed and, taking the theory of sense as input, assigns a propositional content to it. The theory of understanding has, in effect, the task of certifying the legitimacy of the theory of sense as input to the theory of force; it tells what knowledge of the theorems of the theory of sense consists in, i.e. how that knowledge is manifested. This last component of the total theory is required, according to Dummett, because it is not enough that a theory of language mastery merely record *what* a speaker knows — e.g. that 'snow is white' is true iff snow is white — there is the further obligation, reaching beyond mere description, to supply an *explanation* of what possessing this knowledge consists in; or else, it is claimed, no adequate mesh with use is achieved. We might try to meet this obligation by associating with each theorem of the theory of sense some specific 'sensori-motor routine' (recognitional capacity).[7] Such a sensori-motor routine could be represented as a finite sequence of instructions of the form 'find an object satisfying such and such conditions, determine whether it is thus and so . . .'. Each instruction (sub-routine) correlates with a semantic atom contained in the sentence, and the result of following each instruction, until the constituents of the sentence are exhausted, is a decision as to the truth or falsity of the sentence in question. We can think of such a complete routine for a whole sentence as constituting its direct method of verification.[8] And now, in these terms, Dummett's objection to the realist may be stated as the observation that, in the case of undecidable sentences, there is, in a speaker's repertoire of routines, none that corresponds: so grasp of truth-conditions does not always correlate with a practical capacity of such a sort. Examples in natural languages would be: quantification over infinite or unsurveyable domains, past-tense sentences, counter-factual conditionals, psychological sentences, reference to remote regions of space and time, and perhaps others. In each of these cases we appear to have to do with linguistic constructions whose sense, as the realist would claim, takes us (in thought anyway) to sectors of reality inaccessible to our powers of observation and recognition: knowing the truth conditions of sentences of these kinds does not confer upon speakers a practical grasp of a canonically direct route to establishing their truth-value. But then, Dummett insists, the realist cannot discharge his obligation to the theory of understanding. And this may incline us to opt for a verificationist theory of meaning, according to which knowledge of sentence sense just consists in a practical grasp of which states of information would warrant assertion of the sentence.[9] At any rate, the negative point is that, lacking suitable sensori-motor routines for undecidable sentences, knowledge of truth conditions finds no acceptable counterpart in the speaker's dispositions to use the language.

My strategy now is to describe a model case to which Dummett's argument should apply, if it applies at all. I consider and reject three ways a would-be realist might try to meet the argument in the model case, and then suggest and develop a fourth response to the anti-realist challenge. Suppose a community of speakers C using a language L. Members of C are like human beings in their observational powers, save that they are incapable of local motion; they remain fixed at a place, rooted like trees. Their habitat is the north side of a certain mountain, to which they enjoy sensory access; they are able, for example, visually to survey the north side by orienting their head. The south side of the mountain is, however, hidden from them and inaccessible to their sensory capacities. We can suppose there to be sheep that move freely from one side of the mountain to the other, and in whose doings members of C are especially interested. L has the following resources: proper names for sheep, predicates of sheep, the usual truth-functional connectives, quantifiers whose domain is the set of (local) sheep, and two sentence operators, N and S, with the senses respectively of 'On the north side of the mountain it is the case that' and 'On the south side it is the case that'. Sentences of L are either quantified or of the form 'NA' or 'SA'. According to these specifications of the recognitional powers of C and of the resources of L, L contains (with respect to C) an undecidable fragment: that comprising the quantified sentences and those of the 'SA' form. These sentence types are undecidable for C because, given the actual capacities of members of C, it is perfectly possible that they should be systematically unable to determine the truth-value of these sentences, since they cannot transport themselves to the south side of the mountain. We can allow that they occasionally have access to indirect evidence for the truth of sentences belonging to the undecidable fragment; but it can happen that they have available neither verifying nor falsifying information concerning these sentences. (Their predicament with respect to the south side may be compared with ours with respect to the past.) As I glossed it a bit back, they associate no sensori-motor routine with the undecidable sentences corresponding to their semantic structure. Suppose nevertheless that, like us, they are disposed, realistically, to assert bivalence across the board; that is, they take the appropriate notion of truth for their sentences to transcend the epistemic limitations imposed upon them by their truncated recognitional capacities. Now, given all this, we have here, it seems to me, a used language to which Dummett's argument should apply. Since the concept of truth they purport to employ is, for them, recognition-transcendent, the theory of understanding, in terms of ability to determine truth-value, that we are called upon to offer by way of certification of a truth conditions theory of sense for the model language L, will simply give out when we direct it towards the undecidable sentences of L. Because there is nothing in the recognitional capacities of the speakers of L to translate into actual use the conceptions of states of affairs that a truth-conditions theory credits to them, we cannot say in what their knowledge of these transcendent truth-conditions consists, how it is manifested in use. We have no account of what it is about their use of language that confers upon their sentences the kind of sense a truth-conditions theory purports to record. In consequence, their commitment to bivalence is misplaced, and an anti-realist conception of the hidden side of the mountain indicated, at least so far as their conceptual scheme is concerned.

In assessing the cogency of the anti-realist's case for this conclusion it is useful to break the argument into two parts, one part concentrating on acquisition, the other on manifestation.[10] The acquisition argument may be crudely stated as follows: speakers of a public language have, in the course of their training in the use of sentences, been exposed only to states of affairs that they are capable of recognizing (trivially) – in the present case only to conditions as they obtain on the north side of the mountain; and they cannot extract from this training conceptions of conditions that transcend those to which they have been exposed, notably in learning when an assertive utterance is justified – in the present case conditions as they might obtain on the south side. Accordingly, a realist theory of what knowledge of L consists in would leave it quite unexplained – would indeed make it quite mysterious – how it is that speakers have come to bestow upon their sentences truth-conditions that relate to states of affairs that could have played no part in their acquisition of the language, on account of their inaccessibility. Only what obtains recognizably can play a part in endowing sentences with communicable meaning, or in apprising a learner of meanings already endowed. The manifestation argument, on the other hand, is to the effect that recognition-transcendent conditions are not of a sort with respect to which speakers can *display* their knowledge of truth-conditions. The two arguments coalesce in the thought that there can be no more to the semantics of a language than is determined by recognizable conditions in the world – where the relevant notion of recognition attaches directly to the actual capacities of the speakers in question. Both arguments make it seem that a truth-conditions theory for our model language L fails to make out the required connexion between meaning and use.

Three ways of resisting this line of argument suggest themselves.

(i) One might try to warrant the attribution of knowledge of transcendent truth-conditions by exploiting a certain truth-value link: that between the truth-value of a sentence 'SA' when uttered on the north side of the mountain and the truth-value of the same sentence as it might be uttered on the south side. (Compare the link between a present utterance of a past-tense sentence and a past utterance of a corresponding present-tense sentence.[11]) The suggestion, then, is that speakers succeed in extending bivalence to the undecidable sentences by reasoning as follows: 'We have linguistic dispositions that sustain the assertion of bivalence for sentences about the north side; well, the truth-conditions of sentences about the south side are just like that, except that they obtain inaccessibly.' The supposed truth-value link ensures bivalence for the undecidable sentences, and the desired conception of truth conditions is obtained by a sort of projection. But it is plain that this begs, rather than answers, the anti-realist's question: for no southern state of affairs has ever impinged upon the speakers' consciousness while learning their language, and the thought of the alleged link does not equip them to manifest, in acts of recognition, the conceptions it is the design of the above reasoning to induce. The point is simply that the link does not take them, at will, to any state of affairs they are able to recognize directly. If they did have the capacity to transport themselves to the south side, then grasp of the truth-value link would enable them to manifest knowledge of the truth conditions of arbitrary sentences as uttered on the north side: but, of course, this is precisely the capacity they lack. So, as in other areas, appeal to truth-value links cannot remove the underlying difficulty.

(ii) A second attempt, extending an idea of McDowell's,[12] to warrant the attribution of realist truth-conditions to sentences of L might be labelled 'the partial accessibility claim'. The original suggestion, made for the past and for other minds, was that, although the truth-conditions of these sentences are not *always* accessible to direct apprehension, they *sometimes* are: we are, on occasion, non-inferentially aware that the truth-condition of one of the problematic sentences obtains, and this suffices to instil in us a general conception, extensible to other sentences of the given class whose truth-conditions transcend awareness, of the sort of condition that is at issue. Thus we are said sometimes to perceive that another is in pain, and to be vouchsafed direct acquaintance with (certain tracts of) the past via memory. Now, however plausible such a view may be for the past and for the mental states of others, it cannot help the realist in the present case: for there is surely no plausibility in the suggestion that speakers of L sometimes enjoy direct non-inferential apprehension of the fulfilment of truth-conditions for sentences that purport to relate to the hidden side of the mountain; these conditions *always* transcend the recognitional faculties of members of C. So there seems no warranting a truth-conditions theory for L that way. And this suggests, what one may have already suspected for other kinds of sentence for which a realist interpretation has been challenged, that the partial accessibility claim could not be a complete answer to Dummett, and so cannot go to the heart of his argument.

(iii) A third, and initially tempting, thought would be that the problematic conception is acquirable on the basis of analogy. That is to say, speakers of L could come by the desired conception by imaginatively extending the capacities they actually have, or by conceiving of beings with respect to whose capacities conditions on the south side would not be inaccessible; they need only, it seems, hit upon the idea of mobility. The objection to this suggestion, made by Dummett,[13] is not so much, *pace* the acquisition argument in its crude form, that they could not envisage any such extension of capacities, but rather that, even once acquired, we cannot say how the conceptions thus attained manifest themselves in the actual use to which the speakers are able to put their sentences: for the acquired conception does not, *ex hypothesi*, translate into a practical capacity manifestable in acts of truth-value recognition. We cannot justify describing our own language mastery in a certain way by imagining speakers, crucially different from ourselves, for whom that description *would* be correct: we must describe our use of language as it actually is.

What each of these attempts to answer Dummett assumes, one way or another, is that there can be no conception of a state of affairs that isn't a recognitional conception; and indeed Dummett is inclined to assert that the only model we have of what knowledge of truth-conditions consists in (aside from a purely verbal ability) is provided by our grasp of the sense of an observation sentence.[14] This assumption immediately puts the realist in a weak position, just because undecidable sentences are precisely such that their sense cannot be explained in terms of what it would be for the speaker to *observe* that they are true. If determination of their truth-value, where possible at all, is an essentially inferential procedure, the realist, accepting the presupposition of Dummett's argument, finds himself forced to acknowledge that he cannot explain knowledge of truth-conditions in the only way available. This is especially clear in the acquisition argument: we are invited to agree that no conception can enter into understanding a language that is not induced directly by sensorily presented conditions; any going beyond the observational must be either impossible or arbitrary. (Like Hume, we wonder how there could be more to our 'ideas' than can be extracted from our 'impressions'.) This, I think, is precisely why we are ready to be convinced that, given that training in the use of language consists in learning to make assertions in circumstances that justify assertion (i.e. recognizable circumstances), the content of sentences could not transcend that to which we have been thus exposed. Put that way, the argument is suspiciously redolent of a certain reductionist dogma bequeathed to us by classical empiricism: the dogma, to put it shortly, that our conceptual scheme cannot transcend our experience.[15] But it is now, I take it, a commonplace that such reductionism need not be accepted; indeed that, if we are to have an adequate explanation of what is observed, it cannot be accepted. Thus, though my model speakers experience only the north side of their mountain, we may ask what is to *stop* them, as creatures given to speculation and to the search for a coherent picture of the world they inhabit, from arriving at the idea of the south side of the mountain, and from conceiving of it as a determinately constituted stretch of reality. More strongly, it is hard to see how they could *avoid* arriving at that idea. For a conception of that (for them) inaccessible reach of reality seems forced upon them if they are to have any reasonable explanation of the things they do observe: sheep disappearing and reappearing, etc. Their predicament seems much like ours when doing theoretical science, notwithstanding the undecidability. And in answer to the question how this process occurs – how in fact we do arrive at conceptions that transcend the observable – it seems that we can take a leaf out of Quine's book: that is a task for the (possibly speculative) cognitive psychology that goes with naturalized epistemology to discharge; it is not a chapter in the philosophical theory of meaning as such.[16] So I suggest that it is only an empiricist dogma, with few attractions in other contexts, that makes us disposed to deny the possibility of acquiring conceptions of reality that transcend our recognitional capacities.

This response to the acquisition version of the anti-realist argument may be found reasonable, so far as it goes; but it cannot, on its own, be the whole answer, for it does not speak to the original manifestation version of the argument. And here it may seem that the anti-realist has it all his own way. I have just recorded my conviction that we can acquire recognition-transcendent conceptions; but I have signally failed to explain how such conceptions show up in actual linguistic use. In fact, given the conditions the realist has been thus far required to meet, it appears that there is no hope of making good on that crucial obligation, since the acquired conception – in the present case of the hidden side of the mountain – does not correlate with any ability to undertake a decision procedure guaranteed to culminate in a judgment of truth-value. What that suggests is that, though the mountain-dwellers could acquire a conception, encouraging assertion of bivalence, of a sector of reality that transcends their recognitional powers, this conception could not be that in which their grasp of the sense of the relevant sentences consists; for, by Dummett's argument, nothing can qualify as knowledge of meaning unless it relates directly to some linguistic disposition of the speaker – a disposition, we have been agreeing, to engage in a truth-value deciding procedure – and the conception in question precisely does not relate to any such disposition. So are we not back exactly where we started?

I think it must be evident by now that something is going wrong with the anti-realist's argument. For how can we allow that speakers can come by a conception of reality of which they cannot speak? The content of a sentence, Dummett says in one place,[17] is a representation of some facet of reality; but it begins to seem that this representative content *cannot* express the conceptual scheme evidently available to our model speakers. Since it is not plausible to separate acquiring a language from acquiring a conception of reality, it seems that we must choose between two alternatives: either it is, after all, a mistake, an illusion, to suppose ourselves (or others) capable of conceiving a recognition-transcendent reality; or there must be some way of manifesting such a conception in use otherwise than by the exercise of a capacity to conduct a verification procedure. I shall argue for the second alternative.

Suppose we ask what is the proper object of acquiring mastery of a language, what the point of knowing the meaning of sentences is. Then I think we must reply that the point is communication, the business of interpreting the speech of others and having one's own interpreted: that is the end-state at which learning a language aims. We can gain perspective on this capacity by making explicit what a radical interpreter would need to know if he were to become equipped to interpret the speech of a given linguistic community. And we have been taught that what he would need to know is a deductive theory licensing the description of antecedently uninterpreted vocalizations as performances of specific kinds of speech-act possessed of specific propositional contents.[18] But there is no possessing this capacity in isolation from other knowledge about a speaker; it forms an indissoluble part of a more general theory of the actions of the person, a theory that constitutively relates meanings, propositional attitudes and intentional behaviour. If someone knows such a general theory for a language, he has the capacity to use the language; and someone shows himself to possess such a capacity by successfully engaging in communication with speakers of the language. These platitudes prompt the simple thought that one's knowledge of meaning is manifestable in one's capacity to interpret — with all that that involves — the speech behaviour of others. A central component of this ability is correctly ascribing beliefs to the speaker, where these will figure — in combination with suitable desires — in explanations of his behaviour. These beliefs may, or may not, be of realist persuasion. (This is, of course, very different from Dummett's picture of use, where the emphasis is placed upon the solitary individual's capacity to determine truth-value.) Applying this sketch of a description of linguistic use, we get the following: the mountain-dwellers can manifest their knowledge of transcendent truth-conditions, acquired in the way gestured at earlier, by interpreting the assertions of fellow speakers as expressions of the very realist beliefs we have seen no good reason to deny to them (where their assent to bivalence will be of obvious relevance to such an interpretation). It seems that this way of locating knowledge of truth-conditions within the total activity of speech interpretation serves, unambitiously but satisfactorily, to relate conceptions of transcendent states of affairs to a practical linguistic capacity, to actual use.

Identifying sentence use, not with a propensity effectively to determine truth-value, but with the activity of speech interpretation (and production), seems to carry with it a denial that an essential component in the capacity to use and understand a name is an ability to recognize some given object as the bearer of the name. For, on the face of it, one could possess the capacity to interpret sentences containing a certain proper name – i.e. one could know what speech-act was being performed in the sentence's utterance – yet lack any recognitional capacity in respect of the object so denoted;[19] and this raises a number of questions about realism and reference. It is apparent that there are certain connexions between the view one takes of the sense of names and one's position on how the sense of sentences is manifested in use. Dummett urges us to adopt, as a model for the sense of both categories of expression, the idea of a mode of recognition: for names grasping the sense consists in a capacity to judge the truth-value of so-called recognition statements of the form 'that is *a*' accompanied by an ostensive gesture;[20] for sentences it is possessing a capacity to recognize the fulfilment or otherwise of the sentence's truth-conditions. For both semantic concepts – reference and truth – we can formulate realist interpretations, in terms of their allowing of recognition-transcendent application conditions: a sentence may be true though we cannot know it, and a name refer to an object with which we cannot be directly confronted (a past existent, say, or a remote, inferentially postulated, galaxy). And for reference, as for truth, we can construct an anti-realist argument: we have no right to assume a determinate reference for a name whose sense is not such as to present a traversable route to recognizing its bearer, for in such a case there will be no manifesting a grasp of the sense of the name.[21] Reference cannot transcend recognition of reference, as truth cannot transcend recognition of truth. My present question, however, concerns the interdependence of these views of sense. It appears that one might consistently hold that the sense of a name was required to be effective in this way – thus agreeing that the use of a name consists in the exercise of a recognitional capacity – while denying the parallel view of sentence sense, perhaps because of a principled reluctance to assimilate sentences to the prototype of names.[22] But the converse implication seems more compelling, since determining the truth-value of a sentence containing a name of a concrete object will require, in the canonical case, some sort of ostensive identification of its bearer (the direct method of verifying the sentence). Now given (a) that it is such an ability that manifests grasp of a sentence's sense, and (b) that a theory of sense is required to specify what *explicit* knowledge would suffice (and be necessary), when conjoined with certain general principles, for mastery of a sentence's use, it seems to follow, agreeably for Dummett, that some sort of description theory of the sense of names is wanted, since a description is precisely what makes explicit the 'criterion of identification' involved in recognizing the bearer of a name as such.[23] But now we can, I think, reverse the argument: for if we have good reason to reject a description theory of names, as I take it we have,[24] we can infer that the (conjunctive) thesis that entails it is false.

Colin McGinn

Since premise (a) is hard to gainsay, (b) must be the culprit. If this view of the matter is accepted, we can claim an independent ground for rejecting Dummett's picture of sentence use. In fact, it seems to me that the best view of the sense of names conforms exactly with the picture of sentence use I advocate.[25]

It may now be protested that, though apparently answering to the letter of Dummett's argument, the position I have been advancing does not go to its heart. For what I have claimed, in effect, is that the proper locus of manifestation is to be sought in the theory of force — the theory that embeds knowledge of sense in the general theory of interpretation; I have not attempted to ground the theory of sense in some sort of explanation of what it is to know the truth-condition of a sentence. I must acknowledge, therefore, that my remarks have so far left the space reserved for the theory of understanding, as Dummett construes it, quite blank. But we are entitled to question whether the demand for an 'explanation' is really legitimate. Once we separate the request for a link with use from a demand that we explain what knowledge of truth-conditions 'consists in', it begins to seem far less obvious that Dummett's alleged lacuna is one we are obliged to fill. Indeed, it is hard to interpret this latter demand as anything other than an insistence, evidently not mandatory, that we supply some sort of *reduction* of semantic concepts to others — e.g. those we should employ in specifying a sensori-motor capacity.[26] But there seems no instability in a position that declines the invitation to tender such a reduction, while accepting as legitimate the request to relate semantic knowledge to linguistic use.

The cardinal principle of Dummett's conception of language mastery is that it consists solely in, and so cannot go beyond, sensitivity to evidence. This suggests a parallel with Quine that is worth brief exploration. Quine speaks of our total 'theory' as transcending the collated history of our sense experiences: the content of our general conception of the world, notably of theoretical science, is underdetermined by observation.[27] And he sees that genuine underdetermination is possible only under a realist interpretation of scientific (and commonsense) discourse. What these propositions together imply is that grasp of the content of such an experience-transcendent theory cannot be simply equated with or reduced to a complex of (molecular) dispositions to judge of the truth-value of sentences (dispositions to assent and dissent) upon being confronted by recognizable evidential conditions. Nevertheless, for Quine, we are able to acquire the corresponding realist conceptions. Whether undecidability is brought in the wake of such underdetermination is a delicate question: but it does seem that, at least relative to a time, it may be that there are, formulable within our language, sentences of science, e.g. referring to subatomic particles, whose truth-value is not guaranteed to be determinable by us at will, and certainly not by direct verification. So, for such sentences too,

Dummett would be committed to an anti-realist position.[28] The point I wish to make is that Quine and Dummett react somewhat differently to the observation that realist truth-conditions cannot be exhaustively manifested in dispositions to respond to evidential promptings. For both men, the realist must seem to be building more into language than *could* be present in it, since dispositions to recognize truth-value exhaust the objective facts a theory of meaning is required to record. But Quine, taking realism to be obligatory, infers a potential multiplicity of theories from the assumption of underdetermination; the ensuing indeterminacy thesis is itself a form of anti-realism about meaning.[29] Dummett, on the other hand, finds it incredible that meaning should thus outrun linguistic dispositions, and so prefers to relinquish the realism that gives rise to that hiatus, thereby restoring the exhaustive manifestability of sense. The difference could be put by saying that, apropos of the conditional 'If realism, then meaning transcends use', Quine detaches while Dummett contraposes. Both reactions are motivated by the underlying assumption that the capacity to use a language must be represented, fundamentally, as the possession of a complex of dispositions to verify or falsify sentences.

Now, without here taking a stand on the issue of indeterminacy, I can restate my position as follows: I agree with Quine at least in this, that the content of our sentences (or those of my model linguistic community) just does transcend dispositions to determine truth-value by responding appropriately to suitable evidence; and I agree too that how this comes to pass is a fit subject for naturalized epistemology to investigate. This does not entail the kind of subjectivity of sense that Frege was concerned to rebut, for there seems nothing to prevent different speakers sharing the same recognition-transcendent beliefs and meanings. Nor need we give up the virtual truism that mastery of a language is a dispositional capacity: we can characterize it as essentially a set of interrelated (and molecular) dispositions to interpret the speech of others, and to produce speech of one's own, according to a correct theory of sense and force for the language. Knowing a language is possessing an information-processing capacity: but there is no 'explanation' of the operations of that capacity such as Dummett appears to be seeking. A theory of sense aims to describe the core of this capacity, and it needs no support from a theory of understanding that purports to spell out, in a reductionist style, what implicit knowledge of that theory consists in. Indeed, the case of knowledge of a semantic theory seems comparable, in this respect, to knowledge of (say) a theory of chemicals: why *should* we expect an answer to the philosophically loaded reductionist question of what knowledge of such a theory of chemicals would 'consist in'?

I hope it is clear that nothing I have said so far commits me to a blanket endorsement of realism; my argument has been essentially

33

Colin McGinn

permissive. To recapitulate: Dummett presents an argument schema whose instances concern certain kinds of sentence to be found in natural languages; I contended that a model case to which the argument should apply can be argued to escape Dummett's anti-realist critique — we can see, for that model case, how a realist could defend his claim to give an intelligible account of language mastery. If Dummett's argument can be resisted for this model case, then the argument schema of which that case would be an instance cannot be accepted as generally valid. So if an anti-realist case is to be pressed in more familiar areas, it cannot be pressed upon the basis of that general argument. This leaves it open that an anti-realist case might be mounted, with consequences for the theory of meaning, in those other areas. It will be instructive in appraising Dummett's own position to glance at a number of areas for which such a case could be made plausible. For I suspect that Dummett's conclusion can seem compelling for a class of sentences, or sector of reality, not because of his official argument, but because, contrary to his own perspective, specific subject matters may present features that render a realist interpretation in some way problematic, independently of considerations drawn from the general theory of meaning, but with consequences for our understanding of the sense of the sentences in question.

An obvious case is that of statements concerning infinite totalities. Notoriously, the intuitionists insist upon conceiving infinite collections as merely potential, as given to us via the notion of an essentially incompletable process; a platonist conception of the infinite as a completed actual totality misrepresents, according to them, the very nature of the infinite, by illicitly assimilating its character to that of finite collections.[30] Such a view is maintained for mathematical structures, but one can see how it might be extended to space and time. Now, if that were the correct way to construe the infinite, there would be clear point in adopting a constructivist interpretation of the truth-conditions of sentences concerning infinite totalities; and such a decision would be independent of considerations of undecidability as such, but would derive directly from a certain conception of the infinite itself. In consequence, some sort of anti-realist view, involving non-assertion of bivalence for such sentences, might be taken, on the ground that, in advance of constructing appropriate segments of the totality in question, there is no definite reality to speak of. From Dummett's official perspective, however, where undecidability as such is the operative consideration, the properties of infinity and unsurveyability (which can hold of a finite domain) are essentially on a par in their capacity to encourage anti-realist contentions: for both properties block effective manifestation, in recognitional activities, of knowledge of realist truth-conditions. But it seems to me that one might motivate a differential attitude, with respect to the realist/anti-realist dispute, between collections exhibiting these two verification-frustrating properties, on the basis of considerations relating to the intrinsic character of the subject matter in question, independently of facts about our capacity to come to know truths about that subject matter.

A second example of a candidate for a non-generalizable anti-realism is that of statements about abstract objects, particularly numbers. Dummett writes as if the dispute between platonist and intuitionist (or, more generally, non-platonist) could only non-metaphorically consist in a disagreement concerning the relation between meaning and use, as he sets out the form of this disagreement.[31] But there are well-known difficulties in the platonist's conception of the truth-conditions of number-theoretic sentences that are quite special — I mean such problems as how, given plausible assumptions about the causal inertness of abstract objects and causal requirements for knowledge and belief, we can ever come to *know* truths about these objects.[32] It is true, of course, that Dummett's anti-realism is primarily directed at the objectivity of truths and not at the existence of objects; but one can readily appreciate how a platonist picture of mathematical objects should be presupposed to a proof-transcendent view of mathematical truth. So rejection of a platonist ontology might well lead one to a constructivist interpretation of the sense of number-theoretic sentences, perhaps accompanied by local abandonment of classical logic. Not only would such a line of argument fail to generalize to other areas — e.g. the physical universe, other minds; it actually runs directly counter to the direction of argument claimed by Dummett to be the only feasible route to anti-realism: for it takes us *from* a critical thesis about the specific character of the subject matter of mathematics as realistically (i.e. platonistically) construed *to* adoption of a non-realist conception of sense.

Other areas in which arguments of this structure can be envisaged are modal and fictional discourse. Anyone who doubts the existence of hard modal facts corresponding to true modal sentences, preferring instead to construe their truth-conditions as involving some sort of mental construction, will be disposed to take an anti-realist attitude towards the meaning of modal discourse; the more so if the semantics of modal operators is done in terms of quantification over possible worlds. And the reason may, again, derive from supposed epistemological difficulties attending modality. In the case of fictional discourse we take it that fictional entities are defined, roughly speaking, according to the author's intentions, to what he tells us of his creations; we do not suppose that the author brings an entity into existence whose constitution renders determinate the truth-value of every statement we can make about such an entity. The nature of the subject matter of fictional discourse therefore precludes assertion of bivalence, and invites a non-realist interpretation. In each of these areas we can formulate an intelligible anti-realist position, which does not go through a manifestation argument, and so cannot be made to generalize to all areas in which undecidability obtains.

Tensed discourse provides a case in which, not only can we give substance to manifestation-independent arguments, but Dummett's own mode of argument seems to yield bizarre consequences.[33] A natural, and traditional, way to formulate anti-realism with respect to time would be the following. The past exists only in its traces on the present; so where there are no traces there are no past facts; hence bivalence is unassertible for statements about the past. The future has less claim to full-blooded reality, since it leaves no traces, and is in some sense open. The present, however, is fully determinate; it is the foil against which the unreality of the past and future are contrasted. (I do not say that these claims are ultimately defensible, or even properly intelligible; only that they underlie anti-realist thought about time.) Now what is remarkable is that Dummett's anti-realism seems to reverse this intuitive order, rather than coincide with it. For, on his view, realism with respect to a certain subject matter is acceptable in proportion as the corresponding sentences admit of an effective decision procedure for truth-value. But consider sentences concerning some finite initial segment of the future starting now: if such a sentence contains no other problematic construction, we can, it seems, generally guarantee that we shall be able so to position ourselves as to determine the truth-value of the sentence when the appropriate time comes; and this decidability will, according to Dummett, warrant assertion of bivalence, and hence realism. The past, on the other hand, is less well placed: lacking presently available evidence, through memory or traces, statements about the past are apt to remain undecidable, and so present, according to Dummett's argument, prime candidates for anti-realist interpretation. The present, however, occupies a curious position: for it may be that the assertion of a present-tense sentence cannot be effectively verified because the condition that, according to the realist, makes it true no longer obtains at the time of verification; and whether it did, at the time of assertion, obtain becomes a matter subject to the problems of decidability afflicting the past tense. So the verification of many present-tense sentences is at best indirect and at worst unavailable. But surely, we want to insist, this is, as it were, a merely incidental fact about time and verification; it is irrelevant to the question whether, at the time a present tense sentence is uttered, the assertion made thereby was determinately either true or false. The inaccessibility, in this sense, of present states of the world does not seem a good ground for denying their reality. I think that if Dummett's position has these consequences for tensed statements it is reduced to something approaching absurdity.

Dummett places the theory of meaning — the theory of what it is to have mastery of a language — in a position prior to metaphysics. We are to come at traditional metaphysical questions concerning realism and anti-realism by asking what notion of truth can give an adequate account of linguistic use; metaphysical disputes about whether a given class of sentences admits of a realist interpretation turn into a general question as to the relation between meaning and use. It is chiefly for this reason, I think, that Dummett views the philosophy of language as the foundation of philosophy.[34] I have argued that the general considerations about meaning and use that he broaches cannot themselves compel abandonment of realism; disputes of this kind must, accordingly, be settled in other ways. If that is the right way of looking at the matter, we shall have reason to doubt the doctrine that the philosophy of language is the basis and medium of philosophical disputes at large, at least as Dummett intends that doctrine.

Notes

1 Writings of Dummett relevant to this topic include: 'Truth', *Proceedings of the Aristotelian Society*, vol. 59 (1958-9); 'The Reality of the Past', *Proceedings of the Aristotelian Society*, vol. 69 (1968-9); *Frege: Philosophy of Language* (London, Duckworth, 1973); 'What is a Theory of Meaning?', in *Mind and Language*, ed. S. Guttenplan (Oxford, Clarendon Press, 1975); 'The Philosophical Basis of Intuitionistic Logic', in *Logic Colloquium 1973*, eds H. E. Rose and J. C. Shepherdson (Amsterdam, North Holland, 1975); 'What is a Theory of Meaning? (II)', in *Truth and Meaning*, eds G. Evans and J. H. McDowell (Oxford University Press, 1976); *Elements of Intuitionism* (Oxford, Clarendon Press, 1977). See also Crispin Wright's 'Truth Conditions and Criteria', *Proceedings of the Aristotelian Society*, supp. vol. 50 (1976).

2 Cf. the final pages of Dummett, 'Truth'.

3 See especially Dummett, 'What is a Theory of Meaning? (II)', 'The Philosophical Basis of Intuitionistic Logic', *Elements of Intuitionism*, chapters 1 and 7, 'The Reality of the Past'; also Wright's 'Truth Conditions and Criteria'.

4 See H. Putnam, 'The Meaning of "Meaning" ' in *Mind, Language and Reality, Philosophical Papers*, vol. II (Cambridge University Press, 1975).

5 See Dummett, *Frege: Philosophy of Language*, pp. 236-9, 515, 634-6.

6 It might be maintained, plausibly, that 'natural' extensions of language fragments which exhibit transcendence without undecidability will introduce the latter property. Admitting this would not, however, spoil my point, so long as the speaker's competence is confined to the unextended decidable fragment.

7 My use of this notion is not, of course, intended to suggest that the

capacity in question is in some way nonconceptual, only that it typically involves perceptual processes and action.

8 Cf. J. Hintikka's game-theoretic interpretation of the procedures of seeking and finding that he associates with quantifiers; see 'Language-Games for Quantifiers' in *Logic, Language-Games and Information* (Oxford, Clarendon Press, 1973).

9 Dummett is apt to write as if his censure of the realist notion of truth would count against Davidson's conception of a systematic semantics (see 'What is a Theory of Meaning? (II)', p. 67). This seems to be mistaken. So far as I can see, nothing in Davidson's programme is inconsistent with adoption of a verificationist-type construal of the truth theory, either in the weak form described by J. McDowell in 'Truth Conditions, Bivalence and Verificationism' in *Truth and Meaning*, op. cit., or more full-bloodedly as in Wright's 'Truth Conditions and Criteria', section VI.

10 In 'The Reality of the Past' Dummett offers us an acquisition argument; in 'What is a Theory of Meaning? (II)' the argument is presented more or less exclusively in terms of manifestation. McDowell tends to expound Dummett in an acquisition way — see 'Truth Conditions, Bivalence and Verificationism' and 'On "The Reality of the Past" ' (forthcoming). Wright, for his part, is more purely manifestational. As will emerge, it seems to me essential to separate the two arguments.

11 Truth-value link realism is discussed by Dummett in 'The Reality of the Past' and by McDowell in 'On "The Reality of the Past" '.

12 To be found in his 'On "The Reality of the Past" '.

13 See Dummett, 'What is a Theory of Meaning? (II)', pp. 100–1.

14 See *Frege: Philosophy of Language*, p. 465; cf. W. V. Quine's (unsuccessful) attempt to explain knowledge of truth conditions in terms of dispositions to assent and dissent in 'Mind and Verbal Dispositions' in *Mind and Language*, op. cit.

15 That is, Quine's second dogma — see 'Two Dogmas of Empiricism' in his *From a Logical Point of View* (Cambridge, Mass., Harvard University Press, 1953). This doctrine characterizes the position of McDowell's 'strong verificationist' — see 'Truth Conditions, Bivalence and Verificationism'. Dummett's position differs from his, it appears, only by countenancing a more liberal standard of what is recognizable.

16 See W. V. Quine's 'Epistemology Naturalized' in *Ontological Relativity and Other Essays* (New York, Columbia University Press, 1969). It is arguable, indeed, that the intrusion of such considerations into the theory of meaning would be a form of psychologism. But then perhaps verificationist theories in general attract that epithet, because of the relativity to speakers' recognitional capacities they inevitably introduce.

17 M. Dummett, 'The Justification of Deduction', *British Academy Lecture* (1973), p. 24.

18 See D. Davidson's 'Radical Interpretation', *Dialectica*, XXVII (1973), J. McDowell's 'Truth Conditions, Bivalence and Verifica-

tionism' and his 'On the Sense and Reference of a Proper Name', *Mind* (April 1977). The perspective I here wish to endorse construes the theory of meaning as an empirically testable, though possibly underdetermined, explanatory theoretical representation of a speaker's linguistic behaviour, as it interlocks with his psychological properties and dispositions to action.

19   This is not to deny that in order to be able to use a name in ascriptions of propositional content one needs some sort of *de re* attitude in respect of its bearer: but it appears evident that such an attitude may be present in the absence of any corresponding recognitional capacity.

20   See *Frege: Philosophy of Language*, pp. 232f.

21   This issue obtrudes itself at p. 231 of *Frege: Philosophy of Language*; but Dummett does not explicitly remark upon the possibility of an anti-realist conception of reference parallel to that he advocates for truth.

22   Despite his overt rejection of Frege's assimilation Dummett is to be found passing somewhat too readily from the recognitional conception of the sense of a name to the same view of sentence sense. See, e.g., *Frege: Philosophy of Language*, p. 589. (I do not here mean to deny that our grasp of transcendent truth conditions might somehow involve knowledge of ideal procedures of truth-value determination; my point is rather that, even admitting that such procedures belong to the strict sense of a sentence, the knowledge a speaker has of them could show up in use otherwise than in his carrying them out.)

23   If we characterize such a recognitional capacity merely as a disposition to apply the name in ostensive judgments upon being causally prompted by certain properties of its bearer, rather than as consisting in some sort of implicit propositional knowledge, then, even still, the explicit propositional knowledge that would suffice to possess the capacity will involve a description, its predicates recording the causally relevant properties. In any case, there seems no avoiding a rich conception of sense if (a) and (b) are granted.

24   See , e.g., S. Kripke, 'Naming and Necessity' in D. Davidson and G. Harman, eds, *Semantics of Natural Language* (Boston, Reidel, 1972); K. Donnellan, 'Proper Names and Identifying Descriptions', ibid., and C. Peacocke, 'Proper Names, Reference, and Rigid Designation' in *Meaning, Reference and Necessity*, ed. S. Blackburn (Cambridge University Press, 1975).

25   The kind of view adumbrated by McDowell in 'On the Sense and Reference of a Proper Name'. I think, however, that McDowell neglects the motivation for a description theory deriving from the conception of the sense-manifesting use of a sentence as consisting in a determination of its truth-value; it is not (or not merely) motivated by some gratuitous psychologistic picture of what guides the activity of speech. What has to be noted is that, if my argument is right, McDowell too is committed to rejecting that view of sentence use.

Colin McGinn

26 McDowell too diagnoses an underlying reductionism, but construes it as behaviourist in spirit (see 'On the Sense and Reference of a Proper Name', p. 181). To the empiricist reductionism I claim to discern he seems less unsympathetic (see the final section of 'Truth Conditions, Bivalence and Verificationism'). In fact the two types of reductionism are connected, since if all meaning is empirical meaning a speaker's semantic knowledge will correlate with dispositions to assent and dissent behaviour under appropriate stimulation. I think, however, that in the present context the latter type of reductionism is the more basic, and does not in itself *entail* the former type. And there is also, I should say, a more general reductionist strain in Dummett's thinking.

27 See especially Quine, 'Epistemology Naturalized', where the word 'transcend' is used at p. 83.

28 It must be said that Dummett seldom, if ever, in his published writings on this topic addresses himself to the question of scientific realism.

29 See W. V. Quine, 'On the Reasons for Indeterminacy of Translation', *Journal of Philosophy*, lxvii (1970). One can see the indeterminacy thesis as Quine's attempt to resolve the deep tension in his views between, on the one hand, a realistic face-value interpretation of scientific and commonsense discourse and, on the other, his doctrine that there can be no more to meaning than is recoverable from dispositions to assent and dissent under sensory stimulation. What would take up the resulting slack is adherence to some form of 'mentalistic semantics' which repudiates the doctrine of empirical meaning: essentially, that is my position.

30 See, for a discussion of the intuitionistic conception of the infinite, Dummett's *Elements of Intuitionism*, pp. 55f.

31 This is pretty plainly asserted in Dummett, 'The Philosophical Basis of Intuitionistic Logic'.

32 Cf. P. Benacerraf, 'Mathematical Truth', *Journal of Philosophy*, lxx (1973). The case of mathematics in fact exemplifies a general antirealist argument, applicable (e.g.) to some forms of ethical realism, to the effect that the realist's ontology can play no part in *explaining* how knowledge of the area in question is acquired.

33 See 'The Reality of the Past'. I detect no sign that Dummett anticipates the consequences I allege.

34 See chapter 19 of *Frege: Philosophy of Language*. No doubt Dummett has other reasons for holding this view.

3 Causal modalities and realism*

Christopher Peacocke

I

My aim is to question, and to provide the outline of an alternative to, one major component in the views of Hume and his followers on causation. A typical expression of the component in question is given by Ramsey:[1]

> The world, or rather that part of it with which we are acquainted, exhibits as we must all agree a good deal of regularity of succession. I contend that over and above that it exhibits no feature called causal necessity, but that we make sentences called causal laws from which (i.e. having made which) we proceed to actions and propositions connected with them in a certain way, and say that a fact asserted in a proposition which is an instance of a causal law is a case of causal necessity.

The view Ramsey expresses here can be labelled 'actualist'; but it is necessary to distinguish various views that may be so labelled.

We can distinguish two kinds of actualist doctrine with respect to any given modal operator, including causal necessity (' $\square$ '). There is *quantifier* actualism, the doctrine that there is no ineliminable quantification over nonactuals, in the sense of 'actual' appropriate to the operator. In the case of metaphysical possibility, this is the plausible doctrine that all intelligent apparent quantification over possibilia, as in 'the possible person who would have come from this pair of gametes would have had blue eyes', can be reduced to quantification over actual objects, modal operators and predicates of actual objects. Quantifier actualism is to be distinguished from *operator* actualism, the doctrine that all sentences containing occurrences of the given modal operator have equivalents that speak only of what is actually the case; that is, equivalents that do not contain that operator at all. Obviously, it is consistent to be a quantifier actualist about a given modal operator while not being an

*I am very grateful to Michael Dummett and Barry Stroud for comments on earlier versions of this paper, and to Gareth Evans both for discussions about quantification and for advice about the presentation of these claims.

Christopher Peacocke

operator actualist with respect to it. From now on in this paper I will use 'actualism' for operator actualism applied to the causal modalities. I will also include as actualists those who, though declining to give any interpretation to causally modal sentences themselves, nevertheless hold that an account can be given of what it is to believe a causally modal statement which does not itself employ causal modalities; for those who hold this view will also equally claim that an account of our linguistic practices with operators for causal modalities can be given that does not itself use causal modalities.

My strategy in questioning the views of the actualist tradition will be this. First I will criticize the positive accounts actualists have offered of what it is to treat a generalization as a law, and their accounts of why laws but not generalizations of fact entail — or as they are likely to prefer to say sustain — counterfactuals. Actualists often have another idea. They often hold that there is a firm base of nonmodal categorical truths knowledge of which is unproblematic; in forming theories we generalize these particular categorical truths; and we are then prepared to extend these generalizations to nonactual instances. I will also question this idea. After that, I will go on to make some more positive contributions to the development of a nonactualist conception of causal necessity. Some of these positive suggestions are partial and provisional: I am uncertain about the details of what I say. What I am really suggesting is the *form* of a position.

These issues have not only their intrinsic interest, but also a more general one. Ⓒ is a recognition-transcendent notion, if anything is. It applies in the first instance to generalizations whose truth is liable to transcend our capacity to recognize it. So any systematic defence of an anti-actualist position about causal necessity — a notion that is absolutely pervasive in our everyday thought about the world — cannot fail to be a suggestion about *one* way of meeting anti-realist doubts about realist semantics. More than this, we shall touch on a number of points that suggest special links between causal modalities and realism.

The distinction between generalizations of law and generalizations of fact ('accidentally true generalizations') has always provided a challenge to actualist writers in a neo-Humean tradition. We shall look soon at what actualist writers have offered in response to this challenge. (J. L. Mackie writes that this difficulty 'can be completely resolved so that it no longer tells against the thesis that natural laws, in so far as they have any claim to truth, are contingent unrestricted universals'.[2]) My own view is that it is not enough to consider these actualist responses and to give grounds for rejecting them. If we are not actualists, we ought also to answer the following questions. Why does the distinction between the causally necessary and the accidental matter to us? What else would we have to abandon if we abandoned the distinction? How is our belief in its application manifested and how do we reasonably apply such a distinction? We ought to attempt to answer all these questions. But as a first step we would do well to note two points about accidental generalizations here. First, they can be about physically fundamental entities (e.g. about the uniform co-occurrence of two kinds of quark), they can hold in a wide variety of circumstances and they can be both free of singular terms and spatio-temporally unrestricted. Second, if *s* is such an accidentally true generalization, the counterfactual 'If we were to test *s* under certain empirically possible conditions, it would be falsified' is true, but it is not at all clear that the actualist can admit that it is, since the generalization is of a kind of which he is likely to say that if actually true it sustains the opposite counterfactual.

Let us now turn to the examination of some actualist surrogates for the notion of law and some actualist explanations of phenomena that causal necessity might be invoked to describe. I am going to argue that these actualist accounts either are inadequate or else they tacitly use notions of the kind their advocates are trying to avoid.

We will look first at the account Ayer presents in his paper, 'What is a Law of Nature?'[3] Ayer's idea is this:[4]

> I believe that all the cigarettes in my case are made of Virginian tobacco, but this belief would be destroyed if I were informed that I had absent-mindedly just filled my case from a box in which I keep only Turkish cigarettes. On the other hand, if I took it to be a law of nature that all the cigarettes in this case were made of Virginian tobacco, say on the ground that the case had some curious physical property which had the effect of changing any other tobacco that was put into it into Virginian, then my belief would not be weakened in this way.

(We had better take it that Ayer is using 'Virginian' and 'Turkish' for kinds of tobacco rather than as words for place of origin: not even God could change now the origin that a particular quantity of tobacco already has.) Ayer generalizes from this case and holds that, provided we fully specify the generalizations and do not leave some conditions unspecified and taken for granted, we can say:[5]

> a person A was treating a statement of the form 'for all x, if ϕx then ψx' as expressing a law of nature, if and only if there was no property X which was such that the information that a value α of x had X as well as ϕ would weaken his belief that α had ψ.

(He adds the restrictions that X does not entail not-ψ and that the presence of X is not regarded as a manifestation of not-ψ.)

Clearly something has gone wrong here. A man may hold it to be a law of nature that plants of a certain kind grow only where the temperature never falls below freezing point, even if his belief that the temperature around a given plant has never fallen below freezing point is weakened when he is informed that it originally grew in Iceland for several years and was transplanted from there. But the property of growing in Iceland does not *entail* that the temperature around the plant fell below freezing point — it does so only in conjunction with other factual beliefs. Ayer's suggestion about what it is to treat something as a law of nature seems to stem from an incorrect generalization from the tobacco example. If an object, such as Ayer's cigarette case, turns all F things that are put into it into $F\&G$ things, then obviously a belief that all the F things it contains are G things is not going to be undermined by the information that a different kind of F thing — but an F thing none the less — was put into it. But there are many other ways the belief could be weakened, which are analogues of the case of the plant from Iceland. If I know a friend enjoys smoking only non-Virginian tobacco, and enjoys smoking a cigarette from the case, then my belief that that particular cigarette from the case is Virginian must be weakened.

Can we revise Ayer's criterion to avoid this problem? The obvious revision would be this:

a person A was treating a statement of the form 'for all x, if ϕx then ψx' as expressing a law of nature iff there is no property X such that
(i) the information that a value α of x had X as well as ϕ would weaken A's belief that α had ψ, where
(ii) the information that α is X does not appear to A to entail in conjunction with the remainder of his beliefs that α is not ψ.

The main objection to any such revision is that the definition now includes some generalizations not held by A to be causally necessary. There is no impossibility in a man's believing a universal generalization, on the basis of its instances, but not believing it to be a law of nature, yet also being such that he will give up the belief in the universal generalization only if he gains information that is, in the context of the rest of his beliefs, incompatible with the generalization. (His not believing it to be a law of nature will be shown in his acceptance of particular counterfactuals.) For this man, there will be no property meeting (i) and (ii), and so the revision wrongly counts him as holding the generalization to be a law of nature.

It is in fact also unclear whether the revised criterion is really necessary for a generalization to be held as a law of nature. A man may hold a generalization to be causally necessary, but still acknowledge the existence of a rival theory in the field. This rival theory may successfully predict an object to be both ϕ and ϕ'; even though in the context of his beliefs being ϕ' does not appear to him to entail being not-ψ, this man may still abandon his previously believed laws in favour of the alternative theory: he may simply no longer believe at all what he previously took to be a law, and hence that object's being both ϕ and ϕ' weakens his belief that it will be ψ in those circumstances. Hence the revised criterion wrongly pronounces it not to have previously been held to be a law.

Ayer was hoping to explain the difference between treating something as a law and treating it as a generalization of fact in terms of different responses to the presentation of information of certain kinds. There is a great danger here of incorrectly identifying two distinctions. The first is the distinction between those generalizations that are retained and those that are not retained under a counterfactual hypothesis: this, in general, *is* indeed the distinction between generalizations of law and of fact. The second is the distinction between those generalizations one will retain and those one would abandon *if those counterfactual conditions were presented to one as actually obtaining.* There are many generalizations one would abandon under such conditions, even though, as things actually are, they are held to be laws. Our man who believes the law about the plants will accept the counterfactual 'if some of these plants were placed in the ground in Iceland, they would die'; this is quite consistent with the truth of the counterfactual about *him* that if he were presented with and accepted the information that one of the plants had been found growing in Iceland, then he would abandon the generalization. We must not conflate a distinction drawn on the basis of the way someone *in fact* reasons about counterfactual situations with one drawn on the basis of the way that person would react if presented with the information that those counterfactual conditions are actually fulfilled.[6] The effect of collateral information is quite different in the two cases.

There is a puzzling feature of the general form of Ayer's theory, which is an account in terms of the *dispositions* of those who take a generalization to be a law. Ayer's aim was to say what it is to believe a generalization to be causally necessary without using the concept of a generalization's *being* causally necessary. Causally necessary generalizations are distinguished from the accidental generalizations by entailing counterfactuals. Now dispositional statements equally entail counterfactuals: why should counterfactuals be any less puzzling when their subject-matter is persons than when their subject-matter is something else? It is as if someone concerned to give an account of statements apparently about the past avoiding use either of the past tense or of quantification over past times were also to say that what makes an expression O translatable as 'in the past' in English is the fact that, memory failures apart, a person assents to OA if in the past he assented to A. That ought not to satisfy *him*.[7]

Ayer himself seems to have felt this dissatisfaction in a later work, *Probability and Evidence*, and he raises essentially that objection against himself. His reply is that[8] we can explain what is meant by treating a generalization as one of law, and so explain how a non-truth-functional conditional can be acceptable, by describing actual instances in which someone makes the required projection. Having learned what it is to extend a generalization to an undetermined or imaginary instance, we can comprehend the case where the generalization which is extended is itself a generalization about the process of extension.

Presumably the generalization that is here being extended is: on all past occasions, the move from 'All examined Fs have been Gs' to 'The next examined F will be G' has been found correct. But when someone is extending this generalization to new unexamined cases, that seems to manifest no more than the belief that all actual Fs are Gs, and not a belief in its causal necessity. If it is meant to be a nonactual, counterfactually specified instance to which the generalization is being extended, the actualist is illegitimately making use of a notion he finds suspect in the way our theorist was in the example about the past: for what is it to extend a generalization to a nonactual instance? For this reason, Ayer does not really have a right to include the words 'or imaginary' in his phrase 'Having learned what it is to extend a generalization to an undetermined or *imaginary* instance . . .'. (In fact, if we *had* learned what it is to extend a generalization to an undetermined or imaginary instance, the problem would already be solved.)

This general problem with the form of Ayer's account, or of any account in terms of the dispositions of the believer in a law of nature, would not be resolved by pointing to the existence of physical brain states that underlie the dispositions. First, the dispositions have not been satisfactorily specified by the terms of the actualist programme — as we have just seen, they must be more than dispositions to project to actual instances. Second, the problem for the actualist is doubled up by this move to underlying brain states, since the underlying state is meant to explain causally the manifestations of the disposition, and causal explanation seems to take us back to causal laws.

Like Ayer, Mackie also holds that 'there is nothing in the sustaining of counterfactuals to show that causal laws have a meaning or content that in any way differs from that of a straight-forward factual universal';[9] but he also offers a positive account of why we take laws to sustain counterfactuals. He writes that:[10]

We need consider only the simplest case where [a] law itself is either directly confirmed or inductively su̗pported. If it is, say, the law that potassium when in contact with oxygen ignites, the evidence will be that other samples of potassium, in contact with oxygen under varying conditions, have ignited, that experiments have been made in which potassium has at first been kept away from oxygen and has not ignited, and then, some oxygen having been brought into contact with it, but nothing else, so far as we can tell, that could possibly be relevant having changed, the potassium has burst into flame, and so on. Now consider how this body of evidence is related to the following other cases: first, some potassium will be brought into contact with oxygen tomorrow; secondly, some potassium was brought into contact with oxygen yesterday, but we have not heard what happened on that occasion; thirdly, someone may be bringing some potassium into contact with oxygen just now in the next room; fourthly, suppose that this bit of potassium, which has not in fact been exposed to oxygen, had been so exposed. The evidence does, by hypothesis, support the proposed law. It does, therefore, give us some reason to believe that the potassium in the first case will ignite; equally, that the potassium in the second case did ignite; and equally that if in the third case the potassium in the next room is now being exposed to oxygen, it is igniting. But that body of evidence bears the same logical relation to the fourth, the counterfactually supposed case, as it bears to the other three. It therefore makes it reasonable for us to assert, within the scope of that counterfactual supposition, that the potassium ignited.

Now it appears that on this account, an accidentally true generalization that held in a wide variety of different kinds of circumstance would count as sustaining counterfactuals: certainly the argument that the evidence 'bears the same logical relation' to the counterfactually supposed case as to the unknown actual cases applies equally to the accidentally true generalization. I do not mean to suggest that there is not in these circumstances evidence that the generalization is a law — on the contrary, there obviously is — but I do mean to suggest that our notion of causal modality is such that we have a conception of how the evidence could hold and yet the counterfactuals fail to hold: in Mackie's example it requires no more than that there are empirically possible circumstances such that, if they were to obtain, the generalization would be falsified. Mackie's account seems not to leave room for this possibility.

The general form of Mackie's account is this. An explanation is given of why a sentence $\ulcorner$it is a law that $p\urcorner$ sustains a corresponding sentence, a counterfactual p', in terms of the existence of evidence of a certain kind for p. But if the evidence can hold, and in fact is consistent with the truth of some weaker condition, an accidentally true generalization q, which does not sustain a corresponding q', then the account in terms of evidence will leave it unexplained why q does not sustain the corresponding q'.[11]

A supporter of Mackie might well object to this, and say 'In your example we are required to make sense of the possibility that a counterfactual is well supported by the evidence but is nevertheless false. But since they do not concern what is actually the case, counterfactuals cannot be simply true or simply false:[12] they can only be more or less well supported by the evidence, in that what is actually the case can make it more or less reasonable to develop the consequence of a supposition in a particular way. Hence I do not find your example intelligible.'

I shall make three remarks on this, besides the obvious one that the possibility in the example does not really seem hard to understand.

(i) Suppose the accidental generalization that has been found to hold in a wide variety of circumstances is that all Fs are Gs. If in fact later we come across an F that is not a G and we believe that background conditions have not altered, then we will say that the earlier evidence supported belief in the law, yet an assertion of the law was not in fact correct (though it was not unreasonable to make the assertion). But I think we ought to accept the following general principle:

If it is sufficient for r to fail to be the case that the counterfactual 'If p were the case, q would be the case' is true, then we understand what it is for r to fail to be the case even though it is not actually the case that p and that q.

(ii) Examples can be given of which we can make sense but which are parallel to the case that this defence of Mackie claims to be unintelligible. It is plausible that their intelligibility can be supported by appeal to the principle in (i). Suppose we have evidence that animals are never to be found in regions of a certain kind, and consider a region of this kind that is in fact unexplored. Even though the evidence disconfirms it, we understand what it is for the statement that there is a horse at a particular place in that region to be true: it is in general sufficient that the counterfactual 'If we were to go there, we would perceive it' is true.

(iii) It is *not* necessary to suppose, in giving this objection to Mackie's suggestion, that a counterfactual can be barely true or barely false in Dummett's sense:[13] in the kind of example in question, there can be something in virtue of which the counterfactual 'if p were the case, q would be' ($p \mathbin{\Box\!\!\rightarrow} q$) whose truth is incompatible with the law, is true. Because truth-in-virtue-of is here an *a posteriori* notion, we need not be in a position to *know* of a property that a counterfactual is true in virtue of an object's possession of that property – even though we may know the object possesses that property. (Note that in example (ii) there would be something in virtue of which the counterfactual is true.) I shall discuss in more detail in section III the relations between the denial of actualism and doctrines employing the notion of that in virtue of which a statement is true.[14]

Actualist writers in the neo-Humean tradition tend to present the problems about causal modalities as problems about what it is to have a belief in a law or a counterfactual: belief in and knowledge of what is actually the case is taken as, for these purposes, relatively unproblematic. This general picture is given vivid expression by Ayer:[15]

> Our picture of the world is a picture not only of actual events, or events which are believed to be actual, but also of imaginary events which branch out from the actual ones. Logically speaking, the requirement that our beliefs be factually true leaves us free to characterize the imaginary events in any way we please, but, in practice, we limit our freedom by adopting principles of construction which apply to the whole picture.

This general view may be undermined from within by pressing the question: what has to be the case if we are to have this knowledge of what is actually the case, the 'factual' core the actualist takes as unproblematic? Perception cannot fail to play an essential part in gaining knowledge of what is actually the case. But the truth of perceptual statements requires the truth of certain causally modalized statements. A token experience e is a perception of an object x only if there are properties F and G such that x's being F causally explains e's being G, i.e., only if there is a law connecting an object's being F (in certain circumstances) with the occurrence of an experience of the kind G. Let me immediately add some clarifications. I do not mean that perception of an object can be analysed in terms of counterfactuals: in fact I do not believe that claim.[16] The point is that a certain generalization has to be true, but not merely accidentally so. The second disclaimer is this: it is not being denied that the relevant law may be statistical. A perceptual mechanism may contain probabilistic components. Although it is more difficult to apply, the distinction between the nomologically and the accidentally true applies as much within the class of statistical generalizations as it does within the class of non-statistical generalizations.

This connection between perception and causal modalities is not something we could peel off from the concept to obtain a concept just as serviceable as perception itself, a notion of perception*, say. The fact that perceptual sentences require for their truth the truth of some causally modalized sentences is linked with the fact that to perceive an object is a way of gaining knowledge of it. On the concept of perception*, one can perceive* an object even though the properties of one's experience are to be explained not by the states of that object, but (if they are explained by anything at all) by the states of something else. It is alien to our concept of knowledge to suppose that experiences can be a source of *knowledge* about an object if their relevant properties are not explained by the object being as it is. (Indeed, in these circumstances the experiences would not be *of* that object at all.)

These considerations suggest that it is incoherent to say that our knowledge of what is actually the case can be extended, in the ways specified by the actualist, to counterfactual cases so as to yield knowledge of laws. But that would be too strong, and unfair to the actualist: obviously the clear-headed actualist will apply his favoured account of lawhood also to the laws true perceptual statements require. The considerations do however suggest a weaker conclusion: if we find one-by-one that actualist analyses of lawhood do not work, and if we find some system in the failures, this must cast doubt upon the availability to the actualist of a core of categorical truths, knowledge of which is unproblematic. For if causal necessity is ineliminable, then, according to these considerations from the theory of perception, an account of what makes our beliefs in these actual truths knowledge cannot avoid employment of causal modalities.

The same connection between perception and causal modalities can also be presented from another angle. The empirical evidence that a person has that he is located, say, in Oxford and not in Cambridge is expressed by such counterfactuals as 'if I were in Cambridge, I would not be having an experience (as I in fact am) as of the Radcliffe Camera'. It seems very difficult to express this evidence adequately if one replaces the counterfactual by an indicative conditional. For, first, if I am having an experience as of the Radcliffe Camera, then the indicative conditional 'if I am in Cambridge, then there is a building like the Radcliffe Camera in Cambridge' *is* acceptable. But let us set that aside for a more fundamental problem. On what grounds can we in the statement of the evidence that I am in Oxford and not in Cambridge assert the indicative version of the conditional, that is 'if I am in Cambridge then I am not having an experience as of the Radcliffe Camera'? It cannot be asserted on the basis of its components: its consequent is in the imagined circumstances false, and its antecedent is one of the statements for which we wish to use the whole conditional as evidence. Nor can it be asserted on the basis of past constant conjunction. That would produce far too many conditionals, some of which would be evidence for sentences that, in conjunction with other truths, would entail that the person is not located at the place at which he is in fact located. A man may know for instance that in the past people have always entered Oxford by coming down from Headington Hill. (We can pick suitable qualitative properties of Oxford and Headington Hill and suppose them to occur in a generalization free of singular terms.) This would be evidence for the conditional that, if he is in Oxford now, then in the past he had an experience as of coming down Headington Hill. But anyone with mastery of the spatial scheme will realize that (absence of barriers permitting) a person could enter Oxford by a different route, and would not use the counterfactual analogue of such a conditional as any evidence about his present location.[17] If someone has mastery of the spatial scheme, he will always be able to draw a distinction between coincidental and non-coincidental generalizations about experiences, based on the idea that a perceiver could always have taken a different route through the spatial world. (Physical objects in space are permanent possibilities of counterfactuals.) This could not of course supply a basis for the general distinction between such generalizations, since the distinction so founded is one between generalizations about experience only, and is also relative to a contingent distribution of objects in space. Nevertheless, it is plausibly a case where the causal modalities are not easily replaced in favour of indicative sentences.

II

On an anti-actualist view, we form hypotheses about what is causally necessary and what is not on evidence much less than conclusive. This necessarily allows for the possibility that there are some accidental generalizations we wrongly count to be causally necessary: but as we noted, such generalizations are not unknowably accidental — there are empirically possible circumstances in which the generalization would be falsified.

A plausible anti-actualist view also has, and is required to have, a more positive component: an account of how a belief in causal necessity is manifested which shows how ascriptions of belief in causal necessities (and not something weaker or stronger) can be empirically confirmed. The distinctive feature of the anti-actualist view I want to put forward is that the account of manifestation makes essential use of the notion of causal necessity and related concepts. This account thus forms part of the case for the homophonic treatment of ' $\boxed{c}$ ' in a meaning theory for a language containing it: it would be a misunderstanding to think that the manifestation condition developed in this section of the paper is intended to supplant rather than to go in tandem with the view that ' $\boxed{c}$ ' has a certain sense.[18]

I should also note here that the account to be given is strictly an account of what it is to believe that something is *at least* causally necessary. (Henceforth I shall not explicitly insert the 'at least'.) It will be striking to those interested in Quinean issues about necessity that there does not seem to be a satisfactory account for $\square$ corresponding to the one I shall suggest for $\boxed{c}$. Those who believe that there are satisfactory accounts of the manifestation of beliefs in stronger notions of necessity should imagine the manifestation condition that I will give to be supplemented with a clause to the effect that the conditions for manifestation of a stronger belief are not met; what I have to say here will be neutral on whether there are satisfactory accounts of manifestation for the stronger notion.

In setting out an account of manifestation, we will find it helpful to pursue a comparison with the manifestation of a belief in an unmodalized, universally quantified condition. The account we will use for comparison will be essentially Ramsey's. Ramsey wrote[19]

> To believe that all men are mortal — what is it? Partly to say so, partly to believe in regard to any x that turns up that if he is a man he is mortal.

Let us concentrate on the second half of this, since it is implausible that general beliefs cannot be attributed to languageless creatures. An important first point to note is that, when we consider just the second part of Ramsey's account, the disposition in which belief in the general statement is said to consist is one the specification of which *uses* a universal quantifier — 'to believe in regard to *any x* that turns up . . .'. This is quite unobjectionable: if we know what it is to have singular beliefs, one can inductively confirm or disconfirm the presence of the disposition in which on a Ramseyan account belief in the general statement consists.

There is a point to notice in passing. A man can have a general belief yet fail to think of instantiating it with respect to a particular object, much as he may fail to connect up two of his beliefs that entail a third. Ramsey is presuming that we can have good reasons for distinguishing such cases from those in which he does not have the general belief at all. Let us grant that for the present. But now once that *is* granted, it would be all right to replace Ramsey's

> belief in regard to any x that turns up that if he is a man he is mortal

i.e. a disposition to believe singular conditionals, with a conditional relating singular beliefs, i.e.

> in regard to any x that turns up to be such that if one believes that he is a man, one believes he is mortal.

The difference between these two dispositions arises only in the case in which a man fails to connect two of his beliefs. In Ramsey's case the distinction between the two versions is not of great significance because belief in an indicative conditional does not raise problems of a kind the account is meant to be resolving. In other cases this is not so (we will see that the case of causal necessity is one of them), and, where $ is some binary sentence-forming operator on sentences, the distinction between

> a believes that (p,q)

and

> $(a$ believes that p, a believes that $q)$

can be crucial in removing a threat of circularity in the account of what it is to have a belief of the kind in question.

Some revisions and elucidations of Ramsey's account are evidently needed, but let us first give the analogue for belief in a causal necessity of this simple account, an analogue that will itself need corresponding revision and elucidation. The analogue, which uses causal modalities just as the Ramsey condition uses the universal quantifier, is: for *a* to believe that $\boxed{c}$ *p* is for it to be the case that

(C) for any *q* such that $\diamondsuit\!\!\!\!\!c\;\; q$, (*a* believes it has come to be the case that *q*) $\Box\!\!\rightarrow$ (*a* still believes that *p*).

(Here '*p*' and '*q*' are schematic for complete sentences.) The application of this condition can be empirically tested by trying out various causally possible *q*s just as the Ramsey condition is empirically testable. Just as in the case of the Ramsey condition, it would be wrong to represent (C) as giving an account of manifestation that invokes circumstances that are in fact completely inaccessible to us. It turns on what is accessible to us granted inductive reasoning.

It is also important that '$\Box\!\!\rightarrow$' has wider scope than either occurrence of 'believes': if that were not so, (C) could be applied only if we already knew what it is to have a counterfactual belief — a belief in a causal modality of the kind for which we purport to be giving an account.

(C) pronounces differently from Mackie's account on some examples. For instance, a man who comes to believe a universally quantified conditional only after testing it in various circumstances certainly need not believe it to be a law: he may just take this as evidence that the circumstances that would falsify the law do not, as it happens, occur in nature. We have seen that it is not easy to see how Mackie could accommodate this fact. But it presents no difficulty for (C). The imagined person is not counted as believing the generalization to be causally necessary according to (C) because he *would* cease to believe the generalization if these circumstances that he supposes not to arise in nature were in fact to do so.

Like any adequate manifestation condition for a given expression with a given sense, (C) specifies a goal that must be achieved by any training programme designed to produce in a person the proper use of that expression. In the case of Ramsey's condition, if *we* have inductive reasons for believing a universally quantified condition is true of the trainee, then we have reason to believe that the goal of the training programme has been achieved. Similarly, if *we* have reasonable beliefs about what is causally necessary, we can have reason to believe that the goal of a training programme that (C) specifies for the use of '$\boxed{c}$' has been achieved.

If (C) is accepted, it will function as a constraint on the interpretability of an expression in a person's language as a sign for causal modality.

If we know a sentence $\$A$ to be sincerely uttered, when the speaker does not meet the condition resulting from (C) when a translation of A is substituted for 'p' then $\$$ should not be interpreted by '$\boxed{c}$'. For this reason, our ability to *ask* someone whether he believes that $\boxed{c}\,p$ can never obviate the need for a condition like (C) in an account of what it is to have such a belief. For such a condition will have to be used in the identification of a particular expression in the person's language as an expression for causal necessity and hence to frame the question we would have to ask him.

Why is the antecedent of the counterfactual 'a believes it has come to be the case that q' rather than just 'a believes it is the case that q'? The answer is that it helps to solve the problem raised for Ayer by the case of the plants in Iceland. It is true that if the subject in that example were to believe there are plants of the given kind growing in Iceland, then he would abandon his belief in the law. But we are not interested in the subject's reaction on the hypothesis that he accepts that such plants grow in Iceland, with no other changes in his beliefs: we want to capture his reactions if he not only believes this new piece of information, but also supposes that the adjustments in the world necessary to allow it have taken place, and that consequential adjustments will also take place. This move to belief in its having come about that q has some complications of its own, which we will touch upon later. Of course if it does help towards answering the objection, it is something that Ayer could take over too: but Ayer could not consistently embed the condition, as I have done, within unreduced counterfactual and causal possibility operators.

I now respond to some objections to (C). I shall write in a style suggestive of a greater confidence in the responses I offer than I really feel: I am quite prepared to believe that there are other and better responses to the objections which are consistent with the general strategy outlined in the preceding paragraphs of this section.

(i) Suppose a believes that certain conditions are causally possible that are not in fact causally possible; and suppose too that a believes that p would hold in all those conditions that are in fact causally possible, but believes that it would not hold under those additional conditions that he holds to be causally possible but which are not in fact so. Then surely he does not believe that $\boxed{c}\,p$, yet according to our present account he would do so. Moreover, the revision for which one immediately reaches, to alter 'for any q such that $\diamondsuit q$' to 'for any q such that a believes that $\diamondsuit q$', would produce circularity, since we are trying to give an account of what belief in causal modalities consists in.

There is an analogous problem in the Ramseyan account of the universal quantifier, and the natural solution to it suggests a parallel solution for the problem in the causal case. The analogous problem runs as follows. A person may believe there to be some objects that are F and not G: this can be true even though not only are there no such objects, but also there are not in fact any of which he believes that they are F and not G. (Intuitively, he believes only in fact nonexistent things to be F and not G.) Such a person will not believe that all Fs are Gs. But since nonexistent objects cannot, in Ramsey's phrase, 'turn up', then it can still be true that, in regard to any object that turns up, our person will believe that if it is F it is G.

The natural solution to this problem is to require that the person have the given disposition to form beliefs even when a specification of the belief presents the object of the belief under such modes of presentation as 'the next one to be encountered'. For all our man in our last example may know it may be one of the F and not G ones he believes to exist. The general principle being invoked here is that, if someone fails to believe that all Fs are Gs, then there will be *some* mode of presentation ϕ such that given the information that the ϕ (or that ϕ) is F, he will not believe that the ϕ (or that ϕ) is G. As the parenthetical addition suggests, we should allow demonstrative modes of presentation, and in the case of beliefs about real numbers such substituends for 'ϕ' as 'real number determined by the infinite sequence of digits issued by this random number machine'. (There are certainly difficulties here, but they seem to be less acute for beliefs about concrete objects.[20])

A similar move can be made to resolve the problem in the causal case: even if someone believes certain conditions are causally possible which are not in fact causally possible, he will not have the property specified in condition (C) if we interpret (C) in such a way that the conditions it quantifies over can be presented in the form 'the physical condition to be realized in the centre of α-Centauri at midnight tomorrow' or 'the next physical condition to be produced in the accelerator at Stanford'. The assumption that corresponds to the assumption about the modes of presentation of concrete objects that are mentioned above is this: for any person a, if a fails to believe that $\boxed{c}\,p$, then there is some mode of presentation ϕ of a condition such that (a believes the condition meeting ϕ obtains) $\Box\!\!\rightarrow$ (a does not believe that p). Here of course the mode of presentation ϕ must be *a priori* neutral with respect to whether it is the case that p or not.[21]

The original revision in the Ramsey quantifier condition should be welcome for other reasons too. To believe that all Fs are Gs is to believe something stronger than that all the Fs one will encounter are Gs: these two are not conflated when such modes of presentation as 'the next F to occupy such and such a region' are included. Here there is another threat of circularity. The equivalences upon which Russell's theory of descriptions is founded show that unrestricted use of 'the' within the scope of 'believes' may again involve the attribution of general beliefs. We must be able to show that the uses of 'the' required in the specifications of the modes of presentation that are invoked to solve

Christopher Peacocke

these problems are uses that can be mastered prior to full mastery of quantification. (This has some plausibility in the case of 'the next F in place p to be so and so'.) In developing such a programme one would expect mastery of functors such as 'the object to the north of ( )' to be important.

(ii) A complication is also provided by the converse possibility: that in which some p comes to be the case that the believer thought not to be causally possible. In such circumstances it may be true that, if he were to believe it had come to be the case that p, then he would abandon belief in a law: yet the truth of this counterfactual does not show that he does not actually believe the relevant generalization to be a law.

Once again there is an analogue of this situation in the case of the universal quantifier. For all a man's believing that all Fs are Gs, he might not believe of an object that 'turns up' that is manifestly F and not G that if it is F then it is G. Here it is natural to say: what matters is that if he had only the information that it is F and no singular information about whether it is G or not, then he would believe it to be G.

We can make a parallel response in the causal case. It is reasonable to hope that, if we can explain what it is to believe in the causal necessity of a law, we can give accounts, derivative from that explanation, of what it is to believe in the causal necessity of other forms of statement. Since the general form of a law is

$$\forall x_1 \ldots \forall x_n \ (F(x_1, \ldots, x_n) \supset G(x_1, \ldots, x_n))$$

(where F and G will in general be complex) then we have the two components F and G that allow us to revise (C) in a way parallel to the revision of Ramsey. In the case in which we confine our attention to monadic F and G and ignore the qualifications prompted under (i) above then we may say that a believes that $\boxed{c}$ $\forall x(Fx \supset Gx)$ iff

for any condition Fx such that $\Diamond_c Fx$ (a believes that it has come to be the case that Fx and a does not have singular evidence other than Fx relevant to whether Gx) $\Box\!\!\rightarrow$ (a believes that Gx).

Can we raise the same difficulty again with respect to the conditions Fx? There are two kinds of case to consider here, that in which all instances of the antecedent are believed to be causally impossible, and that in which only some are. We need not worry about not admitting such believed laws in the former case: a person's belief in such laws could never directly explain his manipulations of the world, except to the extent that we relax the condition that he at all times believes instances of the antecedent to be causally impossible.[22] (To put the point in possible worlds terms: such laws impose no restrictions on the worlds he believes to be causally possible.) It seems there are examples of the other case, in which only some instances of the antecedent are believed to be causally impossible. This phenomenon is particularly noticeable in the case of functional laws — for example, van der Waals's law when the molecules of the gas are extensionless. But these appear to be cases in which certain values are not excluded in order to achieve mathematical simplicity of formulation: in such examples there will be a less convenient form which the believer will accept as of equal explanatory power.

There is a minor irritation about vacuous fulfilment of the quantifier condition 'for any condition Fx such that $\langle\!\!\langle c \rangle\!\!\rangle Fx \ldots$' in this revised condition. Are we to permit vacuous fulfilment? That would then make everyone believe every law that has a causally impossible antecedent. Are we to exclude vacuous fulfilment? That would then exclude anyone from believing to be a law something with an in fact causally impossible antecedent. We should perhaps take the second option, but do so with a more relaxed attitude to the application of the condition. We can discern someone's belief in a law with an in fact causally impossible antecedent if he uses it in the same way as other generalizations directly identified as believed laws by the criterion, if he sincerely asserts the generalization within the scope of an operator identified in more direct cases as an expression for causal necessity, and so forth.

(iii) Another complication of detail is this. Suppose a man believes the generalization $\forall x \, \forall t \, (Axt \supset Bx(t+1))$ to be a law, and believes more firmly for some particular x and t that Axt. Then if he were to believe it has come about that x is not B at time $t+1$, he would abandon belief in the status of the generalization as a law, or even as true. But this formerly believed law may be a source of derived laws having not-B as predicate of their antecedent, and the condition offered would have the consequence that these are not actually believed. One way round this is to add to the antecedent in the counterfactual specifying what it is to believe in a law the hypothesis that the subject loses any beliefs that together with essentially general statements rule out its coming about that Fx. 'Generalization' here need not be restricted to those believed to be causally necessary, so there need be no circularity.

There are, of course, other manifestations of belief in causal necessity: as Ramsey says in a vivid phrase:

> causal laws form the system with which the speaker meets the future.[23]

Thus if 'All past Fs have been Gs' is believed to be causally necessary and not just an accidentally true generalization, and there is a particular object x that a man does not want to be G, he will take precautions to prevent it becoming F, whereas he would not if the generalization were believed to be only accidentally true. But such manifestations are derivable from (C) or its refinements. So in this example, if the person believes that it is causally necessary that all Fs are Gs, then, according to (C), if he were to believe that x is F he would believe that x is G;

and this makes intelligible his attempts to prevent x from becoming F. But this kind of manifestation of belief in a causal necessity does not lend support to the actualist view, as can be seen in this particular example from the fact that the idea of the agent's taking precautions would take us back to a notion of the causal laws in which he believes, and this I have argued is something we can explain only by ourselves using the concepts of causal necessity and possibility.

It may however be suggested that there is an important distinction of structure between the Ramseyan condition and the condition I have suggested for the causal modalities. For any given condition that purports to state manifestation conditions for a particular kind of belief, we can distinguish the beliefs (if any) that that condition takes as relatively unproblematic, from those that the condition aims to illuminate. Thus the Ramseyan quantifier condition takes singular beliefs as relatively unproblematic. Now the suggestion is that one difference between the quantifier and causal cases – a difference implicit in our preceding discussion – is this. It is not plausible, it may be said, that there are any cases of quantification in which the beliefs taken as relatively unproblematic by the Ramseyan condition cannot be manifested (or possessed at all) unless corresponding general beliefs are manifested. I am not sure whether this claim is true. (If it is true, it is obviously important to ask *why* it is.) But let us suppose for the moment that it is true: what I want to argue is that, even if it were true, it would not damage the account I have presented. The reason it might be thought to provide a threat is that it *is* plausible that there are some causally modal beliefs such that the beliefs taken as relatively unproblematic by the manifestation condition I have suggested cannot be manifested (or possessed at all) unless those causally modal beliefs are manifested. An example we have already considered that fits this description is the case of beliefs about the spatial location of objects, properties and features. We suggested that it is plausible that the belief that one is located, and that various other objects and features are located, at particular places can be established only by reasoning involving (for any given circumstances) certain counterfactuals. If then our manifestation condition for causally modal sentences is accepted, when applied to cases in which ' $\boxed{c}$ ' operates on a sentence containing the relevant spatial predicates, the beliefs taken as relatively unproblematic by the condition will not be manifestable without beliefs in corresponding causally modal sentences also being manifested.

This situation is not contrary to reason, nor does it undermine the point of specifying a manifestation condition. What it means is that in such examples the manifestation conditions of spatial and causally modal beliefs must be applied to patterns of actions *simultaneously*, and a best theory of a person's beliefs worked out by reference to both conditions. Indeed, the phenomenon of such simultaneous manifestation seems to be found within the spatial scheme itself. There appears for example, to be no possibility of manifesting in action beliefs that particular places have certain properties without manifesting beliefs about one's own location.[24]

It is natural to ask why so many philosophers have taken different attitudes to the cases of universal quantification and causal necessity. Michael Dummett has suggested to me that one reason is that, while the idea of a being able to observe *all* the objects in the range of a universal quantifier exerts a powerful grip, there seems to be nothing analogous in the case of causal necessity. Of course universal quantification itself was not in fact thought to be problematic by many positivists even when it was quantification over unobservables: rather, their position seems to have been that, once singular statements about unobservables had been satisfactorily explained, there were no further problems about the universal quantifier. But this is consistent with the presence of some unconscious influence of the idea of such an ideal observer.

There is another point that suggests that the notion of observation may be relevant to the explanation of the different treatment the two notions have had historically. When we instantiate the universal quantifier in the Ramseyan condition we get a disposition of a person with respect to a particular object that we can effectively check, at least on the assumption that the presence of singular beliefs is not problematic. But in the case of (C) and its refinements, when we instantiate 'for all q' or 'for all conditions Fx', we do not obtain a condition that is decidable (relative to the attribution of the embedded beliefs) because of the presence of '$\Diamond$' and '$\Box\!\!\rightarrow$', both of which, when applied to sentences, yield conditions that cannot be said to be *observed* to be true. Only what is actually the case can be observed to be true. More generally, in the case of both observational and theoretical sentences, on an anti-actualist view, what is actually the case fails to settle the truth value of causally modal sentences but does not fail to settle those of universal generalizations.

All this is an attempt to explain, not to justify, the difference of attitude to the two cases. In the basic case, we finite beings can check the ascription to others of beliefs in universal quantifications of observational predicates only inductively. (Indeed, even if we *could* survey infinitely many objects simultaneously, without corresponding powers we could not manifest belief in such a universal quantification all at once to another.) In both cases it is our ability to use less than conclusive grounds for asserting sentences containing the constructions that makes the general form of the manifestation conditions I have offered unobjectionable.

Christopher Peacocke

III

What of the objections to anti-actualist views? Ramsey offered a one-sentence objection:[25]

> If we regarded the unfulfilled conditional as a fact we should have to suppose that any such statement as 'If he had shuffled the cards, he would have dealt himself the ace' has a clear sense, true or false, which is absurd.

The falsity of a sentence is the truth of its logical negation. Ramsey is here confusing the external negation of a counterfactual $A \mathbin{\Box\!\!\to} C$, viz. $\sim (A \mathbin{\Box\!\!\to} C)$, with its internal negation $A \mathbin{\Box\!\!\to} \sim C$, sometimes called the 'opposite' counterfactual of $A \mathbin{\Box\!\!\to} C$. The former but not the latter gives the falsity condition of $A \mathbin{\Box\!\!\to} C$; and the fact that it can be that neither $A \mathbin{\Box\!\!\to} C$ nor $A \mathbin{\Box\!\!\to} \sim C$ is true in no way shows that it can be that neither $A \mathbin{\Box\!\!\to} C$ nor $\sim (A \mathbin{\Box\!\!\to} C)$ is true.

The difference between the internal and the external negation comes out well in David Lewis's semantics.[26] If, in a sphere of worlds around the actual world, for every world in which $A \& C$ is true there is an equally close or closer world in which $A \& \sim C$ is true, and conversely, then clearly both $A \mathbin{\Box\!\!\to} C$ and $A \mathbin{\Box\!\!\to} \sim C$ are false. Presumably Ramsey believed this kind of situation obtained in his example: the antecedent 'if he had shuffled the cards' is so unspecific that many different, equally small, departures from the actual world can make it true, where some of these departures make the consequent true, and others make it false. But in these circumstances the external negation of the counterfactual, which is true just in case the counterfactual it negates is not true, is simply true: for the truth of the external negation requires (given of course that vacuity of the antecedent is not in question) that it is not the case that in some sphere in the system of spheres around the actual world either A or C holds at every world in that sphere. This requirement is fulfilled in such examples, and it is not 'absurd' to say that Ramsey's counterfactual is false.

A different objection to anti-actualism, one that may have been influencing Ramsey, is the thought that counterfactuals cannot be barely true: when a counterfactual is true, there is actually something in virtue of which it is true. Other than a simple reassertion of actualism, there are at least three different doctrines that might be intended here. I will argue that, in many cases, there is no difficulty presented for anti-actualism by these doctrines; but I will also tentatively raise some problems for these doctrines.

A familiar notion of 'sentence s is true in virtue of the truth of sentence s'' is that on which s reduces to a class of sets of statements, the conjunction of all the members of one of which sets is s', where 'reduces' is used in the sense of Michael Dummett.[27] This is a relation between (or an operator upon) a pair of sentences, not between a sentence and an object or a sentence and a property. On Dummett's notion, a dispositional statement about a particular object can be true in virtue of the truth of a statement of the grounds of that disposition in that object. Now it is not at all obvious that there is an inconsistency between the claim (i) that all counterfactuals about actual objects are true in virtue of statements not involving counterfactuals about the actual properties of those objects, and the claim (ii) that actualism is false. It is not at all obvious because reduction in Dummett's sense is not generally an *a priori* notion, as the case of dispositions shows. The counterfactual 'If this were placed in water, it would dissolve' can be true in virtue of the truth of a statement of the form 'This cube has microstructure M'; but to know the one is true in virtue of the other we must know there is a law of a certain kind connecting microstructure M with dissolving in water.

But though there may be no inconsistency between (i) and (ii), it may be said that there is at least a tension between them, given the role Dummett meant reduction to play. For Dummett explicitly says that, when there is a reduction of a given sentence *s*, 'grasp of the truth condition of *s* is not problematic'; understanding of *s* 'consists in our implicit grasp of the way in which its truth depends upon the truth of the statements in the reducing class'.[28] Given that Dummett allows the family of sets of reducing statements for a given statement to be infinite, there are other questions that could be raised here, but they are not our immediate concern. Our concern is the tension between Dummett's claim that counterfactuals cannot be barely true, and my own claim that we need to *use* causal modalities in specifying what is involved in mastery of the causal modalities and counterfactuals. However, it appears to me that an unreduced use of causal modalities is involved in Dummett's account. Dummett's reductions are not *a priori*: the extension of 'is true in virtue of' need not be available to anyone who understands the language in advance of detailed empirical investigation. So, presumably, one who understands a language containing a class of sentences that has an *a posteriori* reduction must be in possession of a procedure for determining by empirical investigation that in virtue of which a sentence of the kind in question is true. And our earlier arguments were designed to make it plausible that a specification of this procedure must either employ the notion of causal necessity or lead to incorrect answers.[29] (It of course raises questions about the importance of this notion of reduction if the appropriate specification of the procedures of investigation has to make use of recognition-transcendent concepts.)

It is worth developing and considering a possible objection to the view that no counterfactual is barely true. We can state it as follows.

In all of Dummett's examples in which we have an inclination to say that, if a counterfactual is true, then there must actually be something in virtue of which it is true – e.g. the counterfactuals corresponding to *brave* or to *is good at learning languages* – there is, if the counterfactual is true, some predicate that applies to the object in question where this predicate does *not* occur in the counterfactual, but does occur in the law; and it is in virtue of the object's satisfaction of *this* predicate that the counterfactual is true. But of course we also believe counterfactuals of the form

$$(F_1 a \ \& \ \ldots \ \& \ F_n a) \ \Box\!\!\rightarrow Ga$$

where $F_1, \ldots, F_n$ are *all* of the predicates that occur in the antecedent of the relevant law. An example in a Newtonian universe would be 'If this body were to have a mass of n lbs and a force f were applied, it would have such and such acceleration'. *Ex hypothesi*, in these examples there is *no* predicate that occurs in the law that does not occur in the counterfactual.

So in virtue of what are such counterfactuals true? Can we say that they are true in virtue of the law's holding? But then what is the law true in virtue of? One might be inclined to say that it is true in virtue of the truth of all the singular counterfactual instances for both actual and causally possible instances, and these in turn would be true in virtue of actual properties of these objects. But this would be simply to admit that counterfactuals like $(F_1 a \ \& \ \ldots \ \& \ F_n a) \ \Box\!\!\rightarrow Ga$ can be barely true: for this counterfactual is true in virtue of the law, and the law in virtue of singular counterfactuals including this one. Hence it is not the case that there is a statement in virtue of which the counterfactual is true and which does not itself involve counterfactuals. In such examples, we have run out of actual properties to cite in virtue of the possession of which by the object the counterfactual is true.[30]

I think we must admit the inconsistency this argument points out. But one feature of the argument that might be questioned is the assumption that the counterfactual $(F_1 a \ \& \ \ldots \ \& \ F_n a) \ \Box\!\!\rightarrow Ga$ is true in virtue of the holding of the law. An essentially programmatic reply to the objection might be this. That counterfactual is true rather in virtue of (for instance) s's being composed of *matter*. It might be thought that if the term 'matter' is introduced by 'whatever stuff satisfies the set S of laws' for some particular set of laws, the objection is not avoided. But here we must not ignore a distinction of scope between the false sentence

The counterfactual is true in virtue of a's being composed of the kind of stuff satisfying the set S of laws

(in which the description has narrow scope) and the true sentence concerning the kind K of stuff satisfying the set S of laws: the counterfactual is true in virtue of a's being composed of stuff of *that* kind K

(in which the description has wide scope). A fuller elaboration of this somewhat obscure reply would need (i) to show that this is not a distinction without a difference, and (ii) that there is some unity between the different things in virtue of which counterfactuals are said to be true in the two cases of counterfactuals that do and those that do not omit predicates that occur in the antecedent of the appropriate corresponding law. I do not know whether this reply can be made out: in any case, the objection seems to me very serious, and until we are confident that there is some adequate answer, it ought not to be taken as at all obvious that counterfactuals cannot be barely true.

I will very briefly mention two other concepts of 'truth in virtue of'. A second notion of 'true in virtue of' may be defined in terms of the notion we have already considered: if we use subscripts to indicate the first and second notions (the third is still to come), the definition would be

s is true in virtue of$_2$ object x iff $\exists s' \, \exists F$ (s is true in virtue of$_1$ s' and s' states of x that it is F).

The claim that any sentence of a given kind is true in virtue of$_1$ the truth of some other sentence may very well be weaker than the claim that any true sentence of that kind is true in virtue of$_2$ some object or other. For it is disputable whether all sentences are about objects. The first claim might be verified in the case of a particular sentence by that sentence being true in virtue of the truth of 'In the past it rained'. Now if in fact that quoted sentence can be interpreted as not making predication of any kind of object at all (even places and times), then the second doctrine, that all true sentences of the given kind are true in virtue of$_2$ objects, would insist further that there are objects in virtue of the properties of which 'In the past it rained' is true. This is not the place to discuss the stronger claim, once it is distinguished from the first. But for the same reasons as in the case of the weaker doctrine, positive argument is needed that it is incompatible with anti-actualism.

A third doctrine that might be intended can be introduced in the following way. When Dummett states his principle[31]

If a statement is true, there must be something in virtue of which it is true

it may be said that, if the question is not to be begged against the realist, the word 'be' of the consequent should not be read as present-tensed: rather it should require no more than that, for a statement 'In the past it was the case that p' to be true, it be the case that there *was* something in virtue of which the statement is (now) true. Now what is the analogue of this for counterfactuals? Perhaps it is this: the principle requires for the truth of $A \ \Box\!\!\rightarrow C$ not that there is *actually* something in virtue of which it is true but rather this: if A were to be the case, then there *would be* something in virtue of which C was true.

This third doctrine is however so anodyne and apparently inviolable that even Dummett's example of the objects of God's *scientia media* does not violate it. Suppose a theologian holds that God does know counterfactuals about the detailed behaviour of beings not actually created but who, if they had been created, would have had free will. These theologians are not committed to denying the principle read in this third way: 'Of course', they will say, 'if person a were created, he would have acted in such and such a way and this implies that if a were created, then there would be something in virtue of which "a acts in such and such a way" is true — in fact just the kind of thing that makes the statement that a person acts in that way true in the actual world.' So there seems nothing in this third version of the doctrine to threaten even these theologians, let alone the anti-actualist.

Twenty-five years ago, at the end of an elegant statement of the actualist view, Braithwaite wrote of the complexities of his own account that 'there is no need to suppose they spring from anything transempirical in the world itself'.[32] Transempiricism sounds a heady doctrine. If it is simply the negation of actualism, then I am a transempiricist. But if it is meant to imply that there is something nonempirical about irreducible causal modalities, then I am not a transempiricist. I have suggested that we ourselves, in constructing empirical theories, use a concept of causal necessity that is, like the universal quantifier over unsurveyable domains, recognition-transcendent in Dummett's sense, and that our ascription of causally modal beliefs to others is to be explained in terms of causal necessity itself. For operators and quantifiers, I am not sure what more could be involved in attributing to people beliefs about the world.

Notes

1   F. P. Ramsey, 'General Propositions and Causality', in *The Foundations of Mathematics and Other Essays* (London, Routledge, 1931), p. 252.

2   J. L. Mackie, *The Cement of the Universe* (Oxford University Press, 1974), p. 204.

3   A. J. Ayer, 'What is a Law of Nature?', reprinted in *The Concept of a Person and Other Essays* (London, Macmillan, 1963).

4 Ayer, 'What is a Law of Nature?' p. 231.

5 ibid., pp. 231–2.

6 Ayer's use of the phrase 'the generalization is resistant to the supposition that . . .' on p. 131 of *Probability and Evidence* (London, Macmillan, 1972) is open to the objection that it straddles this distinction.

7 This objection to Ayer's account will not impress anyone who holds that a counterfactual can be true without there existing any appropriately related law. Such a person should also find Ayer's account incomplete, since if that is a real possibility, then to give, as Ayer does, an account of what it is to believe something to be a law is not yet to give an account of what it is to believe a counterfactual. Moreover this person's view does not sit easily with the actualism motivating Ayer unless there is some nonmodal truth about the actual world that in some way corresponds with the truth of those counterfactuals that are not backed by laws. These issues are pursued later in the text.

8 Ayer, *Probability and Evidence*, p. 132.

9 J. L. Mackie, *Truth, Probability and Paradox* (Oxford University Press, 1973), p. 118.

10 Mackie, *The Cement of the Universe*, pp. 201–2.

11 Equally I could not agree that what makes an unrestricted true generalization into a law is that it fits into an (any?) overall true theory. For, on pain of circularity, 'true' must mean 'true in the actual world', and will exclude causally modal truths. But in that case accidentally true generalizations at the level of the explanatorily fundamental objects will wrongly be included as laws, for certainly to include them will greatly increase the power of the theory without introducing falsity. For the same reason, I am committed to disagreeing with the (early) Ramseyan theory of lawhood proposed by David Lewis in *Counterfactuals* (Oxford, Blackwell, 1973), pp. 73–4, according to which laws are those unrestricted generalizations that would be included as theorems or axioms in each true deductive system with a best combination of simplicity and strength. (Lewis's remark (2) on p. 74 makes clear that he also means by 'true' here 'truth in a given world', and his proposal defines a relative notion of a generalization being a law *at a world*.)

12 Mackie, *Truth, Probability and Paradox*, p. 106.

13 'the thesis that a counterfactual cannot be, as I shall say, *barely true*, that is, that a counterfactual cannot be true unless there is some statement, not involving the subjunctive conditional, whose truth renders the counterfactual true' – Michael Dummett, 'What is a Theory of Meaning? (II)' in *Truth and Meaning*, ed. G. Evans and J. McDowell (Oxford University Press, 1976), p. 89.

14 It may be that one reason Mackie does not consider the objection developed in the text to his account of why laws sustain counterfactuals is that in his discussion, immediately before the quoted passage, of why accidental generalizations do not sustain counter-

factuals, he considers only generalizations established by a complete enumerative check of instances. (I have no disagreements with his treatment of such examples.) But since as Mackie himself urges with great clarity later (p. 208), 'Not being made true only by what is locally the case is . . . neither necessary nor sufficient for a contingent universal's having what we intuitively recognize as the status of a law', it must be possible to believe a generalization on inductive grounds and yet not believe it to be a law. (It should also be noted that Mackie's later interesting discussion of 'forms of persistence' is not relevant to our present question of the explanation of why laws sustain counterfactuals: for Mackie agrees that there could be universes in which we would say there were laws which did not guarantee such forms of persistence — yet presumably those laws would still sustain counterfactuals.)

Mackie's general account may then be regarded as a specification of the meaning of 'It is a law that all Fs are Gs' by supplying a list of acceptance and rejection conditions for the sentence. Sometimes the realist can argue against such accounts if they include conclusive acceptance or rejection conditions by saying that if there are conclusive acceptance conditions, then the content of the sentence is that some one of these conditions obtains; if there are conclusive rejection conditions, the content is that none of these conditions obtains; and if there are both a combined condition can be given. But it would be a mistake to apply *this* argument against Mackie. For in the case of 'It is a law that all Fs are Gs' only the rejection conditions are conclusive (an instance of an F that is not G) and these rejection conditions are the *same* as those for the accidental universal generalization. For causal laws the realist's position should be rather that the meaning of the sentence cannot be properly specified by a list of criteria in the first place.

15 Ayer, *Probability and Evidence*, p. 124.
16 For reasons given in my *Holistic Explanation* (forthcoming, Oxford University Press, 1979), chapter 2.
17 Examples in which the time references are the same in the two halves of the conditional can be constructed by considering a true generalization 'In the past, there has never been an F at place p' and supposing that a certain F is following a regular path in space that will make it occupy place p at the present time.
18 Where 'A' ranges over complete sentences and ' $\boxed{c}$ ' means the same as 'it is at least causally necessary that', a case can be made for the principle

$$\forall A(\text{True} (\ulcorner \boxed{c} \ A \urcorner) \equiv \boxed{c} (\text{True} (A))).$$

Some arguments that can be used in defence of this claim will be found in my 'Necessity and Truth Theories' (*Journal of Philosophical Logic*, 1978). Of course the major question raised by this paper, a question I leave for future work, is: is there a *uniform* relation between meaning-theory clauses and manifestation conditions?
19 Ramsey, *The Foundations of Mathematics*, pp. 240–1.

20   The problem is that this account of what it is to believe that all *F*s
     are *G* collapses that belief into the belief that all specifiable *F*s are
     G. Will not this account have the consequence that any intelligent
     person will believe that all real numbers are specifiable?

21   It may be objected – fairly, given what has so far been said – that
     the mode of presentation ϕ needs to be *a priori* not only neutral
     with respect to *p* but also neutral in the context of *a*'s beliefs about
     what is causally necessary. For suppose the mode of presentation
     specifies that a certain object is both *F* and not *H*, and suppose that
     our person believes that it is a law that all *F*s are *G*s and that it is a
     law that all *G*s are *H*s. If his latter belief is the stronger, then he
     would not on believing that such a condition had come to be the
     case continue to believe that all *F*s are *G*s. This kind of example can
     be constructed for the nonmodal quantifier case, and also to force
     some refinements to the claims below. A proper development of
     the account would presumably have to apply in a series of steps,
     giving manifestation conditions in the first instance to all of a per-
     son's strongest beliefs in causal necessities, and then working down
     to less strong ones. The example of this note cannot be made to
     apply to the conjunction of all of a person's strongest causal beliefs.

22   Laws about ideal cases, if their antecedents really are believed to be
     causally impossible, are not counterexamples to this claim: for what
     are employed in explanation and prediction are not strictly these
     laws, but approximations to them.

23   Ramsey, *The Foundations of Mathematics*, p. 241.

24   See my *Holistic Explanation*, chapter 4.

25   Ramsey, *The Foundations of Mathematics*, p. 253.

26   David Lewis, *Counterfactuals* (Oxford, Blackwell, 1973). The rele-
     vant semantical clause is on p. 16. Note also that there is an onus
     upon anyone who takes Lewis's account to be illuminating on mat-
     ters of validity, but who wants to have an absolute theory of truth
     for counterfactual conditionals that does not attribute an ontology
     of possible worlds to an object language containing them, to say
     how the truth- and model-theoretic concepts are linked.

27   Dummett, 'What is a Theory of Meaning? (II)', p. 94.

28   ibid., p. 95.

29   The fact that the procedure would have to be specified using causal
     modalities has the important consequence that there is no simple
     argument from (i) the failure of supervenience of causally modal
     sentences upon what is nonmodally actually the case to (ii) the fal-
     sity of the doctrine that for every counterfactual, there is some-
     thing in virtue of which it is true. (i) entails that there is some
     causally modal sentence *s* the truth value of which varies even
     though what is actually the case is held fixed: but nevertheless any
     true counterfactual *s* sustains could still be true in virtue of the
     truth of something actually the case since whether such a counter-
     factual is true in virtue of the truth of another sentence may depend
     upon causally modal truths too (i.e. upon what the laws are).

30   Note that this objector's objection is *not* that the notion of a law

4   Moral reality and the end of desire*

Mark Platts

The moral realist view I want to examine takes off from a semantic thesis, a thesis about the proper form of a semantic account of moral discourse. This thesis has two components: the first is that moral discourse is descriptive in character, that moral judgments are assertoric in force; the second is an identification of the correct semantic treatment of descriptive discourses as the now-familiar truth-theoretic treatment. The first component seems already to commit us to holding that a moral judgment and its negation are incompatible, cannot both be true. Taking the two components together we obtain the thought that giving the truth-conditions of a particular moral sentence is a way of giving the meaning of that sentence. To such a semantic thesis the moral realist adds a claim about the world: namely, that it is such that it is how a number of non-negative moral sentences claim it is. This claim about reality thus licenses use of moral discourse without revision in our understanding of that discourse as descriptive. Finally, a full-blown moral realist view emerges with the addition of two claims about the applicability of the notion of truth to moral discourse: the first is that if a moral judgment is true, if it hits its target, that is so in virtue of an independently existing moral reality; the second is that the realistic truth-conditions of a moral sentence, the conditions that determine its meaning, can transcend the recognitional capacities of those who can use and understand that sentence.

There seems no clear reason for thinking that such a realist view has to be applied either to the whole of moral discourse or to none of it. I wish to consider the realist view primarily as it applies to moral evaluations, to judgments expressible by sentences of forms like 'x is loyal', 'x is kind', 'x is malicious', and so on, where x can be (at least) a person, an action or an attitude. That is, I do not want to consider the particular problems that arise in applying the realist view to sentences like, for

*I have profited greatly, and hope that this paper has too, from discussions of the topics dealt with here with John McDowell. I am also indebted to Paul Snowdon and David Wiggins for their comments on earlier versions of the paper.

example, 'That is what you ought to do', 'That is the right thing (for you) to do', or 'That is what you must do'. In fact, my subject matter is narrower still, since I shall not directly consider general evaluations like 'x is good' and 'x is bad'. The realist treatment of specific moral evaluations is the central concern.

At the sub-sentential level, the realist gives the meaning of a particular moral evaluative expression by specifying its systematic contribution to the truth-conditions of those sentences in which it can figure. In the homophonic case — e.g. where we are attempting to give the semantics of English in English — such a specification will generally exhibit the feature that John McDowell has labelled 'austerity'[1]; that is, it will rely upon the structure of designation and use with no attempt at decompositional analysis (although informal heuristic glosses may be given). So we might have, for example,

(S_n) An object α satisfies 'is courageous' if, and only if, α is courageous.

The simple structure of designation and use, of quoting an expression on the LHS of the biconditional and using it on the RHS, ensures that there is nothing trivial about such specifications. (S_n) records a contingent, learnable, forgettable fact *about* the English language *in* the English language.[2] The realist claims that (S_n) expresses something knowledge of which would ensure, assuming competence in the usage of at least some of the rest of the language, competence in the usage of the expression designated. This competence can be had by a speaker even if it is beyond that speaker's present recognitional capacities to recognize particular instantiations of courageousness; and this competence, this grasp upon the concept of courage, can persist through, can transcend, changes in the speaker's recognitional capacities, including such changes brought about by changes in the speaker's beliefs about the grounds of his recognitional capacities, his changing *conceptions* of courage. Such a competence (and such a persisting competence) is reasonably attributed to a speaker when that attribution enables us to make sense of what he says in view of all that we know and believe about him, particularly in view of all we believe about other things he says and does; that is to say, such a competence is reasonably attributed to a speaker when it is part of our making sense of him.

These doctrines reflect a distinctive view of part of the moral life. The picture is presented of moral language resulting from epistemic interactions between tawdry, finite moral epistemic beings on the one hand, and a moral reality of perhaps infinite moral complexity on the other. We have a picture of at least one dimension of moral self-development as the persistent endeavour to be open to the influence of things as they morally are, not as we would wish them to be, the endeavour to increase our sensitivity to the presence of moral features, to the full complexity and recurrent presence of the moral veins of the world. As life goes on, our tendencies to wishful thinking and to self-deception may be controlled a little, and our tendency, even need, to shelter behind a few simplistic rules may be restrained a little. As life goes on, our grasp upon what, for example, courage is can improve (or degenerate) without end, bringing with it an increased sensitivity to (or blindness towards) its instances. With luck, our moral beliefs about particular circumstances are more likely to be approximately true. But approximate truth, and improved understanding, are all that can be hoped for; the limit is, for us, unattainable.[3] And so, for most of us, the realistic limit of moral ambition is to be 'a poor sort of good man'.

Such a picture serves to remind that, although moral realism begins from a semantic thesis, it cannot be assessed in isolation from other areas of philosophical inquiry. A realist will have to meet, for example, the epistemological challenge from one form of moral scepticism, since it is precisely the realist divorce of truth-conditions from actual recognition-conditions that lends deep plausibility to sceptical arguments of that form. The realist will also have to meet the challenge raised by the relativist. This challenge is often mis-stated since realism neither implies nor is implied by either intersubjective agreement or emergent consensus; if there is intersubjective agreement or emergent consensus, there are many other possible explanations besides the realist one; while if there is not, all the realist requires is realistic explanation of the differences obtaining. Any substantial relativist challenge will come from considerations *internal* to a moral system relating to its view of other (actual or possible) moral systems. These considerations will only have much purchase upon judgments of the forms 'x is the right thing to do', 'x is not to be done', and so on. Such judgments are outside the scope of this paper, but one example will serve to illustrate the indecisiveness of most relativist arguments. Gilbert Harman has argued for relativism and against realism by emphasizing the fact that we do not, for example, condemn primitive tribesmen for cannibalism.[4] What is right for us may be wrong for them, and vice versa, so that our judgment that cannibalism is wrong is not incompatible with their judgment that it is not wrong. Now, there are surprising difficulties about making this clearly incompatible with realist talk of the incompatibility of moral judgments – talk that will enter for *any* descriptive treatment of moral discourse – but these need not now delay us since Harman's point is anyway far from decisive. We do not condemn the same primitive tribesmen for believing that the sun goes around the earth or for acting upon that belief; given the kinds of beliefs they were brought up to hold, the kinds of observations they make and the kinds of theories currently available to them, their error is natural and comprehensible. Indeed, given their situation, there is a sense in which they are right to believe what they do believe and to act as they do, a sense

Mark Platts

in which they ought to believe it and to act on that belief. Saying that is quite compatible with astronomical realism, and quite compatible with saying that, in another sense, they ought to believe that the earth goes around the sun because it is true that it does and that they ought to act on that true belief. Likewise, it is not at all clear that we cannot attach sense and truth to the claim that the tribesmen ought not to indulge in cannibalism even if, in view of the form of life they have inherited, we do not wish to condemn them for doing so. If anything, the moral case is slightly easier for the realist since it is rather less easy in that case to attach sense to the thought that, given their circumstances, they are right to eat their fellows.

The moral realist also faces a challenge, partly epistemological, partly metaphysical, from what J. L. Mackie calls 'the argument from queerness'.[5] Mackie writes:

> If there were objective values, then they would be entities or qualities or relations of a very strange sort, utterly different from anything else in the universe. Correspondingly, if we were aware of them, it would have to be by some special faculty of moral perception or intuition, utterly different from our ordinary ways of knowing everything else.[6]

The queerest thing about this as it stands is the claim that it is an *argument*. ('As it stands', since the main subject of this paper is one area in which life might be injected into the queer.) The world *is* a queer place. I find neutrinos, aardvarks, infinite sequences of objects, and (most pertinently) impressionist paintings peculiar kinds of entities;[7] but I do not expect nuclear physics, zoology, formal semantics or art history to pay much regard to that. While the invention of a special faculty of the mind does not follow, is not needed, and may not even be intelligible; we discover moral truths in the ways we discover most (if not all) truths: by attention, perception, and reflection.

Deeper metaphysical challenges arise elsewhere. There are general anti-realist arguments of the kind that Michael Dummett attempts to derive from truths about meaning and language use; these, however, will be, in a mundane enough way, of less present interest than arguments, whether originating in explicitly metaphysical considerations or not, designed only to establish the incoherence of the realist view of moral values as part of the real world. Which leads to the central concern of this paper, a family of considerations deriving from philosophical psychology which have been deemed incompatible with the realist view of moral evaluative judgments.

II

'These things can be so independently of our ability to tell': this element of the realist treatment of evaluative moral judgments, the element unacceptable to Dummett, plays a crucial role in the attraction of the realist view of moral life just sketched. The challenge to realism from philosophical psychology I wish to consider focuses attention upon another element of the realist view, an element whose connections with that of recognition-transcendence are unclear. This new element could be put like this: 'these things can be so independently of our desires'. (Connections between the elements only come clear on a specific assumption about what recognition *would* be.) The realist treats evaluative judgments as descriptions of the world whose literal significance (viz. truth-conditions) make no reference, or generally make no reference, to human desires, needs, wants or interests. Such a view appears incompatible with a conjunction of two doctrines, one a dogma of moral philosophy, the other a dogma of philosophical psychology. The moral thesis, which will be clearer after we have elaborated upon the psychological one, is that moral judgments, including evaluative moral judgments, always (or at least frequently) purport to give at least *prima facie* reasons for doing (or not doing) some possible, or already performed, action, together with the claim that, when an agent has indeed performed some intentional action, his acceptance of some moral judgment, which may be an evaluative moral judgment, can have been his reason, his motivating reason, for doing it. (*Prima facie* contrasts with *conclusive*, not with *not really*.)

The dogma from philosophical psychology is that any complete specification of even a *prima facie* reason for action must make reference to the potential agent's desires or possible desires. The idea, crudely, is that even any *prima facie* reason for doing something will make reference, in the antecedent of a conditional, to the potential agent's actual or possible desires — 'if you desire that . . . , then, *prima facie, you* have a reason to make it the case that . . .'. Such a reason becomes the potential agent's own reason, a motivating reason for him, if he has, and recognizes himself to have, the desire specified in the antecedent of the conditional. If, then, the agent performs the appropriate action, and does so for that reason, then he does so *because* he has, and recognizes himself to have, that desire. It is just that the *prima facie* motivating reason was, in the circumstances (including his other desires), a sufficient reason for acting; it sufficed for action.

Note that, even if all reference in the statement of the dogma from philosophical psychology to desire were replaced by reference to, say, pro-attitude, the apparent incompatibility of that claim with the conjunction of the moral thesis and the realist treatment of moral evaluative judgments would remain. I shall therefore work with the apparently more exact version of the psychological dogma phrased in terms of desire.

III

The claim that any complete specification of a motivating reason for an action — complete in revealing it *as* a motivating reason — must make reference to the agent's desires and to his recognition thereof could be challenged in an obvious enough way by trying to cite counter-examples of which at least some moral judgments might be deemed an important case.[8] In general, however, the track record of this procedure does not invite much hope for outcome; and in the present context our view of the putative counter-examples will be far too much determined by our antecedent views on moral realism.

What has to be explored is the ground for the persistent manoeuvre of *reading* a desire into any apparent counter-example to the dogma. The ground for that manoeuvre must have at least this structure: there is some condition upon a motivating specification of a reason for action which is met only by the introduction of reference to desire (and to recognition of desire) *and which is at least sometimes met by that introduction*. Put like that, two obviously connected questions arise. Why does reference to desire together with recognition of desire sometimes meet the unstated condition? And does reference to any recognized desire appropriately connected with the agent's beliefs meet that condition?

An answer for each question is found in the thought: that is what desires are like! Desire is that state of an agent such that, when the agent recognizes that state's obtaining, he is thereby given a motivating *prima facie* reason for acting so as to satisfy it. Thus citation of any desire recognized will meet the condition of motivation specification, and will do so because that is part of the essential functional role embodied in the concept of desire. Now, I do not wish to say that there is something inherently unsatisfactory because ultimately non-explanatory about this answer; nor do I wish to say that it is the only answer that can be given; I simply want to emphasize that, if that is the answer given, it has as a consequence that each and every recognized desire serves to provide motivation.

An instructive parallel in understanding this view of desire is pain. David Wiggins has recently given the following characterization of pain: 'that functional state n of the central nervous system which accounts for the patient's tendency, while such and such state persists in consciousness, to avoid objects he believes to be responsible for initiating or aggravating the state'.[9]

Two aspects of this characterization should be noted. First, the functional role of pain is given in such a way as to forge, via the references to tendency, consciousness, and beliefs, a connexion between pain and *prima facie* motivating reason for action. Pain is that state such that, when its characteristic phenomenological manifestation is present, and is recognized to be present (which may, for this kind of phenomenological manifestation, be the invariable consequence of its presence), and is believed to be present because of (or is believed to be aggravated by) causal interaction with an object, the agent is thereby provided with a motivating reason for changing that causal interaction. *If* this account were meant to be a complete treatment of the connexions between pain and action, it would be too narrow. It does not cover, unless inadmissible play is made with the notion of belief, the connexion of pain with a large amount of pain-avoiding or pain-ameliorating behaviour, the instinctive, like the withdrawing of a hand from a hot plate. Not all pain-manifesting behaviour is belief-expressing behaviour. Such instinctive behaviour can be *aversive* behaviour too. And even as regards intentional behaviour, the account given seems too narrow: a crucial part of the aversion induced by pain is the *avoidance* of objects one has learnt to connect with painful experiences even though there is at the time no painfulness present. Still, doubtless Wiggins would accept these additions to the functional role of pain. And note, importantly, that none of this implies that aversions will always, or even generally, be acted upon.

That spelling-out of the functional role of pain brings out the second crucial feature of the account offered, which is that it is not just functional but is also phenomenological. Reference is made to such and such state persisting 'in consciousness'. One reason for this is clear: a slot is thereby provided (although not in Wiggins's account filled) through which pain can be distinguished from a number of other states with a broadly similar functional role, like irritation, boredom, and dislike. Going beyond the account given we can fill this slot, and so make the requisite demarcation, by reference to the essential *painfulness* of pain. There is nothing trivial about this specification of the phenomenological character of pain; it is precisely what distinguishes pain from irritation and the like. If we ignore the painfulness of pain, we shall mirror within this functionalist account the inadequacy that the propounder of the account detects in any consistent dualist analysis of pain — viz. the assimilation of pain to a kind of sadness, to, so to speak, a purely intellectual perception.

What may be a philosophically deeper reason for stressing the painfulness of pain connects with the motivating role assigned to pain by the functionalist account of it. About the original account of pain we might be tempted to ask: why should reference to pain ever fully specify the motivating force of a reason for an action? And does such a reference always specify that, will any and every pain do? Here, I think, we find a case in which we can reasonably say: that is what pains, all pains, are like. If a creature is capable of feeling pain and is capable of intentional action and is capable of forming beliefs about the object of pain, then we can make sense of that creature only if that creature is at least *prima facie* motivated by his perceptions of his pains and his beliefs about their objects in the ways that our functionalist account has described. Maybe that *prima facie* motivation can be over-ridden (courage under torture); maybe the pain state can be changed as a result of reflection and attention in such a way that it no longer persists to provide even a *prima facie* motivation, so that the pain ceases (certain forms of ascetic stoicism). But as long as pain persists, potential motivation is present; and that is precisely because as long as pain persists, painfulness persists.

Pain has, essentially, a distinctive phenomenological character which serves, not just to distinguish it from other functionally similar states, but also to fix the connection with reasons for actions; and that phenomenological character shows why all pains have that connection with reasons for action.

If, now, we compare pain's functional role with that of desire we shall be struck by two (connected) dissimilarities. The first is that the general phenomenological quality of desire, if any, is somewhat elusive. Are all desires essentially desireful? And the second difference is that desires have a logical content in a way that pains do not. One desires *that p*; and it is at least arguable that any description of a desire using the form *desiring object x* can be rewritten using the *desire that* construction. But one does not pain *that p*; at most, one has a pain *like* . . . , where what follows is either an introspective characterization of the phenomenological feel of the pain or an analogical characterization of it, say by reference to the circumstances in which one would expect to have that kind of feeling. Pains have a phenomenological quality, not a logical content.

These dissimilarities are crucial to understanding and assessing the dogma from philosophical psychology about reasons for actions and desires. For pain it is the essential phenomenological component which brings to an end the question, 'Why should that motivate?'. But there is, generally, no comparable phenomenological characteristic in desire. What, then, replaces the phenomenological component in giving the motivating force of desire, in silencing the question? One answer is obvious and seems the only obvious answer: desires, unlike pains, have a logical content, and desires motivate an agent because of his view of the objects of his desires *as desirable*. But this answer would be no answer at all if that view of the object of desire was seen by the agent simply as being a consequence of its *being* the object of his desire; for then there would be nothing to constitute the motivating force.

What needs emphasizing here is that the dogma from philosophical psychology has been construed – as it must be if it is to have any direct force against the realist view, if the inconsistency outlined in section II is to be more than *appearance* – as implying that the agent's desires account for any desirability attributed to the object of desire in a reason-giving explanation. Someone might say: 'All right, desirability *elicits* desire; still, the desire thesis from philosophical psychology is true. That is, to explain an action, by giving a full motivating reason, you still have to cite not only the desirability of the object but also the desire it elicits.' The point is that saying that – interpreting the dogma in that way – is quite compatible with moral realism; for saying that is simply obtaining the dogma from the conjunction of the realist treatment of desirability characterizations together with two further claims. The first is that to explain an agent's action the desirability has to be *recognized* by the agent. The other is a thesis, which I shall for the moment concede without argument, about what is involved in the recognition of the obtaining of such a desirability characterization. You only see the desirability of some object if you desire it, so that desirability can be *your* reason for acting, or a source of motivation *for you* (as opposed to being a possible reason for you to act), only if you desire the desirable object. But the logical independence of the desirability remains to give the motivation in the absence of any distinctive phenomenological quality. That it is the view of the content of the desire rather than its phenomenological quality that constitutes its motivating force still serves to yield an argument that desirability is prior to desire; it is merely that recognition of desirability brings desire with it.

Wiggins, while exploring this territory from a different vantage point, has written this:

> Surely it can be true both that we desire x because we think x good, and that x is good because we desire x. It does not count against the point I am making that the explanation of the 'because' is different in each direction.[10]

With slight modification, this encapsulates the conclusions of the foregoing discussion. 'We desire x because we see x as desirable': this 'because' embodies the conceptual requirement needed to take account of the motivating force of our desires. 'We see x as desirable because we desire x': this 'because' embodies the concession just made to the standard dogma, a concession rendering that dogma compatible with moral realism, to the effect that we can only recognize the desirability of some state of affairs if we desire it. It is no part of this dual conclusion, however, that moral evaluative reasons for actions can be atomized into, can be explained as the product of, two (or more) distinct components, say, the desire and the perception of the desirability of the object of desire.

IV

Discussion of human motivation and human perception is the discussion of *human* motivation and perception. Conceptual understanding of such motivation and perception should reflect facts about human beings, their natures and experiences. Some of the conceptual points just made straightforwardly reflect some such facts.

Consider, again, the case of pain. The motivating force of pain is intelligible because of the phenomenological character of pain, its painfulness; that suffices, in conjunction with appropriate beliefs, to motivate action. Suppose, for example, that I have a certain pain which I believe to be caused by my proximity to an object — say, a fire; then I am given a motivating reason for moving away from that fire. But I can, of course, conceive of myself having a similar pain in similar circumstances where I believe (and, let us say, truly believe) the pain to be caused by my distance from the fire; I should then be motivated to move closer to the fire. The interesting fact is this: in this world, where I believe the pain to be caused by my being too close to the fire, the motivating force of the pain is quite unaffected by my thinking, at the point of action, of this other world in which I should be motivated to do some quite different action.

Some desires can be like this because some desires — especially *appetitive* desires — can have (although do not always have) a comparatively distinct phenomenological quality. In the back row of the cinema, my base *lust* for the person on my left can remain just as effective a source of motivation even if, at the point of action, I have the (not always implausible) thought that my desire could be just as intelligibly directed towards the person on my right. (I do not say that its motivating force is always so unaffected by reflections on other possibilities; that may depend, not just on the strength of the lust and its degree of unconnectedness with the object of lust, but also upon one's general capacity for ironic disengagement from the self (among other things).)

But consider now a desire lacking, like most desires, such a distinctive phenomenological quality. Suppose that the person whose desire it is sees the desirability of the object as stemming solely from his desiring it; that is, he subscribes to the dogma from philosophical psychology in the form in which it is incompatible with moral realism. What has been said suggests that the motivating force of that desire is, for him, quite mysterious. And this emerges in a tidy way. He might, of course, have desired some other object – he might even have desired *that not p* instead of his actual desire *that p*. (I mean: there seems no reason for him to think this not possible; whether it is possible for a realist is a more complicated question.) Given his general view of desires and desirability, if he thinks of this possibility he will be thinking of a possibility in which it is desirable *that not p*. My point now is that it seems to me a brute fact about human motivation and human desires that if this agent, at the point of action, considers this other possibility in his own terms, then he will cease to be motivated by his desire *that p*. This is the brute human fact that reflects the conceptual priority accorded to the desirable over desire in the philosophical account of motivation just sketched. If this is right, then, for such an agent, reflection will eliminate the motivating force of his desire; and since, *ex hypothesi*, his desire lacks any phenomenological quality, his desire will then cease to be as the motivating force ceases to be. For a reflective being with a nature like ours, the price of abandoning moral realism can be the end of desire.

In the world as it is conflicting pairs of desires do occur without the motivating force of each of the pair being undermined. I think it a strength of the moral realist view of evaluative moral judgments that it can acknowledge such conflicts of even non-appetitive, non-phenomenologically grounded desires and account for their peculiarly tortuous nature. For the anti-realist, such occurrences are much more philosophically troublesome. He can try to assimilate them to conflicts of appetitive or phenomenologically grounded desires, but that seems simply wrong. Without that assimilation, however, it is difficult to see why the anti-realist should take either of his desires seriously; the hypothetical thought of a world with a different desire invoked a moment ago will apparently be forced upon him by the actuality of that other desire. In consequence, the emptiness of his motivation will be forced upon him; lacking any motivating force and lacking any phenomenological quality, each of the conflicting desires will cease to persist.

Philosophers (and others – more excusably) have tended to treat the questions of whether someone has a desire, and, if so, of which desire he has, far too simply. This tendency is doubtless encouraged by an undue attention to appetitive desires, whether of a general kind – the desire for water – or of derivative more specific kinds – the desire for *this* glass of water. In cases like the latter, cases of comparatively specific derivative appetitive desires, such desires rest, of course, upon beliefs – say, the belief that this *is* a glass of water. If the belief goes, so, presumably, will the desire for *this*; but the general appetitive desire will live on, searching, so to speak, for another object to attach itself to. But what has to be acknowledged is that we have many non-appetitive desires in our having which beliefs are involved in complex ways. For us, desires frequently require an appropriate belief about the independent desirability of the object of desire, in such a way that loss of that belief terminates that desire. Of course, all our desires might have been appetitive, or, at least, have been such that the entrenched belief-connections do not obtain or do not obtain in this way. But that is not how *our* desires all are; so that is not how we are.

Aside from the appetitive model, another conception of desire tacitly prevalent in the thoughts of philosophers and others is the *random choice* model: with no appetitive, phenomenologically grounded desire present, I simply choose some object and so desire it. It is, of course, desperately unclear that desire could enter in this way. What do I choose it for? But even if we acknowledge the skeleton of a kind of desire here, it does not take much reflection to see that such random choice desires together with appetitive and phenomenologically grounded desires do not exhaust the range of kinds of desires we have. And given that we are beings capable of the detachment involved in reflecting upon the nature of our lives, it does not take much sensitivity to be glad that we have other kinds of desires. Ironic detachment without realism becomes at the limit a self-indulgence that destroys all but its animal self. A false understanding of the world and of his relation to it in action and perception can be the end for a reflective being like us by being the beginning of a life that is empty, brutish, and long.

V

For desires lacking any distinctive phenomenological quality, the only obvious answer to the question of what serves to fix their connexion with motivation is the subject's view of the logical object of desire as independently desirable. That the obvious answer might be true is suggested by *our* inability to be motivated upon reflection by such desires, to take them seriously, except by accepting that answer. And what that reflects is that *we* have desires into which the belief that the object of desire is independently desirable is built, desires for which that belief is essential.

Let me end by taking up one of the more central of the many issues treated too slightly thus far. Earlier, I conceded a thesis about recognition of desirable features in the world in order to eliminate the appearance of incompatibility presented in section II. The thesis conceded was that to *recognize* the obtaining of, say, some desirable moral feature in a possible state of affairs *is* to desire the obtaining of that state of affairs (though not just that). One cannot see the loyal, the courageous, and so forth *as* the loyal, the courageous, etc., without desiring them.

This concession raises problems elsewhere, notably about both weakness of will and the possibility of evil.[11] It also resurrects a (sophisticated) version of the argument from queerness: what very strange states of affairs these moral states must be if recognition of their obtaining requires a response like *desire* from the one doing the recognizing. But my present concern about the recognition thesis conceded is another one.

It follows from that thesis that if someone else claims to see the same evaluative features in the world as I do while differing from me in the obtaining or the not obtaining of desires directed to those states of affairs, then what he has seen is not the same as what I have seen, that how it looks to him must be different from how it looks to me. This consequence worries for two connected reasons. First, we can in many cases separate sameness of looks (tastes, smells, etc.) from sameness of accompanying response. You can smell the same smell as I can (smell it *as* the same smell), but you grimace while I grin; I can at one time taste the same taste as at another time, but on one occasion I shun it, on the other pursue it; you and I can both see the humour in a joke, but you are amused while I am not (I am the butt). Second, we feel, in general, that there must be some constraint upon employment of the manoeuvre: 'If you respond differently, then how it looks to you is different from how it looks to me'. Why is there no such constraint upon moral looks? And why is there no *detaching* moral looks from elicited desires?

The issues here are complex, and I shall merely make some brief comments. The first is that, even in the cases of 'simple' sensations — tastes, smells, etc. — I am utterly unclear what the controls are upon our descriptions of them. Second, I think there are clear cases of perception of value where some *non-cognitive* response is internal to, or suffuses, the perception. I have in mind cases like Wittgenstein's examples of seeing value in the world: feeling wonder at the existence of the universe and feeling absolutely safe.[12] It seems simply wrongheaded to think that one who sees the universe with wonder at its existence sees the same as one who just *notices* that it is there, differing only in some accompanying external response, or to think that one who feels absolutely safe literally sees the world around him in the same way as one who notices, say, the complete absence of threat and danger around him. Third, when we consider perception of *moral* value, I think it clear that, if introspective phenomenology can be our guide, moral perceptions manifest a unity of such a kind that potential motivation is indeed internal to them. But, finally, I am still unsure as to whether in such cases we should always see that potential motivation as being grounded in an elicited desire; such a view is obvious only for those who treat the notion of desire as a mental catch-most. In the context of this paper, however, this last doubt need not concern us: for if the potential motivation internal to perception of moral value is not

Mark Platts

grounded in an elicited desire, the dogma from philosophical psychology that raised the apparent difficulty for the moral realist emerges, in its strict formulation,[13] as false.

Notes

1 John McDowell, 'On the Sense and Reference of a Proper Name', *Mind*, LXXXVI, no. 342 (April 1977), pp. 159–85; reprinted in this volume as chapter 8.
2 Cp. the editors' introduction to *Truth and Meaning: Essays in Semantics*, ed. Gareth Evans and John McDowell (Oxford University Press, 1976), p. xi.
3 Cp. Iris Murdoch, *The Sovereignty of Good* (London, Routledge and Kegan Paul, 1970), especially chapter 1.
4 Gilbert Harman, *The Nature of Morality: An Introduction to Ethics* (Oxford University Press, 1977), pp. 97–8.
5 J. L. Mackie, *Ethics: Inventing Right and Wrong* (Harmondsworth, Penguin, 1977).
6 ibid., p. 38.
7 'Most pertinently' because the fact that a painting is an impressionist painting is clearly a *supervenient* fact. Are all supervenient truths and properties unacceptably queer?
8 Cp. Michael Woods, 'Reasons for Actions and Desires', *Proceedings of the Aristotelian Society supp. vol.* XLVI (1972), pp. 189–201.
9 David Wiggins, 'Identity, Designation, Essentialism and Physicalism', *Philosophia*, vol. 5 (1975), p. 23.
10 David Wiggins, *Truth, Invention, And The Meaning Of Life* (London, British Academy, 1976), p. 348. Compare Hume: 'We do not infer a character to be virtuous, because it pleases: But in feeling that it pleases after such a particular manner, we in effect feel that it is virtuous.' (*A Treatise of Human Nature*, ed. L. A. Selby-Bigge (Oxford University Press, 1958), p. 471.)
11 These problems are briefly discussed in the final chapter of my *Ways of Meaning: An Introduction to a Philosophy of Language* (London, Routledge and Kegan Paul, 1979).
12 Ludwig Wittgenstein, 'A Lecture on Ethics', *Philosophical Review*, LXXIV (1965), at p. 8.
13 See, again, the last paragraph of section II above.

5   Tarski's theory of truth*

Hartry Field

In the early 1930s there was prevalent, among scientifically minded philosophers, the view that semantic notions such as the notions of truth and denotation were illegitimate: that they could not or should not be incorporated into a scientific conception of the world. But when Tarski's work on truth became known, all this changed. 'As a result of Tarski's teaching, I no longer hesitate to speak of "truth" and "falsity",' wrote Popper;[1] and Popper's reaction was widely shared.[2]

A philosopher who shared Popper's reaction to Tarski's discoveries would presumably argue as follows. 'What Tarski did was to define the term "true", using in his definitions only terms that are clearly acceptable. In particular, he did not employ any undefined semantic terms in his definitions. So Tarski's work should make the term "true" acceptable even to someone who is initially suspicious of semantic terms.'

This contention has an initial plausibility, but I will argue that it is radically wrong. My contrary claim will be that Tarski succeeded in reducing the notion of truth *to certain other semantic notions*; but that he did not in any way explicate these other notions, so that his results ought to make the word 'true' acceptable only to someone who already regarded these other semantic notions as acceptable.

By claiming that Tarski merely reduced truth to other semantic notions, I don't mean to suggest that his results on truth are trivial. On the contrary, I think that they are extremely important, and have applications not only to mathematics but also to linguistics and to more directly philosophical problems about realism and objectivity. I think, however, that the real value of Tarski's discoveries for linguistics and philosophy is widely misunderstood, and I hope to eradicate the most central misunderstandings by clarifying and defending the claim that Tarski merely reduced truth to other semantic notions.

*Reprinted by permission of the author and of the editors from *The Journal of Philosophy*, vol. LXIX, no. 13 (1972), pp. 347–75.

This paper grew out of a talk I gave at Princeton in the fall of 1970, where I defended T1 over T2. Donald Davidson and Gilbert Harman – and later, in private conversation, John Wallace – all came to the defence of T2, and their remarks have all been of help to me in writing the paper. I have also benefited from advice given by Michael Devitt, Paul Benacerraf, and especially David Hills.

Hartry Field

I

I believe that Tarski presented his semantic theory in a very misleading way, one which has encouraged the misinterpretations just alluded to. In this section I will present Tarski's theory as I think he should have presented it. However, I do not expect instant agreement that this new way is better than the old, and so I will use the name 'Tarski*' for a logician who gave the sort of semantic theory I will now sketch. Later in the paper I will compare Tarski*'s semantics to the semantics that the real Tarski actually gave; by doing this I will cast light on the issues raised in my introductory paragraphs.

In sketching Tarski*'s theory, I will focus my attention on a particular object language L. The language L that I choose will be a quantificational language, with names ('c_1', 'c_2', . . .), one-place function symbols ('f_1', 'f_2', . . .), and one-place predicates ('p_1', 'p_2', . . .). The language of course cannot be viewed as an 'uninterpreted' language, i.e. as just a bunch of strings of meaningless marks, for then there would be no truth to worry about. Instead, the language should be regarded as something that people actually speak or write; and it is because the speakers speak or write the way they do that the words of the language have the meaning they have.[3]

Initially I will follow Tarski in supposing that in L 'the sense of every expression is unambiguously determined by its form',[4] i.e., that whenever two speakers use the same name (or one speaker uses it on two occasions) they are referring to the same thing; that whenever two speakers use the same sentence either both are saying something true or neither is, etc. In these circumstances it makes sense to speak of the names of the language denoting things (a name denotes whatever the users of the name refer to) and the sentences being true or false (true when speakers who use it say something true by so doing). The more general situation, in which there are expressions whose 'sense' is not determined wholly by their form, will be dealt with later. (We'll see that it is one of the advantages of Tarski*'s semantics that it can easily handle this more general situation.)

The syntax of L can be given by two recursive definitions: first we define the *singular terms* by saying that all names and variables are singular terms, and a function symbol followed by a singular term is a singular term; then we define the *formulas* by saying that a predicate followed by a singular term is a formula, as is the negation of a formula, the conjunction of two formulas, and the universal quantification of a formula with any variable. The *sentences*, or *closed formulas*, are then singled out in the usual way.

Now we can proceed to Tarski*'s semantics. Rather than characterize truth directly, we characterize it relative to some assignment of objects to the variables, say s_k to 'x_k'. The idea is going to be to treat the variables, or at least the free variables, as sort of 'temporary names' for the objects assigned to them. So we proceed by fixing a sequence $s = \langle s_1, s_2, \ldots \rangle$ of objects, to be assigned to 'x_1', 'x_2', ..., respectively; and we want to say what it is for a formula to be true$_s$, i.e. true relative to the assignment s. As a preliminary we say what it is for a term to denote an object, i.e. to denote it relative to the assignment s. The denotation of 'x_k' relative to s is evidently s_k, for this is the object assigned to 'x_k'. But what is the denotation relative to s of 'c_k'? Evidently what objects are assigned to the variables here is irrelevant, and the denotation$_s$ of 'c_k' is some fixed object that users of the language refer to when they use the name 'c_k'. Just what this object is depends on facts we have not yet been given about the use of 'c_k'. Similarly there are facts we have not yet been given about the use of 'p_k' and 'f_k' which we need in order to fix the truth value of sentences containing them. For 'p_k' the relevant facts concern the extension of the predicate — what objects the predicate *applies to* — for it is this which affects the truth value of all utterances containing 'p_k'. For 'f_k', the relevant facts concern what pairs of objects *fulfil* that function symbol — in the sense that the pair ⟨John Adams, John Quincy Adams⟩ and every other father–son pair fulfil the function symbol 'father of'.

With these points in mind it is now easy to give an inductive characterization of denotation$_s$:

T1 (A) 1 'x_k' denotes$_s$ s_k.

2 'c_k' denotes$_s$ what it denotes.

3 $\lceil f_k(e) \rceil$ denotes$_s$ an object a if and only if (i) there is an object b that e denotes$_s$ and (ii) 'f_k' is fulfilled by $\langle a,b \rangle$.

(Here 'e' is a variable ranging over expressions of L.) Similarly we define 'true$_s$' for formulas — what Tarski calls satisfaction of a formula — by s:

(B) 1 $\lceil p_k(e) \rceil$ is true$_s$ if and only if (i) there is an object a that e denotes$_s$ and (ii) 'p_k' applies to a.

2 $\lceil \sim e \rceil$ is true$_s$ if and only if e is not true$_s$.

3 $\lceil e_1 \wedge e_2 \rceil$ is true$_s$ if and only if e_1 is true$_s$ and so is e_2.

4 $\lceil \forall x_k(e) \rceil$ is true$_s$ if and only if for each sequence s^* that differs from s at the kth place at most, e is true$_{s^*}$.

This completes the characterization of truth relative to an assignment of objects to the variables. In the case of sentences it is easily seen that we get the same results whatever such assignment we pick; we can say

(C) A sentence is true if and only if it is true$_s$ for some (or all) s.

This completes my elaboration of Tarski*'s 'truth definition' T1 for

L – or his truth characterization (TC), as I prefer to call it. What is its philosophical significance? The obvious answer, and the correct one, I think, is that the TC reduces one semantic notion to three others. It explains what it is for a sentence to be true in terms of certain semantic features of the primitive components of the sentence: in terms of what it is for a name to denote something, what it is for a predicate to apply to something, and what it is for a function symbol to be fulfilled by some pair of things. It is convenient to introduce the expression 'primitively denotes' as follows: every name *primitively denotes* what it denotes; every predicate and every function symbol *primitively denotes* what it applies to or is fulfilled by; and no complex expression primitively denotes anything. In this terminology, what T1 does is to explain truth in terms of primitive denotation. Similarly we can explain denotation for arbitrary closed singular terms [such as '$f_1(c_1)$'] in terms of primitive denotation, i.e. in terms of the semantic features of the names and function symbols from which the complex singular term is composed – we merely say that a closed singular term denotes an object a if it denotes$_s$ a for some (or all) s, where denotation$_s$ is defined as before. We see then that *Tarski*'s semantics explains the semantic properties of complex expressions* (e.g., truth value for sentences, denotation for complex singular terms) *in terms of semantic properties of their primitive components.*

To explain truth in terms of primitive denotation is, I think, an important task. It certainly doesn't answer *every* question that anyone would ever want answered about truth, but for many purposes it is precisely what we need. For instance, in model theory we are interested in such questions as: given a set Γ of sentences, is there any way to choose the denotations of the primitives of the language so that every sentence of Γ will come out true given the usual semantics for the logical connectives?[5] For questions such as this, what we need to know is how the truth value of a whole sentence depends on the denotations of its primitive nonlogical parts, and that is precisely what T1 tells us. So *at least for model-theoretic purposes*, Tarski*'s TC is precisely the kind of explication of truth we need.

I want now to return to a point I mentioned earlier, about Tarski's restriction to languages in which 'the sense of every expression is unambiguously determined by its form'. Natural languages are full of expressions that do not meet this requirement. For instance, different tokens of 'John takes grass' can differ in 'sense' – e.g., one token may be uttered in saying that John Smith smokes marijuana, and another may be uttered in saying that John Jones steals lawn material, and these differences may give rise to differences of truth value in the tokens. (I say that a complete[6] token of a sentence is true if the person who spoke or wrote that token said something true by so doing; I also say that a name token denotes an object if the person who spoke or wrote the token referred to the object by so doing.) The prevalence of such examples in natural languages raises the question of whether Tarski's type of semantic theory is applicable to languages in which the sense is *not* determined by the form; for if the answer is no, then Davidson's very worthwhile project[7] of giving truth characterizations for natural languages seems doomed from the start.

It seems clear that if we stick to the kind of TC that Tarski actually gave (see next section), there is no remotely palatable way of extending TCs to sentences like 'John takes grass'. But if we use TCs like T1 there is no difficulty at all. The only point about languages containing 'John' or 'grass' or 'I' or 'you' is that for such languages 'true', 'denotes' and other semantic terms make no clear sense as applied to expréssion types; they make sense only as applied to tokens. For this reason we have to interpret clause (B)2 of T1 as meaning

A token of $\ulcorner \sim e \urcorner$ is true$_S$ if and only if the token of e that it contains is not true$_S$

and similarly for the other clauses. Once we interpret our TC in this way in terms of tokens, i.e. individual occasions of utterance, that TC works perfectly: someone who utters 'John is sick' (or 'I am sick') says something true if and only if his token of 'sick' applies to the person he refers to by 'John' (or by 'I'); and the fact that other speakers (or this speaker on other occasions) sometimes refer to different things when they use 'John' (or 'I') is beside the point.

This analysis leaves entirely out of account the ways in which 'I' and 'John' differ: it leaves out of account, for instance, the fact that a token of 'I' always denotes the speaker who produced it. But that is no objection to the analysis, for the analysis purports merely to explain truth in terms of primitive denotation; it does not purport to say anything about primitive denotation, and the differences between 'I' and 'John' (or their analogues in a language like L) are purely differences of how they denote. (The word 'I' denotes according to the simple rule mentioned two sentences back; 'John' denotes according to much more complex rules that I have no idea how to formulate.)

Of course, the fact that a theory of denotation for a word like 'I' is so simple and obvious, makes it possible to alter the TC so that the theory of denotation for such a word is built into the TC itself — such a course is adopted, for instance, by Davidson at the end of 'Truth and Meaning'. I myself prefer to preserve the analogies of the word 'I' to words that function less systematically, e.g., 'we', 'she' and 'John'. How one treats 'I' is more or less a matter of taste; but the less systematic words I've just mentioned cannot be handled in the way that Davidson handles 'I', and the only reasonable way I can see to handle them is the way I have suggested: use a truth characterization like T1 (except stated in terms of tokens rather than types), and leave it to a separate theory of primitive denotation to explain the relevant differences between tokens of 'John' that denote John Adams and tokens of 'John' that denote John Lennon, and between tokens of 'bank' that apply to things along rivers and tokens of 'bank' that apply to the Chase Manhattan.[8]

There are other advantages to T1 besides its ability to handle ambiguous sentences, i.e. sentences for which the sense is not determined by the form. For instance, Tarski required that the vocabulary of the language be fixed once and for all; but if we decide to give truth characterizations of type T1, this is unnecessary: all that is required is that the general structure of the language be fixed, e.g. that the semantic categories[9] (name, one-place predicate, etc.) be held constant. In other words, if a language already contained proper names, the invention of a new name to baptize an object will not invalidate the old TC; though introduction of a name into a hitherto nameless language will.

To show this, we have merely to reformulate the given TC so that it does not rely on the actual vocabulary that the language contains at a given time, but works also for sentences containing new names, one-place predicates, etc., that speakers of the language might later introduce. To do this is trivial: we define denotation$_s$ by

1 The kth variable denotes$_s$ s_k.
2 If e_1 is a name, it denotes$_s$ what it denotes.
3 If e_1 is a singular term and e_2 is a function symbol, then $\ulcorner e_2(e_1) \urcorner$ denotes$_s$ a if and only if
  (i) as before,
  and (ii) e_2 is fulfilled by $\langle a,b \rangle$.

And we can generalize the definition of truth$_s$ in a similar manner.[10] This shows that, in giving a TC, there is no need to utilize the particular vocabulary used at one temporal stage of a language, for we can instead give a more general TC which can be incorporated into a diachronic theory of the language (and can also be applied directly to other languages of a similar structure). *If*, that is, we accept the modification of Tarski proposed in this section.

II

The kind of truth characterization advocated in the previous section differs from the kind of TC Tarski offered in one important respect. Tarski stated the policy 'I shall not make use of any semantical concept if I am not able previously to reduce it to other concepts' (CTFL 152/3), and this policy is flagrantly violated by T1: T1 utilizes unreduced notions of proper names denoting things, predicates applying to things, and function symbols being fulfilled by things.

Tarski's truth characterizations, unlike T1, accorded with his stated policy: they did not contain any semantic terms like 'applies to' or 'denotes'. How did Tarski achieve this result? Very simply: first, he translated every name, predicate, and function symbol of L into English; then he utilized these translations in order to reformulate clauses 2 and 3(ii) of part (A) of the definition and clause 1(ii) of part (B). For simplicity, let's use '$\bar{c}_1$', '$\bar{c}_2$', etc. as abbreviations for the English expressions that are the translations of the words 'c_1', 'c_2',... of L: e.g., if L is simplified German and 'c_1' is 'Deutschland', then '$\bar{c}_1$' is an abbreviation for 'Germany'. Similarly, let '$\bar{f}_1$' abbreviate the translation into English of the word 'f_1' of L, and let '$\bar{p}_1$' abbreviate the translation of 'p_1' into English. Then Tarski's reformulated truth definition will read as follows:

T2 (A) 1 as before

2 'c_k' denotes$_s$ $\bar{c}_k$

3 $\ulcorner f_k(e) \urcorner$ denotes$_s$ a if and only if

(i) as before

(ii) a is $\bar{f}_k(b)$

(B) 1 $\ulcorner p_k(e) \urcorner$ is true$_s$ if and only if

(i) as before

(ii) $\bar{p}_k(a)$

2–4 as before

(C) as before

What T2 is like depends of course on the precise character of the translations of the primitives that are utilized. For instance, if we translate 'c_1' as 'the denotation of "c_1"', translate 'p_1' as 'is something that "p_1" applies to', etc., then T2 becomes identical with T1. This of course is *not* what Tarski intended. What Tarski intended is that T2 not contain unexplicated semantic terms, and if we are to get this result we must not employ any semantic terms in our translations.[11]

But other restrictions on translations are also necessary: if we were to translate 'Deutschland' as 'Bertrand Russell', a truth characterization T2 that was based on this translation would grossly misrepresent L. In order to state the matter more generally, I introduce the term 'coreferential': two singular terms are coreferential if they denote the same thing; two predicative expressions are coreferential if they have the same extension, i.e., if they apply to the same things; and two functional expressions are coreferential if they are fulfilled by the same pairs. It is then easily seen that any departure from coreferentiality in translation will bring errors into T2. For instance, suppose we translate the foreign predicate 'glub' as 'yellow', and suppose 'glub' and yellow are not *precisely* coreferential; then clause (B)$_1$

will say falsely that 'glub(x)' is true of just those objects which are yellow.

Let us say, then, that

(1) An adequate translation of a primitive e_1 of L into English is an expression e_2 of English such that
  (i) e_1 and e_2 are coreferential, and
  (ii) e_2 contains no semantic terms.

This notion of an adequate translation is of course a semantic notion that Tarski did not reduce to non-semantic terms. But that is no objection to his characterization T2 (at least, it isn't obviously an objection), for the notion of an adequate translation is never built into the truth characterization and is not, properly speaking, part of a theory of truth. On Tarski's view we need to adequately translate the object language into the metalanguage in order to give an adequate theory of truth for the object language; this means that the notion of an adequate translation is employed in the methodology of giving truth theories, but it is not employed in the truth theories themselves.

In what follows I shall assume that the language L with which we are dealing is so related to English that all its primitives *can* be adequately translated into English, according to the standards of adequacy set forth in (1). (This is another restriction that we avoid if we give TCs of the type T1; quite a significant restriction, I think.) If we then suppose that the translation given ('$\bar{c}_1$' for 'c_1', etc.) is one of the adequate translations, then T2, like T1, is a correct recursive characterization of truth for the language L. There is, of course, a simple procedure for transforming recursive characterizations such as these into explicit characterizations. To carry the procedure through in these cases would be pretty complicated, but it could be done; so we could regard T1 (or T2) as implicitly specifying a metalinguistic formula '$A_1(e)$' (or '$A_2(e)$'), and saying that an utterance e of L is true if and only if $A_1(e)$ (or $A_2(e)$). If we regard T1 and T2 as written in this form, then the key difference between them is that '$A_1(e)$' *contains semantic terms and* '$A_2(e)$' *does not*. The question then arises: is the fact that '$A_2(e)$' does not contain semantic terms an advantage of T2 over T1? If so, then *why* is it an advantage?

In order to discuss the possible advantages of T2 over T1, I think we have to go beyond mathematical considerations and focus instead on linguistic and other 'philosophical' matters. It is not enough to say that T2 *defines* truth without utilizing semantic terms, whereas T1 defines it only in other semantic terms; this is not enough until we say something more about the purpose of definition. If the purpose of giving a 'definition' of truth is to enable you to do model theory, then the elimination of semantic terms from T1 gives no advantage. For what purpose do we want definitions for which the elimination of semantic terms is useful?

One purpose to which definitions are sometimes put is in explaining the meaning of a word. This of course is very vague, but I think it is clear enough to enable us to recognize that neither T1 nor T2 has very much to do with explaining the meaning of the word 'true'. This is especially obvious for T2: a T2-type truth definition works for a single language only, and so if it 'explains the meaning of' the word 'true' as applied to that language, then for *any* two languages L_1 and L_2, the word 'true' means something different when applied to utterances of L_1 than it means when applied to utterances of L_2! I make this point not in criticism of T2, but in criticism of the idea that the significance of T2 can be explained by saying that it 'gives the meaning of' the word 'true'.

We still need to know what purpose a truth characterization like T1 or T2 could serve that would give someone reason to think that a TC without unexplicated semantic terms would be better than a TC with unexplicated semantic terms. Tarski hints at such a purpose in one place in his writings, where he is discussing the importance of being able to define the word 'true', as opposed to merely introducing axioms to establish the basic properties of truth. If a definition of semantic notions such as truth could not be given, Tarski writes, 'it would then be difficult to bring [semantics] into harmony with the postulates of the unity of science and of physicalism (since the concepts of semantics would be neither logical nor physical concepts)'.[12] This remark seems to me to be of utmost importance in evaluating the philosophical significance of Tarski's work, and so I will now say something about the general philosophical issues it raises. When this is done we will be in a better position to understand Tarski's choice of T2 over T1.

III

In the early 1930s many philosophers believed that the notion of truth could not be incorporated into a scientific conception of the world. I think that the main rationale for this view is hinted at in the remark of Tarski's that I quoted at the end of the last section, and what I want to do now is to elaborate a bit on Tarski's hint.

In the remark I have quoted, Tarski put a heavy stress on the doctrine of physicalism: the doctrine that chemical facts, biological facts, psychological facts and semantical facts are all explicable (in principle) in terms of physical facts. The doctrine of physicalism functions as a high-level empirical hypothesis, a hypothesis that no small number of experiments can force us to give up. It functions, in other words, in much the same way as the doctrine of mechanism (that all facts are

Hartry Field

explicable in terms of *mechanical* facts) once functioned: this latter doctrine has now been universally rejected, but it was given up only by the development of a well-accepted theory (Maxwell's) which described phenomena (electromagnetic radiation and the electromagnetic field) that were very difficult to account for mechanically, and by amassing a great deal of experiment and theory that together made it quite conclusive that mechanical explanations of these phenomena (e.g., by positing 'the ether') would never get off the ground. Mechanism has been empirically refuted; its heir is physicalism, which allows as 'basic' not only facts about mechanics, but facts about other branches of physics as well.[13] I believe that physicists a hundred years ago were justified in accepting mechanism, and that, similarly, physicalism should be accepted until we have convincing evidence that there is a realm of phenomena it leaves out of account. Even if there *does* turn out to be such a realm of phenomena, the only way we'll ever come to know that there is, is by repeated efforts and repeated failures to explain these phenomena in physical terms.

That's my view, anyway, but there are philosophers who think that it is in order to reject physicalism now. One way of rejecting physicalism is called 'vitalism': it is the view that there are irreducibly biological facts, i.e. biological facts that aren't explicable in nonbiological terms (and hence, not in physical terms). Physicalism and vitalism are incompatible, and it is because of this incompatibility that the doctrine of physicalism has the methodological importance it has for biology. Suppose, for instance, that a certain woman has two sons, one haemophilic and one not. Then, according to standard genetic accounts of haemophilia, the ovum from which one of these sons was produced must have contained a gene for haemophilia, and the ovum from which the other son was produced must not have contained such a gene. But now the doctrine of physicalism tells us that there must have been a *physical* difference between the two ova that explains why the first son had haemophilia and the second one didn't, if the standard genetic account is to be accepted. We should not rest content with a special biological predicate 'has-a-haemophilic-gene' — rather, we should look for nonbiological facts (chemical facts; and ultimately, physical facts) that underlie the correct application of this predicate. That at least is what the principle of physicalism tells us, and it can hardly be doubted that this principle has motivated a great deal of very profitable research into the chemical foundations of genetics.

So much for vitalism; now let us turn to other irreducibility doctrines that are opposed to physicalism. One such irreducibility doctrine is Cartesianism: it is the doctrine that there are irreducibly mental facts. Another irreducibility doctrine has received much less attention than either vitalism or Cartesianism, but it is central to our present concerns: this doctrine, which might be called 'semanticalism', is the doctrine that there are irreducibly semantic facts. The semanticalist claims, in other words, that semantic phenomena (such as the fact that 'Schnee' refers to snow) must be accepted as primitive, in precisely the way that electromagnetic phenomena are accepted as primitive (by those who accept Maxwell's equations and reject the ether); and in precisely the way that biological phenomena and mental phenomena are accepted as primitive by vitalists and Cartesians. Semanticalism, like Cartesianism and vitalism, posits nonphysical primitives, and as a physicalist I believe that all three doctrines must be rejected.

There are two general sorts of strategy that can be taken in rejecting semanticalism, or Cartesianism, or vitalism. One strategy, illustrated two paragraphs back in discussing vitalism, is to try to explicate the terms of a biological theory in nonbiological terms. But there is another possible strategy, which is to argue that the biological terms are illegitimate. The second strategy seems reasonable to adopt in dealing with the following predicate of (reincarnationist) biology: 'x has the same soul as y'. A physicalist would never try to find physical or chemical facts that underlie reincarnation; rather, he would reject reincarnation as a myth.

Since biological theory is as well developed as it is, we usually have a pretty good idea which biological terms require explication and which require elimination. When we turn to psychology and semantics, however, it is often not so obvious which strategy is the more promising. Thus in semantics, physicalists agree that all *legitimate* semantic terms must be explicable nonsemantically − they think in other words that there are no irreducibly semantic facts − but they disagree as to which semantic terms are legitimate. That disagreement has become fairly clear in recent years in the theory of meaning, with the work of Quine: the disagreement is between those physicalists who would look for a nonsemantic basis for terms in the theory of meaning, and those who would follow Quine in simply throwing out those terms. Our concern, however, is not with the theory of meaning, but with the theory of reference, and here the disagreement has been less clear, since there haven't been many physicalists who openly advocate getting rid of terms like 'true' and 'denotes'. There were such physicalists in the early 1930s; part of the importance of Tarski's work was to persuade them that they were on the wrong track, to persuade them that we should explicate notions in the theory of reference nonsemantically rather than simply get rid of them.

The view that we should just stop using semantic terms (here and in the rest of this paper, I mean terms in the theory of reference, such as 'true' and 'denotes' and 'applies to') draws its plausibility from the apparent difficulty of explicating these terms nonsemantically. People utter the sounds 'Electrons have rest mass but photons don't', or 'Schnee ist weiss und Gras ist grün', and we apply the word 'true' to

93

their utterances. We don't want to say that it is a primitive and inexplicable fact about these utterances that they are true, a fact that cannot be explicated in nonsemantic terms; this is as unattractive to a physicalist as supposing that it is a primitive and inexplicable fact about an organism at a certain time that it is in pain. But how could we ever explicate in nonsemantic terms the alleged fact that these utterances are true? *Part* of the explication of the truth of 'Schnee ist weiss und Gras ist grün', presumably, would be that snow is white and grass is green. But this would only be part of the explanation, for still missing is the connection between snow being white and grass being green on the one hand, and the German utterance being true on the other hand. It is this connection that seems so difficult to explicate in a way that would satisfy a physicalist, i.e. in a way that does not involve the use of semantic terms.

If, in face of these difficulties, we were ever to conclude that it was *impossible* to explicate the notions of truth and denotation in nonsemantic terms, we would have either to give up these semantic terms or else to reject physicalism. It seems to me that that is essentially what Tarski is saying in the quotation at the end of the last section, and I have tried to make it plausible by sketching analogies to areas other than semantics. Tarski's view, however, was that, for certain languages at least, semantic terms *are* explicable nonsemantically, and that truth definitions like T2 provide the required explication. It is understandable that as far as *philosophical* purposes go Tarski should think that T1 leaves something to be desired: after all, it merely explicates truth in terms of other semantic concepts; but what good does that do if those other concepts can't be explicated nonsemantically? T2, then, has a strong *prima facie* advantage over T1. In the next section I will show that it is not a genuine advantage.

IV

The apparent advantage of T2 over T1, I have stressed, is that it appears to reduce truth to nonsemantic terms; and I *think* this is why Tarski wanted to give a truth definition like T2 rather than like T1. This interpretation makes sense of Tarski's remark about physicalism, and it also explains why someone who was certainly not interested in 'meaning analysis' as that is usually conceived would have wanted to give 'definitions' of truth and would emphasize that, in these 'definitions', 'I will not make use of any semantical concept if I am not able previously to reduce it to other concepts'. In any case, the problem of reducing truth is a very important problem, one which T1 and T2 provide a partial solution to, and one which T2 *might* be thought to provide a full solution to; and it is not at all clear what *other* interesting problems T2 could be thought to solve better than T1.

In Tarski's own exposition of his theory of truth, Tarski put very little stress on the problem of reduction or on any other problem with a clear philosophical or mathematical motivation; instead, he set up a formal criterion of adequacy for theories of truth without any serious discussion of whether or why this formal criterion is reasonable. Roughly, the criterion was this:[14]

(M) Any condition of the form
>   (2) $(\forall e)\ [e\ \text{is true} \equiv B(e)]$
> should be accepted as an adequate definition of truth if and only if it is correct and '$B(e)$' is a well-formed formula containing no semantic terms. (The quantifiers are to be taken as ranging over expressions of one particular language only.)

The 'only if' part of condition M is not something I will contest. It rules out the possibility of T1 *by itself* being an adequate truth definition; and it is right to do so, if the task of a truth definition is to reduce truth to nonsemantic terms, for T1 provides only a *partial* reduction. (To complete the reduction we need to reduce primitive denotation to nonsemantic terms.) T2, on the other hand, meets condition M; so either T2 is superior to T1 as a reduction, or else condition M is too weak and the 'if' part of it must be rejected. My own diagnosis is the latter, but the other possibility seems initially reasonable. After all, how could condition M be strengthened? We might try requiring that '$B(e)$' be not only *extensionally* equivalent to 'e is true', but *intensionally* equivalent to it; but this clearly won't do, for even if we grant that there is an intelligible notion of intensional equivalence, our concern is not with analysing the meaning of the word 'true' but with performing a reduction. A clear and useful standard of equivalence that is stronger than extensional equivalence but not so strong as to rule out acceptable reductions is unknown at the present time, so I know no way to improve on condition M. My view is that we have a rough but useful concept of reduction which we are unable to formulate precisely; but I must admit that the alternative view, that extensional equivalence is adequate, has an initial appeal.

A closer look, however, will reveal quite conclusively that extensional equivalence is not a sufficient standard of reduction. This can be seen by looking at the concept of valence. The valence of a chemical element is an integer that is associated with that element, which represents the sort of chemical combinations that the element will enter into. What I mean by the last phrase is that it is possible — roughly, at least — to characterize which elements will combine with which others, and in what proportions they will combine, merely in terms of their valences.

95

Because of this fact, the concept of valence is a physically important concept, and so if physicalism is correct it ought to be possible to explicate this concept in physical terms — e.g., it ought to be possible to find structural properties of the atoms of each element that determine what the valence of that element will be. Early in the twentieth century (long after the notion of valence had proved its value in enabling chemists to predict what chemical combinations there would be) this reduction of the concept of valence to the physical properties of atoms was established; the notion of valence was thus shown to be a physicalistically acceptable notion.

Now, it would have been easy for a chemist, late in the last century, to have given a 'valence definition' of the following form:

(3) $(\forall E)(\forall n)$ (E has valence $n \equiv E$ is potassium and n is $+ 1$, or . . .
or E is sulphur and n is $- 2$)

where in the blanks go a list of similar clauses, one for each element. But, though this is an extensionally correct definition of valence, it would not have been an acceptable reduction; and had it turned out that nothing else was possible — had all efforts to explain valence in terms of the structural properties of atoms proved futile — scientists would have eventually had to decide either (a) to give up valence theory, or else (b) to replace the hypothesis of physicalism by another hypothesis (chemicalism?). It is part of scientific methodology to resist doing (b); and I also think it is part of scientific methodology to resist doing (a) as long as the notion of valence is serving the purposes for which it was designed (i.e. as long as it is proving useful in helping us characterize chemical compounds in terms of their valences). But the methodology is not to resist (a) and (b) by giving lists like (3); the methodology is to look for a real reduction. This is a methodology that has proved extremely fruitful in science, and I think we'd be crazy to give it up in linguistics. *And I think we are giving up this fruitful methodology, unless we realize that we need to add theories of primitive reference to* T1 *or* T2 *if we are to establish the notion of truth as a physicalistically acceptable notion.*

I certainly haven't yet given much argument for this last claim. I *have* argued that the standard of extensional equivalence doesn't guarantee an acceptable reduction; but T2 is obviously not trivial to the extent that (3) is. What *is* true, however, is roughly that T2 minus T1 is as trivial as (3) is. One way in which this last claim can be made more precise is by remembering that really we often apply the term 'valence' not only to elements, but also to configurations of elements (at least to stable configurations that are not compounds, i.e. to radicals). Thus, if we abstract from certain physical limitations on the size of possible configurations of elements (as, in linguistics, we usually abstract from the limitations that memory, etc., impose on the lengths of possible utterances), there is an infinite number of entities to which the term 'valence' is applied. But it is an important fact about valence that the valence of a configuration of elements is determined from the valences of the elements that make it up, and from the way they're put together. Because of this, we might try to give a recursive characterization of valence. First of all, we would try to characterize all the different *structures* that configurations of elements can have (much as we try to characterize all the different grammatical structures before we give a truth definition like T1 or T2). We would then try to find rules that would enable us to determine what the valence of a complicated configuration would be, given the valences of certain less complicated configurations that make it up and the way they're put together. If we had enough such rules, we could determine the valence of a given configuration given only its structure and the valences of the elements that make it up. And if we like, we can transform our recursive characterization of valence into an explicit characterization, getting

V1 $(\forall c)(\forall n)$ $(c$ has valence $n \equiv B(c,n))$

The formula '$B(c,n)$' here employed will still contain the term 'valence', but it will contain that term only as applied to elements, not as applied to configurations. Thus our 'valence definition' V1 would characterize the valence of the complex *in terms of the valences of the simple.*

It would now be possible to eliminate the term 'valence' from '$B(c,n)$', in either of two ways. One way would be to employ a genuine reduction of the notion of valence for elements to the structural properties of atoms. The other way would be to employ the pseudo-reduction (3). It is clear that we could use (3) to give a trivial reformulation V2 of V1, which would have precisely the 'advantages' as a reduction that T2 has over T1. (V2, incidentally, would also have one of the disadvantages over V1 that T2 has over T1: V1 does not need to be overhauled when you discover or synthesize new elements, whereas V2 does.)

That is a sketch of one way that the remark I made two paragraphs back about 'T2 minus T1' could be made more precise. But it is somewhat more fruitful to develop the point slightly differently: doing this will enable me to make clearer that there is unlikely to be *any* purpose that T2 serves better than T1 (not merely that T2 is no better at reduction).

To get this result I'll go back to my original use of the term 'valence', where it applies to elements only and not to configurations. And what I will do is compare (3) not to Tarski's theory of *truth*, but to Tarski's theory of *denotation* for names; the effect of this on his theory of truth will then be considered. Tarski states his theory of denotation for names in a footnote, as follows ('CTFL', p. 194):

To say that the name x denotes a given object a is the same as to stipulate that the object a ... satisfies a sentential function of a particular type. In colloquial language it would be a function which consists of three parts in the following order: a variable, the word 'is' and the given name x.

This is actually only part of the theory, the part that defines denotation in terms of satisfaction; to see what the theory looks like when all semantic terms are eliminated, we must see how satisfaction is defined. The definition is given by the (A) and (B) clauses of T2, for, as I've remarked, 'satisfaction' is Tarski's name for what I've called 'truth$_s$'. What Tarski's definition of satisfaction tells us is this: for any name N, an object a satisfies the sentential function $\ulcorner x_1$ is $N \urcorner$ if and only if a is France and N is 'France' or ... or a is Germany and N is 'Germany'. Combining this definition of satisfaction (for sentential functions of form $\ulcorner x_1$ is $N \urcorner$) with the earlier account of denotation in terms of satisfaction, we get:

(DE): To say that the name N denotes a given object a is the same as to stipulate that either a is France and N is 'France', or ... or a is Germany and N is 'Germany'.

This is Tarski's account of denotation for English proper names. For foreign proper names, the definition of denotation in terms of satisfaction needs no modification (except that the 'is' must be replaced by a name of a foreign word, say 'ist' for German). Combining this with the definition (again given by T2) of satisfaction for foreign sentential functions like $\ulcorner x_1$ ist $N \urcorner$, we get:

(DG): To say that the name N denotes a given object a is the same as to stipulate that either a is France and N is 'Frankreich', or ... or a is Germany and N is 'Deutschland'.

DE and DG have not received much attention in commentaries on Tarski, but in fact they play a key role in his semantic theory; and it was no aberration on Tarski's part that he offered them as theories of denotation for English and German names, for *they satisfy criteria of adequacy exactly analogous to the criteria of adequacy that Tarski accepted for theories of truth.*[15] Nevertheless, it seems clear that DE and DG do not really reduce denotation to nonsemantic terms, any more than (3) reduces valence to nonchemical terms. What would a real explication of denotation in nonsemantic terms be like? The 'classical' answer to this question (Russell's) is that a name like 'Cicero' is 'analytically linked' to a certain description (such as 'the denouncer of Catiline'); so to explain how the name 'Cicero' denotes what it does you merely have to explain

(i) the process by which it is linked to the description (presumably you bring in facts about how it was learned by its user, or facts about what is going on in the user's brain at the time of the using)

and (ii) how the description refers to what it does.

Because of (ii), of course, the project threatens circularity: the project is to explain how names refer in terms of how descriptions refer; but the natural way to explain how descriptions refer is in terms of how they're built up from their significant parts,[16] and how those significant parts refer (or apply, or are fulfilled), and those significant parts will usually include names. But Russell recognized this threat of circularity, and carefully avoided it: he assumed that the primitives of the language were to be partially ordered by a relation of 'basicness', and that each name except a most basic ('logically proper') name was to be analytically linked to a formula containing only primitives more basic than it. The most basic primitives were to be linked to the world without the intervention of other words, by the relation of acquaintance.

This classical view of how names (and other primitives) latch onto their denotations is extremely implausible in many ways (e.g., it says you can refer only to things that are definable from 'logically proper' primitives; it requires that there be certain statements, such as 'If Cicero existed then Cicero denounced Catiline', which are analytic in the sense that they are guaranteed by linguistic rules and are immune to revision by future discoveries). I conjecture that it is because of the difficulties with this classical theory, which was the only theory available at the time that Tarski wrote, that Tarski's pseudo-theories DE and DG seemed reasonable — they weren't exciting, but if you wanted something exciting you got logically proper names. The diagnosis that any attempt to explain the relation between words and the things they are about must inevitably lead to either a wildly implausible theory (like Russell's) or a trivial theory (like Tarski's) seems to be widely accepted still; but I think that the diagnosis has become less plausible in recent years through the development of *causal* theories of denotation by Saul Kripke[17] and others. According to such theories, the facts that 'Cicero' denotes Cicero and that 'muon' applies to muons are to be explained in terms of certain kinds of causal networks between Cicero (muons) and our uses of 'Cicero' ('muon'): causal connections both of a social sort (the passing of the word 'Cicero' down to us from the original users of the name, or the passing of the word 'muon' to laymen from physicists) and of other sorts (the evidential causal connections that gave the original users of the name 'access' to Cicero and give physicists 'access' to muons). I don't think that Kripke or anyone else thinks that *purely* causal theories of primitive denotation can be developed (even for proper names of past physical objects and for natural-kind predicates); this however should not blind us to the fact that he has suggested a kind of factor involved in denotation that gives new hope to

99

the idea of explaining the connection between language and the things it is about. It seems to me that the possibility of *some such* theory of denotation (to be deliberately very vague) is essential to the joint acceptability of physicalism and the semantic term 'denotes', and that denotation definitions like DE and DG merely obscure the need for this.

It might be objected that the purpose of DE and DG was not reduction; but what was their purpose? One answer might be that (DE) and (DG) enable us to eliminate the word 'denote' whenever it occurs. ('To explain is to show how to eliminate.') For instance,

(4) No German name now in use denotes something that does not yet exist.

would become

(4') For any name N now in use, if N is 'Frankreich' then France already exists, and . . . , and if N is 'Deutschland' then Germany already exists.

provided that (DG) is a correct and complete list of the denotations of all those German proper names that have denotations. It seems reasonably clear that we could specify a detailed procedure for transforming sentences like (4) into materially equivalent sentences like (4'). A similar claim could be made for the 'valence definition' (3). Such a valence definition makes it possible to eliminate the word 'valence' from a large class of sentences containing it, and in a uniform way. For instance,

(5) For any elements A and B, if one atom of A combines with two of B, then the valence of A is -2 times that of B.

is materially equivalent to

(5') For any elements A and B, if one atom of A combines with two of B, then either A is sodium and B is sodium and $+1 = -2$ $(+1)$, or . . . , or A is sulphur and B is sodium and $-2 = -2$ $(+1)$, or. . . .

provided that (3) is a correct and complete list of valences. So if anyone ever wants to eliminate the word 'denote' or the word 'valence' from a large class of English sentences by a uniform procedure, denotation definitions and valence definitions are just the thing he needs. There are, however, sentences from which these words are not eliminable by the sketched procedure. For instance, in semantics and possibly in chemistry there are problems with counterfactuals; e.g., 'If "Germany" had been used to denote France, then . . .'. Moreover, there are special problems affecting the case of semantics, arising from the facts

(i) that the elimination procedure works only for languages in which nothing is denoted that cannot be denoted (without using semantic terms) in one's own language,

(ii) that it works only for languages that contain no ambiguous names,

and

(iii) that the denotation definitions provide no procedure for eliminating 'denote' from sentences where it is applied to more than one language; e.g., it gives no way of handling sentences like ' "Glub" denotes different things in different languages.'

But, subject to these three qualifications (plus perhaps that involving counterfactuals), the elimination procedure for 'denote' is every bit as good as that for 'valence'!

What value did Tarski attach to such transformations? Unfortunately he did not discuss the one about valences, but he did discuss the one that transforms 'Smith used a proper name to denote Germany' into something logically equivalent to 'Smith uttered "Deutschland".' And it is clear that to this definition he attached great philosophical importance. After defining semantics as 'the totality of considerations concerning those concepts which, roughly speaking, express certain connexions between the expressions of a language and the objects and states of affairs referred to by those expressions' ('ESS', p. 401), he says that with his definitions, 'the problem of establishing semantics on a scientific basis is completely solved' ('ESS', p. 407). In other places his claims are almost as extravagant. For instance, the remark about physicalism that I quoted at the end of section II is intended to apply to denotation as well as to truth: if definitions of denotation like DE and DG could not be given, 'it would . . . be impossible to bring [semantics] into harmony with . . . physicalism' ('ESS', p. 406); but because of these definitions, the compatibility of the semantic concept of denotation with physicalism is established. By similar standards of reduction, one might prove that witchcraft is compatible with physicalism, as long as witches cast only a finite number of spells: for then 'cast a spell' can be defined without use of any of the terms of witchcraft theory, merely by listing all the witch-and-victim pairs.

In other places Tarski makes quite different claims for the value of his denotation definitions. For example:[18]

We desire semantic terms (referring to the object language) to be introduced into the meta-language only by definition. For, if this postulate is satisfied, the definition of truth, or of any other semantic concept [including denotation, which Tarski had already specifically mentioned to be definable], will fulfil what we intuitively expect from every definition; that is, it will explain the meaning of the term being defined in terms whose meaning appears to be completely clear and unequivocal.

But it is no more plausible that DE 'explains the meaning of' 'denote' as applied to English, or that DG 'explains the meaning of' 'denote' as applied to German, than that (3) 'explains the meaning of' 'valence' — considerably *less* so in fact, since for 'valence' there is no analogue to the conclusions that 'denote' means something different when applied to English than it means when applied to German. In fact, it seems pretty clear that denotation definitions like DE and DG have no philosophical interest whatever. But what conclusions can we draw from this about Tarski's *truth* definitions like T2? I think the conclusion to draw is that *T2 has no philosophical interest whatever that is not shared by T1*. How this follows I will now explain.

We have seen that Tarski advocated theories of denotation for names that had the form of mere lists: examples of his denotation definitions were DE and DG, and for language L his denotation definition would take the following form:

D2 $(\forall e)(\forall a)$ [e is a name that denotes $a \equiv (e$ is 'c_1' and a is $\bar{c}_1$) or (e is 'c_2' and a is $\bar{c}_2$) or ...]

where into the dots go analogous clauses for every name of L. Similarly, we can come up with definitions of application and fulfilment which are acceptable according to Tarski's standards, and which also have the form of mere lists. The definition of application runs:

A2 $(\forall e)(\forall a)$ [e is a predicate that applies to $a \equiv (e$ is 'p_1' and $\bar{p}_1(a)$) or (e is 'p_2' and $\bar{p}_2(a)$) or ...].

Similarly, we can formulate a list-like characterization F2 of fulfilment for the function symbols. Clearly neither A2 nor F2 is of any more theoretical interest than D2.

Tarski, I have stressed, accepted D2 as part of his semantic theory, and would also have accepted A2 and F2; and this fact is quite important, since D2, A2, and F2 together with T2 imply T1. In other words, T1 is simply a weaker version of Tarski's semantic theory; it is a logical consequence of Tarski's theory. Now, an interesting question is what you have to add to T1 to get the rest of Tarski's semantic theory. Suppose we can find a formula R that we can argue to be of no interest whatever, such that Tarski's semantic theory (T2 $\wedge$ D2 $\wedge$ A2 $\wedge$ F2) is logically equivalent to T1 $\wedge$ R. It will then follow that the whole interest of Tarski's semantic theory lies in T1 — the rest of his semantic theory results simply by adding to it the formula R, which (I have assumed) has no interest whatever. And if there is nothing of interest in the conjunction T2 $\wedge$ D2 $\wedge$ A2 $\wedge$ F2 beyond T1, certainly there can be nothing of interest in T2 alone beyond T1.

An example of such a formula R is D2 $\wedge$ A2 $\wedge$ F2: it is obvious that Tarski's semantic theory is logically equivalent to T1 $\wedge$ D2 $\wedge$ A2 $\wedge$ F2. Because of this, *any interest in Tarski's semantic theory over T1 must be due to an interest in* D2 *or* A2 *or* F2 *(or to confusion): in this sense* D2 ∧ A2 ∧ F2 *is* 'T2 *minus* T1'. But I've already argued that D2, A2, and F2 have no theoretical interest whatever, and so that establishes that T2 has no theoretical interest whatever that is not shared by T1.

V

Much of what I've said in this paper gains plausibility by being put in a wider perspective, and so I now want to say a little bit about why we want a notion of truth. The notion of truth serves a great many purposes, but I suspect that its original purpose — the purpose for which it was first developed — was to aid us in utilizing the utterances of others in drawing conclusions about the world. To take an extremely simple example, suppose that a friend reports that he's just come back from Alabama and that there was a foot of snow on the ground there. Were it not for his report we would have considered it extremely unlikely that there was a foot of snow on the ground in Alabama — but the friend knows snow when he sees it and is not prone to telling us lies for no apparent reason, and so after brief deliberation we conclude that probably there *was* a foot of snow in Alabama. What we did here was first to use our evidence about the person and his situation to decide that he probably said something true when he made a certain utterance, and then to draw a conclusion from the truth of his utterance to the existence of snow in Alabama. In order to make such inferences, we have to have a pretty good grasp of (i) the circumstances under which what another says is likely to be true, and (ii) how to get from a belief in the truth of what he says to a belief about the extralinguistic world.

If this idea is right, then two features of truth that are intimately bound up with the purposes to which the notion of truth are put are (I) the role that the attempt to tell the truth and the success in doing so play in social institutions, and (II) the fact that normally one is in a position to assert of a sentence that it is true in just those cases where one is in a position to assert the sentence or a paraphrase of it. It would then be natural to expect that what is involved in communicating the meaning of the word 'true' to a child or to a philosopher is getting across to him the sorts of facts listed under (I) and (II); for those are the facts that it is essential for him to have an awareness of if he is to put the notion of truth to its primary use (child) or if he is to get a clear grasp of what its primary use is (philosopher).

I think that this natural expectation is correct, and that it gives more insight than was given in sections II and IV into why it is that neither T1 nor T2 can reasonably be said to explain the meaning of the term 'true' – even when a theory of primitive reference is added to them. First consider (I). The need of understanding the sort of thing alluded to in (I), if we are to grasp the notion of truth, has been presented quite forcefully in Michael Dummett's article 'Truth',[19] in his analogy between speaking the truth and winning at a game. It is obvious that T1 and T2 don't explain anything like this (and in fact Dummett's fourth paragraph, on Frege-style truth definitions, can be carried over directly to T1 and T2).

The matter might perhaps be expressed in terms of assertibility conditions that one learns in learning to use the word 'true': part of what we learn, in learning to use this word, is that in cases like that involving the friend from Alabama there is some *prima facie* weight to be attached to the claim that the other person is saying something true. But there are also *other* assertibility conditions that one learns in learning the word 'true', assertibility conditions which have received considerable attention in the philosophical literature on truth. To begin with, let's note one obvious fact about how the word 'true' is standardly learned: we learn how to apply it to utterances of our own language first, and when we later learn to apply it to other languages it is by conceiving the utterances of another language more or less on the model of utterances of our own language. The obvious model of the first stage of this process is that we learn to accept all instances of the schema

$$\text{(T) } X \text{ is true if and only if } p.$$

where 'X' is replaced by a quotation-mark name of an English sentence S and 'p' is replaced by S. This must be complicated to deal with ambiguous and truth-value-less sentences, but let's ignore them. Also let's ignore the fact that certain pathological instances of (T) – the Epimenides-type paradoxical sentences – are logically refutable. Then there is a sense in which the instances of (T) that we've learned to accept determine a unique extension for the predicate 'true' as applied to sentences of our own language.[20] Our views about what English sentences belong to this unique extension may be altered, but as long as we stick to the instances of (T) they cannot consistently be altered without also altering our beliefs in what those sentences express. This fact is extremely important to the functions that the word 'true' serves (as the Alabama example illustrates).

In stressing the assertibility conditions for simple sentences containing the word 'true', I have followed Quine;[21] for, like him, I believe that such assertibility conditions are enough to make the term 'true' reasonably clear. But now it might be asked, 'Then why do we need causal (etc.) theories of reference? The words "true" and "denotes" are made perfectly clear by schemas like (T). To ask for more than these schemas – to ask for causal theories of reference to nail language to reality – is to fail to recognize that we are at sea on Neurath's boat:

we have to work *within* our conceptual scheme, we can't glue it to reality from the outside.'

I suspect that this would be Quine's diagnosis — it is strongly suggested by section 6 of *Word and Object*, especially when that is taken in conjunction with some of Quine's remarks about the inscrutability of reference and truth value, the underdetermination of theories and the relativity of ontology. It seems to me, however, that the diagnosis is quite wrong. In looking for a theory of truth and a theory of primitive reference we *are* trying to explain the connection between language and (extralinguistic) reality, but we are *not* trying to step outside of our theories of the world in order to do so. Our accounts of primitive reference and of truth are not to be thought of as something that could be given by philosophical reflection prior to scientific information — on the contrary, it seems likely that such things as psychological models of human beings and investigations of neurophysiology will be very relevant to discovering the mechanisms involved in reference. *The reason why accounts of truth and primitive reference are needed is not to tack our conceptual scheme on to reality from the outside; the reason, rather, is that without such accounts our conceptual scheme breaks down from the inside.* On our theory of the world it would be extremely surprising if there were some nonphysical connection between words and things. Thus if we could argue from our theory of the world that the notion of an utterer's saying something true, or referring to a particular thing, cannot be made sense of in physicalist terms (say, by arguing that any semantic notion that makes physicalistic sense *can* be explicated in Skinnerian terms, and that the notions of truth and reference *can't* be explicated in Skinnerian terms), then to the extent that such an argument is convincing we ought to be led to conclude that, if we are to remain physicalists, the notions of truth and reference must be abandoned. No amount of pointing out the clarity of these terms helps enable us to escape this conclusion: 'valence' and 'gene' were perfectly clear long before anyone succeeded in reducing them, but it was their reducibility and not their clarity before reduction that showed them to be compatible with physicalism.

The clarity of 'valence' and 'gene' before reduction — and even more, their *utility* before reduction — did provide physicalists with substantial reason to think that a reduction of these terms was possible, and, as I remarked earlier, a great deal of fruitful work in physical chemistry and chemical genetics was motivated by the fact. Similarly, in so far as semantic notions like 'true' are useful, we have every reason to suspect that they will be reducible to nonsemantic terms, and it is likely that progress in linguistic theory will come by looking for such reductions. (In fact, the fruitfulness of Tarski's work in aiding us to understand language is already some sign of this, even though it represents only a partial reduction.) Of course, this sort of argument for the prospects of reducing semantic notions is only as powerful as our arguments for the utility of semantic terms; and it is clear that the question of the utility of the term 'true' — the purposes it serves, and the extent to which those purposes could be served by less pretentious notions such as warranted assertibility — needs much closer investigation.

All these remarks require one important qualification. The notion of valence, it must be admitted, is *not* reducible to nonchemical terms on the *strictest* standards of reduction, but is only *approximately* reducible; yet, in spite of this, we don't want to get rid of the notion, since it is still extremely useful in those contexts where its approximate character isn't too likely to get in the way and where if we did not approximate we'd get into quantum-mechanical problems far too complex for anyone to solve. (Moreover, considerations about the purposes of the notion of valence were sufficient to show that the notion of valence would only be approximately reducible: for the utility of the notion of valence is that it aids us in approximately characterizing which elements will combine with which and in what proportions; yet it is obvious that no such *precise* characterization is possible.)

Similarly, it may well be that a detailed investigation into the purposes of the notion of truth might show that these purposes require only an approximate reduction of the notion of truth. Still, to require an approximate reduction is to require quite a bit; after all, 'is a reincarnation of' isn't even approximately reducible to respectable biology, and 'electromagnetic field' is not approximately reducible to mechanics. Obviously the notion of approximate reduction needs to be made more precise (as in fact does the notion of strict, or nonapproximate, reduction); but even without making it so, I think we can see that T2 is no more of an approximate reduction than is V2, since D2 ∧ A2 ∧ F2 is no more of an approximate reduction than is (3). In other words, the main point of the paper survives when we replace the ideal of strict reduction by the ideal of approximate reduction.

It should be kept carefully in mind that the Quinean view that all we need do is clarify the term 'true', in the sense that this term is clarified by schema T (or by schema T plus a theory of translation to handle foreign languages; or by schema T plus the sort of thing alluded to in connection with Dummett), is *not* Tarski's view. Tarski's view is that we have to provide a truth characterization like T2 (which, when we choose as our object language L a 'nice' fragment of our own language, can be shown correct merely by assuming that all instances of schema T are valid — cf. n. 14); and such a truth characterization does much more than schema T does. It does not do everything that Tarski ever claimed for it, for Tarski attached much too much importance to the pseudo-theories D2, A2, and F2; but even when we 'subtract' such trivialities from his truth characterization T2, we still get the very interesting and important truth characterization T1. T1, I believe, adequately represents Tarski's real contribution to the theory of truth, and in doing this it has a number of positive advantages over T2 (in addition to the important negative advantage I've been stressing, of preventing extravagant claims based on the fact that T2 contains no semantic terms). First of all, T1, unlike T2, is applicable to languages that contain ambiguities and languages that contain terms not adequately translatable into English. Second, T1, unlike T2, can be used in diachronic linguistics: it doesn't need overhauling as you add new words to the language, provided those new words belong to the same semantic category as words already in the language. Third, I think that the reason why Tarski's theory of truth T2 has seemed so uninteresting to so many people is that it contains the vacuous semantic theories D2, A2, and F2 for the primitives of the language. By expressing the really important features of Tarski's results on truth, and leaving out the inessential and uninteresting 'theories' of the semantics of the primitives, T1 should make the philosophical importance of Tarski's work more universally recognized.

Notes

1 K. Popper, *Logic of Scientific Discovery* (New York, Basic Books, 1968), p. 274.

2 Cf. Carnap's 'Autobiography', in P. A. Schilpp, ed., *The Philosophy of Rudolf Carnap* (Lasalle, Ill., Open Court, 1963), p. 61.

3 It is sometimes claimed that Tarski was interested in languages considered in abstraction from all speakers and writers of the language; that the languages he was dealing with are abstract entities to be specified by giving their rules. This seems incorrect: Tarski was interested in giving the semantics of languages that mathematicians had been writing for years; and only as a result of Tarski's work was it then possible for philosophers like Carnap to propose that the clauses of a Tarski-type truth definition for such languages be called rules of the languages and be used in defining the languages as abstract entities.

4 A. Tarski, 'The Concept of Truth in Formalized Languages' ('CTFL'), in *Logic, Semantics, Metamathematics (LSM)* (New York, Oxford University Press, 1956), p. 166.

5 Actually in model theory we are interested in allowing a slightly unusual semantics for the quantifiers: we are willing to allow that the quantifier not range over everything. We could build this generalization into our truth definition, by stipulating that in addition to the denotations of the nonlogical symbols we specify a universe U, and then reformulating clause (B)4 by requiring that the kth member of s^* belong to U. If we did this, then it would be

the range of the quantifiers as well as the denotations of the non-logical primitives that we would have explained truth in terms of.

6 An *incomplete* sentence token is a sentence token which [like the occurrence of '2 + 2 = 4' inside '∼ (2 + 2 = 4)'] is part of a larger sentence token.

7 D. Davidson, 'Truth and Meaning', *Synthèse*, vol. XVII, no. 3 (September 1967), pp. 314–15.

8 Note that the claims I've been making are intended to apply only to cases where different tokens have different semantic features; they are not intended to apply to cases of indeterminacy, i.e., to cases where a particular name token or predicate token has no determinate denotation or extension. To deal with indeterminacy requires more complex devices than I employ in this paper.

9 The notion of a semantic category is Tarski's: cf. 'CTFL', p. 215.

10 To do so in the obvious way requires that we introduce semantic categories of negation symbol, conjunction symbol, and universal-quantification symbol; though by utilizing some ideas of Frege it could be shown that there is really no need of a separate semantic category for each logical operator. The use of semantic categories in the generalized truth characterization raises important problems which I have had to suppress for lack of space in this paper.

11 For simplicity, I have assumed that L itself contains no semantic terms.

12 A. Tarski, 'The Establishment of Scientific Semantics' ('ESS') in *LSM*, p. 406.

13 This, of course, is very vague, but most attempts to explicate the doctrine of physicalism more precisely result in doctrines that are very hard to take seriously [e.g., the doctrine that for every acceptable predicate '$P(x)$' there is a formula '$B(x)$' containing only terminology from physics, such that '$\forall x(P(x) \equiv B(x))$' is true]. Physicalism should be understood as the doctrine (however precisely it is to be characterized) that guides science in the way I describe.

14 Tarski actually gives a different formulation, the famous Convention T, evidently because he does not think that the word 'correct' ought to be employed in stating a criterion of adequacy. First of all Tarski writes ('ESS', p. 404):

we shall accept as valid every sentence of the form

[T] the sentence x is true if and only p

where 'p' is to be replaced by any sentence of the language under investigation and 'x' by any individual name of that sentence provided this name occurs in the metalanguage.

Is Tarski's policy of accepting these sentences as 'valid' (i.e., true) legitimate? It seems to me that it is, in a certain special case. The special case is where

I The object language is a proper part of the metalanguage (here, English).

II The object language contains no paradoxical or ambiguous or truth-value-less sentences.

In this special case — and it was the case that Tarski was primarily concerned with — I think it will be generally agreed that all instances of Schema T hold. From this, together with the fact that only grammatical sentences are true, we can argue that, if a necessary and sufficient condition of form (2) has the following consequences:

(a) Every instance of Schema T
(b) The sentence '$(\forall x)$ (x is true $\supset S(x)$)', where '$S(x)$' formulates (correct) conditions for an utterance of L to be a sentence

then that necessary and sufficient condition is correct. Let's say that a 'truth definition' for L (a necessary and sufficient condition of truth in L) *satisfies Convention T* if it has all the consequences listed under (a) and (b). Then, restating: when L is a language for which I and II hold, then any truth definition satisfying Convention T is correct; and since only quite uncontroversial assumptions about truth are used in getting this result, anyone will admit to the correctness of a truth characterization satisfying Convention T. If we use the term 'formally correct definition' for a sentence of form (2) in which '$B(e)$' contains no semantic terms, this means that a formally correct definition that satisfies Convention T is bound to satisfy Condition M (when the language L satisfies I and II). As far as I can see, this is the only motivation for Convention T; if so, we can discredit Convention T by discussion Convention M.

Tarski sometimes states a more general form of Convention T, which applies to languages that do not meet restriction I: it is what results when one allows as instances of Schema T the results of replacing 'p' by a *correct translation* of the sentence that the name substituted for 'x' denotes (in some sense of 'correct translation' in which correctness requires preservation of truth value). But then the advantage of the ungeneralized form of Convention T (viz., that anything satisfying it wears its correctness on its face, or more accurately, on the faces of its logical consequences) is lost.

15 A sentence of the form '$(\forall N)$ $(\forall x)$ [N denotes $x \equiv B(N,x)$]' *satisfies convention* D if it has as consequences every instance of the schema 'y denotes z', in which 'y' is to be replaced by a quotation-mark name for a name N, and 'z' is to be replaced by (an adequate translation of N into English, i.e.) a singular term of English that contains no semantic terms and that denotes the same thing that N denotes. Clearly DE and DG are not only extensionally correct, they also satisfy Convention D. Presumably philosophers who are especially impressed with Convention T will be equally impressed with this fact, but they owe us a reason why satisfying Convention D is of any interest.

16 For example, by extending our definition of denotation$_s$ to descriptions by:

⌜$\imath x_k(e)$⌝ denotes$_s$ a if and only if [for each sequence s^* which differs from s at the kth place at most, e is true$_s$* if and only if the kth member of s^* is a].

and then defining denotation in terms of denotation$_s$ by stipulating that a closed term denotes an object if and only if it denotes$_s$ that object for some (or all) s.

17 Some of Kripke's work on names is published in Davidson and Harman, eds., *Semantics of Natural Language* (Dordrecht: Reidel, 1971). What I've said about Russell's view is influenced by some of Kripke's lectures on which his paper there is based.

18 A. Tarski, 'The Semantic Conception of Truth and the Foundations of Semantics', *Philosophy and Phenomenological Research*, vol. IV, no. 3 (March 1944), p. 351.

19 Michael Dummett, 'Truth', *Proceedings of the Aristotelian Society*, vol. LIX (1958-9), pp. 141-62.

20 Cf. W. V. Quine, *From a Logical Point of View* (New York, Harper & Row, 1961), p. 136.

21 ibid., p. 138.

6 Physicalism and primitive denotation: Field on Tarski*

John McDowell

I

In this paper I want to discuss a contention made by Hartry Field, in his influential article 'Tarski's Theory of Truth' (*Journal of Philosophy*, vol. 59 (1972), p. 347 and Chapter 5 above†). Tarski claimed that his work on truth ('The Concept of Truth in Formalized Languages', in *Logic, Semantics, Metamathematics* (Clarendon Press, Oxford 1956): henceforth 'CTFL') made semantics respectable from a physicalist standpoint ('The Establishment of Scientific Semantics', in *Logic, Semantics, Metamathematics* – henceforth 'ESS' – at p. 406). Field's contention is that Tarski thereby misrepresented what he had done, because of an erroneous belief that he had shown how truth (for formalized languages of finite order) can be interestingly defined without using prior semantic notions. What Tarski in fact did, according to Field, was to show how truth (for those languages) can be characterized in terms of a small number of primitive semantic notions. Physicalism requires something more, which Tarski did not offer: namely explication of those primitive notions in physical terms.

I believe Field is right about Tarski's view of the relation between physicalism and his work on truth. I believe also that, given the physicalism he espouses (which is probably Tarski's doctrine too), Field is right to regard Tarski's claim as overblown. (This is not to suggest that Field depreciates the magnitude of Tarski's formal contribution; that is not affected if Tarski's somewhat incidental claims about physicalism are rejected.) What I want to dispute is how semantics and physics are related, which Field aims to motivate by these considerations about Tarski.

*First published in *Erkenntnis*, vol. 13 (1978), pp. 131–52. I read an earlier version of this paper to an Oxford seminar in 1973. It should be obvious that my debts to Donald Davidson's writings far outrun those signalled in the notes. Gareth Evans and Colin McGinn helped with an intermediate revision, and more recently I have had aid and comfort from Hilary Putnam's 1976 John Locke Lectures.
†Page references to Field's paper are made to this volume.

John McDowell

II

I shall begin by setting out the contrast between what Tarski allegedly should have done and what he actually did, on which Field's argument turns.

We are to consider a simple first-order language L, with names (c_1, c_2, and so on to the appropriate last subscript; we use 'c_k' as a variable to range over the names); one-place function symbols (f_1, f_2, . . . ; variable 'f_k'); one-place predicates (p_1, p_2, . . . ; variable 'p_k'); variables (x_1, x_2, and so on indefinitely; variable 'x_k'); connectives $\sim$ and $\wedge$; and a quantifier $\forall$.[1] L's singular terms are: the names, the variables, and the result of writing any function symbol followed by any singular term. L's atomic well-formed formulae (wffs) are: the result of writing any predicate followed by any singular term. The wffs are: the atomic wffs, the negation of any wff, the conjunction of any two wffs, and the universal quantification of any wff with respect to any variable. Sentences are, as usual, closed wffs.

In the case of languages whose only complex sentences are formed by truth-functional compounding, it is straightforward to characterize truth for complex sentences in terms of truth for simple sentences. With quantification, the straightforward procedure is blocked, since the constituents of complex sentences are no longer necessarily sentences. Tarski saw that the obstacle can be circumvented with the concept of satisfaction. In the truth-functional case, the semantic impact of sentence-forming operations is captured in a recursive characterization of truth itself; when sentence-forming operations operate on open as well as closed sentences, their semantic impact is captured instead in a recursive characterization of satisfaction, in terms of which truth can then be directly defined. Satisfaction (of open or closed sentences, by sequences of objects) is, as the above might suggest, something of which truth can be regarded as a limiting case. For a closed sentence to be satisfied by any sequence whatever simply is for it to be true; for an open sentence to be satisfied by a sequence is for it to be true, so to speak, on the fiction that its free variables denote the corresponding members of the sequence. Field aptly describes the idea (p. 85) as being to treat free variables as 'temporary names', and, in place of satisfaction by a sequence, speaks of truth relative to a sequence.

In more detail: the construction has three components. Working backwards:

(i) Truth *tout court* is defined as satisfaction by, or truth relative to, any sequence whatever.

(ii) Truth relative to a sequence, for complex wffs, is recursively characterized in terms of the truth, relative to that sequence, of their simpler constituents. Obvious clauses handle the connectives:

112

(a) $\sim A$ is true$_s$ iff A is not true$_s$;[2]

(b) $(A \wedge B)$ is true$_s$ iff A is true$_s$ and B is true$_s$;

and the clause for the quantifier is only slightly less obvious:

(c) $\forall x_k A$ is true$_s$ iff, for every sequence s' different from s in at most the kth place, A is true$_{s'}$.

Using these clauses, we could, for any complex wff of L, determine conditions under which it would be true relative to a sequence, in terms of the truth or not, relative to that sequence, of its atomic wffs. What, then, are we to say about the base case: sequence-relative truth for atomic wffs? A *closed* atomic wff is true (*tout court*) just in case its predicate *applies* to what its name *denotes* (as 'is wise' applies to what 'Socrates' denotes, given that Socrates is wise); and we want it to be true relative to any sequence whatever in just those circumstances ((i) above). An *open* atomic wff is satisfied by a sequence just in case a corresponding closed wff, with the variable replaced by a name of the relevant member of the sequence, would be true (see above). Neatness recommends introducing the notion of sequence-relative denotation; then truth relative to a sequence, for atomic wffs open or closed, can be explained as a function of the predicate's application-conditions and the open or closed singular term's denotation relative to that sequence:

(d) $p_k t$ is true$_s$ iff there is something y which t denotes$_s$ and p_k applies to y.

(iii) Now we need an account of denotation relative to a sequence for singular terms. With closed singular terms, the relativity to a sequence is idle; thus, for names:

(a) c_k denotes$_s$ what c_k denotes.

What a variable denotes, relative to a sequence, has already been fixed:

(b) x_k denotes$_s$ the kth member of s.

And obviously, with function symbols:

(c) $f_k t$ denotes$_s$ y iff there is something z which t denotes$_s$ and f_k is *fulfilled* by $\langle y, z \rangle$.

(as 'the capital of' is fulfilled by $\langle$London, Great Britain$\rangle$ in virtue of the fact that London is the capital of Great Britain).

That completes the truth characterization, T1, which, according to Field, Tarski should have given for L.

Truth is defined in terms of the auxiliary semantic notion of truth relative to a sequence, or satisfaction. In the truth characterization as it stands, the extension of the satisfaction relation is fixed only recursively; so we cannot simply write down, from the characterization, a formula coextensive with the truth-predicate from which the terminology of sequence-relative truth is absent. With sufficient set theory, we could convert the recursive characterization of the auxiliary notion into a 'normal' or eliminative definition ('CTFL', p. 193, n. 1). That would enable us to eliminate the terminology of sequence-relative truth from the definition of truth; but the resulting formula would still contain the

113

subsidiary semantic terminology of sequence-relative denotation. The recursive characterization of sequence-relative denotation could similarly be converted into an eliminative definition, yielding an eliminative definition of truth free from the sequence-relative semantic terminology. But the result would still contain, in a way which T1 yields no suggestions for eliminating, the evidently semantic terminology 'applies to', 'denotes', and 'is fulfilled by'.

T2, a truth characterization which Tarski might actually have given for L, differs in just that respect. The difference is achieved by the following modifications:

(i) Instead of the general clause ((ii)(d) above) about sequence-relative truth of atomic wffs, each predicate has sequence-relative truth-conditions, for atomic wffs which contain it, spelled out individually. Thus, say:

> (a) $p_1 t$ is true$_s$ iff there is something y which t denotes$_s$ and y is a country;
>
> (b) $p_2 t$ is true$_s$ iff there is something y which t denotes$_s$ and y is a city;

and so on, one clause for each predicate; or they could all be collected in a disjunction.

(ii) Similarly, instead of the general clause about sequence-relative denotation of names ((iii)(a) above), the denotation of each name, relative to any sequence whatever, is specified individually. Thus, say:

> (a) c_1 denotes$_s$ Germany;
>
> (b) c_2 denotes$_s$ France;

and so on, one clause for each name, or a disjunction as before.

(iii) Correspondingly for function symbols; instead of the general clause ((iii)(c) above), T2 has, say:

> (a) $f_1 t$ denotes$_s$ y iff there is something z which t denotes$_s$ and y is the capital of z;
>
> (b) $f_2 t$ denotes$_s$ y iff there is something z which t denotes$_s$ and y is the president of z;

and so on, one clause for each function symbol, or a disjunction as before.

In T2, explicit employments of the semantic notions of application, denotation, and fulfilment disappear in favour of piecemeal specifications of (what are in fact) application-conditions, denotations, and fulfilment-conditions. The specifications are effected by using, for each simple object-language expression, a coextensive expression of the metalanguage. These metalanguage expressions are free from semantic terminology; obviously the trick would not be turned if they were expressions on the pattern of 'is applied to by p_1', 'what c_1 denotes', or 'the first member of an ordered pair which fulfils f_1 and whose second member is'. If we had a complete T2 for L, with a clause for every simple expression, and converted the recursive characterizations as before, the result would be a formula coextensive with the truth-predicate and, this time, entirely free from semantic terminology.

Notice that the masterstroke of approaching truth indirectly, using the notion of satisfaction to circumvent the problem posed by non-sentential sentence-components, is common to both T1 and T2. That is why Field's favouring of the only partially Tarskian T1 over the Tarskian T2 is compatible with a proper respect for Tarski's technical achievement.

III

There are three incidental points on which Field claims superiority for T1-style truth characterizations over those in the style of T2.

(i) L may fail to conform to Tarski's condition that 'the sense of every expression is unambiguously determined by its form' ('CTFL', p. 166). For instance, a name may have more than one bearer. If the expressions mentioned are taken to be tokens, T1 is unaffected; whereas Field claims that 'there is no remotely palatable way of extending' T2-style truth characterizations to cope with such languages (p. 87).

(ii) If L is enriched, then provided only that the additions belong to semantic categories already represented, T1 needs no alteration; whereas T2 needs new clauses (p. 88).

(iii) T2-style truth characterizations can be given only in metalanguages with vocabularies which match, extension for extension, those of the object languages; whereas T1-style truth characterizations are subject to no such restriction (pp. 89–90).

How solid these points are, as advantages for T1, is open to question. Point (i) is vulnerable to the production of palatable treatments, in the style of T2, for, say, languages with promiscuous names.[3] That point (ii) tells in favour of T1 is a thesis which is not really independent of Field's central contention, to be discussed shortly (see the end of section IV and the end of section VI). And from a certain perspective, to be sketched below, point (iii) simply disappears (see the end of section V). Field's main interest, however, is different, and I shall not devote further attention, except in passing, to the three points listed above.

IV

Field's main concern is with the difference emphasized in my exposition of T1 and T2, namely that T2 does, whereas T1 does not, permit construction of a formula coextensive with the truth-predicate and containing no semantic vocabulary.

The difference means that T1, Field's favoured candidate, is in violation of one of Tarski's ground rules. Tarski announced: 'I shall not make use of any semantical concept if I am not able previously to reduce it to other concepts' ('CTFL', pp. 152-3).

Field argues plausibly (pp. 91, 101) that the motivation for that ground rule was the aspiration (expressed at 'ESS', p. 406, mentioned in section I above) of making the notion of truth respectable from the standpoint of physicalism. Field's version of physicalism (probably close to Tarski's, in view of Tarski's talk, in the 'ESS' passage, of the unity of science) is this: 'the doctrine that chemical facts, biological facts, psychological facts, and semantical facts, are all explicable (in principle) in terms of physical facts' (p. 91). If a physicalist found the notion of truth, and hence putative facts in whose formulation it figures, in some way suspect, he would hardly be content with other semantic notions: in particular those of denotation, fulfilment and application, which Field collectively labels 'primitive denotation' (p. 86). So T1 leaves the job of rehabilitating truth (for L) at best incompletely executed; whereas if one obeyed the ground rule which T1 violates, one might hope to perform the task all at once. In Field's view, however, T2, for all its obedience to the ground rule, does not fulfil the hope.

Obviously a lot depends on what it takes to make the notion of truth acceptable to a physicalist. Consider, for instance, a claim of Tarski's as to what is shown by the possibility of constructing T2-style theories for formalized languages of finite order: he says ('CTFL', p. 265) he has demonstrated that for each such language

> a formally correct and materially adequate definition of true sentence can be constructed in the metalanguage, making use only of expressions of a general logical character, expressions of the language itself [he is speaking of the case in which metalanguage includes object language] as well as terms belonging to the morphology of language, i.e. names of linguistic expressions and of the structural relations existing between them.

If a T2-style theory for L, in a metalanguage which included L (so that the theory could use, in those of its clauses which effect T2's distinctive trick, the very expressions which the clauses deal with), had its recursive characterizations converted as before, and if we agreed for present purposes to count expressions of set theory as 'expressions of a general logical character', the result would exactly conform to Tarski's description. Now suppose a physicalist is satisfied with the physical credentials of logic, set theory, and the morphology of language, and those of the non-logical vocabulary of L (which could not leave him unsatisfied, if we moved to the case in which metalanguage does not include object language, with the physical credentials of translations of that vocabulary in the metalanguage). Why could he not allay any doubts about 'true' by reflecting on the availability of the long-winded substitute which Tarski showed he could construct?

Different languages would need different substitutes, even if the languages differed only in that, say, one contained a predicate which the other did not contain (cf. section III, (ii)). But why should that matter? What Tarski promises is a set of physicalistically acceptable formulae containing a formula coextensive with 'true' in its application to the sentences of each language of the relevant sort. To insist that what is needed, if a semantic predicate is to be respectable, is a physicalistically acceptable formula coextensive with it in all its applications, even across the boundaries between languages, could be justified on the basis of a physicalism that requires a single physical equivalent for every decent predicate; but that is something Field explicitly rejects (p. 108, n. 13).

Field's reason for being unimpressed by a defence of T2 on the above lines comes out very clearly in his use of an analogy from chemistry (p. 95 ff.).

We might have a theory which enabled us to determine the valences of chemical compounds on the basis of the valences of the elements out of which they are compounded. We could write it in this form:

$$(c)(n)(c \text{ has valence } n \text{ iff } B(c, n));$$

where we fix the extension of the valence relation, as it holds between compounds and numbers, in terms of a formula '$B(c, n)$' which would contain the term 'valence' as applied to elements. Then we could go on to specify the valence of each element, on these lines:

$(e)(n)(e$ has valence n iff e is potassium and n is $+ 1$, or . . . or e is sulphur and n is -2).

Substituting the right-hand side of this for occurrences of the predicate 'ξ has valence ζ' in the formula '$B(c, n)$' would yield an open sentence, coextensive with the valence relation as it holds between compounds and numbers, in which 'valence' did not appear. But such a construction would compare unfavourably with what we would have if we eliminated 'valence' from '$B(c, n)$' by means of a *reduction* of the valence relation, as it holds between elements and numbers, to structural (physical) properties of atoms. The 'valence'-free open sentence constructed in the first way would be revealed by the comparison as a pseudo-reduction of the concept of the valence of a compound.

What Field suggests is that T2's way of eliminating 'denotes', 'is fulfilled by', and 'applies to' from the definition of truth parallels that pseudo-reduction. Parallel to what the pseudo-reduction is unfavourably compared with would be a theory like T1, but supplemented with genuine explications of the primitive-denotation relations in physical terms: something which does not merely, like T2, specify the extensions of those relations as far as L is concerned, but describes physical relations between expressions and things on which the semantic relations depend, and from whose description, together with suitable physical facts, the extensions of the semantic relations could be determined.[4]

The idea is, then, that T2 is merely T1 plus bogus reductions of the concepts of primitive denotation. By not purporting complete reduction, T1 advertises the fact that we do not yet have genuine explications of those concepts; T2 simply papers over that gap. Tarski's genuine achievement, reflected in T1, involves seeing how to specify the semantic properties of complex expressions in terms of those of simple expressions. T2 gives the appearance of going further, and eliminating the semantic properties of simple expressions. But the appearance is deceptive: we are told nothing interesting — in fact, nothing at all — by T2 about what it is for a simple expression to have one of the appropriate semantic properties, any more than we are told, by a list of the valences of elements, what it is for an element to have a particular valence.

Chemical concepts applied to compounds are reasonably conceived as relating indirectly to the physical facts on which their applicability depends, by way of the application of chemical concepts to elements; it is at the level of elements and their properties that we expect chemistry to be revealed as, so to speak, adhering to the physical facts. Field's picture of semantics is parallel: the semantic properties of complex expressions, in particular truth, relate to the physical facts about those expressions by way of the semantic properties of simple expressions, and it is at that level — the level of the *axioms* of a truth-characterization — that we must seek to reveal the adherence of semantics to the physical facts.

Given the chemical parallel, the vacuity of what is peculiar to T2, as against T1, seems undeniable. From that perspective, moreover, the differences between T2-style theories for different languages, even with the same semantic structure (see section III, (ii)), look like a symptom of how bogus the explication effected is. Differences between languages, in the extensions of the primitive denotation relations, should be capable of being displayed as consequences of different instantiations of those general physical relations between expressions and things on which primitive denotation depends; not represented as brute differences, as at first glance they seem to be in T2-style theories, where the concepts of primitive denotation disappear in favour of, precisely, specifications of their extensions. (But see the end of section VI below.)

A contrasting view about the point of contact between semantical facts and the underlying physical facts is possible. In order to sketch it, I shall begin (in section V) by rescuing Tarski's 'Convention T' (*Kriterium W*) from the contumelious treatment to which Field subjects it.

V

According to Field, Tarski's 'formal criterion of adequacy for theories of truth' was 'roughly' this (p. 95):

(M) Any condition of the form
$$(2)\ (e)(e \text{ is true iff } B(e))$$
should be accepted as an adequate definition of truth if and only if it is correct and '$B(e)$' is a well-formed formula containing no semantic terms.

Field remarks in a footnote (pp. 108-9, n. 14) that 'Tarski actually gives a different formulation, the famous Convention T, evidently because he does not think that the word "correct" ought to be employed in stating a condition of adequacy.'

Is there not something in that thought? In fact it is a travesty to represent Convention T as merely 'a different formulation' of Convention M; for Convention M's 'if and only if it is correct' begs the very question which Convention T is meant to settle. Convention T, as is well known, requires a truth characterization to entail, for each object-language sentence, an instance of the schema 's is true iff p', where 's' is replaced by a designation of the object-language sentence and 'p' by that very sentence, if the object language is included in the metalanguage; otherwise by a translation thereof ('CTFL', pp. 187-8). Conformity with the requirement is a sufficient condition for the predicate characterized by a theory to have in its extension all and only the true sentences of the object language; that is, precisely, for the truth characterization to be, in Field's term, correct.

Tarski has *two* prerequisites for acceptability in a truth characterization: formal correctness and material adequacy (see, e.g., 'CTFL', p. 265, quoted in section IV above). Convention T is his condition of *material adequacy* (Field's 'correctness'). Convention M does not address the question of material adequacy, but, with its insistence on an eliminative definition free of semantic terms, expresses a view of Tarski's about *formal correctness*. The second is detachable from the first: a truth characterization could conform to Convention T while being, because of sparseness of set theory, incurably recursive in its account of satisfaction, and hence failing to conform to Convention M.

If we want a recipe for constructing truth theories for languages in general (at least those amenable to Tarski's methods), we cannot evade the question when a truth theory is correct (materially adequate). Nothing Field says supersedes Convention T (or some version of it: see section VI below) as a general test of correctness. But T1 as it stands yields no nonsemantical truth-conditions for sentences, and so cannot be subjected to any such test. T1 yields assignments of truth-conditions like this (a simple case for illustration):

$p_1 c_1$ is true iff there is something y which c_1 denotes and p_1 applies to y.

One might suppose that that could not be false, so that Convention T is trivially met. But in a real case, we could not be confident of so much as the categorization of the expressions as a predicate and a name, in advance of checking assignments of truth-conditions which result from specific interpretations of them as such — that is, the sort of thing a T2-style truth characterization would give.

Something in the spirit of Field's contrast can still be drawn, even between theories amenable for subjecting to Convention T. The modified contrast would be between:

(a) T2-style theories, which tell us nothing about the concepts of primitive denotation over and above fixing their extensions for the language dealt with; and

(b) a modified version of T1-style theories: theories which, unlike T1 as it stands, do fix the extensions of the primitive-denotation relations (so that they entail specific assignments of truth-conditions, which can be tested against Convention T); but which, unlike T2-style theories, represent the information as derived from the application, to physical facts about particular expressions, of those explications of the primitive-denotation concepts with which Field seeks to supplement T1.

Note, incidentally, that any truth characterization, of either of the two sorts distinguished in the modified contrast, will have to employ, in its specifications of primitive denotation, metalanguage expressions which aim at coextensiveness with the object-language expressions dealt with. (Conformity to Convention T would indicate success in the aim.) If the metalanguage does not, in advance of construction of the truth characterization, contain expressions with suitable extensions, it must be enriched so as to do so (perhaps — the easiest way — by borrowing from the object language). So once we take seriously the assessment of truth characterizations for correctness, there seems no substance to the idea that it is a merit of T1-style theories not to require object-language vocabulary to be suitably matched in the metalanguage (cf. section III, (iii)).[5]

Once we appreciate the need for a test of material adequacy, we can see the possibility of inverting Field's conception of the point of contact between semantic theories and the physical facts.

Consider what would be involved in the interpretation, from scratch, of a foreign language. To simplify, suppose the language is used only to make assertions and that there is no indexicality.[6] Our interpretative needs would be met by a theory which entailed, for any sentence which might be uttered in the foreign language, a theorem of the (highly schematic) form 's ... p'; where 's' is replaced by a suitable designation of the object-language sentence, and 'p' by a sentence of ours such that, if a foreign speaker utters the object-language sentence, we can acceptably report what he says by using that sentence of ours. If we had a theory which met the requirement, replacements for 'p' in its theorems would translate the sentences designated by the corresponding replacements for 's'. So if our requirement-meeting theory worked by characterizing a predicate, 'ϕ', so that the gap between replacements for 's' and replacements for 'p' was filled by 'is ϕ iff', then, by virtue of the theory's conforming to Convention T, the extension of 'ϕ' would be the extension of 'true'. A sufficient condition of correctness, then, in a truth characterization for the language in question, would be the possibility of putting it to interpretative use in the way described above; that is, treating it as if its theorems were of the form 's can be used to say that p'.[7]

We can picture ourselves equipped with all the physically formulable facts about language use in the community, and aiming to construct, via interpretation as above, a truth characterization for their language. Two interlocking requirements would govern the fit between the truth characterization and the physical facts.

(i) The first requirement is one of *system*. We want to see the content we attribute to foreign sayings as determined by the contributions of distinguishable parts or aspects of foreign utterances, each of which may occur, making the same contribution, in a multiplicity of utterances. This is secured by having the theorems deducible, as in T2-style truth characterizations, from axioms which deal with simple expressions and figure as premises in the deduction of the appropriate theorems for any sentences in which their expressions occur. For the theorems to be so deducible, utterances must be identifiable in terms of structures and constituents assigned to them by a systematic syntax; and it must be possible to match up those structures (if necessary obliquely, through transformations) with configurations observable in physical utterance-events.

(ii) The second requirement is one of *psychological adequacy*. Used as an interpretative theory, the truth characterization is to serve up, in the systematic way sketched under (i), specifications of the content of assertions which we can take speakers to be making. Not just any piece of physically described behaviour can be reasonably redescribed as a saying with a specific content. Whether such redescriptions are acceptable turns on whether the behaviour, as redescribed, is intelligible. That requires the possibility of locating it suitably against a background of propositional attitudes — centrally beliefs and desires — in terms of which the behaviour seems to make sense. Ascription of propositional attitudes, in turn, is constrained in complex ways by the physical facts about behaviour, the environment, and their interconnections; also (circling back) by the possibilities of interpreting linguistic behaviour in conformity with requirement (i). Interpretation can be pictured as the superimposition, on all that is available in physical terms about language use, of the content-specifying mode of discourse: ascriptions of sayings, beliefs, and desires. Partly because requirement (i) demands ramified interdependencies between interpretations of different utterances, and partly for general reasons stemming from the character of intentional discourse, the superimposition has to be in principle holistic (which is not, of course, to deny that in practical theory-construction one would need to proceed by way of piecemeal hypotheses).

The hard physical facts, then, which constrain the construction of a truth characterization for a language actually spoken, are (i) the structural properties of physical utterance-events which permit the language to be given a syntactic description; and (ii) the complex relations between behaviour and the environment which permit (some of) the behaviour to be described and understood in intentional terms.

Now it is at the level of its *theorems* that a truth characterization, on this account, makes contact with those hard physical facts. If the theorems are to be systematically deducible so that requirement (i) is met in the way described above, then replacements for '*s*' must characterize utterances in terms of structures and constituents; so that the relation of match or transformational accessibility, which, according to requirement (i), must hold between the structures assigned to sentences by the syntax with which the theory operates, on the one hand, and configurations observable in physical utterance-events, on the other, is revealed or not at the theorem level. Moreover, interpretations of parts of utterances can be subjected to requirement (ii) only through interpretations of whole utterances; an assignment of denotation, for instance, is tested by whether assignments of truth-conditions derivable from it facilitate ascriptions of sayings which are for the most part intelligible; and of course it is the theorems which record interpretations of whole utterances. So requirement (i) makes itself felt, not only directly, in connection with the match between theoretical syntax and actual utterance-events, but in another way too: we can conceive the deductive shape which the theory assumes, in order to meet requirement

(i), as setting up a complex of channels by which the impact of requirement (ii), bearing in the first instance on interpretations of whole utterances, is transmitted backwards, through the derivations of theorems
licensed by the theory, to the premisses of those derivations, in which
the theory says what it does about sentence-components and modes of
sentence-construction.

Describing, on the lines of requirements (i) and (ii), the nature of the
fit between an acceptable truth characterization's theorems and the
physical facts can be regarded as spelling out what Convention T comes
to, in a case in which what translates what cannot be taken (as it could
in the cases Tarski considered) to be simply given or up for stipulation.

According to this picture, a truth characterization fits the underlying
physical facts from the theorems upward; not, as in Field's conception,
from the axioms downward. The deductive apparatus used in deriving
the theorems needs no anchoring in the physical facts, independently of
the overall acceptability of the derived assignments of truth-conditions.[8]
The relations between language and extra-linguistic reality which a
truth characterization describes hold in the first instance between simple
expressions and things, and only mediately, via the laws of semantic
combination set out in the truth characterization, between complex expressions and the world.[9] But from its being at the level of primitive
denotation that relations between words and the world are set up *within*
a semantic theory, it does not follow — nor, according to the inverted
picture, is it true — that it is at that level that the primary connection
should be sought between the semantic theory *itself* and the physical
facts on which its acceptability depends.

A T2-style truth characterization specifies what are in fact denotations, fulfilment-conditions, and application-conditions. (It does not
matter that the primitive-denotation concepts are not explicitly expressed in the T2-style theory sketched above: see below.) Now the
axioms dealing with names, function symbols, and predicates play roles
which are distinctively parallel within each of the three classes, and dis-
similar between them, in the derivations of assignments of truth-
conditions which the truth characterization licenses. According to the
view which inverts Field's picture, there is nothing to the specific
primitive-denotation concepts over and above those distinctive deductive
powers. To give an account of one of the modes of primitive denotation, what we should do is (a) spell out, on the lines of requirements (i)
and (ii), what it is for a truth characterization's assignments of truth-
conditions to be acceptable; and (b) describe the relevant distinctive
deductive capacity, so that the empirical content which (a) confers on
the notion of truth can be channelled backwards through the licensed
derivations into the relevant sort of premiss. (Clearly the various modes
of primitive denotation will not, on this view, be separately explicable;
that is as it should be.)

If it is at the level of its theorems that a truth characterization makes contact, obeying a version of Convention T glossed by requirements (i) and (ii), with the physical facts, then it does not matter a scrap whether the truth characterization yields an eliminative truth-definition free of semantic vocabulary. What matters is the possibility of eliminating semantic terms from the right-hand sides of the theorems (unless the object language contains semantic vocabulary, so that semantic terms can properly occur in reports of what is, on occasion, said by its speakers). That elimination is possible even if we leave the characterization of satisfaction, in a T2-style theory, in its recursive form, so that the concept of satisfaction is still present in any equivalent which the theory yields for the truth-predicate. From this viewpoint, then, there is nothing to favour a direct truth-definition over an axiomatic truth characterization, so long as the latter yields acceptable theorems.

Similarly, the absence from a T2-style theory of explicit expression of the primitive-denotation concepts is not in itself a virtue. We could construct a trivial variant of the T2-style truth characterization partly sketched above, which would explicitly assign denotations, fulfilment-conditions and application-conditions, labelled as such, so that the theory would lack that putative virtue; that would not matter, since the semantic terminology could still be made to disappear in deriving the final assignments of truth-conditions.

Eliminative 'definitions' of the primitive-denotation concepts through specifications of their extensions, such as T2 yields, are not to be conceived as purporting to say what it is for one of those relations to hold; that task is discharged, rather, by the combination of (a) and (b) above. This should alleviate concern over how T2-style truth characterizations would vary from language to language (section III, (ii)). What is said under (a) would be, details aside, common to anything recognizable as a language; and if there is any point in carrying over a specific batch of primitive-denotation concepts from one language to another, that would show up in similarities in what would be sayable about the deductive powers of the relevant sets of axioms, under (b). So the inter-language variations between T2-style theories would leave invariant that about them which contributes to the task of saying what it is for the relations to hold. If someone supposed that we were freed from obligations to look for further explications of the primitive-denotation concepts solely by virtue of the fact that the concepts were not explicitly expressed in eliminative definitions constructed from T2-style theories, then it would be reasonable to be perturbed by variation in the materials of those eliminative definitions (cf. the end of section IV). But the absence of explicit employment of the concepts is not rightly taken in that way. (Notice that it is not in a T2-style theory itself that, on this view, we find accounts of what it is for the primitive-denotation relations to hold; (a) and (b) would be metatheoretical remarks about T2-style theories.)

Tarski's own insistence on eliminative truth-definitions free of semantic terms, justified as it is by a mention of physicalism ('ESS', p. 406),
suggests that he himself conceived the virtues of T2-style theories, from
a physicalist standpoint, in a way justly parodied by Field's chemical
example. But we can accept Tarski's favoured style of truth characterization without needing to agree with everything he thought about its
merits.

VII

Not only is there no need to look for physical underpinnings for the
deductive apparatus of truth-theories, over and above their output.
There is no reason to expect that the search would turn up anything
interesting.

On the view sketched above, superimposition of a semantic theory
on the physical facts about a language-using community is a subtask in
the superimposition of a way of describing and understanding their behaviour in content-specifying terms. For all its extensionality, the truth
characterization has its relation to the realm of the physical governed
by the conditions which govern the relation of intentional to physical
discourse. Now the nature of those conditions makes it quite implausible that the relation of semantics to physics should be anything like
the relation of chemistry to physics.

When we shift from chemical to physical explanation, we shift to a
style of explanation which, though at a deeper level, is still of the same
general kind: a kind in which events are displayed as unsurprising
because of the way the world works.[10] If we are physicalists, we hold
that physics can in principle give a complete account of all events, so
far as that mode of explanation is concerned. So if there is any substance
in chemical explanations of compounding behaviour, then, since those
explanations purport to reveal events as unsurprising *qua* instances of
the world's workings, the laws which, in those explanations, state how
the world is said to work should, law by law, have physical credentials.
And that is how it turns out: the chemical laws which (roughly) determine the compounding behaviour of composite substances on the basis
of that of elements are, by way of the (approximate) reduction of element valences to physical properties of atoms, (approximately) mirrored
in physical laws which govern compounding transactions described in
terms of atomic and molecular structure.

But the difference between physical explanation and that mode of
explanation which is largely constitutive of the network of intentional
concepts is not a difference within a broadly homogeneous kind.

John McDowell

Intentional explanation makes an action unsurprising, not as an instance of the way the world works (though of course it does not follow that an action is *not* that), but as something which the agent can be understood to have seen some point in going in for.[11] An intentional explanation of an event does not, like a chemical explanation, offer, so to speak, to fill the same explanatory space as a physical explanation would. So we can go on claiming, as physicalists, that physics can completely fill that explanatory space, without requiring that, on pain of seeing intentional explanations as substanceless, we must be able to ground the details of those explanations, detail by detail, in physical counterparts.

Explanations of the semantic properties of complex expressions in terms of the semantic properties of simple expressions, appealing as they do to semantic laws whose formulation is part of the move from the physical to the intentional, should be of a piece with intentional explanations, in respect of their relation to the physical; because of the different explanatory pretensions of the intentional, there is no threat to the completeness of physics, as far as the appropriate kind of explanation is concerned, if those semantic laws and their special conceptual content cannot be physically mirrored in the way exemplified in the chemical case. Physicalism, construed as the doctrine that physics is in principle competent to yield an explanation of that kind for all that happens, affords no reason for insisting that such mirroring be available if semantics is to be other than empty; that is (given the assumption that semantics is not empty) for expecting that such mirroring will be found.

If intentional concepts are largely constituted by their role in a special kind of explanation, which does not compete with the kind which physics yields but offers a different species of comprehension, then we need not expect to be able, even approximately, to reduce those concepts to physical terms. The distinctive point of the intentional concepts makes it intelligible that there should be a kind of incommensurability between them and physical concepts.[12] And if the intentional concepts are not reducible to physical terms, then it is, if anything, still less to be expected that reductions should be available for the concepts of primitive denotation, whose conceptual identity, according to the position sketched in section VI, consists solely in their impact on a semantic property of complex expressions – truth-conditions – the concept of which we can explain only in terms of requirements for the applicability of intentional notions.

Field seeks to motivate the contrary thought that we must look for physicalist explanations of the concepts of primitive denotation by arguing (p. 105) that 'without such accounts our conceptual scheme [as physicalists] breaks down from the inside. On our theory of the world it would be extremely surprising if there were some non-physical connection between words and things'. This remark needs careful consideration.

It is not claimed, on behalf of the position Field opposes, that there are no physical connections between words and things (which would certainly be surprising). Assignments of truth-conditions are partly controlled by, for instance, the possibilities of belief-ascription, and belief-ascription is governed in part by principles about how the content of beliefs is sensitive to the causal impact of their subject matter. That, and similar features in a fuller account of acceptability in assignments of truth-conditions, require the presence of causal, no doubt ultimately physical, connections between the world and words at the level of whole utterances, construed as (in our example) voicings of belief. Such causal connections presumably reflect, in ways corresponding to the derivability of assignments of truth-conditions from specifications of primitive denotation, causal connections between occurrences of simple expressions and physically describable circumstances. The position Field opposes is quite compatible with the thesis that whenever a name, say, occurs in an utterance-event, the event is suitably related, in physically describable ways, with events or circumstances involving the name's denotation.

What need not be true is a corresponding thesis with a quantifier shift: that there is some one physically describable relation which obtains between any occurrence of any name and its denotation. This denial is not just the reflection of a needlessly strict view of when we have a single relation. According to the thesis allowed at the end of the last paragraph, any instance of the denotation relation will have what we might call a physical realization. The physical realizations will differ from instance to instance, but that is not the issue; it is not necessarily Pickwickian to classify as a physical relation one which holds just in case some one of a set of physical relations holds. The question is about the principle on which the members of the set are collected. If the point of the grouping cannot be given in purely physical terms, but consists simply in the fact that those physical relations are the ones which obtain when the denotation relation, explicated on the lines suggested in section VI, obtains, then there is no justification for claiming that a reduction has been effected.[13]

It seems right to conclude that denotation, on this view, is a non-physical relation; and similar considerations apply to the other primitive-denotation concepts. Now just how surprising is it that there should be such relations between words and things?

Semantic relations, on this view, are indeed not like chemical relations; if explicability in terms of physical facts, which is what Field's physicalism demands of all facts worthy of the name, requires the sort of grounding, in physical facts, of the facts into which genuine relations enter that is exemplified in the chemical case, then the idea that semantic relations might be as here suggested is either offensive to physicalism or a condemnation of semantics. But perhaps we should look sceptically at Field's formulation of physicalism. Certainly his assimilation of the thesis of semantical irreducibility to such anti-materialistic theses as Cartesianism is unfair.

A doctrine with some claim to be called 'physicalism' is this: (i) all events are physical events, that is, have physical descriptions; (ii) under their physical descriptions, all events are susceptible of total explanations, of the kind paradigmatically afforded by physics, in terms of physical laws and other physically described events. Field's version of physicalism excludes any thesis according to which there are facts irreducible to physical facts − 'semanticalism' and Cartesianism alike. But the version just given discriminates; it allows some irreducibility theses but rejects others. Cartesianism, as standardly understood, is still excluded; for according to it, mental events have no physical descriptions, in violation of (i), and some physically describable events (for instance limb movements) have such events in their causal ancestry, in violation of (ii). However, 'semanticalism' − the irreducibility thesis outlined above − is compatible with physicalism in the revised formulation. The events which comprise linguistic behaviour have physical descriptions, as required by (i). There is no reason to deny that under those descriptions they are explicable as instances of the way the world works, and if physics delivers on its claim to saturate the relevant explanatory space, it must be possible to put the explanations which reveal them as such, ultimately, into physical shape, as required by (ii). The irreducibility thesis turns on the idea that formulation of a truth characterization subserves the compiling of a way of talking whose point lies in a kind of understanding, of those and other events, quite different from that which physics might afford; so, as emphasized above, it poses no threat to the ambitions of physics to be complete in its own sphere. Cartesianism holds, by contrast, that there are questions of the sort physics purports to be able to handle, to which the answers are stubbornly nonphysical.[14]

In a common usage of 'science', the scope of science is taken to cover just such questions; if physicalism is good scientific methodology − which certainly seems plausible on that understanding of what science is − then doctrines like Cartesianism are unscientific. But it is a different matter to refuse to accept that all questions fall within the province of science so understood. We can agree that semantics, on the view here taken, is not in that sense scientific (though there is plenty to justify its claim to be scientific in some more relaxed sense) without thereby agreeing that it is *un*scientific. A discipline can be both rigorous and illuminating without being related to physics in the way Field wants semantics to be; the strong physicalism which denies that seems to me to be, as Field says (p. 108, n. 13) about a version he himself rejects, hard to take seriously.

Notes

1 I treat 'c_1', etc., as names (in the metalanguage) of L's names, etc., which might be 'Deutschland', etc.; this involves notational divergence from Field. '∀' is the name of L's quantifier, rather than a quantifier of the metalanguage; later in the paper I rewrite some of Field's formula with the bracket notation for universal quantification.

2 Concatenations of metalanguage names of object-language expressions denote corresponding concatenations of the named expressions. In such structural descriptions names may give way to variables. Open sentences are to be read as universally quantified (thus the present formula should be understood with quantifiers binding 'A' and 's'). Brackets round designations of conjunctions (as in (b) below) are a scope-marking convention.

3 I believe we can get such a thing out of an account of names on the lines of Tyler Burge, 'Reference and Proper Names', *Journal of Philosophy*, vol. 70 (1973), p. 425.

4 Field ('Tarski's Theory of Truth', p. 99) cites Saul Kripke's work as a beginning on the task of giving the required explications. I prefer to take seriously Kripke's denial that he intended to produce a theory of denotation for names (see pp. 280, 300–3, of 'Naming and Necessity', in Donald Davidson and Gilbert Harman, eds, *Semantics of Natural Language*, Dordrecht, Reidel, 1972). Construed as correcting an alternative picture, rather than giving a substantive account of denotation, Kripke's work is quite compatible with the view of semantics, divergent from Field's, to be sketched in sections VI and VII below.

5 If truth characterizations have to be got into a form in which they can be subjected to the test of Convention T (or some version of it), then it must be possible to circumvent problems posed by indexicality (cf. section III, (i)). But I shall ignore the complications of doing so.

6 Not making these suppositions would complicate the exposition, but (I believe) introduce no new issues of principle.

7 Cf. D. Davidson, 'Truth and Meaning', *Synthèse*, vol. 17 (1967), p. 304; and the first section of my 'Truth Conditions, Bivalence, and Verificationism', in Gareth Evans and John McDowell, eds, *Truth and Meaning* (Oxford, Clarendon Press, 1976).

8 Cf. D. Davidson, 'In Defense of Convention T', in H. Leblanc, ed., *Truth, Syntax, and Modality* (Amsterdam, North-Holland, 1973), at p. 84.

9 This is a very important fact about Tarskian truth characterizations. We are potentially liberated from much bad philosophy about truth by seeing that sentences need no special extra-linguistic items of their own (states of affairs, facts, or whatever) to be related to. (Talk of facts in this paper is, I hope, only a *façon de parler*.) See D. Davidson, 'True to the Facts', *Journal*

of Philosophy, vol. 66 (1969), p. 748.

10   This is not meant to be more than a crude intuitive gesture in the direction of an account of the kind of explanation in question.

11   Again, this is intended only as a gesture.

12   For the claim of irreducibility, see W. V. Quine, *Word and Object* (Cambridge, Mass., MIT Press, 1960), section 45 (note the references to other authors). On the ground of the irreducibility, see D. Davidson, 'Mental Events', in Lawrence Foster and J. W. Swanson, eds, *Experience and Theory* (Amherst, University of Massachusetts, 1970).

13   This is relevant to Michael Friedman's remarks about weak reduction, in 'Physicalism and the Indeterminacy of Translation', *Noûs*, vol. 9 (1975), p. 353.

14   Similarly vitalism, which Field also cites ('Tarski's Theory of Truth', p. 92).

7 Reality without reference*

Donald Davidson

It is difficult to see how a theory of meaning can hope to succeed that does not elucidate, and give a central role to, the concept of reference. On the other hand, there are weighty reasons for supposing that reference cannot be explained or analyzed in terms more primitive or behavioral. Let me describe the dilemma more fully, and then say how I think a theory of truth in Tarski's style can help resolve it.

'Theory of meaning' is not a technical term, but a gesture in the direction of a family of problems (a problem family). Central among the problems is the task of explaining language and communication by appeal to simpler, or at any rate different, concepts. It is natural to believe this is possible because linguistic phenomena are patently supervenient on nonlinguistic phenomena. I propose to call a theory a theory of meaning for a natural language L if it is such that (a) knowledge of the theory suffices for understanding the utterances of speakers of L and (b) the theory can be given empirical application by appeal to evidence described without using linguistic concepts, or at least without using linguistic concepts specific to the sentences and words of L. The first condition indicates the nature of the question; the second requires that it not be begged.

By a theory of truth, I mean a theory that satisfies something like Tarski's Convention T: it is a theory that by recursively characterizing a truth-predicate (say 'is true in L') entails, for each sentence s of L, a metalinguistic sentence got from the form 's is true in L if and only if p' when 's' is replaced by a canonical description of a sentence of L and 'p' by a sentence of the metalanguage that gives the truth-conditions of the described sentence. The theory must be relativized to a time and a speaker (at least) to handle indexical expressions. Nevertheless I shall call such theories *absolute* to distinguish them from theories that (also) relativize truth to an interpretation, a model, a possible world, or a domain. In a theory of the sort I am describing, the truth-predicate is not defined, but must be considered a primitive expression.

We may take reference to be a relation between proper names and what they name, complex singular terms and what they denote, predicates

*Reprinted by permission of the author, and of the editor, of *Dialectica*, vol. 31 (1977), pp. 247–58.

Donald Davidson

and the entities of which they are true. Demonstratives will not enter the discussion, but their references would, of course, have to be relativized to a speaker and a time (at least).

Now back to the dilemma. Here is why it seems that we can't do without the concept of reference. Whatever else it embraces, a theory of meaning must include an account of truth — a statement of the conditions under which an arbitrary sentence of the language is true. For well-known reasons, such a theory can't begin by explaining truth for a finite number of simple sentences and then assign truth to the rest on the basis of the simples. It is necessary, and in any case would be wanted in a revealing story, to analyze sentences into constituent elements — predicates, names, connectives, quantifiers, functors — and to show how the truth-value of each sentence derives from features of the elements and the composition of the elements in the sentence. Truth then clearly depends on the semantic features of the elements; and where the elements are names or predicates, what features can be relevant but the reference? Explaining the truth-conditions of a sentence like 'Socrates flies' must amount to saying it is true if and only if the object referred to by 'Socrates' is one of the objects referred to by the predicate 'flies'.

A theory of truth of the kind mentioned above does show how the truth conditions of each sentence are a function of the semantic features of the items in a basic finite vocabulary. But such a theory does not, it is often said, explain the semantic features of the basic vocabulary. In a theory of truth, we find those familiar recursive clauses that specify, for example, that a conjunction is true if and only if each conjunct is true, that a disjunction is true if and only if at least one disjunct is true, and so on. (In fact the theory must explain how connectives work in open as well as closed sentences, and so the recursion will be applied to the *satisfaction* relation rather than directly to truth.)

The theory must, we know, entail a T-sentence even for the simplest cases, for example:

(T) "Socrates flies" is true iff Socrates flies.

If nothing is said about the constituents, how does the theory handle such cases? Well, one way might be this: The basic vocabulary must be finite. In particular, then, there can be only a finite number of simple predicates and a finite number of proper names (unstructured singular terms, not counting variables). So it is possible to list every sentence consisting of a proper name and a basic predicate. One way, then, that a theory can entail every sentence like (T) is by having every such sentence as an axiom. Clearly this method avoids (so far) any appeal to the concept of reference — and fails to throw any light on it.

Predicates come in any degree of complexity, since they can be built up from connectives and variables; and constant singular terms can be complex. So the method we were just exploring will fail to work in general. In the case of predicates, Tarski's method, as we know, involves appeal to the concept of satisfaction, a relation between predicates and .n-tuples of entities of which the predicates are true (actually, sequences of such). Satisfaction is obviously much like reference for predicates — in fact we might define the reference of a predicate as the class of those entities that satisfy it. The trouble is, an absolute theory of truth doesn't really illuminate the relation of satisfaction. When the theory comes to characterize satisfaction for the predicate 'x flies,' for example, it merely tells us that an entity satisfies 'x flies' if and only if that entity flies. If we ask for a further explanation or analysis of the relation, we will be disappointed.

The fact that an absolute definition of truth fails to yield an analysis of the concept of reference can be seen from this, that if one imagines a new predicate added to the language — or a language just like the old except for containing a single further predicate — the accounts of truth and satisfaction already given don't suggest *how to go on to the new case.* (This remark doesn't apply to the recursive clauses: they say *in general* when a conjunction is true, no matter what the conjuncts are.)

The fact that satisfaction, which we have been thinking of as recursively characterized, can be given an explicit definition (by the Frege-Dedekind technique) should not lead us into thinking a general concept has been captured. For the definition (like the recursion that serves it) will explicitly limit the application of satisfaction to a fixed finite list of predicates (and compounds of them). So if a theory (or definition) of satisfaction applies to a given language and then a new predicate, say 'x flies,' is added, it will follow that 'x flies' is not satisfied by an object that flies — or by anything else.

Analogous remarks go for constant singular terms. Indeed, if there are complex singular terms, it will be necessary to characterize a relation like reference, using recursive clauses such as: 'the father of' concatenated with a name α refers to the father of what α refers to. But for the underlying proper names, there will again be simply a list. What it is for a proper name to refer to an object will not be analyzed.

The point I have just been laboring, that there is a clear sense in which an absolute theory of truth does not throw light on the semantic features of the basic vocabulary of predicates and names, is familiar. This complaint has often been conflated with another, that a Tarski-style theory of truth gives no insight into the concept of truth. It will do no harm if we accept the idea that in a theory of truth, the expression 'is true' (or whatever takes its place) is understood independently. The reason Convention T is acceptable as a criterion of theories is that (1) T-sentences are clearly true (preanalytically) — something we could recognize only if we already (partly) understood the predicate 'is true,' and (2) the totality of T-sentences fixes the extension of the truth-predicate uniquely. The interest of a theory of truth, viewed as an empirical theory of a natural language, is not that it tells us what truth is in general, but that it reveals how the truth of every sentence of a particular L depends on its structure and constituents.

We do not need to worry, then, over the fact that a theory of truth does not fully analyze the preanalytic concept of truth. The point may be granted without impugning the interest of the theory. (I'll come back to this.) There remains the claim, which I also grant, that the theory does not explain or analyze the concept of reference. And that seems a grievous failure, since it undermines the pretensions of the theory to give a complete account of the truth of sentences.

This property of a theory of truth has been pointed out to me with increasing persistence by a number of critics. Gilbert Harman makes the point in order to question whether a theory of truth can, as I have claimed, do duty for a theory of meaning.[1] He says, in effect, that a theory of truth can only be considered as giving the meaning of the logical constants — it gives the logical form of sentences, and to that extent their meaning — but it cannot put flesh on the bones. Hartry Field develops the ideas I have touched on in the past few pages, and concludes that a Tarski-style theory of truth is only part of a complete theory.[2] We must in addition, he thinks, add a theory of reference for predicates and proper names. (I have drawn on his presentation.) Related criticisms have been made by Kathryn Pyne Parsons, Hilary Putnam and Paul Benacerraf.[3]

I have been saying why it seems that we can't live without the concept of reference; now let me say why I think we should be reluctant to live with it. I am concerned with what I take to be, historically at least, the central problem of philosophy of language, which is how to explain specifically linguistic concepts like truth (of sentences or utterances), meaning (linguistic), linguistic rule or convention, naming, referring, asserting, and so on — how to analyze some or all of these concepts in terms of concepts of another order. Everything about language can come to seem puzzling, and we would understand it better if we could reduce semantic concepts to others. Or if 'reduce' and 'analyze' are too strong (and I think they are), then let us say, as vaguely as possible, understand semantic concepts in the light of others.

To 'live with' the concept of reference means, in the present context, to take it as a concept to be given an independent analysis or interpretation in terms of nonlinguistic concepts. The question whether reference is explicitly definable in terms of other semantic notions such as that of satisfaction, or recursively characterizable, or neither, is not the essential question — the essential question is whether it is *the*, or at least one, place where there is direct contact between linguistic theory and events, actions, or objects described in nonlinguistic terms.

If we could give the desired analysis or reduction of the concept of reference, then all would, I suppose, be clear sailing. Having explained directly the semantic features of proper names and simple predicates, we could go on to explain the reference of complex singular terms and complex predicates, we could characterize satisfaction (as a derivative concept), and finally truth. This picture of how to do semantics is (aside from details) an old one and a natural one. It is often called the building-block theory. It has often been tried. And it is hopeless.

We have to go back to the early British empiricists for fairly clear examples of building-block theories (Berkeley, Hume, Mill). The ambitious attempts at behavioristic analyses of meaning by Ogden and Richards and Charles Morris are not clear cases, for these authors tended to blur the distinction between words and sentences ('Fire!' 'Slab!' 'Block!') and much of what they said really applies intelligibly only to sentences as the basic atoms for analysis. Quine, in Chapter II of *Word and Object*, attempts a behavioristic analysis, but although his most famous example ('Gavagai') is a single word, it is explicitly treated as a sentence. Grice, if I understand his project, wants to explain linguistic meaning ultimately by appeal to nonlinguistic intentions – but again it is the meanings of *sentences*, not of words, that are to be analyzed in terms of something else.

The historical picture, much simplified, shows that as the problems became clearer and the methods more sophisticated, behaviorists and others who would give a radical analysis of language and communication have given up the building-block approach in favor of an approach that makes the sentence the focus of empirical interpretation.

And surely this is what we should expect. Words have no function save as they play a role in sentences: their semantic features are abstracted from the semantic features of sentences, just as the semantic features of sentences are abstracted from *their* part in helping people achieve goals or realize intentions.

If the name 'Kilimanjaro' refers to Kilimanjaro, then no doubt there is *some* relation between English- (or Swahili-) speakers, the word, and the mountain. But it is inconceivable that one should be able to explain this relation without first explaining the role of the word in sentences; and if this is so, there is no chance of explaining reference directly in nonlinguistic terms.

It is interesting that Quine in Chapter II of *Word and Object* makes no use of the concept of reference, nor does he try to construct it. Quine stresses the indeterminacy of translation, and of reference. He argues that the totality of evidence available to a hearer determines no unique way of translating one man's words into another's; that it does not even fix the *apparatus* of reference (singular terms, quantifiers and identity). I think Quine understates his case. If it is true that the allowable evidence for interpreting a language is summed up when we know what the acceptable translation manuals from His to Ours are, then the evidence is irrelevant to questions of reference and of ontology. For a

Donald Davidson

translation manual is only a method of going from sentences of one language to sentences of another, and we can infer from it nothing about the relations between words and objects. Of course we know, or think we know, what the words in our own language refer to, but this is information no translation manual contains. Translation is a purely syntactic notion. Questions of reference do not arise in syntax, much less get settled.[4]

Here then, in brief, is the paradox of reference: there are two approaches to the theory of meaning, the building-block method, which starts with the simple and builds up, and the holistic method, which starts with the complex (sentences, at any rate) and abstracts out the parts. The first method would be fine if we could give a nonlinguistic characterization of reference, but of this there seems no chance. The second begins at the point (sentences) where we can hope to connect language with behavior described in nonlinguistic terms. But it seems incapable of giving a complete account of the semantic features of the parts of sentences, and without such an account we are apparently unable to explain truth.

The two approaches are, I think, naturally associated with two views of proper names. With the building-block approach goes the causal theory of proper names, which Saul Kripke, Hilary Putnam and David Kaplan, among others, have done so much to make plausible. The causal theory maintains that a certain sort of causal chain connecting the object named, the introduction of the name into the language and subsequent uses of the name is crucial to the name relation. It seems correct, then, to suppose that on this theory reference must be given an empirical interpretation that is independent of or prior to an account of how sentences containing those names work.

The other view of names holds that interpreting the sentences (and hence, by abstraction, the names) used by a speaker depends solely on the present dispositions of the speaker (or a community of speakers) and so the causal history of names is strictly irrelevant (except, of course, in so far as it shapes present dispositions). (Perhaps I should add that one can accept this position while rejecting the views of Russell, Strawson, Frege or Searle on proper names.)

To return to the central dilemma: here is how I think it can be resolved. I propose to defend a version of the holistic approach, and urge that we must give up the concept of reference as basic to an empirical theory of language. I shall sketch why I think we can afford to do this.

The argument against giving up reference was that it was needed to complete an account of truth. I have granted that a Tarski-style theory of truth does not analyze or explain either the preanalytic concept of truth or the preanalytic concept of reference: at best it gives the extension of the concept of truth for one or another language with a fixed primitive vocabulary. But this does not show that a theory of absolute truth cannot explain the truth of individual sentences on the basis of their semantic structure; all it shows is that the semantic features of words cannot be made basic in interpreting the theory. What is needed in order to resolve the dilemma of reference is the distinction between explanation *within* the theory and explanation *of* the theory. Within the theory, the conditions of truth of a sentence are specified by adverting to postulated structure and semantic concepts like that of satisfaction or reference. But when it comes to interpreting the theory as a whole, it is the notion of truth, as applied to closed sentences, which must be connected with human ends and activities. The analogy with physics is obvious: we explain macroscopic phenomena by postulating an unobserved fine structure. But the theory is tested at the macroscopic level. Sometimes, to be sure, we are lucky enough to find additional, or more direct, evidence for the originally postulated structure; but this is not essential to the enterprise. I suggest that words, meanings of words, reference and satisfaction are posits we need to implement a theory of truth. They serve this purpose without needing independent confirmation or empirical basis.

It should now be clear why I said, in the opening paragraph, that a theory of truth of the right sort could help resolve the apparent dilemma of reference. The help comes from the fact that a theory of truth lets us answer the underlying question how communication by language is possible: such a theory satisfies the two requirements we placed on an adequate answer (in the second paragraph). The two requirements relate directly to the distinction just made between explaining something in terms of the theory, and explaining why the theory holds (i.e., relating it to more basic facts).

Let us take the second condition first. How can a theory of absolute truth be given an empirical interpretation? What is essential in the present context is that the theory be related to behavior and attitudes described in terms not specific to the language or sentence involved. A Tarski-style truth theory provides the obvious place to establish this relation: the T-sentences. If we knew all of these were true, then a theory that entailed them would satisfy the formal requirement of Convention T, and would give truth conditions for every sentence. In practice, we should imagine the theory builder assuming that some T-sentences are true on the evidence (whatever that is), building a likely theory, and testing further T-sentences to confirm, or supply grounds for modifying, the theory. A typical T-sentence, now relativized to time, might be:

'Socrates is flying' is true (in Smith's language) at t iff Socrates is flying at t.

Empirically, what we need is a relation between Smith and the sentence 'Socrates is flying' which we can describe in non-question-begging terms and that holds when and only when Socrates is flying. The theory will, of course, contain a recursion on a concept like satisfaction or reference. But these notions we must treat as theoretical constructs whose function is exhausted in stating the truth conditions for sentences. Similarly, for that matter, for the logical form attributed to sentences, and the whole machinery of terms, predicates, connectives and quantifiers. None of this is open to direct confrontation with the evidence. It makes no sense, on this approach, to complain that a theory comes up with the right truth-conditions time after time, but has the logical form (or deep structure) wrong. We should take the same view of reference. A theory of this kind does not, we agreed, explain reference, at least in this sense: it assigns no empirical content directly to relations between names or predicates and objects. These relations are given a content *indirectly* when the T-sentences are.

The theory gives up reference, then, as part of the cost of going empirical. It can't, however, be said to have given up ontology. For the theory relates each singular term to some object or other, and it tells what entities satisfy each predicate. Doing without reference is not at all to embrace a policy of doing without semantics or ontology.

I have not said what is to count as the evidence for the truth of a T-sentence.[5] The present enterprise is served by showing how the theory can be supported by relating T-sentences, and nothing else, to the evidence. What is clear is that the evidence, whatever it is, cannot be described in terms that relate it in advance to any particular language, and this suggests that the concept of truth to which we appeal has a generality that the theory cannot hope to explain.

Not that the concept of truth that is used in T-sentences can be explicitly defined in nonsemantic terms, or reduced to more behavioristic concepts. Reduction and definition are, as I said at the beginning, too much to expect. The relation between theory and evidence will surely be much looser.

A general and preanalytic notion of truth is presupposed by the theory. It is because we have this notion that we can tell what counts as evidence for the truth of a T-sentence. But the same is not required of the concepts of satisfaction and reference. Their role is theoretical, and so we know all there is to know about them when we know how they operate to characterize truth. We don't need a general *concept* of reference as a condition of spinning an adequate theory.

We don't need the concept of reference; neither do we need reference itself, whatever that may be. For if there is one way of assigning entities to expressions (a way of characterizing 'satisfaction') that yields acceptable results with respect to the truth-conditions of sentences, there will be endless other ways that do as well. There is no reason, then, to call any one of these semantical relations 'reference' or 'satisfaction.'[6]

How can a theory of absolute truth give an account of communication, or be considered a theory of meaning? It doesn't provide us with the materials for defining or analysing such phrases as 'means,' 'means the same as,' 'is a translation of,' etc. It is wrong to think that we can *automatically* construe T-sentences as 'giving the meaning' of sentences if we put no more constraint on them than that they come out true.

The question to ask is whether someone who knows a theory of truth for a language L would have enough information to interpret what a speaker of L says. I think the right way to investigate this question is to ask in turn whether the empirical and formal constraints on a theory of truth sufficiently limit the range of acceptable theories. Suppose, for example, that *every* theory that satisfied the requirements gave the truth-conditions of 'Socrates flies' as suggested above. Then clearly to know the theory (and to know *that* it is a theory that satisfies the constraints) is to know that the T-sentence *uniquely* gives the truth-conditions of 'Socrates flies.' And this *is* to know enough about its role in the language.

I don't for a moment imagine such uniqueness would emerge. But I do think that reasonable empirical constraints on the interpretation of T-sentences (the conditions under which we find them true), plus the formal constraints, will leave enough invariant as between theories to allow us to say that a theory of truth captures the essential role of each sentence. A rough comparison may help give the idea. A theory of measurement for temperature leads to the assignment to objects of numbers that measure their temperature. Such theories put formal constraints on the assignments, and also must be tied empirically to qualitatively observable phenomena. The numbers assigned are not uniquely determined by the constraints. But the *pattern* of assignments is significant. (Fahrenheit and Centigrade temperature are linear transformations of each other; the assignment of numbers is unique up to a linear transformation.) In much the same way, I suggest that what is invariant as between different acceptable theories of truth is meaning. The meaning (interpretation) of a sentence is given by assigning the sentence a semantic location in the pattern of sentences that comprise the language. Different theories of truth may assign different truth-conditions to the same sentence (this is the semantic analogue of Quine's indeterminacy of translation), while the theories are (nearly enough) in agreement on the roles of the sentences in the language.

The central idea is simple. The building-block theory, and theories that try to give a rich content to each sentence directly on the basis of nonsemantic evidence (for example the intentions with which the sentence is typically uttered), try to move too far too fast. The present thought is rather to expect to find a minimum of information about the correctness of the theory at each single point; it is the potential infinity of points that makes the difference. A strong theory weakly

8 On the sense and reference of a proper name*

John McDowell

I

An interesting way to raise questions about the relation between language and reality is to ask: how could we state a theory knowledge of which would suffice for understanding a language? Donald Davidson has urged that a central component in such a theory would be a theory of truth, in something like the style of Tarski, for the language in question.[1] A Tarskian truth-theory entails, for each indicative sentence of the language it deals with, a theorem specifying a necessary and sufficient condition for the sentence to be true. The theorems are derivable from axioms which assign semantic properties to sentence-constituents and determine the semantic upshot of modes of combination. Now Frege held that the senses of sentences can be determined by giving truth-conditions, and that the sense of a sentence-constituent is its contribution to the senses of sentences in which it may occur.[2] The parallel is striking. It suggests a construal of Davidson's proposal as a proposal about the nature of a theory of (Fregean) sense for a language.

Tarskian truth-theories are extensional, and only minimally richer in ontology than their object languages (no need to mention possible worlds and the like). This attractive economy of resources has a consequence which is crucial to the proper understanding of the suggestion: namely that not just any theory of truth, however true, could serve as a theory of sense.

The job of a theory of sense should be to fix the content of speech-acts which a total theory of the language concerned would warrant ascribing to speakers.[3] Abstracting harmlessly from complications induced by indexicality and non-indicative utterances, we can put the point like this: in the case of any sentence whose utterance command of the language would make fully comprehensible as a saying — any

*Reprinted by permission of the publishers, from *Mind*, vol. LXXXVI (1977), pp. 159–85. I have been reading ancestors of this paper to seminars and discussion groups since 1971: it would be impossible for me to identify all the influences on it. I should like to acknowledge special debts to Gareth Evans and David Wiggins.

indicative sentence – a theory of sense must fix the content of the saying which an intentional utterance of the sentence could be understood to be.

The adequacy of the total theory would turn on its acceptably imposing descriptions, reporting behaviour as performance of speech-acts of specified kinds with specified contents, on a range of potential actions – those which would constitute speech in the language – describable, antecedently, only as so much patterned emission of noise. For that systematic imposing of descriptions to be acceptable, it would have to be the case that speakers' performances of the actions thus ascribed to them were, for the most part, intelligible under those descriptions, in the light of propositional attitudes: their possession of which, in turn, would have to be intelligible, in the light of their behaviour – including, of course, their linguistic behaviour – and their environment. The point of the notion of sense – that which the content-specifying component of a total theory of that sort would be a theory of – is thus tied to our interest in the understanding of behaviour, and ultimately our interest in the understanding – the fathoming – of people. We have not properly made sense of forms of words in a language if we have not, thereby, got some way towards making sense of its speakers. If there is a pun here, it is an illuminating one.

Now to specify the content of a saying we need a sentence. A theory might have the power to give us a sentence to meet the need, for any indicative sentence of its object language, by virtue of the fact that it entailed theorems in which the needed content-specifying sentences were used to state necessary and sufficient conditions for the application, to the relevant object-language sentences, of some predicate. The fact that the used sentences specified the content of sayings potentially effected by uttering the mentioned sentences would guarantee that the predicate could, if we liked, be written 'true'; it would guarantee that the theory, with its theorems written that way, was a true theory of truth.[4] But it would be the guaranteeing fact, and not the guaranteed fact, which suited the theory to serve as a theory of sense. For, given a theory guaranteed to be a true theory of truth, by its serviceability in yielding content-specifications, we could exploit the extensionality of truth-theories to derive a new, equally true theory of truth which, in spite of its truth, would not be serviceable in yielding content-specifications, and so would not serve as a theory of sense.[5]

What emerges is that serving as a theory of sense is not the same as being one, on a certain strict view of what it is to be one. It was clear anyway that a truth-theory of the sort Davidson envisages does not, in saying what it does, *state* the senses of expressions. Why should we hanker after a theory which does that mysterious thing, if a theory which does some utterly unmysterious thing instead can be made to serve the purpose? Pending a good answer to that question, there is only the mildest perversity in shifting our conception of what a theory of sense must be, so that Davidsonian theories are at least not ruled out. As positive justification we still have the striking parallel noted at the outset between the Davidsonian *Ersatz* and Frege's own ideas about the genuine article.

II

I shall restrict attention throughout to occurrences of names in straightforwardly extensional contexts in which they function as singular terms; and I shall, in this paper, ignore names with more than one bearer.

For simplicity, I shall begin by considering theories which aim to deal with (fragments of) English in English (the restriction will be removed in section VII). In a theory of truth of that kind, names might be handled by axioms of which the following is typical:[6]

'Hesperus' stands for (denotes) Hesperus.

The role played by some such clause, in the derivation of assignments of truth-conditions to sentences in which the name occurs, would display the contribution made by the name to those truth-conditions. Given the Fregean doctrine about sense mentioned at the beginning of this paper, this suggests that such a clause, considered as having what it says fixed by its location in a theory which yields acceptable content-specifications, gives — or, more strictly, in that context as good as gives — the sense of the name.

III

If there is to be any affinity between my use of 'sense' and Frege's of '*Sinn*' I must keep room for a distinction between sense and reference. There must be contexts where 'sense' is required and 'reference' would not do. Now clauses of the sort just exemplified specify, surely, *references (Bedeutungen)* of names, and it might be thought that the distinction has disappeared.

That thought would be wrong. Frege's notion of sense belongs with the notion of understanding, and we can get at what is involved in understanding a language by careful employment of the notion of knowledge. Recall my opening question about the nature of a theory knowledge of which would suffice for understanding a language. We can think of a theory of sense as a component of a total theory of that kind: a component which, in the context of principles adequate to determine the force (assertion, instruction, or whatever) with which particular utterances are issued, serves (as suggested in section I) to determine the content of speech-acts performed in issuing those utterances. Semantically simple expressions would be mentioned in axioms of such a theory, designed so that knowledge of the truths they express − in the context of knowledge of enough of the rest of the theory − would suffice for understanding utterances containing those expressions. The hypothetical knowledge involved here, then, is knowledge of truths (French 'savoir', German 'wissen'). The reference (Bedeutung) of a name, on the other hand, is, in Frege's usage, its bearer − an object.[7] To know the reference of a name would be, failing an unpardonable equivocation, to know that object: acquaintance, perhaps, but in any case not knowledge of truths but, what is grammatically distinct, knowledge of things (French 'connaître', German 'kennen'). It is not, then, the sort of knowledge which it would make sense to state in clauses of a theory. The grammatical distinction between knowledge of things and knowledge of truths guarantees a difference of role for 'sense' and 'reference'. Without putting that difference at risk, we can claim that a clause which does no more than state − in a suitable way − what the reference of an expression is may nevertheless give − or as good as give − that expression's sense.

This grammatical way of distinguishing sense and reference promises to free us from any need to worry about the ontological status of senses. As far as names are concerned, the ontology of a theory of sense, on the present suggestion, need not exceed the names and their bearers. To construe knowledge of the sense of an expression (knowledge of a truth) as, at some different level, knowledge of (perhaps acquaintance with) an entity (the sense of the expression) seems from this perspective, gratuitous.[8]

Verbal nouns like 'reference' (and 'Bedeutung') have a curious grammatical property which facilitates temptation to the equivocation alluded to above. We would do well to immunize ourselves to the temptation by exposing its source. A phrase of the form 'the reference of x' can be understood as equivalent to the corresponding phrase of the form 'what x refers to', either (i) in the sense in which 'what' amounts to 'that which' (which yields the official Fregean use of 'Bedeutung') or (ii) in the sense in which 'what' is an interrogative pronoun. In this second sense, 'what x refers to' gives the form of an indirect question, something suitable to follow 'know' where knowledge of truths is what is meant. Knowledge of the reference of a name, in this second (non-Fregean) sense, could reasonably be held to be knowledge which, in the context of appropriate further knowledge not itself involving the name, would suffice for understanding utterances containing the name — that is, precisely, knowledge of its *sense*. It is presumably just this slipperiness of the word 'reference' which motivates the introduction of the term of art 'referent'.

The possibility of equating a distinction between sense and (Fregean) reference with a distinction between (non-Fregean) reference and referent may, for those who are at home in the latter idiom, make it easier to see how crediting names with senses (to persist, with the plural, in an ontologically incautious formulation) is not necessarily crediting them with anything like connotation or descriptive meaning.

IV

Frege's distinction was first put to use to solve a problem about identity sentences. Altered so as to involve undisputable instances of ordinary proper names, the question is this: how could someone possess knowledge sufficient to understand a sentence like 'Hesperus is Phosphorus' without thereby knowing, already, that the sentence is true?[9] That question can be answered in the context of a theory which treats names in the austere way suggested above. The two names would be treated, in a theory of the sort I am envisaging, by clauses to this effect:

'Hesperus' stands for Hesperus.
'Phosphorus' stands for Phosphorus.

Since Hesperus *is* Phosphorus, the right-hand sides of these clauses can of course be interchanged *salva veritate*. But it does not follow, from the truth of the results, that they would be equally serviceable in a theory of sense (cf. section I). The idea was that knowledge that 'Hesperus' stands for Hesperus would suffice, in the context of suitable other knowledge not directly involving the name, for understanding utterances containing 'Hesperus'; and similarly with knowledge that 'Phosphorus' stands for Phosphorus and utterances containing 'Phosphorus'. Now if someone knows that 'Hesperus' stands for Hesperus and that 'Phosphorus' stands for Phosphorus, it does not follow that he knows either that 'Hesperus' stands for Phosphorus or that 'Phosphorus' stands for Hesperus. And for it to seem that knowledge sufficient for understanding the sentence would, of itself, suffice for knowing its truth, one or the other of those implications would have to be thought to hold.[10]

The point does not turn essentially on treating the *deductive apparatus* of the envisaged theory of sense (in particular, its axioms) as spelling out hypothetical knowledge (knowledge which would suffice for understanding). The inadequacy of a theory which used just one of the two names on the right-hand sides of its clauses for both would show in its *consequences*, the theorems assigning truth-conditions to sentences. We would have to use those consequences in fixing the content of sayings, to be found intelligible in terms of propositional attitudes, our specification of whose content would need to be fixed partly by our interpretation of the sayings. And some utterances of 'Hesperus is Phosphorus' would be unintelligible — we would not be able to see their point — if we were reduced to regarding them as expressing the belief that, say, Hesperus is Hesperus.[11] What we have here is a glimpse of the way in which, by requiring the theory's consequences to help us make sense of speakers of the language, we force ourselves to select among the multiplicity of true theories of truth. Bearing directly on the theorems, the requirement bears indirectly on the deductive apparatus which generates them. The failures of substitution exploited above, within contexts which specify hypothetical knowledge, simply make vivid how the indirect requirement operates.

V

According to Michael Dummett's reconstruction, Frege's own view was that the sense of a name is a criterion for, or way of, recognizing or identifying an object as its bearer.[12] I have so far left ways of recognizing objects entirely out of account. It is noteworthy how much of Frege it has nevertheless been possible to preserve. Frege's own examples undeniably manifest a richer conception of how sense might be represented; but the suspicion arises that that might be an unnecessary excrescence, rather than — what Dummett evidently takes it to be — something essential to any elaboration of Frege's basic ideas about sense.

What is the point of the notion of sense? According to Dummett's attractive suggestion, it is to capture (in part) a notion of meaning which makes it true that a theory of meaning is a theory of understanding.[13] A theory of understanding is just what I have been thinking of a theory of a language as being. In my terms, then, the issue is this. Within the present restricting assumptions, would knowledge that 'Hesperus' stands for Hesperus — in the context of suitable knowledge about other expressions, and suitable knowledge about the forces with which utterances may be issued — suffice for understanding utterances containing 'Hesperus'? Or would one require, rather, knowledge to the effect that the bearer of the name may be recognized or identified thus and so? Now patently this second, stronger, requirement, interpreted in any ordinary way, insists on more than would suffice; for it insists on more than, in some cases, does suffice. One can have the ability to tell that a seen object is the bearer of a familiar name without having the slightest idea *how* one recognizes it. The presumed mechanism of recognition might be neural machinery — its operations quite unknown to its possessor.[14]

Understanding a language involves knowing, on occasion, what speakers of it are doing, under descriptions which report their behaviour as speech-acts of specified kinds with specified contents. It helps to picture a possessor and a non-possessor of the state involved being subjected together to speech in the language. Assuming he is awake and attentive, the one will know truths expressible by the application of such descriptions; the other will not. Certain information is made available to both, in their shared sensory experience; certain further information is possessed only by one. Now a theory of a language was described above (section I) as warranting systematic imposition of interpreting descriptions on the range of potential behaviour which would constitute speech in the language, thought of as describable, in advance of receiving the interpreting descriptions, only as emission of noise. Such a theory, then, would have the following deductive power: given a suitable formulation of the information made available to both the possessor and the non-possessor of the state of understanding on any of the relevant potential occasions, it would permit derivation of the information which the possessor of the state would be distinguished by having. The ability to comprehend heard speech is an information-processing capacity, and the theory would describe it by articulating in detail the relation, which defines the capacity, between input information and output information.

In order to acquire an information-processing capacity with the right input–output relation, it would suffice to get to know the theory; then one could move from input information to output information, on any of the relevant occasions, by explicit deduction. It does not follow that to have such a capacity is to know any such theory. Nor, in any ordinary sense of 'know', is it usually true. Comprehension of speech in a familiar language is a matter of unreflective perception, not the bringing to bear of a theory.

It is important not to be misled into a bad defence of the richer conception of the sense of a name. Certainly, it may be said, understanding a language does not consist in *explicit* knowledge of a theory. But we are not precluded, by that concession, from saying — as Dummett indeed does[15] — that understanding a language consists in *implicit* knowledge of a theory. And employment of the concept of implicit or tacit knowledge in the recent history of linguistics[16] might make one suppose that the point of this view of understanding lies in dissatisfaction with the unambitious aim of merely *describing* the state. The attraction of the notion of implicit knowledge, one might suppose, lies

John McDowell

in its promise to permit us, more enterprisingly, to *explain* exercises of the capacity involved, in terms of a postulated inner mechanism. The workings of the mechanism are to be thought of as implicit counterparts of the explicit operations, with an explicitly known theory, whereby we might simulate the behaviour we view as the mechanism's external manifestations. Now a mechanism whose workings include an implicit counterpart to explicitly employing a method for recognizing or identifying the bearer of a name would seem to afford more explanation than an alternative mechanism constituted by implicit knowledge of an austere theory of sense. There is, with a rich theory, a specific operation of the mechanism to account for a person's getting on to the right object, and the austere conception yields nothing of the sort. And, on this view, it is beside the point to appeal to those facts about what speakers explicitly know which were exploited, above, in the argument that the rich conception insists on more knowledge than would suffice.

No such defence of the rich conception is available to Frege, as Dummett interprets him. Expounding Frege, Dummett connects the notion of sense, as remarked above, with the notion of understanding. The notion of understanding is a psychological notion, and there is the threat of an objection to using it in this context, on the ground that it infects the notion of sense with the psychologism which Frege detested. Dummett meets the threat, on Frege's behalf, precisely by denying that the notion of sense is to be thought of as employed in the construction of a purportedly explanatory mechanism (*Frege*, p. 681):

A model of sense is not a description of some hypothesized psychological mechanism . . . A model for the sense of a word of some particular kind does not seek to explain *how* we are able to use the word as we do: it simply forms part of an extended description of what that use consists in.

The point is not just *ad hominem*, since a Fregean detestation of such psychologism is well placed. There is no merit in a conception of the mind which permits us to speculate about its states, conceived as states of a hypothesized mechanism, with a breezy lack of concern for facts about explicit awareness. Postulation of implicit knowledge for such allegedly explanatory purposes sheds not scientific light but philosophical darkness.[17]

It is certainly true that psychological explanations of behaviour are central in the conception of a theory of a language outlined above (section I). But their purpose is to confirm the descriptive adequacy of a theory, not to put an explanatory mechanism through its paces. The demand is that we should be able to see, in enough cases, why speakers might think fit to act in the ways in which, by application of the theory, they are described as intentionally acting – the point being to underpin our confidence that they are indeed acting intentionally in those ways.

That is quite distinct from demanding explanations of how speakers arrive at knowledge of what others are doing, under those descriptions; or how they contrive to embody actions which are intentional under those descriptions in their own verbal behaviour.

Hostility to psychologism, then, is not hostility to the psychological. It is of the utmost importance to distinguish rejection of psychologism, as characterized in the above quotation from Dummett, from anti-mentalism of the sort which issues from Skinnerian behaviourism. Indeed one of the chief objections to the psychologistic postulation of implicit knowledge stems from a concern that the notion of the inner life, the life of the mind, not be made unrecognizable.[18] Hypothesized mechanisms are not the way to save from behaviourist attack the indispensable thought that all is not dark within. We get no authentic and satisfying conception of the mind from either of these philistine extremes.

If Frege meant the notion of sense to figure in theories without the explanatory aspirations of psychologism, why did he hold the richer conception of the sense of a name? Partly, perhaps, because of the metaphorical form in which his treatment of the 'Hesperus'-'Phosphorus' puzzle presented itself to him. The two names must not differ merely as objects — they must not be merely phonetic or orthographic variants for each other — if a genuine puzzle is to arise; they must differ also in their manner of presentation of the object which both present, and therein lies the solution.[19] Now, this metaphor of manners of presentation can be interpreted in the context of the austere conception. Difference in sense between 'Hesperus' and 'Phosphorus' lies in the fact that the clauses in the theory of sense which specify the object presented by the names are constrained to present it in the ways in which the respective names present it. They meet this constraint — surely infallibly — by actually using the respective names. But it takes subtlety to find the metaphor thus already applicable; it can easily seem to necessitate something more like a description theory of names. (Any tendency to find a richer interpretation of the metaphor natural would be reinforced by the view of thought to be discussed in section VIII below.[20])

VI

Someone might be tempted to argue against the austere treatment of names in a theory of sense on the following lines. Knowledge that 'Hesperus' stands for Hesperus is too easily acquired for it to suffice, even in the context of appropriate further knowledge, for understanding utterances which contain the name. To know that 'Hesperus' stands for Hesperus, one needs no more than the merely syntactic knowledge that the expression is a name, together with mastery of a general trick of dropping quotation marks.

The argument is worthless. Even adding the knowledge, hardly syntactic, that the name is not bearerless, what those easily acquired accomplishments suffice for is not knowledge that 'Hesperus' stands for Hesperus, but knowledge that the sentence ' "Hesperus" stands for Hesperus' expresses a truth. What we were interested in was the former state, knowledge of the truth which the sentence expresses, and not the latter.[21]

What exactly does the distinction amount to? Recall that we are concerned with these states of knowledge, not as actually possessed by all competent speakers, but as such that someone who possessed them would be able to use them in order to arrive by inference at the knowledge about particular speech-acts which a fluent hearer acquires by unreflective perception. A clause like ' "Hesperus" stands for Hesperus', on my account, would figure in a theory which, for speech-acts in which the name was uttered, warranted specifying their content by means of sentences in which the name was used, that is, sentences which mentioned the planet. Such a clause would do no work in the description of a linguistic capacity actually possessed by a given speaker — knowledge of what it says would play no part in duplicating, by explicit employment of a theory, anything which he could do without reflection — unless he showed an ability to use the name, or respond intelligently (with understanding) to uses of the name on the part of others, in speech-acts construable as being about the planet. Someone whose knowledge about 'Hesperus' was limited to its being a name with a bearer would simply not be enabled thereby to behave in those ways.

If we are to find such an ability in a person, we must be able to find the relevant speech behaviour, and responses to speech behaviour, intelligible in terms of propositional attitudes possessed by him, in the specification of whose content, again, the planet would presumably need to be mentioned. There is considerable plausibility in the idea that, if we are to be able to find in a person any propositional attitudes at all about an object, we must be able to find in him some beliefs about it. If that is right, these considerations capture what looks like a grain of truth in description theories of the sense of names: a person who knows the sense of a name must have some beliefs about its bearer. But that does not amount to a justification for a less austere treatment of the name in a theory of sense. The concession envisaged is that the person must have some *beliefs* — possibly sketchy, possibly false — about the object; not that he must *know* truths about it, sufficiently full to be true of it alone, and thus capable of generating a definite description which could replace the used name in the relevant clause of the theory of sense.

VII

At this point I shall lift the restriction imposed above (section II), and turn to theories which deal with one language in another. In fact, someone who constructed a theory which used English sentences to state their own truth-conditions might, anyway, think of his theory as using his own sentences to state truth-conditions for sentences which another person might use; and in that case the issues are the same. But it is easy to slip into viewing the sort of theory I have been considering from a solipsistic angle, with oneself as the only speaker who needs to be taken into account. That way, some issues are obscured, which become clearer when there is no mistaking the need for interpretation.

In the simplest case, someone interpreting a foreign language will himself already have a name for a suitable object (say a planet): that is, an object such that foreign utterances containing a certain expression can be interpreted as speech-acts about that object, intelligible in terms of propositional attitudes about it, where generation of the content-specifications which represent the speech-acts as being about the object employs clauses like this:

'Aleph' stands for Jupiter.

In a slightly less simple case, he will not antecedently have a name for a suitable object, having had no occasion to use one. But in the course of his attempt to interpret the foreign speakers, his attention might be drawn to some object in their environment, say a mountain (hitherto unknown to him). He would thereby acquire a batch of theory about the mountain. That theory (the facts about the mountain, as he sees them), together with plausible principles about the impact of the environment on propositional attitudes, might make it intelligible that his subjects should have certain propositional attitudes about the mountain, in terms of which he might be able to make sense of utterances by them containing some expression — say 'Afla' — on the hypothesis that it is their name for that mountain.

As far as that goes, he might deal with 'Afla' in his theory of their language by a clause to the following effect:

'Afla' stands for that mountain.

But the context drawn on by the demonstrative would be difficult to keep track of in using the theory. And it might be hard to come by a context-free unique specification to substitute for the demonstrative specification. A neat solution would be simply to adopt the subjects' name for his own use, both in stating the non-semantic facts he has discovered about the mountain and in expressing his theory about their name — thus:

'Afla' stands for Afla.

So far, then, things are much as before. Discussion of two complications should help to make the general picture clearer.

VIII

The first complication is the case of bearerless names, which brings us, I believe, to the deepest source of the richer conception of the sense of names. Suppose an interpreter finds an expression — say 'Mumbo-Jumbo' — which functions, syntactically, like other expressions which he can construe as names, but for which he can find no bearer, and reasonably believes there is no bearer. Such an interpreter, then, can accept no clause of the form

'Mumbo-Jumbo' stands for b

where 'b' is replaced by a name he could use (as above) to express a theory of his own about an object. Names which, in an interpreter's view, have no bearers cannot, by that interpreter, be handled in a theory of sense in the style considered so far. In his view they can have no sense, if a name's having a sense is its being able to be dealt with in that style.

Here we have a genuine divergence from Frege, and one which goes deep. Frege held that the sense of a name, if expressible otherwise than by the name itself, is expressible by a definite description. Definite descriptions are taken to have whatever sense they have independently of whether or not objects answer to them. Thus a name without a bearer could, in Frege's view, have a sense in exactly the same way as a name with a bearer.[22]

The non-Fregean view can be defended on these lines. An interpreter's ascription of propositional attitudes to his subject is in general constrained by the facts (as the interpreter sees them). This is partly because intelligibility, in ascriptions of belief at least, requires conformity to reasonable principles about how beliefs can be acquired under the impact of the environment; and partly because the point of ascribing propositional attitudes is to bring out the reasonableness, from a strategic standpoint constituted by possession of the attitudes, of the subject's dealings with the environment. Now, whether a name has a bearer or not (in an interpreter's view) makes a difference to the way in which the interpreter can use beliefs he can ascribe to the subject in making sense of the subject's behaviour. A sincere assertive utterance of a sentence containing a name with a bearer can be understood as expressing a belief correctly describable as a belief, concerning the bearer, that it satisfies some specified condition.[23] If the name has no bearer (in the interpreter's view), he cannot describe any suitably related belief in that transparent style. He can indeed gather, from the utterance, that the subject believes himself to have a belief which could be thus described, and believes himself to be expressing such a belief by his words. That might make the subject's behaviour, in speaking as he does, perfectly intelligible; but in a way quite different from the way in which, in the first kind of case, the belief expressed makes the behaviour intelligible. In the second kind of case, the belief which makes the behaviour intelligible is a (false) second-order belief to the effect that the subject has, and is expressing, a first-order belief correctly describable in the transparent style. This second-order belief is manifested by the subject's action, not expressed by his words. No belief is expressed by his words: they purport to express a belief which could be described in the transparent style, but since no appropriate belief could be thus described, there is no such belief as the belief which they purport to express.[24]

Opposition to this, on behalf of Frege, involves, I believe, a suspect conception of how thought relates to reality, and ultimately a suspect conception of mind. The Fregean view would have to seek its support in the idea that thought relates to objects with an essential indirectness: by way of a blueprint or specification which, if formulated, would be expressed in purely general terms. Whether the object exists or not would then be incidental to the availability of the thought. Underlying that idea is the following line of argument. When we mention an object in describing a thought we are giving only an extrinsic characterization of the thought (since the mention of the object takes us outside the subject's mind); but there must be an intrinsic characterization available (one which does not take us outside the subject's mind), and that characterization would have succeeded in specifying the essential core of the thought even if extra-mental reality had not obliged by containing the object. From this standpoint, the argument for the non-Fregean view outlined above goes wrong in its principle that the thought expressed by a sentence containing a name, if there is any such thought, is correctly describable as a thought, concerning some specified object, that it satisfies some specified condition. That would be a merely extrinsic characterization of the thought expressed; it succeeds in fitting the thought only if reality obliges. If reality does not oblige, that does not show, as the argument suggested, that no thought was expressed after all. For the real content of the thought expressed would need to be given by an intrinsic characterization; and that would specify the content of the thought without mentioning extra-mental objects, and thus in purely general terms.[25]

The conception of mind which underlies this insistence on not mentioning objects, in specifying the essential core of a thought, is the conception beautifully captured in Wittgenstein's remark, 'If God had looked into our minds, he would not have been able to see there whom we were speaking of'.[26] It is profoundly attractive, and profoundly unsatisfactory. Rummaging through the repository of general thoughts which, when we find the remark plausible, we are picturing the mind as being, God would fail to find out, precisely, whom we have in mind. Evidently that (mythical) repository is not the right place to look. God (or anyone) might see whom we have in mind, rather, by — for instance — seeing whom we are looking at as we speak. That sort of thing — seeing relations between a person and bits of the world, not prying into a hidden place whose contents could be just as they are even if there were no world — is (in part) what seeing into a person's mind is.[27]

A proper respect for a person's authority on his own thoughts points, anyway, in a quite different direction. When one sincerely and assertively utters a sentence containing a proper name, one means to be expressing a belief which could be correctly described in the transparent style. One does not mean to be expressing a belief whose availability to be expressed is indifferent to the existence or non-existence of a bearer for the name. The availability of the second sort of belief would be no consolation if the first sort turned out to have been, after all, unavailable.

In practice, an interpreter might say things like 'This man is saying that Mumbo-Jumbo brings thunder', and might explain an utterance which he described that way as expressing the belief that Mumbo-Jumbo brings thunder. That is no real objection. Such an interpreter is simply playing along with his deluded subject — putting things his way. There is no serious reason here for assimilating what he has found out about 'Mumbo-Jumbo' to what, in the case described above (section VII), he has found out about 'Afla'.[28]

IX

The second complication is the 'Hesperus'-'Phosphorus' puzzle: we can get a clearer view of it by considering it in a context in which the need for interpretation is explicit.

Suppose a smoothly functioning hypothesis has it that the mountain which some of the interpreter's subjects call 'Afla' (section VII) is also called, by some of them, 'Ateb'.[29] Suppose competence with both names coexists, in at least some cases, with ignorance that there is only one mountain involved. Suppose, as before, that the mountain is new to the interpreter, and that he proposes to take over means for referring to it, in expressing his new theory about it, from his subjects. Since he knows (let us suppose) that there is only one mountain involved, his own needs in geographical description (and so forth) would be met by taking over just one of their names. But a theory of their language which said of both names that, say, they stand for Afla would, as before (section IV), be incapable of making sense of some utterances. To leave room for the combination of competence and ignorance, an interpreter who follows the strategy of adopting names from his subjects needs, at least in his theory of their language, to use both their names: thus, as before (section IV), 'Afla' stands for Afla and 'Ateb' for Ateb.

We should distinguish two sorts of case. In the first, the possibility of combining competence and ignorance is an idiosyncratic accident of an individual's language-learning history. Instances of this are provided by people's possession of both 'official' names and nicknames, under which they may be introduced to the same person in situations different enough for him not to acquire knowledge of the truth of the appropriate identity sentence. In this sort of case, it seems plausible that for a speaker enlightened about the identity the two names are (aside from stylistic considerations) mere variants of each other (differ merely as objects). A theory of sense which aimed to cover only enlightened speakers, excluding even their dealings with unenlightened audiences, could without trouble use the same name on the right-hand sides of clauses dealing with each of the two. Only an aim of comprehensive coverage — enlightened and unenlightened together — would require a theory to handle the two differently, thereby representing them as differing in sense.

In the second sort of case, exemplified by 'Hesperus' and 'Phosphorus', and, in the most probable filling out of Frege's fable, by 'Afla' and 'Ateb', the difference of sense is more deep-seated. Even if everyone knew that Hesperus is Phosphorus, that would not make the two names differ merely as objects; or, if it did, the names would have changed in sense. If someone used the two names indifferently in talking about Venus, so that we could find no interesting correlation between utterances containing 'Hesperus' and (say) beliefs formed in response to evening appearances of the planet, and between utterances containing 'Phosphorus' and beliefs formed in response to its morning appearances,[30] then he would not be displaying competence in our use of the names — or, rather the fictitious use, corresponding to our use of 'the Evening Star' and 'the Morning Star', which I am considering in order to be able to discuss Frege's problem without raising irrelevant issues about definite descriptions. Such connections, between the use of a name and the sort of situation which prompts the beliefs it helps to express, can be, not merely idiosyncratic facts about individuals, but partly constitutive of a shared language. (This suggests the possibility of a well motivated translation of a pair of radically foreign names — not even culturally related to ours, like 'Hespero' and 'Fosforo' — by

John McDowell

our 'Hesperus' and 'Phosphorus'. The strategy of adopting the subjects' names is not essential to the sort of situation we are concerned with.)

The second sort of case can seem to support description theories of the sense of names — at least those which can figure in such examples. But it does no such thing. Recall what, in our terms, the issue would be between the austere conception and treatments of names more congenial to description theories. Would knowledge that 'Afla' stands for Afla and 'Ateb' for Ateb, in the context of suitable further knowledge not directly involving the names, suffice for understanding utterances containing them? Or would one need, rather, knowledge in whose spelling out the bearer of each name is specified in a more informative way? In the present case, the material from which a description theorist might hope to construct more substantial specifications is the obtaining of more or less systematic differences between the evidential situations which ultimately account for utterances containing the names. And here again it seems clear that to insist on knowledge of those differences is to insist on more than would suffice. A competent speaker need not be reflective about the evidential ancestry of his remarks. They have whatever evidential ancestry they do without his needing to know that they do. And it is their having it, not his knowing that they do, which counts.

It is certainly true that speakers are likely to have opinions about their own propensities to respond to different evidential situations with utterances containing different names. It is our possession of such opinions which confers initial plausibility on the idea that, for instance, the sense of 'visible in the evening' is part of the sense of 'Hesperus'. But we should not let that initial plausibility deceive us. Those opinions are the result of an activity which comes naturally to the self-conscious and theory-seeking creatures we are: namely theorizing, not necessarily with much explicitness, about our own verbal behaviour, as just one of the connected phenomena that constitute our world. In theorizing thus about the place of our speech in our world, we are no better placed than external observers of ourselves; indeed we may be worse placed, if we are less well-informed about the extra-linguistic facts (see section VIII). Speakers' opinions about their own diverging evidential susceptibilities with respect to names are products of self-observation from, so far as it is accessible, an external standpoint. They are not intimations, from within, of an implicitly known normative theory, a recipe for correct speech, which guides competent linguistic behaviour. It seems that something like the latter picture would have to underlie insistence that, for competence in the use of pairs of names which differ in sense in the deep-seated way, nothing less than knowledge (no doubt tacit or implicit) of the relevant differences in sensitivity to evidence would suffice. The picture is simply a version of the psychologism which Frege rightly rejected (section V).[31]

Difference in sense between 'Hesperus' and 'Phosphorus' appeared, in the account given earlier (section IV) of how the austere conception copes with Frege's puzzle, as a reflection of failures of substitution in propositional-attitude contexts. That would not satisfy those who look to the notion of difference in sense (as Frege did) to explain the failures of substitution.[32] The present section yields the following amplification of the picture: the failures of substitution, together with the characteristics which those failures force into a theory of sense, are reflections of two different sorts of underlying situation: first, in the trivial cases, the accidental absence, from some speakers' linguistic repertoires, of propensities to behave in ways construable as evidencing assent to the relevant identity sentences; second, in the deeper-seated cases, the different roles of the names in speakers' more or less systematic propensities to respond to different sorts of situation with different sentences. We can picture the failures of substitution and the differences in sense as, jointly and inseparably, products of our attempts at principled imposition of descriptions in terms of speech-acts, and explanations in terms of propositional attitudes, on to the hard behavioural facts about linguistic and other behaviour, with the point of the imposition being to see how sense can be made of speakers by way of sense being made of their speech. In this picture, the differences in sense are located no deeper than the failures of substitution. I entertain the suspicion that the ultimate source of the desire to see the differences in sense as underlying the failures of substitution, and hence as capable of affording genuine explanations of them, is the psychologism about sense which Frege (officially) renounced.

X

Dissatisfaction with theories which handle names in the way I have recommended is likely to focus on the modesty of any claims we could make on their behalf. The sense of a name is displayed, in these theories, by the deductive powers of a clause intelligible only to someone already competent in the use of the very name in question, or else another name with the same sense. This exemplifies, for the case of names, one strand of the quasi-technical notion of modesty, in a theory of meaning, discussed by Dummett in 'What is a Theory of Meaning?'.[33] Dummett makes it appear that a theory which was ineradicably modest, in that sense, would amount to a repudiation of the concept of sense.[34] In this section I want to sketch the reason why I think his argument unconvincing.[35]

As noted earlier (section V), Dummett talks of a theory of under-

standing as specifying (implicit) knowledge in whose possession understanding actually consists; but we can let his argument begin, at least,
without jibbing at that. He insists that it is worthless to consider a practical capacity on the model of knowledge of the members of an articulated set of propositions, if one can give no account of what it would be
to know the individual propositions. One thing such an account must
do is distinguish knowledge of one of the relevant propositions from
mere knowledge that some sentence (which in fact expresses it) expresses
a truth; the latter state would not be to the point. Now in section VI
above some simple remarks seemed adequate to ensure, in the case of
the knowledge that 'Hesperus' stands for Hesperus which I claimed
would suffice, in the context of other knowledge not directly involving
the name, for understanding the name, that it did not crumble into
mere knowledge that the sentence ' "Hesperus" stands for Hesperus'
expresses a truth. Why not say, then, that those remarks constitute (for
that case) something meeting Dummett's demand that we specify not
merely what would be known in the hypothetical state of knowledge,
but also what knowing it would consist in? What is counted as constituting a manifestation in linguistic behaviour of the hypothetical state
of knowledge (or, better, of the capacity with the name for which it is
claimed that that knowledge, in its context, would suffice) is, according
to that suggestion, something like this: whatever behaviour would manifest an ability to use the name, or respond intelligently to uses of it, in
speech-acts construable as being about the planet; more specifically,
speech-acts in stating whose content we can use the name which appears
on the right-hand side of the relevant clause, in a way appropriately tied
to the occurrence, in the utterance being interpreted, of the name mentioned on the left-hand side of the relevant clause.

If we give that sort of description, or purported description, of a
component of the articulated practical capacity which, according to a
theory of a language, constitutes mastery of it, we make essential appeal
to the interpretation of the language afforded by the theory itself. The
manoeuvre preserves modesty, in the sense outlined above; no one
could employ the suggested account, in order to ascertain from someone's behaviour whether he had the relevant ability, without being able
to understand sentences like 'This man is engaging in behaviour construable as his saying that Hesperus is visible above the elm tree' — that is,
without himself already being able to understand 'Hesperus'.

Now Dummett's exposition of the notion of modesty amalgamates
two notions: first, the notion of a theory which, as above, refuses to
make itself intelligible except to someone who already understands the
expressions it deals with (or others with the same sense); second, the
notion of a theory which refuses to say what would count as a manifestation of the individual component abilities into which it purports to
segment the ability to speak the language — that is, refuses to say not

only what would be known, in the knowledge of a structured theory which, it is claimed, would suffice for understanding the language, but also what the ability corresponding to each piece of this hypothetical knowledge would consist in.[36] Thus, on pain of the notion of modesty falling apart, those purported specifications of component abilities suggested above, since they preserve modesty in the sense of the first component notion, must not be allowed to count as other than modest in the sense of the second. They are debarred, then, from being accepted as effecting a genuine segmentation of the ability to speak a language. Dummett equates refusal to say what the knowledge in question would consist in, as well as what would be known – modesty in the sense of the second component notion – with repudiation of the concept of sense.[37] Thus the amalgamation reflects the position mentioned at the beginning of this section: that is, that a theory which is ineradicably modest in the sense of the first component notion cannot but repudiate the concept of sense.

Why are those theory-presupposing specifications not allowed to count? Since they are not even contemplated, Dummett's lecture contains no explicit answer. It is easy to guess, however, that they do not occur to him, even as candidates to be ruled out, because he assumes that the acceptability of the demand to say what the knowledge would consist in is the acceptability of a demand for a reduction. The idea is that a genuine segmentation of the ability to speak a language would segment it into component abilities describable, as nearly as possible, in purely behavioural terms. And the theory-presupposing specifications refuse to attempt any such reduction.[38]

Why, though, should reduction be either necessary or desirable? It is extraordinary that a reductive construal of the demand that one say what the states of knowledge in question would consist in should seem so obvious as not to need explicit acknowledgement, let alone defence.

Dummett's lecture is shot through with intimations of an idea which would make that intelligible: namely the idea that a theory of a language ought to be such that we could picture implicit knowledge of it as guiding competent linguistic behaviour.[39] Obviously a theory could not perform that service if understanding the theory required an exercise of the very ability it was to guide. If a theory is to guide speech it must generate instructions for doing things with sentences, intelligible independently of understanding those sentences. That would make congenial the search for a theory which – to illustrate with a simple case – might, in the case of a sentence combining a name with an unstructured predicate, generate instructions on this pattern: 'First find the object (if any) which is thus and so. Then apply such and such tests to it. If the outcome is thus and so, adopt a preparedness to volunteer the sentence or utter "Yes" on hearing it.'[40] A theory which systematically generated such instructions, on the basis of structure within sentences, would presumably be compelled to handle names by means of clauses which specified ways of identifying or recognizing objects; thus richness (in the sense of section V), as opposed to austerity, is the shape which immodesty takes in the case of names.

If pressed to its extreme, the idea from which that line of thought begins — the idea that a theory of a language ought to be such that we could picture implicit knowledge of it as guiding competent linguistic behaviour — leads to the incoherent notion of a theory which cannot be stated in any language.[41] Coherence might be preserved by demanding no more than an approximation, as close as may be, to the impossible ideal of a theory we could state to a person in order to teach him to talk. But in any case the idea which underlies these aspirations — the idea that linguistic behaviour is guided by implicit knowledge — is nothing but a version of the psychologism which Frege denounced and which Dummett officially disclaims.

If we try to preserve everything Frege said about sense, we characterize a position with an internal tension. On the one hand, there is Frege's anti-psychologism, which in Wittgenstein's hands transforms itself into a coherent and satisfying view of the mind's place in reality, stably intermediate between the crass extremes of behaviourism and a psychologism which is objectionable not because it is mentalistic but because it is pseudo-scientific. On the other hand, there is the idea that a theory of sense would be rich or immodest. My claim is that the latter idea can only be justified on the basis of vestiges of the psychologism rejected in the first component. If I am right, something has to be repudiated. It is a terminological issue whether 'sense' belongs with the second component; but fairness to Frege seems to justify trying to find a place for his terminology in a position purged of those elements which can only be grounded in hidden psychologism. Modesty in our demands on a theory of meaning is, in this view, not a repudiation of Frege's notion but an insistence on the feature which makes it an effort at something truly great; immodesty is not a vindication of Frege but a betrayal.[42]

XI

An adherent of a causal theory of names need not, in the interests of his theory, be unsympathetic to what I have said so far. His concern would be, not to enrich the right-hand sides of those specifications of denotation which I have been considering, but to say something substantial about the relation.[43]

Deduction within a truth-theory moves from axioms which assign semantic properties to sentence-constituents (for instance, denoting some specified thing), by way of clauses dealing with modes of combination, to theorems which assign truth-conditions to sentences. That is what warrants the claim that such a theory displays the sense of a sentence-constituent as, in Frege's metaphor, its contribution to the truth-conditions of sentences in which it occurs. The deductive direction can make it seem that the whole structure floats unsupported unless the nature of the semantic properties and relations from which the derivations start is independently explained. Thus it can seem that we need a general account of what it is for a name to denote something, conceptually prior to the truth-theory itself, from which the truth-theory's assignments of denotation to names can be seen as derivable, and in terms of which, consequently, they can be seen as explained. A causal analysis of the relation between a name and its bearer might seem well suited to meet that apparent need.[44]

But the need is only apparent. It is not true that we condemn a truth-theory to floating in a void, if we reject the alleged obligation to fasten it directly to the causal realities of language-use by way of its axioms. On my account, those truth-theories that can serve as theories of sense are already anchored to the facts of language-use at the level of their theorems: the anchoring being effected by the requirement that assignments of truth-conditions are to be usable in specifications of content of intelligible speech-acts. Since the theorems must be derivable within the theory, the requirement bears indirectly on the theory's deductive apparatus, including assignments of denotation; and the deductive apparatus needs no attachment to the extra-theoretical facts over and above what that affords. Thus we can acquire such understanding as we need of the deductive apparatus (in particular, of the denoting relation) by reversing the theory's deductive direction, starting from our understanding of the requirement of serviceability in interpretation imposed on its consequences. We grasp what it is for a name to denote something by grasping the role played by the statement that it does in derivations of acceptable assignments of truth-conditions to sentences – assignments, that is, which would pull their weight in making sense of speakers of the language we are concerned with.[45]

According to Frege, it is only in the context of a sentence that a word has meaning.[46] What he meant was that we should not look for accounts of the meaning of particular words except in terms of their contributions to the meanings of sentences. But it seems in the spirit of his slogan to suggest also, as above, that we should not look for accounts of the sorts of meaning possessed by words of general kinds – for instance, an account of denotation, as possessed by names – except in terms of the contributions made by words of those kinds to the meanings of sentences.

To reject the quest for a causal analysis of denotation, conceived as prior to interpreting a language by constructing a truth-theory, is not to deny the relevance of causal relations in determining what a name

John McDowell

denotes. In fact causal relations will be involved in any adequate elaboration of the requirement imposed on a theory's consequences. To illustrate: suppose a candidate theory of a language would have us describe a certain speaker as saying that p, where we imagine 'p' replaced by a sentence which mentions a particular concrete object. Can we make sense of his saying that p? Standardly, we make sense of sayings as expressing the corresponding belief. And ascription of the belief that p to our speaker is constrained by a principle on the following lines: one cannot intelligibly regard a person as having a belief about a particular concrete object if one cannot see him as having been exposed to the causal influence of that object, in ways suitable for the acquisition of information (or misinformation) about it.[47] Such principles, operating in that ascription of propositional attitudes which we need to go in for in order to make sense of linguistic behaviour, make causation crucial in the determination of what at least some names denote.

There is, however, not the slightest reason to expect that one could construct, out of such materials, a general relational formula true of every name and its bearer. And even if a formula with the right extension could be constructed out of these materials, it would not constitute that prior fixed point of suspension for a truth-theory which was dreamed of in the argument sketched at the beginning of this section. The ultimate justification for an assignment of denotation would be, not some causal relation between an object and utterances of the name, accessible independently of interpreting the language, but — as ever — the acceptability of interpretations which that assignment helps to confer on whole sentences.

Saul Kripke, who is often described as a proponent of a causal theory of denotation for names, in fact expressed the suspicion that any substantial theory of names — like any philosophical theory — is most likely to be wrong.[48] I think Kripke's suspicion was well placed. In this paper I hope to have indicated how we might find that situation possible to live with.

Notes

1 See Donald Davidson, 'Radical Interpretation', *Dialectica*, vol. xxvii (1973), p. 313.
2 G. Frege, *The Basic Laws of Arithmetic: Exposition of the System*, translated and edited by Montgomery Furth (Berkeley and Los Angeles, University of California Press, 1967), pp. 89–90.
3 See 'On Sense and Reference', in Peter Geach and Max Black, *Translations from the Philosophical Writings of Gottlob Frege* (Oxford,

Blackwell, 1952). The sense of a sentence determines, or is, the thought expressed (p. 62); it would be specified in a 'that' clause (see the remark about reported speech, p. 59).

4   See Donald Davidson, 'Truth and Meaning', *Synthèse*, vol. xvii (1967), at pp. 310–11.

5   See the Introduction to Gareth Evans and John McDowell, eds, *Truth and Meaning* (Oxford, Clarendon Press, 1976), pp. xv–xvii.

6   Smoothness in treatment of predicates (whose argument-places can be filled with variables as well as names) dictates, rather, the statement that each of a certain set of functions from singular terms (definite or indefinite) to objects assigns Hesperus to 'Hesperus'; but it comes to the same thing.

7   Notwithstanding Michael Dummett's assertion that Frege had two other uses of '*Bedeutung*' as well (Frege, *Philosophy of Language* (London, Duckworth, 1973), pp. 93–4). Casual occurrences of that ordinary German word should carry no weight against the intention which is plain in Frege's official exposition of the doctrine.

8   I am not suggesting that Frege attained this perspective himself.

9   See 'On Sense and Reference', pp. 56–7.

10 Michael Dummett alludes to an earlier version of this paper, in 'What is a Theory of Meaning?' (in Samuel Guttenplan, ed., *Mind and Language* (Oxford, Clarendon Press, 1975)), at p. 122. This paragraph should make it clear that he has indeed misinterpreted me, as he conjectures (in his Appendix) at p. 126.

11 What about a theory which used both names, but interchanged them? The inadequacy of this will emerge in Section IX.

12 Dummett, *Frege*, pp. 95ff. Whether the way of identifying is expressible in words or not seems unimportant, *pace* Dummett, who makes much of the fact that it need not be so expressible, as against those who attack Frege as a description theorist. The profound unsatisfactoriness of treating the sense of a name as essentially descriptive (see section VIII below) is not cured by allowing that there need be no explicitly descriptive *expression* which expresses that sense.

13 Dummett, *Frege*, pp. 92–3.

14 Neural, not psychological machinery: cf. Dummett's revealing misconception, 'What is a Theory of Meaning?', p. 122. I mean to be denying what Dummett (*Frege*, pp. 102–3) thinks uncontroversial, namely that a speaker always has 'a route that he uses' for getting from a name to its bearer.

15 For a clear statement, see Dummett, 'What is a Theory of Meaning? (II)', in Evans and McDowell, *Truth and Meaning*, at p. 70.

16 See, e.g. Christina Graves and others, 'Tacit Knowledge', *Journal of Philosophy*, vol. lxx (1973), p. 318.

17 The points of Thomas Nagel, 'The Boundaries of Inner Space', *Journal of Philosophy*, vol. lxvi (1969), p. 452, and Stephen P. Stich, 'What Every Speaker Knows', *Philosophical Review*, vol. lxxx (1971), p. 476, have not been adequately answered.

18 Self-styled Cartesians in modern linguistics are in this respect notably unfaithful to Descartes himself.

163

19 'On Sense and Reference', p. 57.

20 There is also the wish (not satisfied in the austere conception) that differences in sense should not reflect but explain failures of substitution: see the last paragraph of section IX.

21 See Dummett, 'What is a Theory of Meaning?', pp. 106-7.

22 See 'On Sense and Reference', pp. 62-3; especially (p. 63) the remark that the thought expressed by the sentence 'Odysseus was set ashore at Ithaca while sound asleep' 'remains the same whether "Odysseus" has reference or not'.

23 That is, describable by way of a transparent, or relational, attribution of belief: see, for instance, W. V. Quine, *Word and Object* (Cambridge, Mass., MIT Press, 1960), pp. 141-56. Of course that does not stop it being describable by way of an opaque belief-attribution too. Note that there is no withdrawing here from the position outlined in section IV. From 'He is expressing a belief that Hesperus is visible above the elm tree' (an opaque attribution) one can, according to the principle stated in the text, move to the transparent 'He is expressing a belief, concerning Hesperus, that it is visible above the elm tree'. From there, since Hesperus is Phosphorus, one can get to 'He is expressing a belief, concerning Phosphorus, that it is visible above the elm tree'. But there is no route back from there to the opaque 'He is expressing a belief that Phosphorus is visible above the elm tree'.

24 Frege's difficulties over truth-value gaps (see Dummett, *Frege*, chapter 12) reflect the pressure he is under, in consequence of his wish to see denoting as a genuine relation between expressions and objects, towards accepting the view of this paragraph.

25 I owe the formulation in terms of intrinsic and extrinsic characterizations to Brian Loar.

26 L. Wittgenstein, *Philosophical Investigations* (Oxford, Blackwell, 1953), p. 217.

27 Ironically, Wittgenstein's dismantling of the conception of mind deplored here — that which underlies the Fregean idea that the sense of a name is indifferent to the existence of a bearer for it — can be seen as carrying Frege's hostility towards mechanistic psychologism to its extreme (and satisfactory) conclusion.

28 Names of fictional characters are another thing again, not discussed in this paper.

29 This completes an example of Frege's (from a letter: Dummett, *Frege*, p. 97).

30 This is meant to be only the crudest sketch of the sort of consideration that counts.

31 Dummett's discussion of this matter (at p. 123 of 'What is a Theory of Meaning?') seems to me to be vitiated by a non-explicit adherence to the essentially psychologistic idea that mastery of a language is possession of a recipe which guides linguistic behaviour.

32 Simon Blackburn made me see this.

33 Dummett's formulation in terms of concepts (p. 101) may suggest that only general terms are in question, but that is not his intention.

34 In the Appendix, which (among other things) relates the arguments of the lecture (not originally couched in Fregean terminology) to Frege: see especially pp. 126–8.

35 I regard what follows as a minimal defence of my continuing to attempt to locate myself in a place which Dummett thinks he has shown non-existent. His subtle and powerful argument needs much more discussion.

36 Note, in 'What is a Theory of Meaning?' on p. 101, the oscillation between explanation of concepts and explanation of what it is to have concepts.

37 See n. 34.

38 That this is how the demand for segmentation is understood emerges, I believe, from Dummett's employment of it to make difficulties for realist (truth-conditions) theories of meaning: see 'What is a Theory of Meaning? (II)', *passim*, and cf. *Frege*, p. 467. 'As nearly as possible' is meant to allow, as Dummett does, for the employment of concepts like that of assent (see 'What is a Theory of Meaning? (II)', p. 80).

39 He speaks throughout of theories of meaning as being *used to obtain* understanding of a language (e.g. p. 114). Note also his talk of 'the undoubted fact that a process of derivation of some kind is involved in the understanding of a sentence' (p. 112). See also n. 31 above.

40 Another part of the theory of a language (the theory of force) is needed to get one from this sort of thing to an ability actually to engage in conversation: see 'What is a Theory of Meaning? (II)', e.g. at pp. 72–4. It is clear that such a theory, on this conception, will have a great deal of work to do.

41 See, What is a Theory of Meaning?', pp. 103–4, where Dummett comes close to imposing the incoherent requirement on those full-blooded theories of meaning which he recommends.

42 I hope it is clear that I want no truck with the theory devised by Dummett in his Appendix under the title of 'holism'. That theory is an attempt (wholly unconvincing, as Dummett rightly says) to meet the reductionist demand which I reject. The topic of holism is too difficult (and confused) to be dealt with *ambulando* in this paper.

43 *Pace* (apparently) Dummett, 'What is a Theory of Meaning?', p. 125.

44 Cf. Hartry Field, 'Tarski's Theory of Truth', *Journal of Philosophy*, vol. lxix (1972), p. 347; reprinted in this volume as ch. 5.

45 Cf. Davidson, 'In Defense of Convention T', in H. Leblanc, ed., *Truth, Syntax and Modality* (Amsterdam, North-Holland, 1973), especially p. 84.

46 G. Frege, *The Foundations of Arithmetic*, translated by J. L. Austin (Oxford, Blackwell, 1953), p. 73.

47 See Gareth Evans, 'The Causal Theory of Names', *Aristotelian Society Supplementary Volume*, vol. xlvii (1973), at pp. 197–200.

48 See 'Naming and Necessity', in Donald Davidson and Gilbert

singular terms pays well-known dividends but fails to account for natural language as it is actually used. Frege's stipulation that intuitively non-denoting singular terms denote the null set forces one to formalize certain negated existence statements in syntactically unnatural ways. Moreover, by thus 'identifying' all non-denoting singular terms, the theory counts sentences like 'Pegasus is the smallest unicorn' true. Although some analytical enterprises can perhaps overlook such results, an account of truth in natural languages cannot.

In the last decade or so, a number of free logics have been developed to account for, rather than do away with, non-denoting singular terms (cf. [10], [21], [13], [14], [11], [20], [23], [19], [15], [8]). These logics seem to me to be on the right track. But there has been little agreement over precisely which inferences such logics should validate or block. The restriction on existential generalization and universal instantiation which is common to all free logics has frequently been justified by reference to various purportedly true singular sentences, like 'Pegasus is winged', from which one cannot existentially generalize. Literally taken, these sentences are, I think, untrue. In so far as they are counted true, they are best seen as involving an implicit intensional context: '(A well-known myth has it that) Pegasus is winged.' The strategy is an extension of Frege's approach to apparent failures of substitution. In our sample sentence (regarded as true), we cannot substitute for 'Pegasus' other singular terms which do not differ in denotation ('the tallest unicorn'), and still preserve truth. So we regard the context as oblique.

One might object that different 'non-existents' are denoted by these singular terms in *all* their occurrences. But as regards the intended interpretation of non-denoting singular terms, this way of speaking is, I think, misleading. Currently, the temptation to speak this way seems to arise only in the face of sentences which are easily seen to be related to one of the standard sorts of intensional contexts (indirect discourse, subjunctives, psychological contexts). The point is clear in our example. When native speakers are asked whether 'Pegasus is winged' is true, they rely on common knowledge and contextual clues to determine what the questioner intends. It is now common knowledge among people who use 'Pegasus' in the relevant contexts that the name is part of, and is meant to be related to, a mythical story. The prefix to the sentence that we supplied above will generally be accepted as producing a paraphrase. But if asked whether the myth itself is true — whether it is a matter of fact (rather than a matter of fiction) that Pegasus is winged — native speakers will reply that the sentence is not literally or 'factually' true. And they will justify this by saying that Pegasus does not exist, 'except in the myth.' I take this behavior as evidence for embedding the sentence in an intensional context when it is regarded as true. Non-denoting singular terms simply do not have anything as their 'ordinary' (non-oblique) denotation. It is just that the oblique reference of some singular terms is the reference they most often have in their everyday uses. Talk of 'non-existents' in contexts like the above can perhaps be assimilated to the strategy of finding the oblique reference for singular terms in intensional contexts.[2]

Implementing the strategy and providing an account of oblique contexts, is, of course, beyond our present purpose. It is enough to note here that the motivation for free logic may be regarded as independent of issues about apparent substitution failures of singular terms. Consider the sentence '$(x)(x = x)$' from identity theory. By universal instantiation, we derive 'Pegasus = Pegasus;' and by existential generalization we arrive at '$(\exists y)(y = \text{Pegasus})$,' which is clearly false. Unless we regress to Russell or Frege, we must either alter identity theory or restrict the operations of instantiation and generalization. Experimentation with the latter two alternatives indicates that the restriction strategy is simpler and more intuitive.

II A sketch of a theory of singular terms

We now characterize a logic underlying a formalized metalanguage *ML* and a theory of truth couched in that language for the sentences of a natural object-language *OL*. The grammar of *ML* is that of first-order quantification theory with predicate constants, identity, function signs, and the definite-description operator. The logical axioms and rules underlying *ML* are as follows:

(A1) If A is a tautology, $\vdash A$.

(A2) $\vdash (x)(A \to B) \to ((x)A \to (x)B)$.

(A3) $\vdash (x)(x = x)$.

(A4) $\vdash t_1 = t_2 \to (A(x/t_1) \leftrightarrow A(x/t_2))$.

(A5) $\vdash (x)A \ \& \ (\exists y)(y = t) \to A(x/t)$.

(A6) $\vdash (x)(x = (\imath y)A \leftrightarrow (y)(A \leftrightarrow y = x))$, where variable $x \neq$ variable y, and x is not free in A.

(A7) $\vdash (x)(\exists y)(x = y)$.

(A8) $\vdash (x)(x = t_1 \leftrightarrow x = t_2) \to (A(y/t_1) \leftrightarrow A(y/t_2))$, where x is not free in t_1 or t_2.

(A9) $\vdash At_1 \ldots t_n \to (\exists y_1)(y_1 = t_1) \ \& \ldots \& \ (\exists y_n)(y_n = t_n)$, where A is any atomic predicate, including identity, and where y_i is not free in t_i.

(A10) $\vdash (\exists y)(y = f(t_1, \ldots, t_n)) \to (\exists y_1)(y_1 = t_1) \ \& \ldots \& \ (\exists y_n)(y_n = t_n)$, where y is not free in $t_1, \ldots, t_n$, and y_i is not free in t_i.

(R1) If $\vdash A$ and $\vdash A \to B$, then $\vdash B$.

(R2) If $\vdash A \to B$, then $\vdash A \to (x)B$, where x is not free in A.

'*A*' and '*B*' range over well-formed formulas of *ML*; '*t*,' '*t*₁,' . . . , '*t*ₙ,' over terms (including variables); and '*x*,' '*y*,' '*y*₁,' . . . , '*y*ₙ,' over variables. '$A(x/t_1)$' signifies the result of substituting t_1 for all occurrences of x in A, rewriting bound variables where necessary.

Axioms (A3), (A5), and (A8) are non-independent. (For the details, see [1].) They are included for the sake of clarifying our motivation. Alternatively, one might take (A3), (A4), and (A5) as non-independent and the others as primitive, adding the symmetry and transitivity axioms of identity. The value of this formulation is that it focuses on (A8) instead of (A4). As will be seen, (A8) constitutes the main principle of interchange in the system.

The logic of *ML* is nearly classical. If (A7) were changed to '$(\exists y)(x = y)$,' and if singular terms other than variables were excluded from the language, the logic would revert to classical quantification theory with identity. The chief motivation for (A7) is that, unlike '$(\exists y)(x = y)$,' it allows some of the free variables (like some of the other terms) to be uninterpreted. 'Non-denoting' free variables are useful in representing sentence utterances which involve failure of reference with demonstrative constructions.[3]

Axiom (A9) differentiates the syntax of *ML* from that of Scott [20]. It expresses a deep and widely held intuition that the truth of simple singular sentences (other than those implicitly embedded in intensional contexts) is contingent on the contained singular terms' having a denotation.[4] The pre-theoretic notion seems to be that true predications at the most basic level express comments on topics, or attributions of properties or relations to objects: lacking a topic or object, basic predications cannot be true. Given that *ML* is bivalent, simple singular predications containing non-denoting terms are counted false, and negations of such sentences are true. ('Pegasus is an animal' is false. 'It is not the case that Pegasus is an animal' is true.) Within *ML*, logical operations such as negation should be intuitively seen as working on simpler sentences as wholes, not as forming complex comments on purported topics or complex attributions to purported objects. This remark would admit of exceptions if we were to provide for singular terms with wide scope ('Pegasus is such that he is not an animal').[5] Then negation operates on an open sentence rather than on a closed one. Non-denoting singular terms with wide scope should cause the sentences they govern, no matter how complex, to be untrue.

Axiom (A9) rests weight on the notion of atomic predicate. As just indicated, I think that the weight has intuitive support, support associated with semantical intuitions about truth and with the pre-theoretic notions of property and relation. The axiom should be regarded as a methodological condition on investigations of predication in natural language: count an expression an atomic predicate in natural language only if one is prepared to count simple singular sentences containing it untrue whenever they also contain non-denoting singular terms.[6] Scott's and Lambert's systems show that it is possible to arrange a logically coherent language with atomic predicates that violate our condition. But it is another question whether such predicates have natural-language readings that are best construed as having the logical form of atomic predicates. In numerous cases, intuition backs our condition; the present proposal is that the condition should be used to guide intuition. Needless to say, it must be judged by the quality of its guidance.

Axiom (A9) enables us to derive the Russell equivalence

$$B(\imath x)Ax \leftrightarrow (\exists y) ((z) (Az \leftrightarrow z = y) \,\&\, By)$$

where B is atomic. (This latter restriction amounts to the proviso that the iota operator always takes smallest scope; cf. note 5.) The present system thus captures Russell's intuitions without using his means of doing so. Whereas we agree with Russell about truth conditions, we disagree with him about logical form. Rather than regarding singular terms on the model of abbreviations for *other* language forms, we take them as primitive in natural language and in formal languages whose purposes include representing natural language. Consequently, rather than give a semantical analysis for singular terms only indirectly, as Russell did, via a semantical analysis for the grammar of quantification theory with identity, we do so directly (cf. Kaplan [12]).

It is worth remarking that in languages where some singular terms fail to denote, (A9) is inconsistent with $\ulcorner t = t \urcorner$. Since some free logics have included this principle, (A9) will be discussed at greater length in section IV.

Axiom (A10) complements (A9): If n-ary function signs are to be regarded as potentially explicable in terms of $(n + 1)$-ary predicates in the usual way, then where function signs are given primitive status (as they are here), (A10) must be added if (A9) is. Axiom (A10) is Fregean in motivation. The value of a function was, on his view, the result of completing the function with an argument — where 'argument' is understood to apply to objects rather than to substituted linguistic items (terms) (cf. [5], 24–5; [7], 33–4, 84).

The model theory for the logic is straightforward. The domain may be empty. Under each interpretation, all sentences are either true or false. Variables, function signs, and complex singular terms are defined by the interpretation function, if at all, on the domain. Only values identical and within the domain satisfy the identity predicate. The clauses for other atomic predicates are as usual. Completeness is provable (for details, see [1]).

We turn now to a theory of truth in *ML* for a natural object-language (or, better, a canonical reading of a natural object-language) *OL*. We assume that *ML* has resources capable of describing the syntax of *OL*. Further, we assume a general correspondence between the vocabulary

Tyler Burge

of *OL* and a sub-vocabulary of *ML*. This correspondence may be understood in terms of inclusion or in terms of translation. Details of such a translation relation conceived generally are, of course, difficult to state and well beyond the scope of this paper.

I shall first indicate the postulates of the theory of truth and then explain how to read the indications:

(T1) $\vdash (\exists\alpha)\,(v)\,(\exists x)\,(\alpha(v) = x\,)))$.

(T2) $\vdash (\alpha)\,(v)\,(x)\,(\exists\beta)\,(\alpha \underset{x}{\overset{v}{\approx}} \beta)$.

(T3) For each atomic function sign $\bar{f}_j^{\,n}$,

$\vdash (x)\,(x = \alpha(\bar{f}_j^{\,n}(\bar{t}_1, \ldots, \bar{t}_n)) \leftrightarrow x = f_j^{\,n}(\alpha(\bar{t}_1), \ldots, \alpha(\bar{t}_n)))$.

(T4) $\vdash (x)\,(x = \alpha(iota(v, \bar{A})) \leftrightarrow x = (\imath y)\,((\exists\gamma)\,(\alpha \underset{y}{\overset{v}{\approx}} \gamma \;\&\; \gamma \text{ satisfies } \bar{A})))$.

(T5) For each atomic predicate $\bar{A}_j^{\,n}$,

$\vdash \alpha \text{ satisfies } \bar{A}_j^{\,n}(\bar{t}_1, \ldots, \bar{t}_n) \leftrightarrow A_j^{\,n}(\alpha(\bar{t}_1), \ldots, \alpha(\bar{t}_n))$.

(T6) $\vdash \alpha \text{ satisfies } nega\,(\bar{A}) \leftrightarrow \neg(\alpha \text{ satisfies } \bar{A})$.

(T7) $\vdash \alpha \text{ satisfies } condit\,(\bar{A}, \bar{B}) \leftrightarrow (\alpha \text{ satisfies } \bar{A} \rightarrow \alpha \text{ satisfies } \bar{B})$.

(T8) $\vdash \alpha \text{ satisfies } unquant\,(v, \bar{A}) \leftrightarrow (\beta)\,(x)\,(\alpha \underset{x}{\overset{v}{\approx}} \beta \rightarrow \beta \text{ satisfies } \bar{A})$.

Greek letters 'α,' 'β,' and 'γ' vary over sequences. '$\alpha(v)$' is written for 'the assignment of α to v;' analogously for other uses of 'α' in function-sign position. 'v' ranges over variables of *OL*; '$\bar{A}$' and '$\bar{B}$,' over wffs; and '$\bar{t}_1$,' . . . , '$\bar{t}_n$,' over terms. '$\alpha \underset{x}{\overset{v}{\approx}} \beta$' is read '$\beta$ agrees with α in all assignments except that it assigns x to v.' Schematically, we use '$\bar{A}_j^{\,n}$' as a name of an *OL* predicate which translates into *ML* as '$A_j^{\,n}$'; analogously for the schematic function-sign name '$\bar{f}_j^{\,n}$.' '$\bar{A}_j^{\,n}\,(\bar{t}_1, \ldots, \bar{t}_n)$' is read, 'the result of applying the predicate $\bar{A}_j^{\,n}$ to any singular terms $\bar{t}_1, \ldots, \bar{t}_n$ in the n-place predicative way.' Functional application is analogous. The operation sign '*nega*' is read 'the negation of.' The readings of the other signs will be obvious. The various styles of variables can be eliminated in favor of a single-sorted, first-order quantification theory.

We omit the usual relativization of the quantifiers to the domain of *OL*. If we were attempting an *explicit* definition of truth for *OL*, this omission would lead to inconsistency. But since we are content with a finitely axiomatized recursive characterization of truth, the omission may be tolerated. The dividend is that we may intuitively think of the quantifiers of *OL* (a fragment of our natural language) as ranging over all that there is.

The material adequacy of the theory is shown by proving that $\vdash Tr(\bar{A}) \leftrightarrow A$, for all closed wffs $\bar{A}$ of *OL*, where $Tr(\bar{A}) =_{df} (\alpha)\,(\alpha$ satisfies $\bar{A})$. (Intuitively, '*Tr*' is the truth predicate for *OL*.)[7] The proof of adequacy is reasonably straightforward and can be largely ignored here (for details, see [1]). What is important for our purpose is the treatment of singular terms.

An aim of the proof is to derive biconditionals like:

(1) α satisfies $\overline{\text{Is-a-number}}$ $\overline{(\text{the successor of} (\overline{\text{the successor of} (\bar{0})}))}$
$\leftrightarrow$ the successor of (the successor of (0)) is a number.

If all singular terms denoted something, the steps would be quite ordinary. We would begin by deriving:

(2) $\alpha \, \overline{(\text{the successor of} (\overline{\text{the successor of} (\bar{0})}))}$
$= $ the successor of (the successor of (0)).

(The assignment of every sequence α to 'the successor of the successor of 0' is the successor of the successor of 0.) Then we would obtain (1) by using Leibniz's law and (2) to substitute on the right side of this instance of axiom schema (T5):

(T5a) α satisfies $\overline{\text{Is-a-number}}$ $\overline{(\text{the successor of} (\overline{\text{the successor of} (\bar{0})}))}$

$\leftrightarrow \alpha \, \overline{(\text{the successor of} (\overline{\text{the successor of} (\bar{0})}))}$ is a number.

The derivation of (2) would utilize an axiom for '0' (taken as a 0-place function sign):

(3) $\alpha(\bar{0}) = 0$.

(The assignment of every sequence α to '0' is 0.) And it would utilize an axiom for 'the successor of':

(4) $\alpha \, \overline{(\text{the successor of} (\bar{t}))} = $ the successor of $(\alpha(\bar{t}))$.

(The assignment of every sequence α to the result of applying 'the successor of' to any term $\bar{t}$ is the successor of the assignment of α to $\bar{t}$.) These two axioms together with Leibniz's law would suffice to derive (2) and thence (1).

But since some singular terms do not have a denotation (or a sequence assignment), we cannot follow this route. For the use of axioms like (3) and (4) would undermine the truth of the semantical theory in the metalanguage. Axiom (4) is false because, say, 'the successor of $\alpha \, \overline{(\text{the Moon})}$' is improper (since there is no successor of the Moon). Though (3) is probably true, other axioms relevantly like it are not. Thus

(5) the assignment of every sequence α to 'Pegasus' = Pegasus

is intuitively untrue because the terms on both sides of '=' are improper.

Axioms of the form of (T3) and (T4) circumvent this problem. For example, we have instead of (5):

(T3a) $(x) (x = \alpha \, \overline{(\text{Pegasus})} \leftrightarrow x = \text{Pegasus})$.

This axiom is true despite the fact that there are non-denoting singular terms in it. Instead of (4), we have

(T3b) (x) $(x = \alpha$ $(\overline{\text{the successor of }} (\bar{t})) \leftrightarrow x$ = the successor of $\alpha(\bar{t})))$.

Whereas in the case of (3) and (4) we could rely on Leibniz's law to make the substitutions needed to prove sentences like (1), that law is not strong enough to make recursive transformations using (T3a) and (T3b). This is where (A8) is required. It enables us to substitute *different* non-denoting singular terms (e.g., 'Pegasus' and '$\alpha(\overline{\text{Pegasus}})$') without relying on false identities like (4) or (5).

III   Criticism of other accounts

I make no claims of final acceptability for the account set out in the previous section. But I shall put it to normative use in judging other accounts. Roughly speaking, my view is that the published accounts with relatively strong logical axioms yield falsehoods, and that accounts with relatively weak axioms cannot justify substitution of the relevant non-denoting singular terms in the adequacy proof of a truth theory.[8]

The description theories which, I think, are most interesting from a semantical viewpoint are those of Scott [20]; Lambert [13], [23] (*FD2*); and Grandy [8]. Given uncontroversial empirical assumptions, each of these logics implies sentences which are uncontroversially untrue under their intended interpretation. Thus, Lambert uses the axiom $\ulcorner (x)(x \neq t_1 \ \& \ x \neq t_2) \rightarrow t_1 = t_2 \urcorner$, and Scott invokes $\ulcorner -(\exists y)(y = t) \rightarrow t = * \urcorner$, where '*' is a constant denoting an object outside the domain of the object-language. Since it is not the case that either the present King of France or the only unicorn on the moon exists, we derive from each axiom

> (6)   The present King of France is identical with the only unicorn on the moon.

Grandy, who takes these intuitive difficulties with the Lambert and Scott systems seriously, employs in his truth theory two axiom schemas (numbered 'T3' and 'T4') which have untrue instances.[9] For example, they yield the instances:

> (7)   What any sequence α assigns to 'the successor of the Moon' is identical with the successor of what α assigns to 'the Moon.'

> (8)   What any sequence α assigns to 'der Vater von Pegasus' is identical with the father of what α assigns to 'Pegasus.'

> (9)   What any sequence α assigns to 'the only unicorn on the Moon' is identical with the unique object assigned to the variable v by some sequence β which satisfies 'is a unicorn on the moon.'

Sentence (8) is untrue because there is no father of what every sequence α assigns to 'Pegasus,' there is no assignment by α to 'Pegasus,' and there is nothing which α assigns to 'der Vater von Pegasus.' Analogously for (7) and (9). To give another, slightly oversimplified, example, we can derive in Grandy's truth theory:

(10) The present King of France is the denotation of 'The present King of France.'

and

(11) The father of Pegasus is the denotation of some expression.

I think (10) and (11) are uncontroversially untrue on intuitive grounds. Intuitively, they do not differ in truth value from (6) or

(12) The present King of France is bald.

It should be emphasized that the standard defense of consequences like (6) and (7)–(12) (which I think is doubtful in any case) is clearly inappropriate in the present context. It is not sufficient to say that such sentences are unimportant to most cognitive sciences and that a smoother theory is obtained by counting them true. For from the present viewpoint – that of a semantical theory which takes native intuitions as part of its evidence – sentences like the above are not unimportant. And as ordinarily intended, they are untrue. Nor is it evident that significant differences in smoothness of theory are at issue.

The logical principles which lead to untrue conclusions should not be dismissed without taking account of their purpose. Scott notes as reason for 'identifying' all non-denoting singular terms the resulting ability to derive the following principle of extensionality:

(13) $(x)(A \leftrightarrow B) \to (\imath x)A = (\imath x)B.$

Together with Leibniz's law, (13) provides substitutivity for non-denoting singular terms as well as for singular terms that denote. As we have seen in the previous section, the availability of substitutivity for different non-denoting singular terms is critical in the recursion steps of a theory of truth. But the logic of section II yields a principle which together with (A8) seems to justify all the reasonable substitutions which (13) and Leibniz's law justify, without leading to untrue sentences like (6), and without depending on axioms like (7)–(10) for their usefulness in a truth theory. This principle is

(14) $(x)(A \leftrightarrow B) \to (x)(x = (\imath x)A \leftrightarrow x = (\imath x)B).$

Several free logics which have been regarded as having the advantage of producing no untrue consequences are too weak to provide the substitutivity needed in a theory of truth. For example, Van Fraassen and Lambert's *FD* ([23] and [24]) and most of the very early proposals do not allow for substituting *any* two (different) non-denoting singular terms. Even slightly stronger logics (e.g., Lambert's *FD*1, [13]) do not appear capable of combining with true semantical axioms such as (T3) and (T4) to yield the needed substitutions. Of course, it is conceivable that one might find semantical axioms other than (T3) and (T4) which are intuitively true and yet strong enough to combine with relatively weak logics to derive the biconditionals, like (1), which are the touchstones of a truth theory. But the prospects for most of the published logics are, I think, dim.

IV Self-identity and existence

By translating each occurrence of '*' as '$(\imath x) (x \neq x)$' and each occurrence of $\ulcorner t_1 = t_2 \urcorner$ as $\ulcorner (z) (z = t_1 \leftrightarrow z = t_2) \urcorner$, we can prove that a sentence is a theorem of Scott's system if and only if its translation is a theorem of ours. By translating each occurrence of $At_1 \ldots t_n$ as $\ulcorner (\exists y) (y = t_1) \& \ldots \& (\exists y) (y = t_n) \& At_1 \ldots t_n \urcorner$ (where A is atomic), we can prove that a sentence is a theorem of our system if and only if its translation is a theorem of Scott's. (I ignore function signs since Scott's system does not contain them.)

The latter result serves simply to place in a different perspective the view of natural-language predication I urged in section II. The former result indicates that, from the viewpoint of our system, Scott's system is sound (truth-preserving) if and only if his $\ulcorner t_1 = t_2 \urcorner$ is read not as $\ulcorner t_1$ is identical with $t_2 \urcorner$, but as $\ulcorner$ anything is identical with t_1 iff it is identical with $t_2 \urcorner$. On our view, Scott's $\ulcorner t_1 = t_2 \urcorner$ says that t_1 and t_2 do not differ in denotation, not that their denotations are the same. In section III, I argued from the assumption that Scott's $\ulcorner t_1 = t_2 \urcorner$ was read $\ulcorner t_1$ is identical with $t_2 \urcorner$ to the conclusion that the system was unsound. What can be said for characterizing identity our way?

In the first place, our representation satisfies the minimum restrictions on any identity predicate — the logical laws of identity, (A3) and (A4). The fact that $\ulcorner x = x \urcorner$ is not valid in our system does not show that the self-reflexive law fails, since formulations of the law as $\ulcorner x = x \urcorner$ in classical systems presuppose that variable x always receives a value. That is, the law is standardly interpreted as (A3).

Analogous remarks apply to the Hilbert–Bernays method of simulating identity within a language (cf. Quine [16]: 230). In so far as the method has been regarded as relevant to understanding identity, it has been seen as a means of expressing indiscernibility of *objects* x and y from the viewpoint of the predicates of a given language. Our identity predicate is coextensive with the Hilbert–Bernays open sentence (for any given language) – it is true of just the same objects. If, however, non-denoting singular terms are attached to the identity predicate, one will get a falsehood, whereas if they are substituted into the Hilbert–Bernays open sentence, one will get a truth. Insisting on equivalence of the closed sentences (in addition to the above-mentioned coextensiveness) would commit one to holding that sentences like (6), (10) or (11) are true in the fragments of English that we have been discussing. I know of no good reason for such insistence. It cannot be justified by the claim that the Hilbert–Bernays open sentence *expresses* or *characterizes* identity (as opposed to merely simulating it by being coextensive with it within the given language). For such a claim is quite unintuitive: indiscernibility via a given stock of predicates just does not seem to give the intended interpretation of identity (cf. Quine [17]: 63).

The main ground for characterizing identity our way, of course, is intuitive. It avoids the unattractive results of the other systems and accords with those intuitions which are held generally. The intuitions of some, though by no means all, will be crossed by the fact that (A9) contradicts

(15) $t = t$

in a language containing non-denoting singular terms.[10] It would be easy to dismiss acceptance of (15) as the result of misguided applications of universal instantiation to (A3). But a deeper consideration of the matter is worthwhile.

Testing instances of (A9) and (15) on intuition does not resolve the question of which to take as valid. Whereas native speakers are clear and nearly unanimous in their rejection of sentences like (6), they react differently to sentences like

(16) The present King of France is identical with the present King of France.

Some find them clearly untrue. Others take them to be just as clearly acceptable. Hesitations (on both sides) can be elicited by further discussion. Negative reactions seem to become somewhat more widespread in the face of sentences like

(17) The only square circle is identical with the only square circle.

But on the whole, the evidence from intuition as to whether or not all instances of (15) are true is unclear. The decision must rest on more general considerations.

One reason for doubting the validity of (15) is an application of the Fregean considerations raised in section I. We cannot preserve the purported truth of (16) if we substitute for one occurrence of 'the present King of France' other singular terms (e.g., 'the only unicorn on the moon') which do not differ in denotation. Together with (A8) and (8)

Tyler Burge

we can use (15) to derive (6) — a sentence rejected by native speakers in unison. One may, of course, wish to doubt (A8) rather than (15).[11] But (A8) served an important purpose in justifying transformations needed for proving the material adequacy of a theory of truth. It seems fair to ask of anyone who rejects the principle to provide a replacement which effects the relevant transformations without leading to untrue consequences or relying on untrue semantical axioms. Since (A8) is non-independent in the logic of section II largely because of (A9), we may regard the latter as tentatively preferable to (15).

There is a further consideration against (15) — one that is vaguer and less compelling but none the less philosophically interesting. An extremely intuitive feature of Tarski's theory of truth is that it explicates what it is for a sentence to be true in terms of a relation (satisfaction) between language (open sentences) and the world (sequences of objects). The notion of correspondence which had always seemed so integral to truth came clean in Tarski's theory. (This point is forcefully made by Davidson in [3].) It is difficult to see how the purported truth of, say, (16) can be explicated in terms of a correspondence relation.

As mentioned earlier, some may want to give correspondence a toehold by assigning 'Pegasus' an unactualized possible. But quite apart from questions about the propriety, clarity, and credibility of the move, it does not apply to (17). Assigning 'Pegasus' itself is not very satisfying either, because it encounters difficulty in explicating '$-(\exists y)$ $(y = \text{Pegasus})$.' The fault is the one we found with Frege's account of singular terms: there is too much correspondence rather than too little.

Loosely speaking, self-identity is a property of objects and all objects have it; sentences expressing identities are true or false by virtue of the relation that the identity predicate and its flanking singular terms bear to the world — never merely by virtue of the identity of the singular terms. Philosophical questions regarding identity seem bound to the notions of existence and object. The point is summed up more austerely by the principle

(18) $(\exists y) (y = t) \leftrightarrow t = t,$

which is easily derived in the logic of *ML*.

In their focus on the intended interpretation of the symbols we employ, our truth theory and its underlying logic help clarify how with respect to singular terms we can use the language we use and in the same language believe in the world we believe in. Alternative combinations of theory and logic should be required to do at least as much.

178

Notes

1 I am grateful to Alonzo Church, Donald Kalish, Dana Scott, and especially Richard Grandy for criticisms and suggestions regarding earlier drafts.

2 Some of what Meyer and Lambert say in [15] is congenial with these remarks. However, their distinction between 'nominal truth' and 'real truth' appears superfluous. 'Nominal truth' may be assimilated to 'real truth' as applied to sentences involving oblique contexts. One advantage of making explicit the oblique contexts in sentences like the above is that by doing so one uncovers grounds for confirming or disconfirming otherwise puzzling sentences. For example, to confirm or disconfirm fictional sentences, we look at the relevant fiction. Whereas some authors have felt that a sentence like 'Pegasus had fewer than 7 million hairs' should be counted truth-valueless because they could find no plausible reason to count it true or false, our view counts it false (even taken as implicitly oblique) because it is easily disconfirmed.

3 Application of this idea is discussed briefly in [2]. The axioms governing the proper name 'Pegasus' which we discuss below ignore for the sake of brevity the considerations of that paper.

4 Donnellan in [4], esp. pp. 295–304, may seem to be in disagreement with this intuition. But I think that the disagreement is only apparent. It should be noted that the bivalence of ML and the account of negation in the object language OL (cf. below) are incompatible with some treatments of presupposition in terms of truth-value gaps. I think that the intuitions backing these accounts can be explicated in other ways. But this issue may be left aside here.

5 Provisions for scope distinctions will be important in a full account of the logical behavior of singular terms in natural languages, especially in treating certain ambiguities which occur with non-denoting terms and in dealing with singular terms in and out of intensional contexts. Such provisions can be added to the present system, but the philosophical issues are complex and will not be discussed here. For a detailed discussion of the problem and an attempt to solve it from a different standpoint than ours, see Grice [9].

6 It is tempting but mistaken to suppose that the condition prohibits taking both a predicate and another predicate understood as its 'contradictory' or 'negation' as primitive. In such cases, the condition may be seen as forcing us merely to construe the singular term as having wider scope than the 'negative element' attributed to the predicate. As long as the predicate is atomic, it is hard to imagine the situation any other way.

7 Cf. Tarski [22]. In our formulation, relativizations of 'Tr' to a canonical reading, a person, and a time are suppressed for the sake of brevity.

8 An exception is Schock [19]: 94. Subsequent to arriving at the

theory of section II, I found that he uses axioms very like (A9) and (A10). Schock gives a Frege-type model theory for his logic using the empty set as the denotation of intuitively non-denoting singular terms.

9   It would be a mistake to think that Grandy 'identifies' only logically equivalent singular terms. In order to prove the adequacy of his truth theory for the iota case, he must derive an identity sentence containing two non-denoting definite descriptions.

10   Smiley [21] and Hintikka [11] are in accord with us on this matter. So, with qualifications, is Russell [25]: 184.

11   (A8) is derivable in both Scott's system and Lambert's *FD2*. It is not derivable in Grandy's system or in the weaker ones.

References

[1] BURGE, TYLER, *Truth and Some Referential Devices* (dissertation, Princeton University, 1971).

[2] BURGE, TYLER, 'Reference and Proper Names,' *The Journal of Philosophy*, 70 (1973), pp. 425–39.

[3] DAVIDSON, DONALD, 'True to the Facts,' *The Journal of Philosophy*, 66 (1969), pp. 748–64.

[4] DONNELLAN, KEITH S., 'Reference and Definite Descriptions,' *Philosophical Review* (1965), pp. 281–304.

[5] FREGE, GOTTLOB, 'Function and Concept,' in *Translations from the Philosophical Writings of Gottlob Frege*, ed. P. Geach and M. Black (Oxford, Blackwell, 1966); first published 1892.

[6] FREGE, GOTTLOB, 'On Sense and Reference,' in *Translations from the Philosophical Writings of Gottlob Frege*, ed. P. Geach and M. Black (Oxford, Blackwell, 1966); first published 1892.

[7] FREGE, GOTTLOB, *The Basic Laws of Arithmetic*, ed. M. Furth (Berkeley, University of California Press, 1967), first published 1903.

[8] GRANDY, RICHARD, 'A Definition of Truth for Theories with Intensional Definite Description Operators,' *Journal of Philosophical Logic* 1 (1972), pp. 137–55.

[9] GRICE, H. P., 'Vacuous Names,' in *Words and Objections*, ed. D. Davidson and J. Hintikka (Dordrecht, D. Reidel Publishing Company, 1969).

[10] HAILPERIN, T. and H. LEBLANC, 'Non-Designating Singular Terms,' *Philosophical Review* (1959), pp. 239–43.

[11] HINTIKKA, JAAKKO, 'Definite Descriptions and Self-Identity,' *Philosophical Studies* (1964), pp. 5–7.

[12] KAPLAN, DAVID, 'What is Russell's Theory of Descriptions?', in *Physics, Logic and History*, ed. Wolfgang Yourgrau (New York, Plenum, 1969).

[13] LAMBERT, KAREL, 'Notes on "E!" III: A Theory of Descriptions,' *Philosophical Studies* (1962), pp. 51–9.

[14] LAMBERT, KAREL, 'Notes on "E!" IV: A Reduction in Free Quantification Theory with Identity and Descriptions,' *Philosophical Studies* (1964), pp. 85–8.

[15] MEYER, ROBERT and KAREL LAMBERT, 'Universally Free Logic and Standard Quantification Theory,' *Journal of Symbolic Logic* (1968), pp. 8–26.

[16] QUINE, W. V., *Word and Object* (Cambridge, Mass., MIT Press, 1960).

[17] QUINE, W. V., *Philosophy of Logic* (Englewood Cliffs, Prentice Hall, 1970).

[18] RUSSELL, BERTRAND, 'On Denoting,' *Mind* (1905), pp. 479–93.

[19] SCHOCK, ROLF, *Logics Without Existence Assumptions* (Stockholm, Almquist and Wiksell, 1968).

[20] SCOTT, DANA, 'Existence and Description in Formal Logic,' in *Bertrand Russell: Philosopher of the Century*, ed. Ralph Schoenman (London, Allen and Unwin, 1967).

[21] SMILEY, TIMOTHY, 'Sense Without Denotation,' *Analysis* (1960), pp. 125–35.

[22] TARSKI, ALFRED, 'The Concept of Truth in Formalized Languages,' in *Logic, Semantics, Metamathematics* (Oxford, Clarendon Press, 1956); first published 1936.

[23] VAN FRAASSEN, BAS, and KAREL LAMBERT, 'On Free Description Theory,' *Zeit. für Math. Logik u. Grundlagen d. Math.*, 13 (1967), pp. 225–40.

[24] VAN FRAASSEN, BAS, and KAREL LAMBERT, *Derivation and Counterexample* (Encino, Dickenson Publishing Company, 1972).

[25] WHITEHEAD, A. N. and BERTRAND RUSSELL, *Principia Mathematica*, Vol. I (Cambridge, England, 1925–27); first published 1910.

10 Truth-theory for indexical languages

Barry Taylor

I Bare demonstratives

Where L is a first-order language, let its *simple indexical* extension LI be
the language obtained from L by adding the demonstrative ⌜that⌝,
construed (for the present at least) as an indexical term functioning
syntactically in precisely the same way as an individual constant. Then
there is a well-known problem about how the familiar Tarskian methods
for constructing a truth-theory for L need to be modified or extended
so as to yield a truth-theory for LI. The problem arises as a particularly urgent one within a Davidsonian framework, which assumes that,
underlying a natural language like English, there exists a formal language ('Base English') in which every surface sentence of English finds
at least one paraphrase (a 'base paraphrase'); surface sentences are
further supposed linked to their base paraphrases by a series of meaning-
preserving Chomskyan transformations, and the task of constructing a
theory of meaning for English identified with that of finding a recursive truth-theory for Base English meeting appropriate constraints. For
the manifest presence in English of indexical elements renders it extremely plausible that Base English will need to extend first-order
resources at least to the point of being a simple indexical extension of
a first-order language. Thus, on Davidsonian assumptions, the problem
of the extension of Tarskian methods from first-order languages to their
indexical extensions is one not merely of a technical interest, but one
that poses key questions for the theory of meaning for natural languages.

Evidently, an important element in the problem lies in the fact that
the simple Tarskian conception of truth as a unary predicate of sentences (i.e. sentence-*types*), though adequate for a first-order language
L, must perforce be modified when its indexical extension LI comes
into question, for the obvious reason that there are sentences of LI that
intuition is prepared to count both true and false, depending on the
context in which they are supposed uttered. Two ways of modifying
Tarski's truth-predicate suggest themselves. The first is to cleave to the
idea that it is a unary predicate, but to deny it is a predicate of sentences; the second is to regard it still as a predicate of sentences, but as

relativized to appropriate parameters. Of these two possible approaches, I shall concern myself entirely with the second, as that promising to do least *prima facie* violence to Tarskian conceptions – since it allows us to construe Tarski's truth-predicate for L as one in which the simplicity of the language has permitted parameters to be suppressed as idle, rather than as one defined over a totally wrong domain.[1]

The truth-predicate for LI, then, is to be relativized to some suitable parameter(s); which? Since the problem about LI is just that its sentences may vary intuitively in truth-value according to the context in which they are supposed uttered, a first answer might be that we should simply regard its truth-predicate as relativized to contexts; but we can improve on this. For the truth-value which a demonstrative sentence S (i.e. a sentence containing occurrences of the demonstrative $\ulcorner$that$\urcorner$) assumes in a context depends not on all features of the context, but just on the objects which, in that context, the various occurrences of the demonstrative in S are taken to denote. The feature of the context on which S's truth-value depends can therefore be taken to be a finite sequence of objects having as its ith element the item which, in the given context, the ith occurrence of $\ulcorner$that$\urcorner$ in S is to be taken as denoting. The suggested refinement of our first answer to which we are led[2] is thus that the truth-predicate for LI should be relativized to finite sequences, interpreted as representing the semantically relevant features of possible contexts in which demonstrative sentences might be evaluated; I shall (following Scott) call these finite sequences *points of reference* for LI, and shall use $\ulcorner\sigma\urcorner$, $\ulcorner\sigma'\urcorner$ etc. as metalinguistic variables over them.

Given the intuitive basis thus sketched underlying the points of reference approach, it is easy to see what standards should be met by an adequate truth-theory for LI based upon it. Suppose the metalanguage ML in which the truth-theory is to be cast contains L, along with the standard Tarskian auxiliary apparatus; then we will, for example, expect an adequate theory to yield as a consequence, for any nonempty σ,

$$T_{LI}(\ulcorner Red(that)\urcorner, \sigma) \leftrightarrow Red(\sigma_1)$$

or, equivalently,

$$T_{LI}(\ulcorner Red(that)\urcorner, \sigma) \leftrightarrow \exists x(x = \sigma_1 \ \& \ Red(x))$$

where, for any i, σ_i is the ith element of σ (if such there be; and is otherwise undefined). One natural way of stating a generalized adequacy condition is therefore the following. For each i, let v_i be the ith variable of LI in the alphabet ordering $\ulcorner x\urcorner$, $\ulcorner y\urcorner$, $\ulcorner z\urcorner$, $\ulcorner x'\urcorner$, $\ulcorner y'\urcorner$, $\ulcorner z'\urcorner$, . . . ; let the *indexical degree* of a wff A of LI be the number of occurrences it contains of the demonstrative $\ulcorner$that$\urcorner$; and let us say that a point of reference σ is *apt for* a wff A just in case the length of σ is at least as great as A's indexical degree. Then:

Barry Taylor

[TIi] An adequate truth-theory for LI in ML should yield as a theorem, for any closed wff A of LI of indexical degree n, that instance of the schema

σ is apt for Ω . $\rightarrow$.

$T_{LI}(\Omega,\sigma) \leftrightarrow \exists v_1 \ldots \exists v_n(v_1 = \sigma_1 \& \ldots \& v_n = \sigma_n \& \Phi)$

in which (a) the schematic letter $\ulcorner \Omega \urcorner$ is replaced in both occurrences by a structural description in ML of A

and (b) the schematic letter $\ulcorner \Phi \urcorner$ is replaced by the wff $A^{\#}$ formed from A by (i) replacing each variable v_i at each of its occurrences in A by v_{i+n}; and (ii) for each $j \leqslant n$, replacing the jth occurrence of $\ulcorner$that$\urcorner$ in A by v_j.

Moreover, it is a straightforward matter to fashion a truth-theory adequate by this standard out of a truth-theory for L in ML which, in standard Tarskian fashion, proceeds via the characterization of a satisfaction predicate true of formulae of L and denumerable sequences s, s' etc.; all we need do, e.g., is to add to such a truth-theory the requirement that, if A has indexical degree n and σ is apt for A,

$T_{LI}(A,\sigma) \leftrightarrow \forall s \, \mathrm{Sat}_L(A^{\#},\sigma * s)$

where $A^{\#}$ comes from A as in [TIi] above, and $\ulcorner * \urcorner$ is a metalinguistic functor of sequence-concatenation.

In sum, then, the approach to the semantics of LI via points of reference combines the virtue of a certain intuitive plausibility with that of ease of formal implementation; nevertheless, there is apparent room for improvement. The intuitive underpinning of the approach lay in the sound insight that the truth-value assumed by a demonstrative sentence S in a given possible utterance-context C depends on the items which, in that context, the demonstratives in S come to denote; but, before agreeing with the conclusion that the relevant features of C should simply be identified with the point of reference constituting the sequence of the denotations thus assumed, we might inquire whether there are not other, more fundamental, features of C which in some systematic way determine what the elements of this point of reference are to be. If there are, then surely it is these that are the fundamental relevant features of C to which the truth-predicate should be relativized; surely too a perspicuous truth-theory should articulate the way in which the truth-value which S assumes in C derives from these features, via a determination of the elements of a point of reference. Moreover, evident candidates for the role of such fundamental relevant features of C emerge in the shape of the purported utterer u of S in C and the time t of his supposed utterance; for in terms of these two, the elements of an associated point of reference can apparently be specified by invoking the pragmatic notion of *speaker-demonstration* — the ith element of that point of reference (i.e. the denotation assumed in C by the ith occurrence of $\ulcorner$that$\urcorner$ in S) being the object which u demonstrated in his

184

*i*th utterance of ⌐that⌐ during *t*.

Such considerations make plausible the adoption of a new approach to the truth-theory of LI — Davidson's, in essence.[3] The truth-predicate for LI we now suppose relativized not to points of reference, but to the utterers and times now identified with the fundamental relevant features of contexts of utterance; and the metalanguage ML in which the truth-theory is to be case equipped with the pragmatic predicate ⌐Dem$_i$$(u,t,x)$⌐, read: *x* is an object demonstrated by *u* in his *i*th utterance of ⌐that⌐ during *t*. The aim will then be to construct a truth-theory yielding such consequences as

$$T_{LI}(⌐Red(that)⌐, u, t) \leftrightarrow Red(\imath x Dem_1(u,t,x))$$

or, equivalently,

$$T_{LI}(⌐Red(that)⌐, u, t) \leftrightarrow \exists x(x = \imath x Dem_1(u,t,x) \ \& \ Red(x)).$$

More generally, the new adequacy condition will be this:

[TIii]   An adequate truth-theory for LI in ML should yield as a theorem, for any closed wff *A* of LI of indexical degree *n*, that instance of the schema
$$T_{LI}(\Omega, u, t) \leftrightarrow \exists \nu_1 \ldots \exists \nu_n(\nu_1 = \imath x Dem_1(u,t,x) \ \& \ldots \& \ \nu_n = \imath x Dem_n(u,t,x) \ \& \ \Phi)$$
in which the schematic letter ⌐Ω⌐ is replaced by a structural description of *A* in ML, and ⌐Φ⌐ is replaced by the wff $A^{\#}$ coming from *A* as in [TIi].

Before precipitating ourselves into a search for a truth-theory adequate by this standard, however, it behoves us to pause and consider a problem raised for this whole Davidsonian approach by cases of *demonstrative equivocation*, in which a speaker manages in a single utterance of the demonstrative simultaneously to demonstrate two or more distinct items. For a simple example of the phenomenon, take the case where I am involved in a tedious telephone conversation — say, one with a colleague outlining at length a fatuous proposal on some administrative matter; my wife, perceiving my plight, slips me a note suggesting she should facilitate my escape by making noises as of the arrival of a guest. Waiting for a gap in the flow from the earpiece, I say ⌐That's a good idea⌐ (perhaps, but not necessarily, accompanying the remark with a wife-directed wink), thereby in a single utterance of the demonstrative indicating the diverse proposals of wife and colleague (and going on to commend each, though with different degrees of sincerity). Clearly, this case and its ilk must raise problems for the Davidsonian approach, since the crucial notion of *the* object demonstrated by a speaker in an utterance of the demonstrative fails to have application.

Putting the matter more abstractly, what these cases of demonstrative equivocation show is that no *unique* set of context-relative denotations

Barry Taylor

for demonstratives can be specified in terms of the Davidsonian fundamental features of the context (utterer and time) and the notion of speaker-demonstration; and putting the matter this way suggests two ways in which the Davidsonian approach might be modified to accommodate the recalcitrant cases. One way would be to cleave to the conception of the truth-predicate as relativized just to utterers and times as the sole fundamental relevant features of the context, but to replace the notion of speaker-demonstration with some more powerful conceptual machinery capable of uniquely recovering a set of denotations from these indices; I am, however, at a loss to find a candidate suited to the role this new apparatus must play. The second way, initially more promising, would be to seek to identify further fundamental features of the context to set beside utterers and times as parameters of the truth-predicate, in the hope that from this enlarged set of indices a unique set of denotations for the demonstratives will be recoverable via the notion of speaker-demonstration (as suitably relativized to the new indices). One suggestion for the role of such a further fundamental feature of context might be *audience*, and certainly this would suffice to deal with the last example — the sentence ⌜that's a good idea⌝ being true in my mouth at the time t of my utterance as directed towards my wife as audience (since the object demonstrated by me to her in my first demonstrative utterance during t was indeed a good idea) but false in my mouth at t as directed to my colleague (since the item I simultaneously demonstrated to him was not). But this suggestion fails to generalize, since it is a simple matter to construct cases of demonstrative equivocation involving only a single audience; and indeed I can find no feature or set of features whose addition to the familiar parameters of utterer and time will suffice in the necessary way to disambiguate all cases of demonstrative equivocation. Conclusion (subject to correction if it transpires that ingenuity can after all manage to produce a successful implementation of one of these strategies): in face of cases of demonstrative equivocation, the attempt to eliminate relativization of the truth-predicate to an explicit specification of the denotations of the demonstratives — i.e. to a point of reference — in favour of a relativization to fundamental relevant features of the context must be judged a failure, since no systematic way emerges adequate to recover a unique set of denotations for the demonstratives in such cases.

It does not follow, however, that we should altogether abandon the Davidsonian approach and revert to the points of reference line. For the Davidsonian approach was surely correct in emphasizing the central role played in the way a sentence assumes a truth-value in a context of utterance by the utterer, the time of his utterance, and the demonstrations he then makes; correct too in requiring that an illuminating truth-theory should articulate the nature of this role, and faulty only in supposing that attention to these points would eliminate altogether the

186

need to call on points of reference as arguments to the truth-predicate. This suggests that the best truth-theory for LI will be a hybrid one, retaining the Davidsonian emphasis on the role of speaker-demonstration in determining truth-conditions for demonstrative sentences, but relativizing the truth-predicate to points of reference as well as to utterers and times.

How should such a hybrid theory work? Its leading idea will be this: a demonstrative sentence S counts as true relative to utterer u, time t and point of reference σ just in case for every i, the ith element σ_i of σ was something demonstrated by u in his ith utterance of ⌜that⌝ during t, and S counts as true when the successive occurrences of the demonstrative in it are construed as denoting the corresponding elements of σ. So, for example, we should expect an adequate hybrid truth-theory for LI cast in the familiar metalanguage ML to deliver as a theorem, for any nonempty σ,

$$T_{LI}(⌜\text{Red(that)}⌝,u,t,\sigma) \leftrightarrow \text{Dem}_1(u,t,\sigma_1) \ \& \ \text{Red}(\sigma_1)$$

i.e. equivalently

$$T_{LI}(⌜\text{Red(that)}⌝,u,t,\sigma) \leftrightarrow \exists x(x = \sigma_1 \ \& \ \text{Dem}_1(u,t,x) \ \& \ \text{Red}(x)).$$

Generalizing by plastering together appropriate requirements from [TIi] and [TIii], we obtain the following as a new adequacy requirement:

[TIiii] An adequate truth-theory for LI in ML should yield as a theorem, for any closed wff A of LI of indexical degree n, that instance of the schema
σ is apt for Ω . → .
$$T_{LI}(\Omega,u,t,\sigma) \leftrightarrow \exists v_1 \ldots \exists v_n(v_1 = \sigma_1 \ \& \ldots \& \ v_n = \sigma_n$$
$$\& \ \text{Dem}_1(u,t,v_1) \ \& \ldots \& \ \text{Dem}_n(u,t,v_n) \ \& \ \Phi)$$
in which the schematic letter ⌜Ω⌝ is replaced in both occurrences by a structural description of A in ML, and ⌜Φ⌝ is replaced by the wff $A^{\#}$ formed from A as in [TIi] above.

But, although this adequacy condition appears to arise naturally out of the intuitive considerations underlying the hybrid approach, it is doubtful whether it genuinely requires truth-conditions to be assigned to demonstrative sentences in accordance with our preanalytic intuitions. The source of the doubt lies in the treatment negation is to receive in the truth-theory. The obvious thing is to suppose it handled by the natural generalization of Tarski, so that for atomic wffs A at least, ⌜$\sim A$⌝ counts as true at given indices iff A itself does not; but this natural assumption combines with [TIiii] to lead to trouble. Thus, let A be the wff ⌜Red(that)⌝, and select u,t, and nonempty σ such that $\sim \text{Dem}_1(u,t,\sigma_1)$. Then by [TIiii] we have $\sim T_{LI}(A,u,t,\sigma)$; hence, by the negation clause, $T_{LI}(⌜\sim A⌝,u,t,\sigma)$. Adoption of [TIiii] combined with a natural treatment of negation thus appears to lead to the counterintuitive result that ⌜that is not red⌝ counts as true at indices $u,t,$ and σ if u either demonstrates nothing during t, or, while demonstrating something, fails to make a demonstration of σ_1.

Two methods suggest themselves for dealing with this difficulty. The first[4] — the method of *conditional assignment* of truth-conditions — locates the problem with [TIiii] in the fact that it requires an assignment of truth-conditions to every closed wff A at all indices $u,t,$ and apt σ, with the stipulation that these indices be appropriately related via speaker-demonstration being part of the truth-condition so assigned; the correct approach, it suggests, should rather be to make the obtaining of the appropriate relation among the indices a condition for the assignment of any truth-condition at all to A at those indices. So, for example, an adequate truth-theory for LI should *not* yield as a theorem the old

$$T_{LI}(⌜Red(that)⌝,u,t,\sigma) \leftrightarrow \exists x(x = \sigma_1 \,\&\, Dem_1(u,t,x) \,\&\, Red(x))$$

(for σ non empty), but in its place the weaker conditional

$$\forall x(x = \sigma_1 \,\&\, Dem_1(u,t,x) \,.\, \rightarrow \,.\, T_{LI}(⌜Red(that)⌝,u,t,\sigma) \leftrightarrow Red(x)).$$

More generally, an adequate truth-theory for LI in ML will be one yielding as a theorem, for each closed wff A of indexical degree n, *not* an instance of the schema enshrined in [TIiii], but instead that instance of the weaker schema

$$\sigma \text{ is apt for } \Omega \,.\, \rightarrow \,.$$
$$\forall v_1 \ldots \forall v_n (v_1 = \sigma_1 \,\&\, \ldots \,\&\, v_n = \sigma_n \,\&\, Dem_1(u,t,v_1) \,\&\, \ldots \,\&\,$$
$$Dem_n(u,t,v_n)$$
$$.\, \rightarrow \,.\, T_{LI}(\Omega,u,t,\sigma) \leftrightarrow \Phi)$$

in which the occurrences of ⌜Ω⌝ are replaced by structural descriptions of A in ML, and ⌜Φ⌝ is replaced by the wff $A^{\#}$ coming from A as in [TIi] above. Evidently, a truth-theory based on this method of conditional assignment will face no difficulties about assigning the wrong truth-conditions to sentences at indices that fail to be appropriately related; for when the appropriate relation fails to hold, no truth-condition will be assigned at all.

The other method for solving the problems about negation that confront [TIiii] — call it the method of *scope-distinction* — proceeds from the idea that there is after all no harm in allowing that ⌜That is red⌝ has one negation (its *external* negation, appropriately read as ⌜It is not the case that that is red⌝) which counts as true at given indices whenever the negated sentence does not, and hence counts trivially as true at u,t,σ when $\sim Dem_1(u,t,\sigma_1)$; the important thing is that we should also have the resources to distinguish a stronger, *internal* negation

188

⌜That is not red⌝ for the sentence, to qualify as true at indices u,t,σ only when $\text{Dem}_1(u,t,\sigma_1)$ but σ_1 is not red. Implementation of this idea, however, evidently demands a reconstrual of the notion of the indexical extension LI of first-order L, as we have operated with it hitherto; for LI as hitherto defined lacks even the syntactic resources necessary to mark the distinction between external and internal negations.

One way to carry out the required revision is to abandon the conception of ⌜that⌝ as functioning syntactically as an individual constant, and to regard it instead as a unary quantifier, i.e. as a variable-binding formula-forming operator on formulae; and to reconstrue LI as coming from L by the addition of such an operator.[5] External and internal negations of ⌜that is red⌝ then become expressible in LI as, respectively,

(i) $\sim$ that x Red(x)

and (ii) that $x \sim$ Red(x)

to which a respectable truth-theory will respectively assign the truth-conditions at indices $u,t,$ and non-empty σ

(i') $\sim (\text{Dem}_1(u,t,\sigma_1) \,\&\, \text{Red}(\sigma_1))$

and (ii') $\text{Dem}_1(u,t,\sigma_1) \,\&\, \sim \text{Red}(\sigma_1)$.

Before advancing to a statement of a more general adequacy condition on truth-theories for LI thus reconstrued, we need to adapt and extend some of our auxiliary apparatus. The *indexical degree* of a wff A of LI will now of course be the number n of occurrences of the demonstrative quantifier in A; if $n = 0$, we say A is *non-indexical*. Where A is a wff of indexical degree n, its *demonstrative-standard equivalent* is to be the wff A' formed from A by (i) replacing every variable v_i at each of its occurrences in A unbound by a demonstrative quantifier by v_{i+n}, and (ii) where v_{j_k} is the variable associated with the kth occurrence of the demonstrative quantifier in A, replacing v_{j_k} by v_k at each of its occurrences bound in A by that occurrence of the quantifier. Finally, the metalinguistic predicate ⌜$\text{Dem}_i(u,t,x)$⌝ should in the present context be read: x is an item demonstrated by u in his ith utterance during t of[6] the demonstrative quantifier. Then:

[TIiv] An adequate truth-theory for LI in ML should yield as a theorem, for any closed wff A of LI of indexical degree n, that instance of the schema

σ is apt for $\Omega . \rightarrow .$

$T_{LI}(\Omega,u,t,\sigma) \leftrightarrow \exists v_1 \ldots \exists v_n (v_1 = \sigma_1 \,\&\, \ldots v_n = \sigma_n \,\&\, \Phi)$

in which ⌜Ω⌝ is replaced in both occurrences by a structural description in ML of A, and ⌜Φ⌝ is replaced by the last member B_m of a shortest sequence $B_1 \ldots B_m$ such that (i) B_1 is the demonstrative-standard equivalent of A, (ii) B_m is non-indexical, and (iii) for each i ($1 \leqslant i < m$), B_{i+1} comes from B_i by replacing some part of the form ⌜that $v_k C$⌝ (where C is non-indexical) by ⌜$\text{Dem}_k(u,t,v_k) \,\&\, C$⌝.

Barry Taylor

There, then, are two methods — those of conditional assignment and of scope-distinction — for fashioning a hybrid theory of truth-conditions for LI, each bringing with it a criterion of adequacy for truth-theories designed to avoid the difficulties about negation attendant upon the imperfect [TIiii]. Of the two, the former is *prima facie* far more attractive. The scope-distinction method's treatment of the demonstrative as a quantifier has little or no prior plausibility, and the suspicion which consequently arises that this construal is quite *ad hoc* is strengthened by the fact that it involves positing a structural complexity within formal paraphrases which appears to be completely idle, corresponding to no intuitive complexity in the interpretation of surface demonstrative sentences — even if the approach is correct in maintaining that the distinction between $\ulcorner\sim$ that $xFx\urcorner$ and $\ulcorner$that $x \sim Fx\urcorner$ corresponds to a surface ambiguity, no parallel surface distinction corresponds to that between e.g. $\ulcorner\exists x$ that $yFxy\urcorner$ and $\ulcorner$that y $\exists xFxy\urcorner$. These are strong methodological reasons for preferring the conditional-assignment approach; despite them, however, it is the method of scope-distinction that I propose to adopt, on the theoretical ground that it will generalize, in a way the conditional-assignment method apparently will not, to handle more complex demonstrative constructions of the sort we shall encounter in the next section. Of this, more below.

The task in hand thus reduces to that of finding some extension of Tarski's method for constructing the truth-theory of a given first-order language L which will suffice for the construction of a truth-theory, adequate by [TIiv], for its indexical extension LI formed by the addition of a demonstrative quantifier; and the task so stated proves easily enough discharged. Let us say that a wff A of LI of indexical degree n is in *demonstrative standard form* iff, for each i s.t. $1 \leqslant i \leqslant n$, the variable associated with the ith occurrence of the demonstrative quantifier in A is v_i; note that the demonstrative-standard equivalent of any wff is in demonstrative-standard form. We define what it is for a wff A of LI to be satisfied by a denumerable sequence s relative to parameters $u,t,$ and σ apt for A; the definition will be particularly geared to the special case where A is in demonstrative-standard form, in which it may be assumed that each contained quantification $\ulcorner$that $v_i\urcorner$ introduces an item which is an object of u's ith utterance of the demonstrative during t. If A is atomic, or has as its main operator a logical connective or logical quantifier, the appropriate Tarskian clause will suffice, with parameters u,t and σ added to the satisfaction predicate. If A is $\ulcorner$that $v_i B\urcorner$ for some B, we require

$$\mathrm{Sat}_{\mathrm{LI}}(A,s,u,t,\sigma) \leftrightarrow \mathrm{Dem}_i(u,t,\sigma_i) \mathrel{\&} \mathrm{Sat}_{\mathrm{LI}}(B,s(\sigma_i/i),u,t,\sigma)$$

where, for any $x,$ $s(x/i)$ is the sequence resulting from s by substituting x for whatever s may have in its ith place. For closed wffs A in

190

demonstrative-standard form, truth then emerges from satisfaction in the standard Tarskian fashion:

$$T_{LI}(A,u,t,\sigma) \leftrightarrow \forall s \; \mathrm{Sat}_{LI}(A,s,u,t,\sigma)$$

while, if A is closed but not demonstrative-standard, we put

$$T_{LI}(A,u,t,\sigma) \leftrightarrow T_{LI}(A',u,t,\sigma)$$

where A' is the demonstrative-standard equivalent of A.

II   Complex demonstratives

The simple indexical extension LI of a suitable first-order language L will evidently suffice to furnish base paraphrases for simple English sentences containing 'bare' demonstratives, i.e. sentences of the form ⌜that is G⌝. But the typical English demonstrative is not bare, but complex; the typical form of the atomic English demonstrative sentence is ⌜that F is G⌝. What should we take as the structure and semantics of the *complex* indexical extension LJ of a first-order language L, designed to furnish paraphrases for these more complex demonstrative sentences?

It might be objected that this question is ill-conceived; that LI itself is adequate to provide the desired paraphrases, since ⌜that F is G⌝ can be represented in LI as ⌜that $x \, (Fx \, \& \, Gx)$⌝. Baldly stated, however, this suggestion is infelicitious in ignoring the intuitive asymmetry one feels in the semantic roles of ⌜F⌝ and ⌜G⌝ in ⌜that F is G⌝. This intuition of asymmetry has a number of manifestations. One is a hesitation to accept the equivalence of ⌜that F is G⌝ with ⌜that G is F⌝, a hesitation that is difficult to explain on a theory like that currently proposed which assigns to the two paraphrases that are trivial logical equivalents; but which would be accounted for if the two were accorded distinct paraphrases in a more sophisticated formalism LJ, paraphrases that were not *logical* equivalents, so that the equivalence between them, if it held at all, would hold only in virtue of substantive nonlogical principles. Another manifestation of the same asymmetry intuition is that the Donnellan-like claim that ⌜that F is G⌝ can be true in some contexts when the demonstrated object is not F, though never when it is not G, is not *self-evidently* absurd; again, this seems to be most happily explained by a theory that assigns to the sentence a truth-theoretic structure from which the falsity of the claim does not follow immediately, so that its mistake (if mistake there be) lies at a deeper level of analysis. (Of course, a champion of the claims of LI would maintain the adequacy of his proffered paraphrases despite these considerations and seek a *pragmatic* explanation for our wayward asymmetry intuitions.

Even if he succeeds, however, in making some such explanation plausible, *ceteris paribus* it is preferable to follow a line that allows for the possibility at least of a genuine *semantic* basis for semantic intuitions.)

The problem, then, is to construct a complex indexical extension LJ of L adequate to furnish for sentences containing complex demonstratives paraphrases able to accommodate, if not ultimately to vindicate, our asymmetry intuitions. Since in the preferred form of the simple extension LI the demonstrative is treated as a unary quantifier, a natural syntactical proposal is that it be treated in LJ as a *binary* one; hence, that we should regard the wffs of LJ as comprising all wffs of L, and in addition count ⌜that $v_i(A;B)$⌝ a wff of LJ whenever A and B so count. ⌜That F is G⌝ will then go over into LJ as ⌜that $x(Fx;Gx)$⌝ – a syntactic proposal which at least promises a stolid neutrality on the asymmetry issue.

The key to constructing a truth-theory for LJ thus construed lies in complicating the notion of speaker-demonstration employed in the semantic description of LI. The notion as we then used it allows the possibility of, and is intended to cover, cases of 'bare' speaker-demonstration, in which the object of the demonstration is identified by an unadorned act of pointing or a suitably-directed twitch of the eyebrows, unsupplemented by any further cues. On the face of it, such bare acts of demonstration do occur (though it is always possible that analysis should reveal this superficial simplicity to mask a hidden complexity); the important point for present purposes is, however, that *prima facie* not all cases of speaker-demonstration are in this way bare. Rather, in many cases, a speaker apparently demonstrates his object *as an F*, supplementing any indicative gestures with a specification of some feature F the object possesses (or which at least the speaker supposes it to possess) to provide an audience with a mode of identifying the object demonstrated. (Typically, this specification is achieved linguistically – I can[7] demonstrate an object as a horse by uttering ⌜horse⌝ in demonstrating it, provided I am speaking (? and am taken to be speaking) in English; but one can imagine the feature specified in some nonlinguistic, though presumably still conventional, manner – e.g., by production of a suitable picture.) Crudely and inaccurately, my semantic proposal is that a truth-theory for sentences containing complex demonstratives should invoke this more complex notion of speaker-demonstration thus: ⌜that F is G⌝ is true relative to u,t and non-empty σ iff at his first demonstrative utterance during t, u demonstrated σ_1 as an F; and moreover, σ_1 is G.

The crudity of the last statement lies in its suppression of complexities of detail, for the sake of initial clarity. Its inaccuracy is more easily localized; for it is not precisely the notion of demonstration as an F that I propose to utilize in the truth-theory. The reason is that that notion is an intensional one – to demonstrate x as an F need not be to demonstrate it as a G, even if all and only F-things are G-things; and not only is it technically inconvenient (and, arguably, ideologically suspect) to allow such notions into the metatheory, but further, the extensionality of the position of $\ulcorner F \urcorner$ in $\ulcorner$that F is $G\urcorner$ suggests that it is inappropriate to assign that sentence a truth-condition in the statement of which $\ulcorner F \urcorner$ is used solely in intensional position. Hence, in place of the intensional $\ulcorner u$ demonstrates x as an $F\urcorner$, my truth-theory will use an extensional analogue $\ulcorner u$ demonstrates x as a member of $\alpha \urcorner$, the two concepts being related thus: u demonstrates x as an α if for some F, α is the set of F-things and u demonstrates x as an F. A more accurate, if still crude, formulation of my semantic proposal is to be obtained from the statement of the last paragraph by replacing the intensional notion there used by this extensional analogue.

To translate this crude formulation into a sharp adequacy criterion on truth-theories for LJ, some technical terminology must be invoked; fortunately, the same form of words as we used in introducing for LI (in its quantifier construal) the concepts of indexical degree, demonstrative-standard form and demonstrative-standard equivalent will suffice to define the same notions in application to LJ. As before, we suppose the metalanguage ML in which the truth theory is to be cast to contain L, along with the standard Tarskian subsidiary apparatus; moreover, that it contains the pragmatic predicate $\ulcorner \mathrm{Dem}_i(u,t,x,\alpha)\urcorner$, read: x is an item demonstrated as a member of α by u in his ith utterance of the demonstrative quantifier during t. Then the adequacy-condition to which we are led is this:

[TIv]   An adequate truth-theory for LJ in ML should yield as a theorem, for any closed wff A of LJ of indexical degree n, that instance of the schema

σ is apt for Ω . $\rightarrow$.

$\mathrm{T_{LJ}}(\Omega,u,t,\sigma) \leftrightarrow \exists v_1 \ldots \exists v_n(v_1 = \sigma_1 \ \& \ldots \& \ v_n = \sigma_n \ \& \ \Phi)$

in which $\ulcorner \Omega \urcorner$ is replaced in both occurrences by a structural description in ML of A, and $\ulcorner \Phi \urcorner$ is replaced by the last member B_m of a shortest sequence $B_1 \ldots B_m$ such that (i) B_1 is the demonstrative-standard equivalent of A; (ii) B_m is non-indexical; and (iii) for each i $(1 \leqslant i < m)$, B_{i+1} results from B_i by replacing some part of the form $\ulcorner$that $v_k(C;D)\urcorner$ (where C and D are non-indexical) by $\ulcorner \mathrm{Dem}_k(u,t,\sigma_k,\{v_k|C\}) \ \& \ D\urcorner$.

Moreover, a truth-theory adequate by this standard is easily constructed by extending the method applied in the last section to LI. As then, we proceed by defining what it is for a wff A to be satisfied by a denumerable sequence s relative to parameters $u,t,$ and σ apt for A with the assignment of satisfaction-conditions once more particularly geared to the case in which A is in demonstrative-standard form. If A is atomic, or has a connective or logical quantifier as its main operator, the satisfaction clause is as before just the Tarskian one, with parameters u,t, and σ restored. If A is $\ulcorner$that $v_i(B;C)\urcorner$ for some wffs B and C, then we require

$$\text{Sat}_{LJ}(A,s,u,t,\sigma) \leftrightarrow \text{Dem}_k(u,t,\sigma_i,\{x | \text{Sat}_{LJ}(B,s(x/i),u,t,\sigma)\})$$
$$\& \ \text{Sat}_{LJ}(C,s(\sigma_i/i),u,t,\sigma).$$

Truth is then defined in terms of satisfaction in the same way as for LI.

The language LJ we have just been studying, with its treatment of the demonstrative as a binary quantifier, was initially constructed by generalizing from a construal of LI in which it was treated as a unary one; but it will be recalled that construal of LI itself had little enough to recommend it, being adopted as the result of applying one method (the method of scope-distinction) to solve difficulties about negation which could apparently be met more elegantly by other means (the method of conditional assignment of truth-conditions). At the time, the reason given for adopting the *prima facie* less attractive method was that it could be generalized to yield a truth-theory for sentences containing complex demonstratives, in a way that its competitor could not. The first part of this claim has been vindicated in the construction above of LJ's truth-theory; it remains to show the grounds for the second part.

Suppose then that we had stuck with the original construal of LI, in which the demonstrative was treated syntactically as a noncomplex singular term. The natural way to extend LI to accommodate complex demonstratives would then have been to treat the demonstrative in LJ as a device for forming complex singular-terms; thus, as a variable-binding term-forming operator on formulae of the same syntactic type as the description operator (so that, e.g., $\ulcorner$that F is $G\urcorner$ would paraphrase as $\ulcorner G(\text{that } x\ Fx))\urcorner$. To avoid semantic problems about negation, the method of conditional assignment of truth-conditions would need once again to be invoked in constructing the metatheory for LJ thus construed. That is, we would aim for a truth-theory having, for each closed wff A, a consequence of the form

$$C. \rightarrow . \ T_{LJ}(\Omega,u,t,\sigma) \leftrightarrow B$$

where $\ulcorner\Omega\urcorner$ is supplanted by a structural description of A in ML; C gives a condition on u's demonstrations of objects as members of appropriate sets whose satisfaction is necessary for A's assuming any truth-value at all relative to u,t, and σ; and B states the condition under which, given that C does hold, the truth-value that A assumes at u,t, and σ is truth. For simple sentences, this seems to work well enough; an adequate theory would, e.g., suffice to prove

$\mathrm{Dem}_1(u,t,\sigma_1,\{x|\mathrm{Man}(x)\})$. → .

$\mathrm{T_{LJ}}(\ulcorner\mathrm{Tall(that}\ x\ \mathrm{Man}(x))\urcorner,u,t,\sigma) \leftrightarrow \mathrm{Tall}(\sigma_1)$.

But the approach fails when what is in question are sentences involving quantification into descriptions embedded inside complex demonstratives, because no consequence of the requisite form can adequately register the manner in which the sets to which demonstrations in the antecedent condition C need to be relativized depend upon the values of variables quantified over in the statement B of truth-conditions. Suppose, for example, A is the wff

$\exists y \mathrm{Loathe}(y,\mathrm{that}\ x\ \mathrm{Denigrate}(x,y))$

— one possible formalization of the surface sentence $\ulcorner$there is someone who loathes *that* denigrator of his$\urcorner$. Clearly, A is not satisfactorily handled by a truth-theory with the consequence

$\mathrm{Dem}_1(u,t,\sigma_1,\{x|\mathrm{Denigrate}(x,y)\})$. → .

$\mathrm{T_{LJ}}(A,u,t,\sigma) \leftrightarrow \exists y \mathrm{Loathe}(y,\sigma_1)$

since the variable $\ulcorner y \urcorner$ in the set-abstract is not bound by the succeeding existential quantifier. Nor does implicit quantification in prenex position fare any better; the consequence

$\mathrm{Dem}_1(u,t,\sigma_1,\{x|\mathrm{Denigrate}(x,y)\})$. → .

$\mathrm{T_{LJ}}(A,u,t,\sigma) \leftrightarrow \mathrm{Loathe}(y,\sigma_1)$

leads to an assignment of incompatible truth-values to A in the case where u simultaneously (why not?) demonstrates σ_1 as a member both of the set of y_1's denigrators and of y_2's denigrators, where y_1 loathes σ_1 but y_2 does not. In fact, there is no specifiable consequence of the given form which will adequately deal with the given sentence A; contrast the ease with which its analogue $A' = \ulcorner \exists y$ that x (Denigrate(x,y); Loathe$(y,x))\urcorner$ in our preferred construal of LJ is dealt with by the truth-theory given, which yields as the relevant theorem

$$\mathrm{T_{LJ}}(A',u,t,\sigma) \leftrightarrow \exists y(\mathrm{Dem}_1(u,t,\sigma_1,\{x\ \mathrm{Denigrate}(x,y)\})$$
$$\&\ \mathrm{Loathe}(y,\sigma_1)).$$

(The debate need not end here. The proponent of the alternative construal may argue, with some justification, that there is no real evidence in surface English that its formalization really does require quantification into descriptions embedded in complex demonstratives, and so propose a corresponding restriction on the syntax of his symbolism legislating out of existence troublesome cases such as that discussed above. This proposal, however, looks dangerously *ad hoc*, involving as it does, e.g., restrictions on the application of existential generalization which will prevent $\ulcorner$someone loathes that denigrator of his$\urcorner$ from following from $\ulcorner$James loathes that denigrator of his$\urcorner$ — an intuitively acceptable entailment our preferred theory accommodates, making the former sentence true at any indices at which the latter is true.

The strength of the alternative proposal lies in the fact that, even on our preferred account, there remains an oddity about a sentence like A', inasmuch as its truth at indices u,t and σ requires a demonstrative feat on u's part at t which he will find it difficult to bring off in an actual utterance of A' itself at t – for our truth-conditions require that, for some *specific y*, he will need to demonstrate σ_1 as a member of the set of denigrators of y, even though A' itself embodies no specification of which y this is to be. However, this oddity should not blind us to the fact that A' may come to count as true at u,t and σ in virtue of an utterance by u at t of some sentence other than A' itself – e.g., of a sentence that entails A' by existential generalization; moreover, even when A' itself is the uttered sentence, the demonstrative feat required of u is, though difficult, not impossible, since he may exploit contextual cues supplied e.g. by the topic of his immediately preceding discourse, to convey to his audience which object y he has in mind. Failing some more convincing demonstration of semantic fault with A' and its ilk, our less restrictive proposal is accordingly to be preferred to the alternative of syntactic gerrymander.)

III   Pragmatic issues

This paper has, in the course of expounding truth-theories for indexical languages, invoked several sophisticated notions of speaker-demonstration which cry out for a systematic analysis, perhaps along Gricean lines, within pragmatics; with the lofty purism of the typical truth-theorist, I have however totally eschewed this analytic task. Still, the real point of this paper is not to downgrade pragmatics, but to clarify its tasks in this area and to provide a framework within which the significance of pragmatic results may be evaluated. I conclude by mentioning a few of the pragmatic issues raised by the truth-theories we have discussed, and their role in the overall theory of demonstrative sentences.

(i) The complex notion of speaker-demonstration used in the semantic articulation of LJ was not the intensional $\ulcorner u$ demonstrates x as an $F\urcorner$, but its extensional analogue $\ulcorner u$ demonstrates x as a member of $\alpha\urcorner$ – though it was found expositorily convenient to introduce the latter in terms of the former. Since, however, the extensional notion appears to suffice to do all that truth-theory demands, it is of some interest to see whether it can be accorded a direct pragmatic analysis, so that the theory overall can be freed completely from intensional taint, or whether a precise pragmatics too must take the intensional notion as primary.

(ii) Another question is whether it turns out to be convenient, in the pragmatic analysis of complex speaker-demonstration, to proceed by first defining a notion of 'bare' demonstration to be utilized in the definition of the complex notion, or whether a more direct elucidation proves possible. In the former case, it would be most natural to take the base language for English as containing the resources of both LI and LJ, and to stick with the section I paraphrases of sentences containing bare demonstratives; in the latter, to regard Base English as containing just the resources of LJ, paraphrasing $\ulcorner$that is $G\urcorner$ as, e.g., $\ulcorner$that x $(x = x; Gx)\urcorner$.

(iii) Our truth-theory for LJ founds the intuitions we have of asymmetry between the roles of $\ulcorner F\urcorner$ and $\ulcorner G\urcorner$ in $\ulcorner$that F is $G\urcorner$ in the *prima facie* distinction between (a) demonstrating an object as an F (or, better: as an element of the set of F-things), and (b) barely demonstrating the object, and saying of it that it is an F; but it could – though I would be surprised – transpire that a systematic pragmatic analysis could find no real ground for this *prima facie* distinction. In such an eventuality, it would be natural to define the five-place predicate of complex speaker-demonstration used in the truth-theory of LJ in terms of the four-place one used in that of LI, thus: $\text{Dem}_i(u,t,x,\alpha) \leftrightarrow \text{Dem}_i(u,t,x)$ & $x \in \alpha$. The upshot would be that our truth-theory for LJ would deliver to sentences containing complex demonstratives precisely the same truth-conditions as they would receive if paraphrased into LI in the manner canvassed at the beginning of section II, and our intuitions of the asymmetry of the roles of $\ulcorner F\urcorner$ and $\ulcorner G\urcorner$ in $\ulcorner$that F is $G\urcorner$ would be revealed as unfounded. The important point, however, is that this conclusion would be a consequence of principles governing speaker-demonstration discovered as a result of pragmatic analysis; not something following trivially from a counterintuitive bludgeoning of sentences into unnatural paraphrases, as it would have been had we uncritically accepted those earlier proposals for direct paraphrase into LI.

(iv) Similarly, the truth of the Donnellan claim that $\ulcorner$that F is $G\urcorner$ can be true in some contexts even when the demonstrated object is not F – sometimes thought to be a further manifestation of the asymmetry of the predicate positions in the sentence – is on the present theory a question of pragmatics rather than of logical form – viz. the question of whether on the best analysis of speaker-demonstration, there can be circumstances in which $\text{Dem}_i(u,t,x,\alpha)$, yet x is not an element of α.

Notes

1 In fact, writers such as Weinstein ('Truth and Demonstratives', *Noûs*, vol. VIII (1974) pp. 179–84) who follow the first of these

Barry Taylor

approaches do find ways of rescuing the significance of Tarski's work; but, for the reasons given above, the second approach still seems to fit more naturally into his framework.

2 Essentially, this is a truth-theoretic analogue of the line pursued in a modal framework by a number of writers – e.g. Scott ('Advice on Modal Logic', in Lambert (ed.) *Philosophical Problems in Logic* (Dordrecht, Reidel, 1970), pp. 143–73) and Lewis ('General Semantics', *Synthèse*, vol. 22 (1970–1), pp. 18–67).

3 See e.g. his 'Truth and Meaning', *Synthèse*, vol. 17 (1967), pp. 304–23.

4 Versions of this method are in effect adopted by Weinstein, 'Truth and Demonstratives' and by Burge, 'Demonstrative Constructions, Reference and Truth', *The Journal of Philosophy*, vol. LXXI (1974), pp. 205–23. See also Davies, *Truth, Quantification and Modality*, (DPhil Thesis, University of Oxford, 1976), pp. 79ff.

5 Another way would be to furnish LI with the apparatus of *predicate-abstraction*, so that the internal negation of ⌜that is red⌝ would become expressible as ⌜$\hat{x}(\sim \text{Red}(x))$ that⌝. From a purely formal standpoint, there is little to choose between this suggestion and the approach discussed in the text; moreover, it has the advantage of enabling the intuitive syntactic construal of the demonstrative as a singular term to be preserved. Still, two considerations incline me to a marginal preference for the approach in the text. The first is an objection specific to this particular employment of predicate-abstraction: there is no prior reason to suppose that the resources needed to be added to L to accommodate demonstratives should recoil upon L itself, in the sense of generating new non-indexical equivalents of L's sentences; this being a feature of the suggestion that predicate-abstraction form part of the apparatus added to L in forming LI, a feature not shared by the proposal in the text, the latter is to be preferred. The second is a general suspicion of the use of predicate-abstraction when it assigns, as here, a role to complex predicates incompatible with the Fregean doctrine that 'the notion of a complex predicate has to be invoked only when we have to deal with quantifiers or other expressions of generality [such as description operators–B.T.]; and, when the argument-place of a complex predicate is filled, not by a bound variable, but by a singular-term, then it is unnecessary, in order to understand the sentence in which that predicate occurs, to recognize the predicate as occurring in it'. (Michael Dummett, *Frege: Philosophy of Language* (London, Duckworth, 1973), p. 30.) To push this objection further would require more space than the issue deserves here; let it simply be observed for present purposes that one weighty authority favours the account in the text.

6 If the language actually spoken by u is not LI itself, but rather one for which LI furnishes base paraphrases, this ⌜of⌝ will need to be replaced by: of an expression deriving transformationally from.

7 But need not: to act in the way described *may* be barely to demonstrate the object, and to say of it that it is a horse. See section III.

198

11 Operators, predicates and truth-theory*

Colin McGinn

An attractive – if not always clearly articulated – conception of the interest of truth-theory as an instrument in the study of the semantics of natural language may be formulated roughly as follows. We begin by stating and motivating a certain general requirement which an adequate interpretative truth-theory for a given natural language must meet; viz. that the theory should, upon the basis of a finite number of axioms, each treating of a semantical primitive of the language, conform to a version of Tarski's Convention T with respect to each of the infinitely many sentences of the language. The thought then is that conformity to the general constraint will perforce reveal significant semantic properties of the expressions of the object-language; i.e., the kinds of axioms needed to fulfil these abstractly stated requirements will, almost algorithmically, determine the semantic category, ontology and contribution to truth-conditions of semantical primitives and compounds thereof. Given the resources of the theory and the goal we set for it, a detailed semantics will be determined; we have only to contrive it.[1] The aim of the present essay is to test the plausibility of this idea against the issues raised for truth-theory by a class of grammatical modifiers to be found in English. In the current state of the art conclusions must be tentatively reached, and my remarks will be exploratory rather than definitive.

The class of constructions I wish to isolate consists of those expressions that function syntactically as sentence modifiers; e.g. 'It is not the case that', 'It is necessary that', 'It is probable to degree n that', 'In the past', 'Make it the case that', 'Ralph believes that', 'It ought to be the case that', 'It is analytic that', 'It is true that', 'and', 'before', 'because', 'If it were the case that . . . it would be the case that _____', and many others. Within this syntactically identified class it has been customary to suppose a partition: into those expressions that function as genuine semantic operators on sentences, and those that are properly viewed as predicative in character. The partition is imposed by the style of semantic axiom appropriate to the expression in question, where this fixes the ontology and semantic role of the expression. In application to

*I am indebted to remarks made in conversation by Tyler Burge, W. D. Hart and Christopher Peacocke.

Colin McGinn

these modifiers the attractive idea is to the effect that the general constraints of the truth-theory will themselves force a decision as to which category — operator or predicate — any given sentence modifier belongs; and, moreover, will do so in such a way as to reflect some significant semantic difference in the expressions thus differently treated. The question is whether this is true.

Suppose we are concerned with classical truth theories framed in terms of a prior recursive definition of satisfaction (nothing I say will depend on this assumption). Then a theory T will treat an n-ary expression E of a language L as an operator if the axiom of T for E has the following form

$$\text{sats } (s, \ulcorner E(A_1, \ldots, A_n)\urcorner, L) \equiv E(\text{sats}(s, A_1, \ldots, A_n, L))$$

where 'A_i' ranges over *sentences* of the object-language and 's' over sequences. T treats E as a predicate if E is governed by an axiom of this form

$$\text{sats}(s, \ulcorner E(t_1, \ldots, t_n)\urcorner, L) \equiv E(s*t_1, \ldots, s*t_n, L)$$

where 't_i' ranges over *terms* of the object-language and '$*$' is a (sequence-relative) assignment functor. The key difference is that the operator clause states the contribution of E to truth (satisfaction)-conditions in terms of the truth (satisfaction)-conditions of the expressions occurring within E's scope; whereas on the predicate clause E contains in its scope only singular terms (including variables), these being interpreted by an assignment of appropriate entities. Both treatments of E proceed by the successive introduction and elimination of semantic vocabulary, on the basis of the theory's disquotational axioms; but the manner of introduction makes for important asymmetries in the availability of the respective clauses, as will emerge. (A parallel distinction of treatment arises for natural language constructions which function syntactically as predicate modifiers, e.g. adverbs and attributive adjectives, and parallel questions can be raised about their semantic status as operators or predicates; but I shall not pursue the issue in their regard.)

The natural language counterparts of the truth-functional connectives are commonly treated as operators by the above criterion. On the other hand, Davidson proposes construing propositional attitude constructions as predicates: on his paratactic theory these sentence modifiers are parsed as two-place predicates, satisfied by persons and utterances.[2] And no wonder, for an operator treatment of psychological modifiers encounters apparently insurmountable difficulties. Thus consider

$$\text{sats } (s, \ulcorner\text{Galileo said that } A\urcorner, L) \equiv \text{Galileo said that sats } (s, A, L).$$

The left-hand side may be true (for a particular A), but the right-hand side will certainly be false; Galileo was no truth theorist. And, even if it were true, it would not follow that Galileo said all the things we get by successive replacements, on the strength of the disquotational axioms of the theory, inside the scope of this metalanguage intensional operator. Tradition and this signal failure may then suggest that the relevant division comes between the truth-functional and the non-truth-functional sentence modifiers, thus confirming a significant prior semantic distinction.[3] However it appears that certain non-truth-functional constructions can be made to submit to operator treatment. Thus consider an operator axiom for a modal modifier '□':

$$\text{sats } (s, \ulcorner \Box A \urcorner, L) \equiv \Box \text{ sats } (s, A, L).$$

It has been argued, plausibly enough, that if we individuate languages by the actual meanings of their words the right-hand side of this biconditional will not differ in truth-value from its left. And the required substitutions inside the scope of the metalanguage '□' can be sustained upon the basis of the necessitation of the axioms of the theory, where the truth of the necessitated axioms can be justified in the same way as was the original axiom for the object-language '□'.[4] If such a theory does indeed avoid falsehood, as apparently it does, then at least some modal constructions can be treated as operators. What is more, other non-truth-functional constructions seem susceptible to the same treatment. Thus consider this axiom for the tense modifier 'In the past':

$$\text{sats } (s, \ulcorner \text{In the past } A \urcorner, L) \equiv \text{In the past sats } (s, A, L).$$

To the objection that a past-tense sentence may be true though the embedded sentence was not in the past true because the sentence meant something different in the past, we can make the reply that we are taking languages to be individuated by their present meanings. And again we shall require corresponding temporal restrictions throughout the axioms of the theory. It thus seems that we can, with a little ingenuity, devise an operator treatment for tense modifiers.[5] Similarly, we could supply operator clauses for certain binary sentence modifiers, e.g. the subjunctive conditional and temporal connectives like 'before'; the style of axiom and accompanying qualifications will by now be obvious. Given the availability of such theories, it is hard to see how truth-functionality could be the differentiating underlying semantic property. We are thus faced with the question whether the feasibility or otherwise of operator treatments correlates with *any* antecedently recognized, or interestingly formulable, semantic distinction. For if it turns out to be more or less arbitrary — a mere artefact of the truth theory's internal workings — then the attractive idea we started with would be brought into serious doubt. Before trying to answer that question it will heighten our sense of the issue to approach the matter from the predicate direction.

I remarked that Davidson (among others) favours a predicate construal of propositional attitude-modifiers. Now, shedding traditional assumptions, we can inquire into the possibility of treating *all* of our modifiers predicatively, perhaps in the paratactic style; and certainly considerations of syntactic similarity would seem to encourage such uniform handling. Thus for necessity we might propose

$$\text{sats } (s, \ulcorner \text{Nec } (t) \urcorner, L) \equiv \text{Nec } (s^* \ t, L)$$

where t is, on the paratactic theory, a demonstrative singular term referring to an utterance or sentence. Similarly for negation

$$\text{sats } (s, \ulcorner \text{Not } (t) \urcorner, L) \equiv \text{Not } (s^* \ t, L)$$

and likewise for the binary truth-functional connectives, paralleling Davidson's treatment of propositional attitudes. If a theory opted for such axioms quite generally, then plainly the object-language would not, by that theory, contain any semantic operators whatever: all would go the way of 'It is true that'. Such a theory is evidently formally feasible, and it is hard to justify resistance to it by usual criteria: we meet Convention T as well here as elsewhere, the ontology invoked is neither intrinsically objectionable nor beyond what is called for when predicate treatments are unavoidable, and structural constraints are adequately respected. It begins to seem that, so far from the theory inexorably imposing its own semantic decisions, there is nothing here to keep us from free-wheeling entirely.

We have, in effect, two questions to answer: (i) Is there significant system in the successes and failures of various operator treatments? (ii) Can we motivate a principled reluctance to treat all sentence modifiers as predicative? It is to be hoped that an answer to the first question will supply an answer to the second. The matter is delicate, but on the evidence now before us a pattern does seem discernible: an operator treatment has succeeded if and only if the construction in question produces a transparent context for (genuine) singular terms; it has failed if and only if the produced context is referentially opaque. Consideration of further cases seems to confirm this hypothesis: e.g., causal contexts on the one hand, and contexts like 'It is tautologous that' on the other. The reason is not far to seek: an operator theory for an expression E is available only if E permits certain substitutions in its scope, sc. of metalanguage singular terms and predicates containing semantic vocabulary, and this requires precisely that E not be absolutely opaque. That is, an operator treatment of E will need to exploit equivalences like

$$E \text{ (Fa)} \equiv E \text{ (denotation 'a' satisfies 'F')}$$

which arguably holds for certain modalities but certainly does not for propositional attitudes. It is true, of course, that an operator theory does not itself require full-width transparency of E, only the substitutivity properties needed to sustain the semantic ascent and descent called upon in the derivation of the T-sentences. But it is hardly surprising that contexts permitting such replacements should also permit others, and that those that do not should not.

To treat a construction as an operator is to specify its contribution to truth-conditions in terms of extensional properties (reference and satisfaction) of expressions that occur in its scope; and the mark of transparency is that the truth-value of sentences containing a transparent context should be sensitive only to extensional properties of the expressions occurring in the context. More intuitively, operator treatments refer us to what a sentence is about in stating its truth-conditions, and transparency is precisely the property of being semantically geared to the entities a sentence speaks of. Predicate treatments, by contrast, gear the statement of a modifier's contribution to truth-conditions to the *sentence* (grammatically) embedded in it, and opacity is precisely the property of sensitivity of truth-value to semantic features more finely distinguished than the entities a sentence refers to (to the senses of expressions or to the expressions themselves). The suggested picture, then, is that the transparency of a modifier and the feasibility of an operator treatment for it appear to coincide, and that this coincidence is unsurprising since operator treatments deploy referential concepts within the scope of the operator in their characteristic axioms. On the other hand, opaque modifiers demand predicate treatment, and this reflects the fact that opaque contexts are geared to the embedded sentence itself, not to extensional properties of its constituents. If this is a correct interpretation, the formal exigencies of truth-theory do correlate with an independently acknowledged semantic distinction, and indeed put that distinction in a new light. If it is incorrect, then I think our initial attractive idea is shown dubious. Let us therefore hope that it is correct.

This neat picture might seem threatened by the modifier 'It is analytic that', and in two ways: first, as a counter-example in its own right to the suggested picture; and second, as affording a means to making propositional attitudes, the paradigm opaque modifiers, operator-like. Taking the second point first, Baldwin has proposed 'slightly reconstruing' (!) propositional attitude constructions along the following lines:[6]

Ralph believes that A = df. ($\exists$ belief b) (Has (Ralph, b) & it is analytic that b is true iff A).

The proposal fails for (at least) this reason: the notion of analyticity needed to make the corresponding operator axiom work will license the very substitutions we saw to defeat a simple operator treatment of the propositional attitudes; but then Baldwin's definiens cannot be equivalent to its intended definiendum, since they will not be intersubstitutable *salva veritate*. But now, even waiving this, are the assumptions needed to secure an operator treatment of analyticity actually true? In short, are the axioms of an adequate truth theory analytic truths? Careful attention to the distinction between use and mention dispels the illusion that they are; for what occurs on the left-hand side of such an axiom is a *name* for a certain object-language expression, not that expression itself; and *its* meaning does not guarantee the truth of the axiom. This is brought out by two (connected) facts: (i) one can understand such semantic statements without knowing their truth-value (consider disquotational axioms for a language you don't know); and (ii) the semantic truths affirmed in an adequately interpretative truth theory are not *a priori*, as analytic truths must be, but are the upshot of empirical theory construction.[7] All analytic truths may be semantic truths of some sort, but not conversely. So 'It is analytic that', along with the propositional attitudes, resists operator treatment. This encourages the tentative conclusion that, according to the dictates of truth-theory, there *are* no opaque sentence operators — an antecedently familiar claim.[8]

Notes

1 I hesitate to attribute exactly this formulation of the conception to any one writer, but its general tenor seems to pervade John Wallace's 'On the Frame of Reference' in *Semantics of Natural Language*, eds D. Davidson and G. Harman (Boston, Reidel, 1972) and his 'Nonstandard Theories of Truth' in *The Logic of Grammar*, eds D. Davidson and G. Harman (Encino, Cal., Dickenson, 1975); also some of Davidson's writings, especially 'The Method of Truth in Metaphysics' in *Midwest Studies in the Philosophy of Language*, ed. French *et al.* (1977).

2 See D. Davidson's 'On Saying That', in *Words and Objections*, eds D. Davidson and J. Hintikka (Dordrecht, Reidel, 1969).

3 This seems to be Wallace's judgment; see 'Nonstandard Theories of Truth', p. 59.

4 I here rely upon the work of Christopher Peacocke, 'Necessity and Truth Theories', *Journal of Philosophical Logic* (1978) and Thomas Baldwin's 'Quantification, Modality and Indirect Speech' in *Meaning, Reference and Necessity*, ed. Simon Blackburn (Cambridge University Press, 1975).

5 I am told that Gareth Evans has worked out the details of such a theory in an unpublished paper, which unfortunately I have not seen.

6 See T. Baldwin, 'Quantification, Modality and Indirect Speech', section IX, for endorsement of the claims here criticized.

7   See D. Davidson's 'Radical Interpretation', *Dialectica*, vol. XXVII (1973).

8   Notably from the writings of W. V. Quine on the (related) difficulty of quantifying into such putative operators; see, e.g., 'Reference and Modality' and 'Quantifiers and Propositional Attitudes' both reprinted in *Reference and Modality*, ed. L. Linsky (Oxford University Press, 1971).

12 Quotation and saying that*

John McDowell

I

Oratio obliqua constructions pose well-known problems for a theory which systematically assigns truth-conditions to utterances in a language.[1] In order to solve these problems, Donald Davidson, in 'On Saying That',[1] offers a paratactic representation of the logical form of sentences containing *oratio obliqua* constructions. Davidson's theory is beautiful and illuminating; perhaps there are difficulties in its further elaboration, but this paper will not criticize it on this or any other score. However, Davidson develops his approach by way of offering to correct 'a subtle flaw' (p. 168) which he claims to find in a promising alternative, namely an approach which employs quotation. In this paper I question the cogency of Davidson's objection to his quotational rival. In the course of doing so, I query the account of quotation which Davidson sketches in 'On Saying That', and elaborate a promising competitor (section VI). The competitor proves subject to difficulties, however (section VII), which help to motivate a different later suggestion of Davidson's own (section VIII). If quotation is understood in this final, and I think satisfactory, way, then Davidson's argument against a quotational account of indirect discourse fails; but the quotational account still will not do (section X). I conclude (section XI) with some remarks about what is achieved by Davidson's paratactic theory.

II

A convenient way to bring out the character of the quotational approach which Davidson discusses is to trace its emergence through the three stages of W. V. Quine's treatment in *Word and Object*.[2]

*I read a version of this paper to an Oxford seminar in 1972, and another at Birkbeck College in 1974; members of those groups, especially Gareth Evans and Mark Platts, have helped to improve it.

At the first stage, the proposal is to regiment sentences like

(1) Galileo said that the earth moves

into sentences containing a two-place predicate, '_____ says-true _____', true of speakers and sentences. (For present purposes we can count proposals for regimentation as proposals about how to represent logical form.[3]) So (1) is represented by

(2) Galileo said-true 'The earth moves'.

The 'said-true' of (2) is not to be confused with the 'said' of direct quotation: (2) is to be true just in case (1) is, even though Galileo did not utter the words quoted in (2).

At the second stage, it is claimed that (2) is vulnerable to a possible indeterminacy of truth-value, over and above anything that affects (1). The claim (to which I shall return: section VII) is that the singular term which fills the second argument-place of (2)'s predicate – the quotation ' "The earth moves" ' – refers to an item which, besides behaving in familiar ways in English, may conceivably also be a sentence of some other language, say Martian. Perhaps in Martian it means something different: something Galileo never said. If this is so, the relation which 'said-true' is meant to express both holds and fails to hold between Galileo and 'The earth moves'. So the two-place predicate gives way to a three-place predicate, '_____ says-true _____ in _____', true of speakers, sentences, and languages; and (1) is now represented by

(3) Galileo said-true 'The earth moves' in English.

Alonzo Church made trouble for this proposal by considering translations of sentences like (3) into other languages.[4] These considerations fail to impress Quine, since they turn on a notion of which Quine takes a dim view: the notion of sameness of meaning. But Quine dislikes the proposal anyway, because of its 'dependence on the notion of *a* language'.[5] Questions about the identity of languages are at least as problematic as those questions about the identity of propositions whose intelligibility Quine doubts; and it was the hope of avoiding these latter questions which made a quotational approach to 'propositional attitudes' attractive in the first place.[6] So Quine moves to a third version, in which the worry which prompted the second is met by having a third argument-place not for a language but for a speaker:

(4) Galileo said-true 'The earth moves' in my sense.

Quine remarks, about this third version, that the third argument-place will 'regularly' be occupied by the speaker of the whole, 'since "that" clauses are always given in our own language'.[7] This may prompt the suspicion that 'in my sense', in (4), is redundant. I shall return to this later (section VII).

John McDowell

III

As Davidson suggests (p. 168), (4) should be paraphrasable by

(5) Galileo uttered a sentence that meant in his mouth what 'The earth moves' means now in mine.

His discussion of (5) runs as follows (pp. 168-9):

We should not think ill of this verbose version of 'Galileo said that the earth moves' because of apparent reference to a meaning ('what "The earth moves" means'); this expression is not treated as a singular term in the theory. We are indeed asked to make sense of a judgment of synonymy between utterances, but not as the foundation of a theory of language, merely as an unanalyzed part of the content of the familiar idiom of indirect discourse. The idea that underlies our awkward paraphrase is that of *samesaying*: when I say that Galileo said that the earth moves, I represent Galileo and myself as samesayers.

And now the flaw is this. If I merely *say* that we are samesayers, Galileo and I, I have yet to *make* us so; and how am I to do this? Obviously, by saying what he said; not by using his words (necessarily), but by using words the same in import here and now as his there and then. Yet this is just what, on the theory, I cannot do. For the theory brings the content-sentence into the act sealed in quotation marks, and on any standard theory of quotation, this means the content-sentence is mentioned and not used. In uttering the words 'The earth moves' I do not, according to this account, say anything remotely like what Galileo is claimed to have said; I do not, in fact, say anything.[8]

Davidson's own proposal is designed expressly to remedy this alleged flaw. The logical form of (1) is represented by

(6) Galileo said that. The earth moves.

To utter this is to make two utterances. In uttering the second sentence, one makes oneself a samesayer with Galileo; so the objection to the quotational account does not apply. The first utterance refers to the second (with the demonstrative 'that'), refers also to Galileo, and predicates of them that the latter is related to the former by a relation expressed by 'said'.[9] This relation can be explained[10] in terms of samesaying, on these lines: the first utterance — which predicates the saying relation — would be true in the same circumstances as an utterance of 'Some utterance of Galileo's, and this one, make us samesayers', with the demonstrative phrase 'this one', like 'that' in (6), heralding and referring to the utterance of the content-sentence by the speaker of the whole.

208

In a typical self-standing utterance of 'The earth moves', 'the earth' would refer to the earth; that is, probably, the planet most referred to in discussions of Galileo. Given the identity, the truth of 'The earth moves' guarantees the truth of 'The planet most referred to in discussions of Galileo moves'; accepting such inferences is part of what it means to accept that 'the earth', in 'The earth moves', functions as a referring expression. If the sentence 'The earth moves' is a semantic component of (1), and if 'the earth' in this sentence — the content-sentence — has its ordinary semantic role, then a similar substitution in (1) should preserve truth. But Galileo did not say that the planet most referred to in discussions of Galileo moves.

Frege's response is to abandon the assumption that the expressions of the content-sentence have their usual semantic role.[11] But according to Davidson's proposal, the expressions of the content-sentence function exactly as they would be said to function by a satisfactory semantic account of the content-sentence on its own.[12] This thesis is freed from unacceptable inferential implications by the fact that the content-sentence is not represented as a semantic component of the utterance whose truth-value is at issue when we assess the truth or falsehood of an *oratio obliqua* report. The truth of an utterance of 'Galileo said that', with 'that' taken as a demonstrative whose reference is fixed by pointing, as it were, in the direction of a certain item, could not entail (by virtue of the form of the sentence which expresses the truth in question) the truth of a different utterance of the same sentence, with the reference of the demonstrative fixed by pointing at a different item. But the items pointed at are utterances, by the utterer of the whole report, of sentences whose component expressions are functioning as they would function in ordinary utterances of those sentences: if I say 'Galileo said that the earth moves', the phrase 'the earth' normally refers, on my lips, to the earth.

An utterance of a content-sentence will not in general be an assertion. (In special circumstances it may be, for instance when prefaced by the explicitly performative 'I hereby assert that'.) But it would be a groundless prejudice to suppose that in uttering 'The earth moves' one cannot be referring to the earth, and predicating of it that it moves, unless one's utterance is an assertion.[13]

IV

Davidson's argument against the quotational approach can be summarized as follows. The primitive predicate which figures in a representation of logical form like (4) would need to be explained in terms of samesaying.[14] (How the explanation goes, for the particular case of (4), is sketched in the 'awkward paraphrase' (5).) But the explanation introduces undesired possibilities of falsehood. An utterer of (4) says something which should be true just in case he and Galileo are samesayers. If he omits to make them so – as he does if all he says is (4) – then his utterance of (4) should be false. But if he had said (1), he would have been uttering a truth. Under a rephrasing which ought simply to make the primitive clear, the regimentations may be false when what they regiment is true. So the account of logical form cannot be correct.

I shall question this argument on two counts. First, Davidson does not show that the explanation of the quotational primitive would need to appeal to samesaying in such a way as to introduce surplus possibilities of falsehood; another option is open which he does not argue against. I shall elaborate this in section V. Second, the argument relies on the questionable thesis that to mention a sentence by quoting it is not to use it. I shall elaborate this in sections VI–VIII.

V

The first criticism is independent of the second. So let us assume, for the moment, that to quote the sentence 'The earth moves' is not to use it.

Does it follow that someone who only quotes the sentence cannot be a samesayer with Galileo? Obviously it depends on the nature of the samesaying relation. Davidson uses the term in forms like this: 'a's utterance b, and c's utterance d, make a and c samesayers'. So it seems that samesaying is a relation which utterances cause to hold between speakers. But the relation which really does the work, in the suggested explanations of primitives, would be the four-place relation between utterances and speakers, or perhaps the relation between utterances on which the samesaying relation is consequential.[15]

Now one reasonable way to think of utterances is as concrete particular events.[16] We might plausibly say that actual occurrence is to concrete particular events what actual existence is to material objects. So, just as we should be suspicious of the idea that there are possible but non-existent particular people,[17] we should equally be suspicious of the idea that there are possible but non-occurrent particular concrete events. If there are not, then unless one actually makes a suitable utterance – as the quotational approach, on our present assumption, fails to ensure that one does – one cannot be a samesayer with Galileo; there is nothing to fill one of the argument-places of the four-place relation formulated above.

But must samesaying be thought of this way?

Davidson proposes that we should try to construct Tarskian truth-characterizations for natural languages. At first sight, this project is vulnerable to objection on the ground that, if a language contains indexical elements, it cannot be sentences which are the bearers of truth-values. Davidson's standard response is to modify Tarski: the truth-predicate to be characterized is not, as in Tarski, a one-place predicate of sentences, but a three-place predicate of sentences, utterers and times. An expression of the three-place truth-predicate takes this form: '*a* is true as potentially uttered by *b* at *c*'.[18] This predicate, then, can hold of a sentence, a person, and a time even though the sentence is not then uttered by the person. The predicate gives a way of saying, in effect, that a certain potential utterance would have been true (this is a different use of 'true', as a one-place predicate of utterances); but it does not require an ontology of non-actual concrete particulars.[19]

Why should samesaying not be reconstrued on similar lines? On this reconstrual, two speakers will be made samesayers not only by actual utterances of theirs which are, as Davidson puts it, 'the same in import' (p. 169), but also by potential utterances which would match in import. As before, the appearance of quantifying over potential utterances is dispensable. We can capture the idea in a formulation like Davidson's formulation of his truth-predicate: if sentence *a*, as potentially uttered by person *b* at time *c*, is the same in import as sentence *d*, as potentially uttered by person *e* at time *f*, then *b* and *e* are samesayers in respect of those sentences and times. (As in the truth-predicate, 'potentially' need not exclude 'actually'; it simply signals that an actual utterance is not required.) On this account of samesaying, I need not utter a sentence in order to be a samesayer with Galileo, any more than I need utter a sentence in order to stand to it and the present moment in the relation expressed by Davidson's truth-predicate. When I claim to be a samesayer with Galileo, with respect to a certain sentence, I can specify the sentence in any way I choose; I need not be embarrassed by the accusation that I have only mentioned the sentence and not used it. So if the quotational primitive is explained in terms of samesaying as reconstrued here, Davidson's 'subtle flaw' disappears.

On occasion Davidson seems to suggest that there is no fundamental difference between truth-characterizations which deal with his three-place predicate, on the one hand, and truth-characterizations which deal with a one-place predicate of utterances, on the other.[20] We can certainly effect a simple connection between them if we construe utterances as ordered triples of sentences, persons and times, so that what appears in one theory as a relation between three items becomes, in the other, a monadic property of a triple. But if utterances are construed in this way, there is no doubting the existence of utterances which do not get uttered; at any rate not on the sort of grounds considered above. Given the existence of the relevant sentence, person and time, the existence of an utterance is guaranteed by part of set theory, whether the person utters the sentence at the time or not. Scepticism would have to be about the required part of set theory. On this construal, utterances are not concrete but abstract particulars. If utterances are thought of in this way, the six-place relation of the last paragraph can be seen as a spelling out of the original four-place relation; and if no suitable sentence gets uttered by me, it no longer follows that we have no occupant for one of the argument-places of the four-place relation.

What objection could there be to this reinterpretation of samesaying? Is the modified relation unintelligible? Surely not; we can explain it in terms of the relation which Davidson considers, as follows: if the relevant sentences are actually uttered by the relevant people at the relevant times, the relations coincide; if either or both of the sentences are not uttered, then the modified relation holds if and only if, had the sentences been uttered by the people at the times, they would have been producing utterances that would have occupied the appropriate argument-places in a true ascription of the four-place relation which Davidson considers.

This partly counterfactual explanation spells out the force of 'potentially' in an earlier formulation. Is it objectionable? We have already seen that there is something similar in the theorems of a Davidsonian truth-characterization for a natural language. This is for good reasons. The point and interest of Davidson's truth-characterizations lies in this fact: they would show how the truth-conditions of utterances depend first on how the sentences uttered are constructed, by modes of construction exemplified in other sentences too, out of parts which occur in other sentences too; and second on the identity of the utterer and the time of utterance. No theory which had this sort of interest, and dealt with a language of even moderate complexity, could restrict itself to actual utterances; it would be bound to have implications about sentences which were constructed in ways it discussed out of parts it discussed, but which happened never to be spoken at all, and similarly implications about sentences as uttered by people who did not utter them, or as uttered at times at which they were not uttered, even if they were uttered by other people and at other times. This is analogous to the way in which, if a language is sufficiently complex, a systematic syntax for it is bound to certify as grammatical some strings which are never actually uttered.

On these lines it appears that, if a truth-theorist does aim to characterize truth as a monadic predicate of utterances, he will need to find a way of construing merely potential utterances as subjects of predication. But, as we saw above, this undermines Davidson's argument against the quotational approach.

We cannot, then, eliminate 'potentially' from our formulation of the truth-predicate. Now this is not merely parallel to the partly counterfactual construal of samesaying whose intelligibility I am concerned with. The same considerations apply, in the end, to both cases.

Davidson's claim is that his truth-characterizations would be appropriate components of theories of meaning; that is, theories such that knowledge of what they say would suffice for interpreting utterances in the languages which they deal with. The role of a truth-characterization in such a theory would be that the sentences used on the right-hand sides of its theorems — specifications of truth-conditions — could be employed to specify the content of speech acts effected by uttering the sentences mentioned on the left. If a truth-characterization of the appropriate kind tells us that a certain sentence *a*, as uttered by a person *b* at a time *c*, is true if and only if *p*, then it is to be acceptable to interpret *b*'s utterance of *a* at *c* as his saying that *p*. (The implicit limitation to the indicative is an eliminable simplification.[21])

Now we cannot dispense with the restriction 'of the appropriate kind'; not all truth-characterizations which are correct, in that they specify conditions under which utterances really are true, will serve this interpretative purpose.[22] And we cannot explain the restriction without an appeal to the interpretative purpose itself. We cannot first construct a theory about the conditions under which utterances are true, and then draw conclusions about what speakers are saying; rather, we attempt to construct a truth-characterization precisely with a view to the acceptability of using its specifications of truth-conditions as specifications of what speakers are saying.[23]

Of course we can test this acceptability only by how well our interpretations make sense of actual utterances. But the system in the theory means that our theorizing will go beyond the actual. And this will be so not only in specifications of truth-conditions for merely potential utterances, as already noted, but also, and by the same token, in hypotheses about what speakers would be saying if they made those potential utterances. To try to construct a truth-characterization of the appropriate kind is inevitably to theorize about the acceptability of counterfactual *oratio obliqua* reports. If these reports must be understood in terms of samesaying, then no one who is prepared to theorize in this way can object to the counterfactual used above in the explanation of the modified samesaying relation.[24]

(It may be thought that we ought not to allow people to be actual samesayers by virtue of merely potential utterances. But if it is conceded that the counterfactual reports are intelligible, this point is only terminological. Say, if you like, no more than the following: if the people had made the utterances, they would have been samesayers — Davidson's samesaying, counterfactually employed. This still gives materials for an explanation of the quotational primitive, even if quoting a sentence is not using it. Thus: if I were now to utter the sentence 'The earth moves', then that utterance and an utterance which Galileo made would have rendered Galileo and me samesayers. On this account, a more perspicuous 'awkward paraphrase' than (5) would be

(7) Galileo uttered a sentence that meant in his mouth what 'The earth moves' would mean now in mine.

And (7) is certainly less economical than (6). But this is not Davidson's point. Given the intelligibility of counterfactual *oratio obliqua* reports, (7) is immune to Davidson's argument against (5).)

There is a sense in which, on the view sketched above, the 'judgments of synonymy' involved in ascriptions of samesaying are at the foundations of a theory of a particular language; this seems to contradict a remark of Davidson's quoted above ('On Saying That', p. 168).[25] The point Davidson should be making is not that judgments of samesaying are not fundamental in constructing a theory of a language, but rather that such judgments are not grounded in some deeper level, at which one recognizes that there is a single meaning, shared by the utterances which underlie a case of samesaying. (Cf. section XI below.)

Dealing with formal languages, Tarski could take the notion of translation for granted, as determined by stipulation, and work from there to a characterization of truth. Davidson points out that when we say what it is to construct a semantic description of a natural language, we cannot simply recapitulate Tarski's procedure, since translation can no longer be taken for granted.[26] Now I am not suggesting that firm judgments of samesaying are made in advance of constructing a truth-characterization, when one interprets a foreign language from scratch; nor that the question what someone is saying — a question whose true answer is systematically determined by the words he utters and the context of utterance — is intelligible independently of the idea of something like a truth-characterization. So I am not making myself liable to Davidson's strictures.

But it seems wrong to suggest, as Davidson does, that we should reverse Tarski's direction.[27] I claimed above that we do not know independently what a truth-characterization of the appropriate kind is, and use the construction of such a truth-characterization as a route to judgments of samesaying (judgments about what people are saying). On the contrary, we have no notion of what the appropriate kind is except in terms of the acceptability of judgments about what people are saying. Constructing a truth-characterization of the appropriate kind, and putting oneself in a position systematically to interpret what people say, are a single activity; no worthwhile procedure moves in either direction. Nevertheless, there remains this sense in which we can say that the second description of the activity is nearer the foundations: it is by way of the question whether its implications about what people say are acceptable that a truth-characterization is confronted with the behavioural facts on which it rests.

VI

The second objection to Davidson's argument is this: he does not show that there is no workable account of quotation according to which, if one quotes a sentence, one is thereby effecting an utterance of it. Armed with such an account of quotation, we could defend the quotational approach without needing to query whether actual utterances are required for the samesaying relation.

A workable account of quotation, for the purpose at hand, is one which shows how the occurrence of quotation in a stretch of discourse does not block the systematic assignment of truth-conditions.

It is natural to begin with the assumption that quotations are singular terms. (This was taken for granted in the development of the quotational approach outlined in section II.) Systematic assignment of truth-conditions requires that the singular terms be seen as structured combinations of components from a finite stock.[28]

Davidson (p. 162) sketches an account which exploits the structure articulated by spelling. A full-dress version might be as follows. There would be somewhat over thirty base clauses, each fixing what is denoted by the result of enclosing a letter (including spaces and punctuation marks) in quotation marks — namely, in each case, the letter itself; and a recursive clause dealing in the obvious way with concatenation, treated perhaps as an iterable two-place functional expression which yields complex quotations when its argument-places are filled with quotations. The quotation ' "the" ' (say) is treated as abbreviating '("t" concatenated with "h") concatenated with "e" '. The upshot is that any string consisting of left-hand quotes, a concatenation of letters and right-hand quotes denotes the concatenation of letters: ' "The earth moves" ' denotes 'The earth moves'.

This account treats quotation as a variant notation for spelling out the quoted material. Reformulated in a way which makes explicit the semantic structure credited to it on this view, (4) becomes something like this:

(8) Galileo said-true, in my sense, the result of concatenating the following in this order: 't', 'h', 'e', ' ', 'e', 'a', 'r', 't', 'h', ' ', 'm', 'o', 'v', 'e', 's'.

As Davidson says (p. 169), an utterance of 'The earth moves' is not to be found in an utterance of (8). If this reformulation accurately reflects the semantic structure of (4), then any appearance that in uttering (4) one utters the sentence quoted is a mere accident of notation.

But this conclusion is rather hard to believe. (Try saying (4) aloud.) Davidson claims to find the spelling account of quotation 'all but explicit in Quine' (p. 162), but Quine's discussion of spelling is offered not as a theory of the semantics of quotation but as an account of 'an alternative device to the same purpose'.[29] This seems the right description. Besides its desirable results (such as ' " 'The earth moves' " ' denotes "The earth moves" '), the spelling account also serves up consequences like this: ' "zxwt prt gjh" ' denotes 'zxwt prt gjh'. Not that this is to be objected to on the ground that it assigns a semantic property to something we cannot say (let alone understand); we can write ' "zxwt prt gjh" ', and if it is written for an appropriate purpose — namely to say something about that string of letters — we do understand it. But we are under no obligation to suppose that what we write and understand in such a case is a quotation.[30]

The structure articulated by spelling is not the only structure discernible in written quotation. There is also the superficial syntactic structure marked by spaces between words; and (with some complications) we can find the same structure in spoken language, marked by possibilities of alternative combinations. Exploiting this, we could construct an account that would be formally parallel to the spelling account. I shall sketch the idea, to begin with, in a version suited to quotations written according to standard modern English practice. Each base clause would assign a denotation to the result of enclosing a word in quotation marks, namely the word itself. (The number of base clauses, in an account which deals with quotation of, say, English, would still be finite, though of course much larger.) The recursive clause would be as before. As before, ' "The earth moves" ' denotes 'The earth moves'. (Equally, ' "Moves earth the" ' denotes 'Moves earth the'. But ' "zxwt prt gjh" ' is not given a denotation by this theory.) There is an informal version of this account of quotation in P. T. Geach's *Mental Acts*.[31]

We can take the semantic treatment just described as formalizing the following view of quotation, in a way appropriate, so far, for the quotation-mark notation. All words are ambiguous in one extra dimension, over and above any we need to recognize apart from quotation: any word can occur as a name of itself. When words which require this autonymous interpretation are concatenated, concatenation is not, as usual, a mere method of syntactic construction, but takes on the descriptive significance registered in our recursive clause. So the concatenation of the words 'the', 'earth' and 'moves', in that order, with the words bearing their autonymous interpretation, denotes the concatenation of the words 'the', 'earth' and 'moves', in that order.

Actual marks of quotation are treated here as a dispensable notational convention.[32] The purpose of the convention is to disambiguate: the notation allows us to indicate explicitly which interpretation of ambiguous expressions is intended. Apart from the greater generality of the convention, flanking words with quotation marks is on a par with writing 'bank$_1$' when one means a financial institution and 'bank$_2$' when one means a configuration of terrain. No one could suppose that embellishing an occurrence of 'bank' with a subscript prevented it from being a use of a word. Similarly, then, with quotation marks: on the present account of quotation, there is nothing to stop us saying that words written within quotation marks are used, with the quotation marks serving the purpose of explicitly requiring the autonymous interpretation (and also of indicating, as noted above, that concatenation in the context acquires a descriptive significance).

On this view, it is after all misleading to state the semantic theory in terms of the quotation-mark notation. What we want is a general account of how words work in contexts of quotation. The effect of the previous base clauses can be achieved by a simple quantification over words: any word in such a context denotes itself.[33] (The domain of this quantification would be fixed by the syntax which is anyway a prerequisite to a semantic description of a language.) Otherwise the theory can be as before. Where we mention quotation marks is in a general account of the contexts in which this fragment of the semantics of the language applies. One such context is the kind indicated in writing by quotation marks. But we can recognize that there are other ways in which the intention to quote is signalled. (Sometimes we discern quotation simply because no other interpretation makes sense.)

Quotation marks, or — better now — inverted commas, serve not only to indicate quotation as here understood. We have already envisaged examples like

(9) The machine printed out 'zxwt prt gjh'.

And there is also transcription of vocal sounds, as in

(10) The song begins 'a wop bop a loo bop a lop bam boom'.

For (9), if we assume (as so far with quotations) that ' "zxwt prt gjh" ' is a singular term, we need something like Davidson's spelling account. We might parallel the suggested treatment of quotation marks in quoting: the spelling theory is labelled as applicable to contexts of copying, with inverted commas figuring, again, in a general gloss on the label, as a device for signalling such contexts. For (10), a spelling account would miss the point. Here we need an analogue to the spelling account, with phonemes substituted for letters. (There is a complication: a straightforward analogue would have concatenations of phonemes denoting themselves, but what is written between inverted commas in (10) is not a string of phonemes. The phoneme-spelling theory would apply to a spoken version of (10); we should think of (10), as it stands, as our written representation of what is primarily a spoken form. Similarly, (9) is primarily a written form.)

According to this picture, then, inverted commas signal one of at least three kinds of context: quotation, letter-by-letter copying, and vocal mimicry. This diversity is not a ground for disliking the theory, or set of theories, which I have described. The roles of inverted commas have a common feature which makes the diversity intelligible. In each case inverted commas signal autonymy: in the first case selecting the autonymous interpretation from among others to which the surrounding matter might be susceptible, in the other two indicating the only way in which the surrounded matter can in general be interpreted at all.

(The idea of autonymy helps to explain the sense in which (9) is primarily a written form and (10) primarily a spoken one. We have autonymy — letters denoting letters — only in the written form of (9). A spoken version might be transcribable thus:

(11) The machine printed out zed-ex-doubleyu-tee pee-ar-tee gee-jay-aitch;

where it is names of letters which denote letters, rather than the letters themselves. Analogously, we have autonymy — phonemes denoting phonemes — only in the spoken form of (10). As we noted above, the written version uses, to denote phonemes, something other than the phonemes themselves: namely strings of letters such that to read them aloud as if they were words, according to standard principles of English spelling, is to utter the phonemes.[34]).

On the present view, the quotation fragment of a semantic description of English would deal with the autonymous use of English words only. (Recall that the domain of quantification, in what replaces the base clauses, is to be fixed by a syntax for our object language.) So such a theory would not handle sentences like

(12) He said 'Sprechen Sie Deutsch?'.

We might consider dealing with (12) in terms of spelling or mimicry; no doubt such an account would accurately reflect any understanding of (12) which is available to someone wholly ignorant of German. But we can also countenance another possible level of understanding, in which what follows 'said' is understood as quotation in a sense which contrasts with spelling or mimicry. A semantic treatment which reflected this level of understanding would draw on the quotation fragment of a semantic description of German, and so represent (12) as a hybrid, not wholly in English.[35] (Notice that this level of understanding would not require comprehension of the standard meaning of the quoted words; the semantic treatment would draw on no more than a syntax for German and that fragment of the semantics which deals with the autonymous use of words.)

The account of quotation sketched in this section seems to protect the possibility of systematically assigning truth-conditions, by showing how denotations can be systematically assigned to quotations. But quoting the concatenation of words which constitutes a sentence is regarded as a (special) use of that concatenation of words. Certainly someone who utters (4) or (5) does not assert the sentence 'The earth moves'; this matches Davidson's own (6), and is as it should be. But on the proposed view of quotation, such a person does utter the sentence. So if this account of quotation is acceptable, it undermines Davidson's complaint that an utterer of (4) or (5) has not made himself a same-sayer with Galileo.

VII

If quoting words is mentioning them by using them in a special, self-denoting way, then the denotation of a quotation depends on the identity of the words used in it. Now, what is a word? A view urged by Geach is that inscriptional or phonetic match does not suffice for word-identity; according to Geach, the German word 'ja' (meaning 'yes') and the Polish word 'ja' (meaning 'I') are two different words.[36]

From the standpoint of this view of Geach's, there was something wrong with the development of the quotational approach outlined in section II. The ground for adding a third argument-place to the regimentations was that, in its intended interpretation, the original two-place relation of saying-true could both hold and fail to hold between a person and a sentence, since one and the same sentence might also belong to, say, Martian, and have a different sense in that language. But according to Geach's view of word-identity this ground was false. Whatever it is that conceivably belongs to Martian, it cannot be the very sentence we use in English, since it does not consist of the same words. If we do specify a language in a quotational regimentation, it must be as in

(13) Galileo said-true the English sentence 'The earth moves'

where 'English' must be taken as part of a complex singular term, designating the second argument of a two-place predicate. Its point is to make clear which sentence is used in the quotation, and hence which sentence is denoted by it.[37]

'In my sense', in (4), took over the purpose of 'in English', in (3); and we are now seeing that purpose as being to make clear the identity of the second argument of a two-place predicate. Now it might seem that we could reason as follows. The reconstrued purpose of 'in my sense' is presumably to indicate that the sentence designated is the one which the utterer of (4) would be using if, in uttering the quotation, he were using a sentence. But on the present view of quotation he is using a sentence when he utters the quotation. It would be pointless to preface everything one said with 'This is in my sense'. So must not 'in my sense', in (4), be superfluous? (Recall the suspicion of redundancy mentioned at the end of section II.)

But this line of thought is superficial. It would be equally pointless to make a general practice of specifying the language in which one was speaking. But one need not always speak one's own usual language or that of one's interlocutors. On the assumption that one speaks the words one quotes, sentences like (12) yield examples of slipping into another language, though of course such slipping is possible independently of quotation. Equiformities between languages can thus generate real possibilities of misunderstanding, which one can sensibly aim to avert by specifying the language to which a potentially confusing utterance is to be taken as belonging. Similarly, one can slip out of one's own usual idiom, while remaining, in any ordinary sense, in the same language — perhaps in a kind of play-acting, but equally in quoting words as they would be used by speakers of a different dialect; and here adding 'in my sense' or 'in your sense' might be the best way to avert similar possibilities of misunderstanding. So 'in my sense' is not generally superfluous. If changing the dialect, like changing the language, gives a new word, 'in my sense' must be thought of, like 'in English', as part of a complex singular term, with the qualification helping to make it clear what is designated by a quotation.

Now there are at least two difficulties here for an account of quotation on Geach's lines.

First, how exactly do the qualifying phrases work? Geach says that the specifications of languages 'logically attach not to the predicates ... but to the subject'.[38] But how does 'English sentence' (for example) function in the putative complex singular term 'the English sentence "The earth moves" '?

We cannot assimilate its functioning to that of 'whom we met yesterday' in 'the Jones whom we met yesterday'. For 'Jones' in this phrase must be understood as a predicate univocally true of Joneses.[39] The Jones we met yesterday and the Jones we met the day before would each be a Jones in the same sense. The sense is, roughly, that they are named 'Jones': 'Jones' — one and the same name — is a name of each Jones. A parallel account of 'the English sentence "The earth moves" ' and 'the Martian sentence "The earth moves" ' would represent ' "The earth moves" ' — one and the same name, in an extended sense — as a name of each of the two sentences. But this contradicts Geach's account of the identity of quoted words.

Perhaps we could preserve that account by claiming that the qualifying phrases function like subscripts, in the disambiguating notation envisaged in section VI. The subscripts signal that 'bank' in 'bank$_1$' (a word for a financial institution) and 'bank' in 'bank$_2$' (a word for a configuration of terrain) are not a single word;[40] just as, according to Geach, ' "The earth moves" ', in 'the English sentence "The earth moves" ', and ' "The earth moves" ', in 'the Martian sentence "The earth moves" ', are not a single expression. However, it would be pointless to look for semantic structure within 'bank$_1$'. The subscript is inscriptionally attached to 'bank', but not semantically attached to anything. There is no semantic unit (for instance a word; in this notation 'bank' is not a word) for it to be attached to. If this is a good parallel to what Geach's account requires, the account is hard to swallow. Geach's phrase 'logically attach' suggests that he would not like the parallel; but if the phrase is meant to imply semantic attachment, then the manner of semantic attachment needs explaining.

Second, if the identity of words depends on the identity of languages (or, in the extension considered above in connection with 'in my sense', on the identity of dialects), then words become problematic as objects of reference. Recall the motivation ascribed to Quine, in section II above, for preferring the third version of the quotational approach to the second. From a Quinean standpoint, languages as a kind of entity should be no more acceptable than meanings. Indeed, the ideas seem interdefinable: two speakers speak the same language when a sufficient number of their equiform utterances have the same meaning.[41] Words, conceived in Geach's way, would be in the same boat. When Geach puts forward a quotational account of indirect discourse, he discusses objections that presuppose a notion of synonymy sharp enough to warrant the thought that there is a meaning that two synonymous expressions both have. He responds like this: 'I should demand of such a critic: "What is your criterion of synonymy?" – with very little hope of getting a coherent answer.'[42] But it appears that, in order to give the identity-conditions of the objects of reference required by his account of quotation, Geach needs the very sort of conceptual apparatus whose availability he here concurs with Quine in doubting.

Geach's view of word-identity is not a mere afterthought, readily detachable from an account of quotation like the one outlined in section VI. The only plausible alternative is a view of word-identity as determined by inscriptional or phonetic indistinguishability, or a combination of the two. But on such a view, given the conceivability of our speculation about Martian, there is no reason to say that, when one utters ' "The earth moves" ' in the course of uttering (4) or (5), one is designating (by making a special use of) English words in particular. Davidson's argument is thus reinstated: if I am not speaking English words when I utter sounds transcribable as 'The earth moves', only an illusion could seem to justify confidence that I thereby make myself a samesayer with Galileo. On this view, the quotation is a self-sufficient singular term; what it designates is, once more, something found equally in English and in our hypothetical Martian, and we are back to the justification for a third argument-place originally envisaged in section II. In this context there no longer seems to be any reason to object to the idea that quotation functions by sheer reproduction of strings of letters or phonemes. But the point of the account of quotation in section VI was largely to insist on a distinction between quotation and mere reproduction.

VIII

The difficulties disappear if we change tack, and query the assumption, so far unchallenged, that quotations are structured singular terms.

In his John Locke lectures (given in Oxford in 1970), Davidson pointed out that the assumption is anyway untenable for sentences like

(14) Geach says that they 'logically attach to the subject'.

This is a grammatical sentence, but it could not be (barring intolerably *ad hoc* modifications to syntactic theory) if what follows the first four words were a singular term. Such sentences cry out for a paratactic account of logical form. (14) is well regimented by

(15) Geach says that they logically attach to the subject,
      in part by uttering this;

where the arrow and bracket indicate the reference of the demonstrative.

In (14) the material surrounded by quotation marks is part of the sentence in which the quotation marks appear.[43] But once we have a paratactic account of sentences like (14), it is natural to extend it to sentences like (2), yielding a representation of form like Davidson's (6) in that the quoted material is not part of the sentence asserted by one who asserts (2):

(16) Galileo said-true this. The earth moves.

What is referred to by the demonstrative in an utterance of (16)? It is not, at first sight, obvious that there is anything to stop us saying this: it is an item indistinguishable in all respects from that referred to by the demonstrative in an utterance of Davidson's own (6). In that case, if an utterer of (6) is immune to criticism on the ground that he has failed to make himself a samesayer with Galileo, an utterer of (16) should be likewise immune, and the quotational approach seems, once more, not liable to Davidson's objection. (The details of this argument will be modified in section X.)

Our question about the semantic role of expressions like 'the English sentence', in 'the English sentence "The earth moves" ', is answered by obvious applications of the paratactic machinery. (13), for instance, becomes something like this:

> (17) The earth moves. That is an English sentence, and it was saidtrue by Galileo.

We can now bypass the problem about the identity-conditions of words. The theory need not speak of reference to anything over and above utterances: concrete particular events of writing or vocalizing. Many sentences seem, at first sight, to involve reference to words. But our theory can shirk the commitments which would be imposed by such an interpretation; we find reference only to utterances, and ensure acceptable construals of the sentences by means of an appropriate understanding of their predicates.[44]

The desirable distinction between quoting and mere reproduction is now located as a distinction between different sorts of predicate of utterances. Suppose someone makes inscriptions equiform with 'The earth moves' and 'zxwt prt gjh'. In both cases he does what is, at a certain level of description, the same kind of thing, namely effecting an utterance (in a broad sense). But there are properties which are not shared. In the first case the inscriber and his inscription may well stand in a certain complex relation to an equiform inscription by me: a relation which will serve to explain a two-place predicate, '____ writes the English words ____', which we can find in

> (18) He wrote the English words 'The earth moves'.

In the second case the inscriber stands in no such relation to any inscription of mine. He stands in a different relation to an inscription I can produce: a relation which will serve to explain a different two-place predicate, discernible in

> (19) He wrote the letters 'zxwt prt gjh'.

(This second relation holds in the first case also, but the first relation holds only there.) Predications explicable in terms of the first relation are typical cases of quoting; predications explicable in terms of the second are typical cases of reproduction.

The paratactic account of quotation has the advantage that concatenation no longer need be thought to play the dual role noted in section VI. We might have wondered whether the utterance of 'The earth moves' which we managed to find in, say, (4) could really be an utterance of the familiar sentence 'The earth moves', as it needed to be for the aim of defending the quotational approach against Davidson's objection. In the quotation, concatenation would be playing the role of a descriptive quasi-expression; but surely it plays no such role in the sentence. (I suppressed this doubt in section VI because I wanted to make the account of quotation as attractive as possible.)

Our current understanding of the quotational (2) is represented in (16). It is a question how, if at all, this differs from Davidson's (6).[45] I shall argue, in section X, that there is a difference, and that (6) is superior. But first I want to mention a consideration which has been thought favourable to quotational accounts of *oratio obliqua*.

IX

Quine has made us familiar with a distinction, within a set of idioms which includes *oratio obliqua* reports, between forms which block the intersubstitution of co-referring singular terms and forms which do not.[46] As noted in section III, from (1) and the identity of the earth with the planet most referred to in discussions of Galileo, we cannot standardly infer

(20) Galileo said that the planet most referred to in discussions of Galileo moves.

But we seem to be able to understand a different form of report, happily expressed by

(21) Galileo said of the earth that it moves,

in which we can, *salva veritate*, make such substitutions for 'the earth'. One reason why it seems that we must recognize the distinct form of (21) is that we appear to understand quantifications like

(22) There is something which Galileo said to move.

And we cannot see this, or some such regimentation as

(23) ($\exists x$) (Galileo said that x moves)

as constructed by quantification from a complex predicate, 'Galileo said that ＿＿＿moves', found also in (1), from which (23), on this view, would be seen as derivable by existential generalization. For we could make sense of such a derivation only if 'the earth' occurred in (1) as a singular term, and one which referred there to the earth, since it would be the earth which made (23) true. But, as noted in section III, the failure of substitution stops us supposing that this is so.[47] The upshot is that we seem to need two different primitive forms, exemplified in (1) and (21). A unification would be desirable.

Now consider the quotational regimentation (2). On an account of quotation like that outlined in section VI, the quotation in (2) is a 'structural description'. It consists of a concatenation of denoting expressions. There is no reason why the positions occupied by these expressions should not be accessible to variables bound by initial quantifiers. We can register this by constructing, from (2), the open sentence

(24) Galileo said-true α & 'moves'

where the Greek letter is a variable to range over expressions,[48] and '&' is a sign of concatenation. (2) can be reconstituted from (24) by constructing, out of the putative singular term ' "the earth" ', what we might call 'an individual quantifier', and using it to bind (24)'s variable, thus:

(25) 'The earth' is an α such that Galileo said-true α & 'moves'.

The item denoted by the putative singular term (on an account of quotation like that of section VI) stands in various relations to the earth: for instance, denoting it. A schematic representation of the form in which such relations are ascribed is

(26) R (' "the earth" ', the earth).

Here again, 'the earth' occupies a position accessible to a variable; we can write

(27) 'The earth' is an α such that R (α, the earth).

From (25) and (27) we have

(28) $(\exists\alpha)$ ($R(\alpha$, the earth) and Galileo said-true α & 'moves').

And, since 'the earth' occupies a referential position in (28), we can derive

(29) $(\exists x)(\exists\alpha)$ ($R(\alpha,x)$ and Galileo said-true α & 'moves').

Now it is attractive to suppose that, with a suitable interpretation of 'R', (28) will serve as an analysis of (21), and (29) as a rendering of (22). And the only primitive relation of saying expressed in (28) and (29) is the relation expressed in (2), the quotational regimentation of (1). This unification of the conceptual apparatus of (1) and (21) might seem a reason in favour of a quotational approach.[49]

But unification of primitives is possible on the paratactic approach too. There is an independent argument for finding further structure, not hitherto needed, in Davidson's (6), thus:

(30) $(\exists x)$ (Said (Galileo, x, this)). The earth moves.[50]

And now (21) can be represented thus:

(31) $(\exists x)$ (Of(the earth, x) and Said (Galileo, x, this)). It moves.[51]

Once again, the same primitive saying relation is expressed in both.

An inclination to prefer the former unification may be fuelled by

John McDowell

the currency of such labels as 'exportation',[52] for the inference from forms like (1) to forms like (21), or 'quantifying in',[53] for the inference from forms like (1) to forms like (22). The quotational approach does not treat these inferences as formally valid, but it does treat them as proceeding, in the presence of an extra premiss expressed in terms of 'R', by formal manipulations of expressions which occur in the sentences from whose truth the inferences proceed ((1) in our case); and this conforms to what the labels suggest. Nothing similar could be said about an inference from (30), together with a further premiss formulated in the terms used in an acceptable account of what it is for an utterance to be 'of' something, to (31). But of course what the labels suggest is simply a denial of the paratactic theory's most striking claim, namely that the expressions in question do not occur in the sentences in question. And the currency of the labels is not in itself an argument in favour of this denial.

In any case, the quotational unification depends essentially on an account of quotation like that outlined in section VI; and the difficulties mentioned in section VII still threaten any such account.[54]

X

What is the difference between (6) and (16)?

Consider first what should be paradigm cases of quotation, namely *oratio recta* reports like

(32) He said 'The earth moves'.

On a paratactic account of quotation this becomes

(33) He said this. The earth moves.

The primitive 'said' of Davidson's (6) is explicable in terms of samesaying, which is intuitively expressible in terms of a match in content between a pair of utterances. Analogously, the different primitive 'said' of (33) should be explicable in terms of a relation intuitively expressible by 'is an utterance of the same sentence as'.[55]

A pair of ordinary utterances by me of a sentence like 'That cat is hungry' will not, in general, make me a samesayer with myself. Context may determine that the reference is to different cats. But the relation which underlies the *oratio recta* 'said' (call it 'the quoting relation') holds between such utterances.

Such a sentence may serve as content-sentence in an *oratio obliqua* report, thus:

(34) He says that that cat is hungry.

226

A quotational regimentation, parallel to (2), is

(35) He says-true 'That cat is hungry'.

And the paratactic account of quotation yields, parallel to (16), this:

(36) He says-true this. That cat is hungry.

Now obviously the *oratio obliqua* 'says-true' of (36) cannot, like the *oratio recta* 'said' of (33), be understood simply in terms of the quoting relation (cf. section II above). As Davidson urges (cf. section III above), something like samesaying must also enter into an account of it. But if there is to be any point in claiming that (36) exploits the apparatus of quotation in representing the logical form of (34) — that 'says-true' is a quotational *oratio obliqua* primitive — then varying the identity of the utterance demonstrated in an utterance of (36) should not affect truth-value as long as the substitutively demonstrated utterance bears the quoting relation to the original.

But if this is right, the quotational approach to *oratio obliqua* is in trouble. If a given utterance of (36) by me does indeed lay bare the logical form of an utterance of (34), I should be able to achieve the same again with a subsequent utterance of (36), in circumstances in which, if I were saying 'That cat is hungry' on my own behalf, I would be referring to a different cat. But if the first demonstrated utterance made me a samesayer with the person I aim to report when I utter (34), it will only be an accident if the second does so too. And if the context in which the second demonstrated utterance is made is somehow blocked from determining reference to the wrong cat, how could the context in which the first demonstrated utterance was made determine reference to the right one?

The utterance which, according to a paratactic account of quotation, is demonstratively referred to when one quotes 'That cat is hungry' — call it 'u_1' — may be indistinguishable, in respect of all properties other than those it acquires or loses by virtue of the fact that what one predicates of it is quotational, from the utterance demonstratively referred to in a version of (34) on the lines of Davidson's (6) — call it 'u_2' (cf. section VIII above). Utterance u_1 may occur in a context in which, if it were not made for purposes of quotation, reference would be fixed, by interaction between the context and the sense of 'that cat', to a certain cat. But given that what is said about u_1 is quotational, an utterance of the same sentence in a context in which, quotation aside, reference would not be fixed to the same cat should serve just as well as a subject of the predication in question; this is the claim of the last two paragraphs. It follows that when an utterance is made in order to quote it, even if it occurs in a context which would otherwise determine references for expressions whose sense is insufficient to do so, like 'that cat', the fact that what is said about it is quotational divests it of what

John McDowell

would otherwise be a property consequential on occurrence in such a context, namely that the expressions refer as so determined. Thus u_1 and u_2 do after all differ (cf. section VIII), even if made in similar contexts, in that context enters into the interpretation of u_2 but is precluded from doing so with u_1 by the fact that what is predicated of it is quotational.

This generates a fatal tension in the putatively quotational *oratio obliqua* primitive 'says-true'. A samesaying component is evidently required in any explication of it that fits it to be an *oratio obliqua* primitive; and this demands that context operate to determine reference where the sense of a referring expression does not suffice on its own. But the quotational component thwarts this demand.[56]

On a paratactic account of quotation, there is no reason to say that quoted words are not uttered. This is not why an utterer of (35) fails to make himself a samesayer with someone who says that a certain cat is hungry. So the modification, two paragraphs back, to the argument of section VIII does not reinstate Davidson's objection to a quotational account of *oratio obliqua*. But the present objection suggests a different reading of his words 'the theory brings the content-sentence into the act sealed in quotation marks' (p. 169): not that the words of the content-sentence are not used at all, but that the quotation marks seal them off from their context in such a way as to prevent interpretation of context-dependent referring expressions.[57]

It might seem possible to repair the quotational approach. Can we not construct predicates of utterances which are quotational but whose sense nevertheless cancels the usual sealing-off effect of quotation? Then we should be able to achieve the effect of an *oratio obliqua* report by making sure the demonstrated utterance is in a suitable context, and applying to it a suitable predicate, explicable in terms of samesaying and quoting together, which has the cancelling force. But why should we count a paratactic form which lacks the sealing-off effect as quotational? In particular, it would be a confusion to suppose that Davidson's three-place truth-predicate, with quotation paratactically construed, is just such a form. The truth-predicate does not in general cancel insulation from context. It makes room for explicit mention of relevant features of potential contexts. Certainly if the extra argument-places are occupied by the utterer of the demonstrated utterance and the time at which he utters it, the upshot is tantamount to a cancellation of the sealing-off effect. But the sealing-off effect of quotation is required for a proper understanding of such uses of the truth-predicate as

(37) 'I am hot' is true as said by you now.

Intuitively speaking, quotation is a device for talking about words in abstraction from the circumstances in which the words happen to be produced for purposes of such talk. The account of quotation sketched in section VIII does not allow us to put it quite like that: in quotation, on this account, we talk not about words but about utterances. But the thesis that quotational predicates insulate quotationally demonstrated utterances from the usual interpretative impact of context is a suitable substitute, in the environment of this account, for the intuitive formulation.

There seems to be no point in calling a paratactic form 'quotational' unless its predicate has the sealing-off effect. But in the end there is no need to insist on this terminological policy. What we can say is this: a quotational account of *oratio obliqua*, with quotation understood paratactically, is either unsatisfactory or indistinguishable from Davidson's account.

XI

Failures of inferences involving substitution and quantification have seemed to some philosophers to justify the thesis that *oratio obliqua* reports relate speakers to propositions, construed as meanings of sentences. Words in 'that' clauses are taken to denote their own meanings – items which determine the meanings of sentences in which the words occur – and it becomes unsurprising that words whose normal denotation is the same should not be intersubstitutable in these contexts if their meanings differ. On this view, it is an application of a principle indispensable in the plainest extensional logic that pairs of words with the same meaning are intersubstitutable, *salva veritate*, in 'that' clauses of *oratio obliqua*.[58] However, pairs of synonyms which behave as expected fail to come to light (the Paradox of Analysis), and this might make us suspicious of the whole idea. Davidson's theory makes the idea superfluous: it yields accounts of logical form such that, without finding reference to meanings, we can see that there was no reason on grounds of form to expect the problematic inferences to go through (see section III).

This avoidance of reference to meanings may seem only a temporary subterfuge. Surely, it may be said, the idea of propositions, as entities which *oratio obliqua* reports are to be construed as referring to or quantifying over, will re-emerge when we look into the samesaying relation. What is it for a pair of utterances to make their utterers samesayers, if not that they are utterances of the same proposition?[59]

If this is to be damaging, however, the claim must be that there is no way to explain what samesaying is except in terms of a prior notion of meanings as objects of reference. Such a claim could not survive appreciation of Quine's writings on translation,[60] or – more to the point, since samesaying is not, in general, a relation exactly of translation – of Davidson's writings on interpretation.[61]

Given an equivalence relation between entities of a certain kind F, we can introduce entities of a new kind G, reconstruing the obtaining of the equivalence relation between two members of F in terms of the idea that both stand in a suitably expressed relation to one and the same member of G. For instance, a direction can be explained as what two parallel lines both have.[62] If samesaying – as explicated independently in behavioural and psychological terms, on the lines suggested by Davidson's work on radical interpretation – is an equivalence relation, it will similarly justify the introduction of things said (propositions) as possible objects of reference. This is not the place to discuss the Quinean considerations which cast doubt on the idea that we can make sense of such a samesaying relation. But one beauty of Davidson's account of *oratio obliqua* is that we do not need to raise the question. We can see that the problematic inferences need not have been expected to preserve truth, without being obliged to suppose that there is an intelligible samesaying relation of the kind which Quine doubts: one which would admit of reconstrual in terms of a common relation which utterances have to a single proposition. To understand the logical behaviour of *oratio obliqua* reports, we can make do with the rough and ready relation of samesaying which we actually use in reporting others, a relation whose describability and intelligibility nobody denies;[63] and, if we like, we can be agnostic about Quinean objections to propositions.

Quotation yields an instructive parallel. If we are to be faithful to the intuition that quoting differs from sheer reproduction, we cannot explicate the 'quoting relation' (see section X) entirely in terms of equiformity. To capture what lies behind the intuition, and accounts for the plausibility of Geach's view about word-identity, we need to ensure that two utterances which bear the quoting relation to each other are made, as we may intuitively put it, in the same language. What this comes to, if we avoid the appearance of quantifying over languages, is something like this: each utterance issues from a practice or disposition of its utterer, such that some sufficient number of equiform utterances issuing from the two dispositions would be intertranslatable (cf. section VII). If Quine is right about the notion of translation, a quoting relation explained in terms of translation will not be the sort of relation from which we could generate words, conceived in Geach's way, as possible objects of reference. Geach finds reference to words, conceived his way, in quotations, and this puts him in conflict with Quine, much as finding reference to meanings in *oratio obliqua* reports would (see section VIII). But we can achieve an approximation to Geach's intuitions, without being vulnerable to Quinean attack, if we suppose, as in section VIII, that the only relevant reference is to utterances. We can make do with a quoting relation which is at least as rough and ready as the translation relation appealed to in its explication.

Confidence that there can be no substance to qualms about propositions may be reinforced by arguments designed to show that Davidson's account of *oratio obliqua* reports does not even get their truth-conditions right.[64] But the arguments I have in mind are inconclusive.

A preliminary clarification may help to blunt their edge. In 'On Saying That' (p. 170), Davidson says that

(38) $(\exists x)$ (Galileo's utterance x and my last utterance make us samesayers)

becomes 'Galileo said that' — the second part of a reversed version of (6) — by way of 'definitional abbreviation'. This is misleading. It suggests the idea of a concise way of expressing exactly what some longer form expresses. But there is no reason to say that an utterer of (6) refers, for instance, to himself; whereas an utterer of (38) does refer to himself. A formulation like (38) should be thought of, not as an expansion justified by analysis (definition) of the saying primitive of (6), but as 'an expository and heuristic device':[65] an aid in instructing novices in the use of the saying primitive. We instruct a novice by saying: when you could truly utter (38), then you may follow the utterance in question with an utterance of 'Galileo said that', with the demonstrative referring to the utterance in question. This is a form of explanation of the primitive which need not confer on (6), the idiom explained, all the entailments of (38), in terms of which it is explained. Now an utterer of (6) not only does not refer to himself; he says nothing whatever about what he refers to with the demonstrative 'that' (except that Galileo said it). 'Galileo said that', uttered in the course of uttering (6) or its reversed version, no more entails

(39) $(\exists x)$ (x is an utterance of mine)

than 'That's a red one', said of what is in fact a billiard ball, entails '$(\exists x)$ (x is a billiard ball)'. Given a sufficiently careful account of the role of (38) in explaining (6)'s primitive, the fact that (38) entails (39) is irrelevant to this claim.[66]

Still, it may be said, Davidson directs us to understand (6) in such a way that an utterance of it cannot be true unless an utterance, by the same speaker, of (38) with 'next' substituted for 'last' would be true; this cannot be explained away by pedantry about entailment, and is sufficiently embarrassing for the account of *oratio obliqua*. But what exactly is the embarrassment supposed to be? Simon Blackburn's version of the argument comes to this:[67]

There is no logical equivalence between [(1)] and [(6)]. For I cannot now make an utterance such that [(1)] entails that [Galileo said — an occurrence of the saying primitive of (6) —] that utterance.

Suppose we rewrite the second sentence of this as follows: 'I cannot now make an utterance — call it "u" — such that an utterance of (1) by me cannot be true unless Galileo said u.' The point of the paratactic theory is that I cannot make an utterance of (1) without, in the course of doing so, making just such an utterance u. If the utterance of 'The earth moves' which I make in the course of uttering (1) had meant something different, thereby falsifying the claim that that utterance and one of Galileo's make him and me samesayers, then (by the same token) the utterance of (1) would itself have been false. Modal considerations like this, which are what Blackburn appeals to, cannot make the truth-values of utterances of (1) diverge from the truth-values of utterances of (6) in the same circumstances.[68]

It may be replied that we should be concerned with the truth-conditions, not of utterances of (1), but of what (1) says — something which might have been sayable even if (1) had not been a way to say it. But to assume that this topic of concern is so much as available is to presuppose, at the outset, the acceptability of the contentious notion of a proposition. 'Should' suggests that the notion must be acceptable, since we have a theoretical need for it. But it is really not at all clear why we should find it insufficiently ambitious to try to assign correct truth-conditions to all actual and possible utterances of our object language. And Blackburn's argument does not show that a paratactic account of *oratio obliqua* thwarts this aim.[69]

Davidson's account of *oratio obliqua* obviates the need for the full panoply of Frege's doctrine of sense. But there is still room for Frege's terminology, and in a theoretical context which makes employments of it echo Frege himself. We are bound to go on asking questions like this: if an utterance of a certain sentence makes me a samesayer with someone, why does an utterance of a sentence exactly like the first except that it substitutes for one name another name of the same thing not also make me a samesayer with him? Answers can be taken to spell out differences in the contributions made by the names to what is said in utterances of sentences containing them; that is — this equation is justifiable from Fregean texts[70] — differences in sense between the names. The crucial difference is that, although the terminology is thus preserved, reference to senses is nowhere needed. A follower of Quine need have no reason to object to this emasculated version of Frege. There is something very satisfying about this projected rapprochement.[71]

Notes

1 D. Davidson, 'On Saying That', *Synthèse*, vol. xix (1968), p. 130; reprinted in Donald Davidson and Jaakko Hintikka, eds, *Words and Objections* (Dordrecht, Reidel, 1969), p. 158; page references henceforth are to *Words and Objections*.

2 W. V. Quine, *Word and Object* (Cambridge, Mass., MIT Press, 1960), pp. 212–14. (Quine does not endorse even the final version, preferring something simpler; against which, see Davidson, 'On Saying That', pp. 167–8.)

3 See W. V. Quine, 'Reply to Davidson', in *Words and Objections*, p. 333.

4 Alonzo Church, 'On Carnap's Analysis of Statements of Assertion and Belief', *Analysis*, vol. x (1950), p. 97.

5 Quine, *Word and Object*, p. 214.

6 This sentence actually owes more to Davidson's purported exposition of Quine ('On Saying That', p. 164) than to *Word and Object*.

7 Quine, *Word and Object*, p. 214.

8 These remarks are clearly meant to refute (5)'s claim to paraphrase (1). Contrast R. J. Haack, 'On Davidson's Paratactic Theory of Oblique Contexts', *Noûs*, vol. v (1971), p. 351, which (at pp. 351–2) takes (5) as Davidson's own proposed paraphrase.

9 Predicates, not necessarily asserts. This disposes of one of Haack's difficulties (p. 356) about iterated *oratio obliqua* constructions.

10 Not analysed: see section XI below.

11 See G. Frege, 'On Sense and Reference', in Peter Geach and Max Black, eds, *Translations from the Philosophical Writings of Gottlob Frege* (Oxford, Blackwell, 1952), p. 56.

12 If the content-sentence itself contains an *oratio obliqua* construction, the paratactic account (*ex hypothesi* a satisfactory semantic account of such constructions) is applied to it in turn. As far as I can see, this answers the question which leads to the rather mysterious second difficulty Haack finds in iterated *oratio obliqua* constructions (pp. 357–8).

13 Against the prejudice, see P. T. Geach, 'Assertion', *Philosophical Review*, vol. lxxiv (1965), p. 449.

14 This would not be an analysis, any more than the similar explanation of the primitive which figures in (6); see n. 10 above, and section XI below.

15 See Ian McFetridge, 'Propositions and Davidson's Account of Indirect Discourse', *Proceedings of the Aristotelian Society*, vol. lxxvi (1975–6), at pp. 138–9. In 'True to the Facts', *Journal of Philosophy*, vol. lxvi (1969), at p. 763, Davidson says that samesaying 'holds between speech acts', i.e. presumably utterances.

16 Davidson's way: see 'Eternal vs. Ephemeral Events', *Noûs*, vol. v (1971), at p. 349, n. 12.

17 Cf. Quine on the possible fat men in a doorway: 'On What There Is', in *From a Logical Point of View* (Cambridge, Mass., Harvard

John McDowell

University Press, 1953), at p. 4.

18 See D. Davidson, 'Truth and Meaning', *Synthese*, vol. xvii (1967), pp. 319–20.

19 Talk of the truth-predicate as predicated of sentences may need a non-face-value construal, in view of sections VII and VIII below; similarly with talk of words and sentences as subjects of predication elsewhere in this paper.

20 See, e.g., Davidson, 'Truth and Meaning', p. 319; 'On Saying That', p. 174, n. 14.

21 See, e.g., section 1 of my 'Truth Conditions, Bivalence, and Verificationism', in Gareth Evans and John McDowell, eds, *Truth and Meaning* (Oxford, Clarendon Press, 1976), p. 42.

22 See the Introduction to Evans and McDowell, eds, *Truth and Meaning*, at pp. xiii–xv.

23 It might seem that Davidson's account of radical interpretation in terms of the idea of holding-true (see 'Radical Interpretation', *Dialectica*, vol. xxvii (1973), p. 313) bypasses the need for checking the acceptability of hypotheses about what people say in testing a truth-characterization. But I believe any such appearance would be misleading.

24 The non-actuality introduced by these counterfactual *oratio obliqua* reports is at the other end of the samesaying relation, so to speak: in the reported utterance, rather than – as in the cases for which modified samesaying was introduced – the reporting utterance. But why should this matter?

25 Contrast 'True to the Facts', p. 763, where Davidson speaks of 'devising a theory of translation that does not depend upon, but rather founds, whatever there is to the concept of meaning'; this is nearer what I want.

26 D. Davidson, 'In Defense of Convention T', in H. Leblanc, ed., *Truth, Syntax, and Modality* (Amsterdam, North-Holland, 1973), at p. 84; 'Radical Interpretation', at p. 321.

27 See n. 22 above.

28 See D. Davidson, 'Theories of Meaning and Learnable Languages', in Y. Bar-Hillel, ed., *Logic, Methodology, and Philosophy of Science* (Amsterdam, North-Holland, 1965), p. 383.

29 Quine, *Word and Object*, p. 143.

30 Cf. P. T. Geach, *Mental Acts* (London, Routledge & Kegan Paul, 1957), pp. 85–6.

31 ibid.: see especially pp. 81–3.

32 Nothing corresponds to quotation marks in standard speech.

33 A simplification not previously available. We might have tried writing: the result of enclosing any word (letter) in quotation marks is an expression that denotes that word (letter). But '(w) ("w" denotes w)' involves quantification into the scope of quotation marks; that this is intelligible, and how, is surely something to be demonstrated by an account of the semantics of quotation, not presupposed in it.

34 Slightly untidily, it is the written form which has the inverted commas.

35   Cf. Geach, *Mental Acts*, p. 90.
36   ibid., pp. 86–7.
37   Cf. ibid., pp. 86–7; and, for a corollary about language-relative truth-predicates, pp. 97–8.
38   ibid., p. 87.
39   See Tyler Burge, 'Reference and Proper Names', *Journal of Philosophy*, vol. lxx (1973), p. 425.
40   Note that any general thesis to the effect that ambiguity is plurality of words would need an exception for the proposed autonymous interpretation; otherwise autonymously used words could not name words which can also be used for other purposes.
41   Cf. Davidson, 'On Saying That', p. 164. We can distinguish dialects, within languages, by altering the conditions for equiformity, or our view of what counts as a sufficient number; this introduces extra indeterminacies, but for present purposes the essential point is the appearance of 'have the same meaning'. A variant of this gloss on 'speak the same language', not designed to certify languages (or words) as proper objects of reference, will emerge in section XI below.
42   Geach, *Mental Acts*, p. 90 (with a reference to Quine's *From a Logical Point of View*).
43   Namely 'They "logically attach to the subject" '; not (14) (see section III above).
44   This manoeuvre is precisely analogous to the way in which Davidson's account of *oratio obliqua* obviates the need to find reference to propositions. Some find the claim to avoid problematic ontology fraudulent in the latter case, and will presumably find it fraudulent in the present case too; I postpone discussion of this until section XI.
45   The difference is not that a form like (2) needs expansion on the lines of (3) or (4). If there is a need to avert potential misunderstanding of which language I am speaking, or in whose sense, when I utter words for purposes of quotation in uttering (2), construed as (16), then there is just the same need in the case of (6).
46   See, e.g., W. V. Quine, 'Quantifiers and Propositional Attitudes', *Journal of Philosophy*, vol. liii (1956), p. 177; reprinted in *The Ways of Paradox* (New York, Random House, 1966), p. 183.
47   If 'the earth' is a singular term referring to the earth, then it does not occur in (1), or, more exactly, does not occur in the utterance which is assessed for truth when we determine the truth-value of an utterance of (1). The consequent of this is Davidson's position: see section III above.
48   On the reason why a special style of variable is advisable, see David Kaplan, 'Quantifying In', *Synthèse*, vol. xix (1968), p. 178; reprinted in Davidson and Hintikka, eds, *Words and Objections*, p. 206; at pp. 213–14 of *Words and Objections*.
49   For this proposal, and suggestions about '*R*' (including giving it an extra argument-place), see Kaplan, 'Quantifying In'; and cf. Geach, *Mental Acts*, pp. 92–5.

50 See D. Davidson, 'The Logical Form of Action Sentences', in Nicholas Rescher, ed., *The Logic of Decision and Action* (Pittsburgh, University Press, 1967), p. 81.

51 For a more precise proposal on these lines, see Jennifer Hornsby, 'Saying of', *Analysis*, vol. xxxvii (1976-7), p. 177.

52 Quine, 'Quantifiers and Propositional Attitudes', at p. 188 of *The Ways of Paradox*.

53 Kaplan's title.

54 There is a further difficulty over whether, in view of the cardinality of the set of expressions, the quotational account can be generally adequate for sentences like (22).

55 This intuitive expression of the relation should not mislead us. We cannot simply assume that 'x is an utterance of the same sentence as y' can be explained as '$(\exists z)$ (z is a sentence and x is an utterance of z and y is an utterance of z)'. Cf. Section VII above and section XI below.

56 Obviously modifying (35) on the lines of (3) or (4) will not meet the difficulty.

57 The sealing-off effect does not work in examples like (14). (If I say 'Davidson finds the spelling account of quotation "all but explicit in Quine" ', it is important that I should be referring to the author of *Word and Object*.) In such cases it is as if the words in question occurred twice, inside and outside quotation marks ((15) brings this out nicely); the occurrence outside quotation explains how context can affect interpretation. There is nothing similar in a form like (35).

58 This is essentially Frege's position; see 'On Sense and Reference'.

59 Cf. Simon Blackburn, 'The Identity of Propositions', in Simon Blackburn, ed., *Meaning, Reference, and Necessity* (Cambridge, University Press, 1975), p. 184.

60 See especially Quine, *Word and Object*, chapter 2.

61 See especially Davidson, 'Radical Interpretation'.

62 Cf. G. Frege, *The Foundations of Arithmetic*, translated by J. L. Austin (Oxford, Blackwell, 1959), pp. 74-5.

63 *Contra* Blackburn, p. 188, suggesting that Quinean doubts about synonymy make, e.g., *oratio obliqua* reports unintelligible.

64 I cannot here discuss the source of such confidence, which I believe to be something profoundly suspect.

65 D. Davidson, 'Reply to Foster', in Evans and McDowell, eds, *Truth and Meaning*, at p. 39.

66 Cf. William G. Lycan, 'Davidson on Saying That', *Analysis*, vol. xxxiii (1972-3), p. 138.

67 Blackburn, 'The Identity of Propositions', p. 185. (I have substituted the authentically Davidsonian form (6) for Blackburn's (D), which misformulates Davidson's proposal.)

68 Cf. Peter Smith, 'Blackburn on Saying That', *Philosophical Studies*, vol. xxx (1976), p. 423.

69 If we take formulations in terms of samesaying to be analyses of *oratio obliqua* constructions, there will seem to be a problem about

an imparallelism between 'Galileo made an utterance which, with my next utterance, puts him and me in the samesaying relation. The earth moves. Now that might have been so however the English language had evolved,' and 'Your car is the same colour as my car. Now that might have been so whatever had happened to my car in the paint shop.' If we construe 'that might have been so' in the first case in a way parallel to the most natural construal of it in the second, we shall not capture the thought that Galileo might have said the very thing he did say, even if my way of ascribing that saying to him had not been available. But we should not take the samesaying formulations as analyses. (This footnote is a partial response to pressure from Christopher Peacocke. The point needs much more elaboration.)

70 See G. Frege, *The Basic Laws of Arithmetic: Exposition of the System*, translated and edited by Montgomery Furth (Berkeley and Los Angeles, University of California Press, 1967), pp. 89–90.

71 I have attempted further elaboration of the pared-down version of Frege, for the case of proper names, in 'On the Sense and Reference of a Proper Name', *Mind*, vol. lxxxvi (1977), p. 159; reprinted in this volume, ch. 8.

13 What metaphors mean*

Donald Davidson

Metaphor is the dreamwork of language, and like all dreamwork its interpretation reflects as much on the interpreter as on the originator. The interpretation of dreams requires collaboration between a dreamer and a waker, even if they be the same person; and the act of interpretation is itself a work of the imagination. So too understanding a metaphor is as much a creative endeavor as making a metaphor, and as little guided by rules.

These remarks do not, except in matters of degree, distinguish metaphor from more routine linguistic transactions: all communication by speech assumes the interplay of inventive construction and inventive construal. What metaphor adds to the ordinary is an achievement that uses no semantic resources beyond the resources on which the ordinary depends. There are no instructions for devising metaphors, there is no manual for determining what a metaphor 'means' or 'says,' there is no test for metaphor that does not call for taste.[1] A metaphor implies a kind and degree of artistic success; there are no unsuccessful metaphors, just as there are no unfunny jokes. There are tasteless metaphors, but these are turns that nevertheless have brought something off, even if they were not worth bringing off or could have been brought off better.

This paper is concerned with what metaphors mean, and its thesis is that metaphors mean what the words, in their most literal interpretation, mean, and nothing more. Since this thesis flies in the face of contemporary views with which I am familiar, much of what I have to say is critical. But I think the view of metaphor that emerges when error and confusion are cleared away makes metaphor a more, not a less, interesting phenomenon.

The central mistake against which I shall be inveighing is the idea that a metaphor has, in addition to its literal sense or meaning, another sense or meaning. This idea is common to many who have written about metaphor; it is to be found in the works of literary critics like Richards, Empson and Winters, philosophers from Aristotle to Max Black, psychologists from Freud and earlier to Skinner and later, and linguists from Plato to Uriel Weinreich and George Lakoff. The idea takes many

*Reprinted from *Critical Inquiry*, 5 (Autumn 1978), pp. 31–47.

forms, from the relatively simple in Aristotle to the relatively complex in Black. The idea appears in writings that maintain that a literal paraphrase of a metaphor can be produced, but it is shared by those who hold that typically no literal paraphrase can be found. Some stress the special insight metaphor can inspire, and make much of the fact that ordinary language, in its usual functioning, yields no such insight. Yet this view too sees metaphor as a form of communication alongside ordinary communication, conveying truths or falsehoods about the world much as plainer language does, though the message may be considered more exotic, profound or cunningly garbed.

The concept of metaphor as primarily a vehicle for conveying ideas, even if unusual ones, seems to me as wrong as the parent idea that a metaphor has a special meaning. I agree with the view that metaphors cannot be paraphrased, but I think this is not because metaphors say something too novel for literal expression but because there is nothing there to paraphrase. Paraphrase, whether possible or not, is appropriate to what is *said*: we try, in paraphrase, to say it another way. But if I am right, a metaphor doesn't say anything beyond its literal meaning (nor does its maker say anything, in using the metaphor, beyond the literal). This is not, of course, to deny that a metaphor has a point, nor to deny that that point can be brought out by using further words.

In the past those who have denied that metaphor has a cognitive content in addition to the literal have often been out to show that metaphor is confusing, merely emotive, unsuited to serious, scientific or philosophic discourse. My views should not be associated with this tradition. Metaphor is a legitimate device not only in literature but in science, philosophy and the law; it is effective in praise and abuse, prayer and promotion, description and prescription. For the most part I don't disagree with Max Black, Paul Henle, Nelson Goodman, Monroe Beardsley and the rest in their accounts of what metaphor accomplishes, except that I think it accomplishes more, and that what is additional is different in kind.

My disagreement is with the explanation of how metaphor works its wonders. To anticipate: I depend on the distinction between what words mean and what they are used to do. I think metaphor belongs exclusively to the domain of use. It is something brought off by the imaginative employment of words and sentences, and depends entirely on the ordinary or literal meanings of those words and hence of the sentences they comprise.

It is no help (I shall argue) in explaining how words work in metaphor to posit metaphorical or figurative meanings, or special kinds of poetic or metaphorical truth. These ideas don't explain metaphor; metaphor explains them. Once we understand a metaphor we can call what we grasp the 'metaphorical truth' and (up to a point) say what the 'metaphorical meaning' is. But simply to lodge this meaning in the metaphor is like explaining why a pill puts you to sleep by saying it has a dormative power. Literal meaning and literal truth-conditions can be assigned to words and sentences apart from particular contexts of use. This is why adverting to them has genuine explanatory power.

I shall try to establish my negative views about what metaphors mean and introduce my limited positive claims by examining some false theories of the nature of metaphor.

A metaphor makes us attend to some likeness, often a novel or surprising likeness, between two or more things. This trite and true observation leads, or seems to lead, to a conclusion concerning the meaning of metaphors. Consider ordinary likeness or similarity. Two roses are similar because they share the property of being a rose; two infants are similar by virtue of their infanthood. Or, more simply, roses are similar because each is a rose, infants, because each is an infant.

Suppose someone says 'Tolstoy was once an infant.' How is the infant Tolstoy like other infants? The answer comes pat: by virtue of exhibiting the property of infanthood, that is, leaving out some of the wind, by virtue of being an infant. If we tire of the phrase 'by virtue of,' we can, it seems, go plainer still by saying the infant Tolstoy shares with other infants the trait of having the predicate 'is an infant' apply to him; given the word 'infant,' we have no trouble saying exactly how the infant Tolstoy resembles other infants. We could do it without the word 'infant'; all we need is other words that mean the same. The end result is the same. Ordinary similarity depends on groupings established by the ordinary meanings of words. Such similarity is natural and unsurprising to the extent that familiar ways of grouping objects are tied to usual meanings of usual words.

A famous critic said that Tolstoy was 'a great moralizing infant.' The Tolstoy referred to here is obviously not the infant Tolstoy but Tolstoy the adult writer; this is metaphor. Now in what sense is Tolstoy the writer similar to an infant? What we are to do, perhaps, is to think of the class of objects that includes all ordinary infants and, in addition, the adult Tolstoy, and then ask ourselves what special, surprising property the members of this class have in common. The appealing thought is that given patience we could come as close as need be to specifying the appropriate property. In any case, we could do the job perfectly if we found words that meant exactly what the metaphorical 'infant' means. What is interesting, from my perspective, is not whether we can find the perfect other words, but the assumption that there is something to be attempted, a metaphorical meaning to be matched. So far I have been doing no more than crudely sketching how the concept of meaning may have crept into the analysis of metaphor, and the answer I have suggested is that, since what we think of as garden variety similarity goes with what we think of as garden variety meanings, it is natural to posit unusual or metaphorical meanings to help explain the similarities metaphor promotes.

The idea, then, is that in metaphor certain words take on new, or what are often called 'extended,' meanings. When we read that 'the Spirit of God moved upon the face of the waters,' for example, we are to regard the word 'face' as having an extended meaning (I disregard further metaphor in the passage). The extension applies, as it happens, to what philosophers call the extension of the word, that is, the class of entities to which it refers. Here the word 'face' applies to ordinary faces, and to waters in addition.

This account cannot, at any rate, be complete, for if in these contexts the words 'face' and 'infant' apply correctly to waters and to the adult Tolstoy, then waters really do have faces and Tolstoy literally was an infant, and all sense of metaphor evaporates. If we are to think of words in metaphors as directly going about their business of applying to what they properly do apply to, there is no difference between metaphor and the introduction of a new term into our vocabulary: to make a metaphor is to murder it.

What has been left out is any appeal to the original or literal meaning of the word. Whether or not metaphor depends on new or extended meanings, it certainly depends in some way on the original meanings; an adequate account of metaphor must allow that the primary or original meanings of words remain active in their metaphorical setting.

Perhaps, then, we can explain metaphor as a kind of ambiguity: in the context of a metaphor, certain words have either a new meaning or an original meaning, and the force of the metaphor depends on our uncertainty as we waver between the two meanings. Thus when Melville writes that 'Christ was a chronometer,' the effect of metaphor is produced by our taking 'chronometer' first in its ordinary sense and then in some extraordinary or metaphorical sense.

It is hard to see how this theory can be correct. For the ambiguity in the word, if there is any, is due to the fact that in ordinary contexts it means one thing and in the metaphorical context it means something else; but in the metaphorical context we do not necessarily hesitate over its meaning. When we do hesitate, it is usually to decide which of a number of metaphorical interpretations we shall accept; we are seldom in doubt that what we have is a metaphor. At any rate, the effectiveness of the metaphor easily outlasts the end of uncertainty over the interpretation of the metaphorical passage. Metaphor cannot, therefore, owe its effect to ambiguity of this sort.[2]

Another brand of ambiguity may appear to offer a better suggestion. Sometimes a word will, in a single context, bear two meanings where we are meant to remember and to use both. Or, if we think of wordhood as implying sameness of meaning, then we may describe the situation as one in which what appears as a single word is in fact two. When Shakespeare's Cressida is welcomed bawdily into the Grecian camp, Nestor says 'Our general doth salute you with a kiss.' Here we are to take 'general' two ways, once as applying to Agamemnon, who is the general; and once as applying to no one in particular, but everyone in general, for she is kissing everyone. We really have a conjunction of two sentences: our general, Agamemnon, salutes you with a kiss; and everyone in general is saluting you with a kiss.

This is a legitimate device, a pun, but it is not the same device as metaphor. For in metaphor there is no essential need of reiteration; whatever meanings we assign the words, they keep through every correct reading of the passage.

A plausible modification of the last suggestion would be to consider the key word (or words) in a metaphor as having two different kinds of meaning at once, a literal and a figurative meaning. Imagine the literal meaning as latent, something that we are aware of, that can work on us without working in the context, while the figurative meaning carries the direct load. And finally, there must be a rule that connects the two meanings, for otherwise the explanation lapses into a form of the ambiguity theory. The rule, at least for many typical cases of metaphor, says that in its metaphorical role the word applies to everything that it applies to in its literal role, and then some.[3]

This theory may seem complex, but it is strikingly similar to what Frege proposed to account for the behavior of referring terms in modal sentences and sentences about propositional attitudes like belief and desire. According to Frege each referring term has two (or more) meanings, one of which fixes its reference in ordinary contexts and another which fixes its reference in the special contexts created by modal operators or psychological verbs. The rule connecting the two meanings may be put like this: the meaning of the word in the special contexts makes the reference in those contexts to be identical with the meaning in ordinary contexts.

Here is the whole picture, putting Frege together with a Fregean view of metaphor: we are to think of a word as having, in addition to its mundane field of application or reference, two special or supermundane fields of application, one for metaphor and the other for modal contexts and the like. In both cases the original meaning remains to do its work by virtue of a rule that relates the various meanings.

Having stressed the possible analogy between metaphorical meaning and the Fregean meanings for oblique contexts, I turn to an imposing difficulty in maintaining the analogy. You are entertaining a visitor from Saturn by trying to teach him how to use the word 'floor.' You go through the familiar dodges, leading him from floor to floor, pointing and stamping and repeating the word. You prompt him to make experiments, tapping objects tentatively with his tentacle while rewarding his right and wrong tries. You want him to come out knowing not only that these particular objects or surfaces are floors, but also how to tell a floor when one is in sight or touch. The skit you are putting on doesn't *tell* him what he needs to know, but with luck it helps him to *learn* it.

Should we call this process learning something about the world or learning something about language? An odd question, since what is learned is that a bit of language refers to a bit of the world. Still, it is easy to distinguish between the business of learning the meaning of a word and using the word once the meaning is learned. Comparing these two activities, it is natural to say that the first concerns learning something about language, while the second is typically learning something about the world. If your Saturnian has learned how to use the word 'floor,' you may try telling him something new, that *here* is a floor. If he has mastered the word trick, you have told him something about the world.

Your friend from Saturn now transports you through space to his home sphere, and looking back remotely at earth you say to him, nodding at the earth, 'floor.' Perhaps he will think this is still part of the lesson and assume that the word 'floor' applies properly to the earth, at least as seen from Saturn. But what if you thought he already knew the meaning of 'floor,' and you were remembering how Dante, from a similar place in the heavens, saw the inhabited earth as 'the small round floor that makes us passionate'? Your purpose was metaphor, not drill in the use of language. What difference would it make to your friend which way he took it? With the theory of metaphor under consideration, very little difference, for according to that theory a word has a new meaning in a metaphorical context; the occasion of the metaphor would, therefore, be the occasion for learning the new meaning. We should agree that in some ways it makes relatively little difference whether, in a given context, we think a word is being used metaphorically or in a previously unknown but literal way. Empson, in *Some Versions of Pastoral*, quotes these lines from Donne: 'As our blood labours to beget / Spirits, as like souls as it can, / . . . So must pure lover's soules descend. . . .' The modern reader is almost certain, Empson points out, to take the word 'spirits' in this passage metaphorically, as applying only by extension to something spiritual. But for Donne there was no metaphor. He writes in his *Sermons*, 'The spirits . . . are the thin and active part of the blood, and are a kind of middle nature, between soul and body.' Learning this does not matter much; Empson is right when he says, 'It is curious how the change in the word [that is, in what we think it means] leaves the poetry unaffected.'[4]

The change may be, in some cases at least, hard to appreciate, but unless there is a change, most of what is thought to be interesting about metaphor is lost. I have been making the point by contrasting learning a new use for an old word with using a word already understood; in one case, I said, our attention is directed to language, in the other, to what language is about. Metaphor, I suggested, belongs in the second category.

This can also be seen by considering dead metaphors. Once upon a time, I suppose, rivers and bottles did not, as they do now, literally have mouths. Thinking of present usage, it doesn't matter whether we take the word 'mouth' to be ambiguous because it applies to entrances to rivers and openings of bottles as well as to animal apertures, or we think there is a single wide field of application that embraces both. What does matter is that, when 'mouth' applied only metaphorically to bottles, the application made the hearer *notice* a likeness between animal and bottle openings. (Consider Homer's reference to wounds as mouths.) Once one has the present use of the word, with literal application to bottles, there is nothing left to notice. There is no similarity to seek because it consists simply in being referred to by the same word.

Novelty is not the issue. In its context a word once taken for a metaphor remains a metaphor on the hundredth hearing, while a word may easily be appreciated in a new literal role on a first encounter. What we call the element of novelty or surprise in a metaphor is a built-in aesthetic feature we can experience again and again, like the surprise in Haydn's 94th Symphony, or a familiar deceptive cadence.

If metaphor involved a second meaning, as ambiguity does, we might expect to be able to specify the special meaning of a word in a metaphorical setting by waiting until the metaphor dies. The figurative meaning of the living metaphor should be immortalized in the literal meaning of the dead. But although some philosophers have suggested this idea, it seems plainly wrong. 'He was burned up' is genuinely ambiguous (since it may be true in one sense and false in another), but although the slangish idiom is no doubt the corpse of metaphor, 'He was burned up' now suggests no more than that he was very angry. When the metaphor was active, we would have pictured fire in the eyes or smoke coming out of the ears.

We can learn much about what metaphors mean by comparing them with similes, for a simile tells us, in part, what a metaphor merely nudges us into noting. Suppose Goneril had said, thinking of Lear, 'Old fools are like babes again'; then she would have used the words to assert a similarity between old fools and babes. What she did say, of course, was 'Old fools are babes again,' thus using the words to intimate what the simile declared. Thinking along these lines may inspire another theory of the figurative or special meaning of metaphors: the figurative meaning of a metaphor is the literal meaning of the corresponding simile. Thus 'Christ was a chronometer' in its figurative sense is synonymous with 'Christ was like a chronometer,' and the metaphorical meaning once locked up in 'He was burned up' is released in 'He was like someone who was burned up' (or perhaps 'He was like burned up').

There is, to be sure, the difficulty of identifying the simile that corresponds to a given metaphor. Virginia Woolf said that a highbrow is 'a man or woman of thoroughbred intelligence who rides his mind at a gallop across country in pursuit of an idea.' What simile corresponds? Something like this, perhaps: 'A highbrow is a man or woman whose intelligence is like a thoroughbred horse and who persists in thinking about an idea like a rider galloping across country in pursuit of . . . well, something.'

The view that the special meaning of a metaphor is identical with the literal meaning of a corresponding simile (however 'corresponding' is spelled out) should not be confused with the common theory that a metaphor is an elliptical simile.[5] This theory makes no distinction in meaning between a metaphor and some related simile, and does not provide any ground for speaking of figurative, metaphorical or special meanings. It is a theory that wins hands down so far as simplicity is concerned, but it also seems too simple to work. For if we make the literal meaning of the metaphor to be the literal meaning of a matching simile, we deny access to what we originally took to be the literal meaning of the metaphor, and we agreed almost from the start that *this* meaning was essential to the working of the metaphor, whatever else might have to be brought in in the way of a nonliteral meaning.

Both the elliptical simile theory of metaphor and its more sophisticated variant, which equates the figurative meaning of the metaphor with the literal meaning of a simile, share a fatal defect. They make the hidden meaning of the metaphor all too obvious and accessible. In each case the hidden meaning is to be found simply by looking to the literal meaning of what is usually a painfully trivial simile. This is like that -- Tolstoy like an infant, the earth like a floor. Trivial because everything is like everything, and in endless ways. Metaphors are often very difficult to interpret and, so it is said, impossible to paraphrase. But with this theory, interpretation and paraphrase typically are ready to the hand of the most callow.

These simile theories have been found acceptable, I think, only because they have been confused with a quite different theory. Consider this remark by Max Black:[6]

> When Schopenhauer called a geometrical proof a mousetrap, he was, according to such a view, *saying* (though not explicitly): 'A geometrical proof is *like* a mousetrap, since both offer a delusive reward, entice their victims by degrees, lead to disagreeable surprise, etc.' This is a view of metaphor as a condensed or elliptical *simile*. [Italics in original]

Here I discern two confusions. First, if metaphors are elliptical similes, they say *explicitly* what similes say, for ellipsis is a form of abbreviation, not of paraphrase or indirection. But, and this is the more important matter, Black's statement of what the metaphor says goes far beyond anything given by the corresponding simile. The simile simply says a geometrical proof is like a mousetrap. It no more *tells* us what similarities we are to notice than the metaphor does. Black mentions three similarities, and of course we could go on adding to the list for ever. But is this list, when revised and supplemented in the right way, supposed to give the *literal* meaning of the simile? Surely not, since the simile declared no more than the similarity. If the list is supposed to provide the figurative meaning of the simile, then we learn nothing about metaphor from the comparison with simile — only that both have the same figurative meaning. Nelson Goodman does indeed claim that 'the difference between simile and metaphor is negligible,' and he continues, 'Whether the locution be "is like" or "is," the figure *likens* picture to person by picking out a certain common feature. . . .'[7] Goodman is considering the difference between saying a picture is sad and saying it is like a sad person. It is clearly true that both sayings liken picture to person, but it seems to me a mistake to claim that either way of talking 'picks out' a common feature. The simile says there is a likeness and leaves it to us to pick out some common feature or features; the metaphor does not explicitly assert a likeness, but if we accept it as a metaphor, we are again led to seek common features (not necessarily the same features the associated simile suggests; but that is another matter).

Just because a simile wears a declaration of similitude on its sleeve, it is, I think, far less plausible than in the case of metaphor to maintain that there is a hidden second meaning. In the case of simile, we note what it literally says, that two things are resembling; we then regard the objects and consider what similarity would, in the context, be to the point. Having decided, we might then say the author of the simile intended us — that is, meant us — to notice that similarity. But having appreciated the difference between what the words meant and what the author accomplished by using those words, we should feel little temptation to explain what has happened by endowing the words themselves with a second, or figurative, meaning. The point of the concept of linguistic meaning is to explain what can be done with words. But the supposed figurative meaning of a simile explains nothing; it is not a feature of the word that the word has prior to and independent of the context of use, and it rests upon no linguistic customs except those that govern ordinary meaning.

What words do do with their literal meaning in simile it must be possible for them to do in metaphor. A metaphor directs attention to the same sorts of similarity, if not the same similarities, as the corresponding simile. But then the unexpected or subtle parallels and analogies it is the business of metaphor to promote need not depend, for their promotion, on more than the literal meaning of words.

Metaphor and simile are merely two among endless devices that serve to alert us to aspects of the world by inviting us to make comparisons. I quote a few stanzas of T. S. Eliot's 'The Hippopotamus:'

The broad-backed hippopotamus
Rests on his belly in the mud;
Although he seems so firm to us
He is merely flesh and blood.

Flesh and blood is weak and frail,
Susceptible to nervous shock;
While the True Church can never fail
For it is based upon a rock.

The hippo's feeble steps may err
In compassing material ends,
While the True Church need never stir
To gather in its dividends.

The 'potamus can never reach
The mango on the mango-tree:
But fruits of pomegranate and peach
Refresh the Church from over sea.

Here we are neither told that the Church resembles a hippopotamus (as in simile) nor bullied into making the comparison (as in metaphor), but there can be no doubt the words are being used to direct our attention to similarities between the two. Nor should there be much inclination, in this case, to posit figurative meanings, for in what words or sentences would we lodge them? The hippopotamus really does rest on his belly in the mud; the True Church, the poem says literally, never can fail. The poem does, of course, intimate much that goes beyond the literal meanings of the words. But intimation is not meaning.

The argument so far has led to the conclusion that as much of metaphor as can be explained in terms of meaning may, and indeed must, be explained by appeal to the literal meanings of words. A consequence is that the sentences in which metaphors occur are true or false in a normal, literal way, for if the words in them don't have special meanings, sentences don't have special truth. This is not to deny that there is such a thing as metaphorical truth, only to deny it of sentences. Metaphor does lead us to notice what might not otherwise be noticed, and there is no reason, I suppose, not to say these visions, thoughts and feelings inspired by the metaphor are true or false.

If a sentence used metaphorically is true or false in the ordinary sense, then it is clear that it is usually false. The most obvious semantic difference between simile and metaphor is that all similes are true and most metaphors are false. The earth is like a floor, the Assyrian did come down like a wolf on the fold, because everything is like everything. But turn these sentences into metaphors, and you turn them false; the earth is like a floor, but it is not a floor; Tolstoy, grown up, was like an infant, but he wasn't one. We use a simile ordinarily only

Donald Davidson

when we know the corresponding metaphor to be false. We say Mr S is like a pig because we know he isn't one. If we had used a metaphor and said he was a pig, this would not be because we changed our mind about the facts but because we chose to get the idea across a different way.

What matters is not actual falsehood, but that the sentence be taken to be false. Notice what happens when a sentence we use as a metaphor, believing it false, comes to be thought true because of a change in what is believed about the world. When it was reported that Hemingway's plane had been sighted, wrecked, in Africa, the New York *Mirror* ran a headline saying 'Hemingway lost in Africa,' the word 'lost' being used to suggest he was dead. When it turned out he was alive, the *Mirror* left the headline to be taken literally. Or consider the case: A woman sees herself in a beautiful dress, says, 'What a dream of a dress!' — and then wakes up. The point of the metaphor is that the dress is like a dress one would dream of and therefore isn't a dream-dress. Henle provides a good example from *Antony and Cleopatra* (II, 2):

> The barge she sat in, like a burnish'd throne
> Burn'd on the water

Here simile and metaphor interact strangely, but the metaphor would vanish if a literal conflagration were imagined. In much the same way the usual effect of a simile can be sabotaged by taking the comparison too earnestly. Woody Allen writes, 'The trial, which took place over the following weeks, was like a circus, although there was some difficulty getting the elephants into the courtroom.'[8]

Generally it is only when a sentence is taken to be false that we accept it as a metaphor and start to hunt out the hidden implication. It is probably for this reason that most metaphorical sentences are *patently* false, just as all similes are trivially true. Absurdity or contradiction in a metaphorical sentence guarantees we won't believe it, and invites us, under proper circumstances, to take the sentence metaphorically.

Patent falsity is the usual case with metaphor, but on occasion patent truth will do as well. 'Business is business' is too obvious in its literal meaning to be taken as having been uttered to convey information, so we look for another use; Ted Cohen reminds us, in the same connection, that no man is an island.[9] The point is the same. The ordinary meaning in the context of use is odd enough to prompt us to disregard the question of literal truth.

Now let me raise a somewhat Platonic issue by comparing the making of a metaphor with telling a lie. The comparison is apt because lying, like making a metaphor, concerns not the meaning of words but their use. It is sometimes said that telling a lie entails saying what is false; but this is wrong. Telling a lie requires not that what you say be

248

false but that you think it false. Since we usually believe true sentences and disbelieve false, most lies are falsehoods; but in any particular case this is an accident. The parallel between making a metaphor and telling a lie is emphasized by the fact that the same sentence can be used, with meaning unchanged, for either purpose. So a woman who believed in witches but did not think her neighbor a witch might say, 'She's a witch,' meaning it metaphorically; the same woman, still believing the same of witches and her neighbor but intending to deceive, might use the same words to very different effect. Since sentence and meaning are the same in both cases, it is sometimes hard to prove which intention lay behind the saying of it; thus a man who says 'Lattimore's a Communist' and means to lie can always try to beg off by pleading a metaphor.

What makes the difference between a lie and a metaphor is not a difference in the words used or what they mean (in any strict sense of meaning) but in how the words are used. Using a sentence to tell a lie and using it to make a metaphor are, of course, totally different uses, so different that they do not interfere with one another as, say, acting and lying do. In lying one must make an assertion so as to represent oneself as believing what one does not; in acting, assertion is excluded. Metaphor is careless to the difference. It can be an insult, and so be an assertion, to say to a man, 'You are a pig.' But no metaphor was involved when (let us suppose) Odysseus addressed the same words to his companions in Circe's palace; a story, to be sure, and so no assertion — but the word, for once, was used literally of men.

No theory of metaphorical meaning or metaphorical truth can help explain how metaphor works. Metaphor runs on the same familiar linguistic tracks that the plainest sentences do; this we saw from considering simile. What distinguishes metaphor is not meaning but use — in this it is like assertion, hinting, lying, promising or criticizing. And the special use to which we put language in metaphor is not — cannot be — to 'say something' special, no matter how indirectly. For a metaphor *says* only what shows on its face — usually a patent falsehood or an absurd truth. And this plain truth or falsehood needs no paraphrase — it is given in the literal meaning of the words.

What are we to make, then, of the endless energy that has been, and is being, spent on methods and devices for drawing out the content of a metaphor? The psychologists Robert Verbrugge and Nancy McCarrell tell us that:[10]

> Many metaphors draw attention to common systems of relationships or common transformations, in which the identity of the participants is secondary. For example, consider the sentences: *A car is like an animal, Tree trunks are straws for thirsty leaves and branches.* The first sentence directs attention to systems of relationships among energy consumption, respiration, self-induced motion,

sensory systems, and, possibly, a homunculus. In the second sentence, the resemblance is a more constrained type of transformation: suction of fluid through a vertically oriented cylindrical space from a source of fluid to a destination.

Verbrugge and McCarrell don't believe there is any sharp line between the literal and metaphorical uses of words; they think many words have a 'fuzzy' meaning that gets fixed, if fixed at all, by a context. But surely this fuzziness, however it is illustrated and explained, cannot erase the line between what a sentence literally means (given its context) and what it 'draws our attention to' (given its literal meaning as fixed by the context). The passage I have quoted is not employing such a distinction: what it says the sample sentences direct our attention to are facts expressed by paraphrases of the sentences. Verbrugge and McCarrell simply want to insist that a correct paraphrase may emphasize 'systems of relationships' rather than resemblances between objects.

According to Black's interaction theory, a metaphor makes us apply a 'system of commonplaces' associated with the metaphorical word to the subject of the metaphor: in 'Man is a wolf' we apply commonplace attributes (stereotypes) of the wolf to man. The metaphor, Black says, thus 'selects, emphasizes, suppresses, and organizes features of the principal subject by implying statements about it that normally apply to the subsidiary subject.'[11] If paraphrase fails, according to Black, it is not because the metaphor does not have a special cognitive content, but because the paraphrase[12]

> will not have the same power to inform and enlighten as the original . . . one of the points I most wish to stress is that the loss in such cases is a loss in cognitive content; the relevant weakness of the literal paraphrase is not that it may be tiresomely prolix or boringly explicit; it fails to be a translation because it fails to give the insight that the metaphor did.

How can this be right? If a metaphor has a special cognitive content, why should it be so difficult or impossible to set it out? If, as Barfield claims, a metaphor 'says one thing and means another,' why should it be that when we try to get explicit about what it means, the effect is so much weaker — 'put it that way,' Barfield says, 'and nearly all the tarning, and with it half the poetry, is lost.'[13] Why does Black think a literal paraphrase 'inevitably says too much — and with the wrong emphasis'? Why inevitably? Can't we, if we are clever enough, come as close as we please?

For that matter, how is it that a simile gets along without a special intermediate meaning? In general critics do not suggest that a simile says one thing and means another — they do not suppose it *means* anything but what lies on the surface of the words. It may make us think deep thoughts, just as a metaphor does; how come, then, no one appeals to the 'special cognitive content' of the simile? And remember Eliot's hippopotamus; there there was neither simile nor metaphor, but what seemed to get done was just like what gets done by similes and metaphors. Does anyone suggest that the *words* in Eliot's poem have special meanings?

Finally, if words in metaphor bear a coded meaning, how can this meaning differ from the meaning those same words bear in the case where the metaphor *dies* — that is, when it comes to be part of the language? Why doesn't 'He was burned up' as now used and meant mean *exactly* what the fresh metaphor once meant? Yet all that the dead metaphor means is that he was very angry — a notion not very difficult to make explicit.

There is, then, a tension in the usual view of metaphor. For on the one hand, the usual view wants to hold that a metaphor does something no plain prose can possibly do, and on the other hand it wants to explain what a metaphor does by appealing to a cognitive content — just the sort of thing plain prose is designed to express. As long as we are in this frame of mind, we must harbor the suspicion that it *can* be done, at least up to a point.

There is a simple way out of the impasse. We must give up the idea that a metaphor carries a message, that it has a content or meaning (except, of course, its literal meaning). The various theories we have been considering mistake their goal. Where they think they provide a method for deciphering an encoded content, they actually tell us (or try to tell us) something about the *effects* metaphors have on us. The common error is to fasten on the contents of the thoughts a metaphor provokes and to read these contents into the metaphor itself. No doubt metaphors often make us notice aspects of things we did not notice before; no doubt they bring surprising analogies and similarities to our attention; they do provide a kind of lens or lattice, as Black says, through which we view the relevant phenomena. The issue does not lie here but in the question of how the metaphor is related to what it makes us see.

It may be remarked with justice that the claim that a metaphor provokes or invites a certain view of its subject rather than saying it straight out is a commonplace; so it is. Thus Aristotle says metaphor leads to a 'perception of resemblances.' Black, following Richards, says a metaphor 'evokes' a certain response: 'a suitable hearer will be led by a metaphor to construct a . . . system.'[14] This view is neatly summed up by what Heraclitus said of the Delphic oracle: 'It does not say and it does not hide, it intimates.'[15]

I have no quarrel with these descriptions of the effects of metaphor, only with the associated views as to *how* metaphor is supposed to produce them. What I deny is that metaphor does its work by having a

Donald Davidson

special meaning, a specific cognitive content. I do not think, as Richards does, that metaphor produces its result by having a meaning that results from the interaction of two ideas; it is wrong, in my view, to say, with Owen Barfield, that a metaphor 'says one thing and means another'; or with Black that a metaphor asserts or implies certain complex things by dint of a special meaning and *thus* accomplishes its job of yielding an 'insight'. A metaphor does its work through other intermediaries – to suppose it can be effective only by conveying a coded message is like thinking a joke or a dream makes some statement which a clever interpreter can restate in plain prose. Joke or dream or metaphor can, like a picture or a bump on the head, make us appreciate some fact – but not by standing for, or expressing, the fact.

If this is right, what we attempt in 'paraphrasing' a metaphor cannot be to give its meaning, for that lies on the surface; rather, we attempt to evoke what the metaphor brings to our attention. I can imagine someone granting this and shrugging it off as no more than an insistence on restraint in using the word 'meaning'. This would be wrong. The central error about metaphor is most easily attacked when it takes the form of a theory of metaphorical meaning, but behind that theory, and statable independently, is the thesis that associated with a metaphor is a cognitive content that its author wishes to convey and that the interpreter must grasp if he is to get the message. This theory is largely false, whether or not we call the purported cognitive content a meaning.

It should make us suspect the theory that it is so hard to decide, even in the case of the simplest metaphors, exactly what the content is supposed to be. The reason it is often so hard to decide is, I think, that we imagine there is a content to be captured when all the while we are in fact focusing on what the metaphor makes us notice. If what the metaphor makes us notice were finite in scope and propositional in nature, this would not in itself make trouble; we would simply project the content the metaphor brought to mind on to the metaphor. But in fact there is no limit to what a metaphor calls to our attention, and much of what we are caused to notice is not propositional in character. When we try to say what a metaphor 'means,' we soon realize there is no end to what we want to mention.[16] If someone draws his finger along a coastline on a map, or mentions the beauty and deftness of a line in a Picasso etching, how many things are drawn to your attention? You might list a great many, but you could not finish, since the idea of finishing would have no clear application. How many facts or propositions are conveyed by a photograph? None, an infinity, or one great unstatable fact? Bad question. A picture is not worth a thousand words, or any other number. Words are the wrong currency to exchange for a picture.

It's not only that we can't provide an exhaustive catalogue of what has been attended to when we are led to see something in a new light;

the difficulty is more fundamental. What we notice or see is not, in general, propositional in character. Of course it *may* be, and when it is it usually may be stated in fairly plain words. But if I show you Wittgenstein's duck-rabbit, and I say 'It's a duck,' then with luck you see it as a duck; if I say 'It's a rabbit,' you see it as a rabbit. But no proposition expresses what I have led you to see. Perhaps you have come to realize that the drawing can be seen as a duck or as a rabbit. But one could come to know this without ever seeing the drawing as a duck or as a rabbit. Seeing as is not seeing that. Metaphor makes us see one thing as another by making some literal statement that inspires or prompts the insight. Since in most cases what the metaphor prompts or inspires is not entirely, or even at all, recognition of some truth or fact, the attempt to give literal expression to the content of the metaphor is simply misguided.

The theorist who tries to explain a metaphor by appealing to a hidden message, like the critic who attempts to state the message, is then fundamentally confused. No such explanation or statement can be forthcoming because no such message exists.

Not, of course, that interpretation and elucidation of a metaphor are not in order. Many of us need help if we are to see what the author of a metaphor wanted us to see, and what a more sensitive or educated reader grasps. The legitimate function of so-called paraphrase is to make the lazy or ignorant reader have a vision like that of the skilled critic. The critic is, so to speak, in benign competition with the metaphor-maker. The critic tries to make his own art easier or more transparent in some respects than the original, but at the same time he tries to reproduce in others some of the effects the original had on him. In doing this the critic also, and perhaps by the best method at his command, calls attention to the beauty or aptness, the hidden power, of the metaphor itself.

Notes

1 I think Max Black is wrong when he says, 'The rules of our language determine that some expressions must count as metaphors.' He allows, however, that what a metaphor 'means' depends on much more: the speaker's intention, tone of voice, verbal setting, etc. 'Metaphor,' in his *Models and Metaphors* (Ithaca, NY, Cornell University Press, 1962), p. 29.

2 Nelson Goodman says metaphor and ambiguity differ chiefly 'in that the several uses of a merely ambiguous term are coeval and independent' while in metaphor 'a term with an extension established by habit is applied elsewhere under the influence of that

Donald Davidson

habit,' and he suggests that as our sense of the history of the 'two uses' in metaphor fades, the metaphorical word becomes merely ambiguous. *Languages of Art* (Indianapolis, Bobbs-Merrill, 1968), p. 71. In fact, in many cases of ambiguity, one use springs from the other (as Goodman says) and so cannot be coeval. But the basic error, which Goodman shares with others, is the idea that two 'uses' are involved in metaphor in anything like the way they are in ambiguity.

3   The theory described is essentially that of Paul Henle, 'Metaphor,' in *Language, Thought and Culture*, ed. P. Henle (Ann Arbor, University of Michigan Press, 1958).

4   William Empson, *Some Versions of Pastoral* (London, Chatto & Windus, 1935), p. 133.

5   J. Middleton Murry says a metaphor is a 'compressed simile,' *Countries of the Mind*, 2nd series (Oxford, University Press 1931), p. 3. Max Black attributes a similar view to Alexander Bain, *English Composition and Rhetoric*, enlarged ed. (London, Longmans, 1887).

6   Black, 'Metaphor,' p. 35.

7   Goodman, *Languages of Art*, pp. 77–8.

8   Woody Allen, *New Yorker*, 21 November 1977, p. 59.

9   Ted Cohen, 'Figurative Speech and Figurative Acts,' *The Journal of Philosophy*, vol. 72 (1975), p. 671. Since the negation of a metaphor seems always to be a potential metaphor, there may be as many platitudes among the potential metaphors as there are absurds among the actuals.

10   Robert R. Verbrugge and Nancy S. McCarrell, 'Metaphoric Comprehension: Studies in Reminding and Resembling,' *Cognitive Psychology*, vol. 9 (1977), p. 499.

11   Black, 'Metaphor,' pp. 44–5.

12   ibid., p. 46.

13   Owen Barfield, 'Poetic Diction and Legal Fiction,' in *The Importance of Language*, ed. Max Black (Englewood Cliffs, NJ, Prentice-Hall, 1962), p. 55.

14   Black, 'Metaphor,' p. 41.

15   I use Hannah Ahrendt's attractive translation of '$\sigma\eta\mu\alpha\acute{\iota}\nu\epsilon\iota$'; it clearly should not be rendered as 'mean' in this context.

16   Stanley Cavell mentions the fact that most attempts at paraphrase end with 'and so on,' and refers to Empson's remark that metaphors are 'pregnant' (*Must We Mean What We Say?* (New York, Scribner's, 1969), p. 79). But Cavell doesn't explain the endlessness of paraphrase as I do, as can be learned from the fact that he thinks it distinguishes metaphor from some ('but perhaps not all') literal discourse. I hold that the endless character of what we call the paraphrase of a metaphor springs from the fact that it attempts to spell out what the metaphor makes us notice, and to this there is no clear end. I would say the same for any use of language.

14 Pronouns, quantifiers and relative clauses (I)*

Gareth Evans

I Introduction

Some philosophers, notably Professors Quine and Geach, have stressed the analogies they see between pronouns of the vernacular and the bound variables of quantification theory. Geach, indeed, once maintained that 'for a philosophical theory of reference, then, it is all one whether we consider bound variables or pronouns of the vernacular'.[1] This slightly overstates Geach's position since he recognizes that some pronouns of ordinary language do function differently from bound variables; he calls such pronouns 'pronouns of laziness'. Geach's characterization of pronouns of laziness has varied from time to time, but the general idea should be clear from a paradigm example:

(1) A man who sometimes beats his wife has more sense than one who always gives in to her.

The pronouns 'one' and 'her' go proxy for a noun or a noun phrase (here: 'a man' and 'his wife') in the sense that the pronoun is replaceable in paraphrase by simple repetition of its antecedent.[2]

However, if we leave such cases out of consideration for the time being, we are left with two main kinds of situation in which pronouns occur, and Geach appears to want to say that in both of them pronouns are functioning in the way bound variables of quantification theory function. In the first kind of situation, the pronoun has a singular term as its antecedent, as, for example, in

(2) John loves his mother
(3) John is happy when he is in love.

In the second kind of situation, the pronoun has a quantifier expression,

*This article is reprinted from Volume VII, Number 3 (September 1977) of the *Canadian Journal of Philosophy* by permission of the Canadian Association for Publishing in Philosophy. The author has made slight emendations to the original version. He would like to thank the following for reading the paper and offering comments and encouragement: M. K. Davies, G. H. Harman, P. F. Strawson, B. Taylor, D. Wiggins, D. Wilson and M. J. Woods.

or what Geach calls 'an applicational phrase', as its antecedent; as, for example, in

(4) Some man loves his mother
(5) No man is happy when he is in love.

From Geach's writings on pronouns it becomes clear in what the analogy between pronouns and bound variables is taken to consist. Time and again, in those writings, his target is the 'lazy assumption' that we can understand the functioning of pronouns by labelling them 'referring expressions' and inquiring into what they refer to. Just as it makes no sense to ask about the reference of any particular occurrence of the variable 'x' in the sentence

$(\exists x)$ $(Fx$ & $Gx)$,

Geach's idea is that it equally makes no sense to inquire into the reference of English pronouns. Correspondingly, just as there are many sentential contexts containing variables which cannot be regarded as having truth-values, on Geach's view there will be many English sentences containing pronouns which cannot be regarded as complete sentences with a truth-value.

For at least some occurrences of pronouns in English, these parallels with bound variables appear quite striking. Geach is surely right that it does make no sense to inquire into the reference of the pronoun in

(4) Some man loves his mother.

And, just as it makes no sense to ask for the truth-value of the sentence 'Gx' in the formula

(x) $(Fx \supset Gx)$,

surely Geach is right that we cannot assign a truth-value to the sentence 'he admires Mozart' as it occurs in

If any man loves music he admires Mozart.

Despite this, I find myself in considerable disagreement with the *general* equation between pronouns and bound variables which Geach has put forward. My disagreement consists of two independent points which I can best summarize as follows.

First, take any sentence containing a pronoun which has a quantifier antecedent, and which is admittedly functioning like a bound variable, e.g. (4) and (5). Paired with any such sentence is a well-formed sentence in which a singular term stands in place of the quantifier expression, as (2) and (3) are respectively paired with (4) and (5). Now, Geach appears to want to insist that pronouns function like bound variables even when they have singular terms as antecedents, so that they too cannot be assigned a reference, nor can their most immediate sentential context always be assigned a truth-value. For example, Geach appears to want to regard the sentence:

If John loves music he admires Mozart

as the result of attaching a complex conditional predicate to the name 'John', so that the function of the pronoun 'he' cannot be said to be that of referring to John nor can the sentence be regarded as the conditional compound of two sentences each of which has a truth-value.

I do not wish to claim that Geach's way of looking at pronouns with singular antecedents is incorrect, though I shall mention one or two advantages of looking at them another way. My first disagreement with Geach is on the question of whether it is *necessary* to adopt his way of looking at such pronouns. Geach believes that if we are to recognize the status of pronouns which have quantifier antecedents as akin to bound variables — as expressions whose function is not to refer — then we must say the same about the pronouns in those singular sentences from which the quantified sentences may be regarded as got by substitution. This seems to me to be a mistake. I shall argue that the semantical significance of these pronoun-antecedent constructions can be exhaustively stated in terms of a simple principle according to which a pronoun refers to whatever its singular antecedent refers to. Such an account is entirely adequate, not merely in the sense that it explains the functioning of pronouns with singular antecedents, but in the sense that no further explanation of the functioning of pronouns with quantifier antecedents is called for.

The fact that there are two equally viable approaches to the semantics of these pronoun-antecedent constructions — Geach's approach and the co-referential approach — is of no great moment in itself. It is an entirely trivial consequence of the fact that there are two different approaches to the semantics of quantified sentences, which I will outline in section II below. As with other points that I shall make in this paper, this point is only worth making because Geach has denied it, many times and with great vehemence.

For the purpose of this first dispute, then, it is common ground that certain pronouns with quantifier antecedents function just like bound variables — the issue is rather how this effect is to be achieved. But my second, and much more important, disagreement with Geach arises over the question of just how many pronouns with quantifier antecedents can be seen as functioning in this agreed way. I want to try to show that there are pronouns with quantifier antecedents that function in a quite different way. Such pronouns typically stand in a different grammatical relation to their antecedents, and, in contrast with bound pronouns, must be assigned a reference, so that their most immediate sentential contexts can always be assigned a truth-value. The relevant grammatical relation appears to be Klima's relation of 'in construction with'.[3] When the pronoun is in construction with its antecedent, as in (4) and (5), the result is a bound pronoun. But when it is not, as in

(6) Mary owns a donkey and John beats it
(7) John owns many sheep and Harry vaccinated them last July,

the pronouns must be regarded as having a reference, so that the second conjunct in both sentences may be assigned a truth-value. I call these pronouns 'E-type pronouns'.

E-type pronouns will occupy us for the bulk of this paper. But first I want to consider the other issue, since it will help us in thinking about pronouns that do not function like bound variables to have considered some that do. And before I can embark upon the question of the proper treatment of pronouns that do function like bound variables, I must first say something about two different approaches — the Tarskian and Fregean approaches — to the semantics of quantified sentences.

II   Two approaches to the semantics of quantified sentences

The major problem posed for semantic theory by quantified sentences of both natural and artificial languages arises because of the curious dual role which connectives and quantifiers play. The connectives 'and', 'not', 'if . . . , then', etc., both have the role of forming complex sentences from sentences, and of forming complex predicates from predicates. Thus we have

It is not the case that snow is white

as well as

Some men are not bald,

and

Snow is white and grass is green

as well as

Some men are young and bald.

The quantifiers also have a dual role. Sometimes they form sentences from predicates, as 'Someone runs' is formed from 'runs', and sometimes they form predicates of degree $n-1$ from predicates of degree n, as 'loves someone' is formed from 'loves'.

This poses the following problem. Our first instinct would be to provide an account of the sentence-forming role of these expressions in terms of the *truth*-conditions of the resulting expression, and of their predicate-forming role in terms of the *satisfaction*-conditions of the resulting expression. So, for example, if we followed our first instinct with the expression 'and', we should have the principle

(A) Any sentence S $\frown$ 'and' $\frown$ S′ is true iff S is true and S′ is true

to deal with the sentence-forming role, and the principle

(B) An object satisfies a predicate of the form F $\frown$ 'and' $\frown$ G iff it satisfies F and it also satisfies G

to deal with the predicate-forming role. But, by having two independent principles for the single semantical unit 'and', we deem it to be ambiguous, which our second instinct would be to say is absurd.

There appear to be two logically possible ways of solving this problem, and theories along both lines have been constructed. Either a theory takes the sentence-forming role as basic, keeps principles like (A), and somehow or other contrives to explain the predicate-forming role in terms of it. Or alternatively, the predicate-forming role is taken as basic, and the sentence-forming role is somehow derived from principles like (B). The first approach is associated with the name of Frege, and the second with that of Tarski.

Tarski was able to manage with principles of the form (B) alone, because he assimilated closed sentences to predicates, assigning to them, as well as to predicates, conditions under which objects satisfy them.[4] The essentials of the trick can be seen if we suppose Tarski's formal language had also contained certain unstructured propositional constants P and Q, with, for example, the meaning of 'Snow is white' and 'Grass is green'. Then, instead of explaining their semantic significance in a natural way,

P is true iff snow is white
Q is true iff grass is green,

but in a way which would not integrate with the clause for conjunction when the sentence 'P and Q' had to be dealt with, Tarski would have had clauses which effectively assigned them an extension:

An object satisfies P iff snow is white
An object satisfies Q iff grass is green.

Since these clauses are of the form '$(x)\,(Fx \equiv R)$' we know immediately that either every object satisfies these sentences or no object satisfies these sentences according to whether or not they are true or false. So it will be open for us to define a true sentence as a (closed) sentence with the universal extension. With this definition of truth, it is easy to show that the truth-functional role of the connective 'and', for example, as forming truths when and only when flanked by truths, is a special case of its role of forming an expression which is satisfied by an object iff that object satisfies both of the expressions which flank it.

Gareth Evans

Perhaps the point comes out most clearly if we look at the matter model-theoretically. 'And' is assigned a function from pairs of sets to their intersection, 'not' is assigned a function from a set to its complement, and so on. It is clear that $f_{and}(a,b)$ = the universal set iff $a = b =$ the universal set, and $f_{not}(a)$ = the universal set iff a = the empty set. So if we define T = the universal set, and F = the empty set, the truth-functional role drops out as a special case.

This will achieve the desired results, but only so long as it is arranged that true closed sentences are satisfied by every object and false closed sentences are satisfied by none. It is easy to arrange this case by case for unstructured propositional constants, but it remains to be seen how Tarski arranged it for structured and closed atomic sentences. Pretend for a moment that the language under consideration contains only monadic predicates, and that the only way of forming a closed atomic sentence is by combining a quantifier with a predicate. Then, the most natural way of stating the semantic effect of the quantifiers would be in clauses which spoke of truth, along the lines of

(C) A sentence of the form 'Something'⌢A is true iff something satisfies A.

To give closed sentences the properties Tarski requires, (C) must be replaced by a principle which states the impact of the quantifiers in terms of satisfaction:

(D) An object satisfies 'Something'⌢A iff something satisfies A.

Once again, this has the form of '$(x)(Fx \equiv R)$', and the effect that a closed sentence is satisfied by all objects iff it is true, and by no objects iff it is not true.

So long as we consider languages all of whose atomic predicates are monadic, the form of (D) could only be explained by a desire to assign closed predicates an extension, in order that the predicate-forming role of the connectives can be taken as basic. But once the language contains polyadic predicates, the quantifier also doubles as a predicate-former, so that a clause of the form of (C) is not adequate by itself, and a clause, like (D), dealing in terms of satisfaction has some independent advantages. In fact it has to be more complex than (D), speaking in terms of satisfaction by ordered n-tuples, or sequences, of objects, and comprising some device for keeping track of which position in a complex predicate goes with which other. But it will have the same effect as (D), in that, when the quantifier is initial and the sentence closed, the conditions under which a sequence of objects satisfies it have nothing to do with the particular properties of that sequence, so that either every sequence will satisfy it, or none will.

Frege's alternative strategy is less well known, and certainly less widely appreciated as a genuinely alternative solution to the problems

260

posed by the dual status of the connectives and quantifiers.[5] The Fregean strategy is to take the sentence-forming roles of the connectives as basic, with principles like (A) which deal in terms of *truth* as exhaustive statements of them. The theory is able to deal with sentences in which connectives operate upon predicates, or expressions which cannot be assigned a truth value, because in the course of evaluating such sentences, and by the time the contribution of the connective is to be accounted for, the sentence will have undergone a metamorphosis, as a result of which the constituents upon which the connective operates are, once again, complete sentences.

The main idea of a Fregean truth theory for quantified sentences is that 'in the case of a complex predicate, the notion of a predicate's being true or false of an object is derivative from that of the truth or falsity of the sentence which results from filling the argument-place of the predicate with a name of that object.'[6] We may use a simple principle for the quantifiers like (C) but the relation of satisfaction which holds between an expression and an object to which that clause directs us is, in the case of a complex predicate, defined in terms of the truth-value of the sentence which results when a singular term referring to that object is substituted in the predicate, or, if the language contains no name for the object, in terms of the truth-value, in some extension of the language, of a sentence which results when a singular term which refers to that object upon that extension of the language is substituted in the predicate. We must assume that for every object there is an extension of the language which contains a name for that object, although at no stage are we obliged to assume that there is an extension of the language which contains a name for every object.

It should be clear how such a conception of satisfaction enables a theorist to dispense with any explanation of the role of connectives and quantifiers other than that stated in terms of truth. Thus, for example, 'Some man is such that he is young and he is bald' is true iff there is a man that satisfies the predicate 'he is young and he is bald'. Now, an object y satisfies this predicate iff upon that extension of the language on which β denotes y, 'β is young and β is bald' is true.[7] At this point we may invoke the simple principle (A) for sentential conjunction, and derive the result that y satisfies 'he is young and he is bald' iff upon that extension of the language on which β denotes y, 'β is young' is true and 'β is bald' is true. Since we know that a sentence of the form 'β is young' is true iff the denotation of β is young and a sentence of the form 'β is bald' is true iff the denotation of β is bald we derive the conclusion that y satisfies the complex predicate iff y is young and y is bald, so that the whole sentence is true iff there is an object that is young and bald.

There are similarities between Fregean truth theories and the substitutional truth-theories familiar from the work of Professor Marcus.[8]

Both run their recursions directly on truth, and both take the sentence-forming roles of operators as basic. But there are crucial differences which I have tried to bring out by separating the clauses for the quantifiers (like (C)) and the clause giving a general explanation of the notion of satisfaction.[9]

Unlike the substitutional truth-theory, the Fregean truth-theory introduces no new concept of existence – the principle (C) uses the perfectly ordinary, objectual, concept of existence. And for every object that we deem to exist in this sense, we are obliged to consider as relevant to the truth-value of quantified sentences, the truth-value of a substitution instance that may be formed with the use of a term denoting that object, while at no point are we permitted to consider as relevant the truth-value of substitution instances formed with the use of non-denoting names.

The net effect of these two provisions is to deprive the Fregean truth-theory of any ontological interest whatever. But, the fact that a Fregean truth-theory is not an ontological rival to a Tarskian theory should not lead us to think that it is not a semantical rival. Using the leading idea of the Fregean theory, it is easy to construct homophonic theories for standard first-order languages which unquestionably take the sentence-forming roles of the quantifiers and connectives as basic. And the idea can be generalized to deal with quantification into any context. From the Fregean point of view, once an operator has been given a clear sense when attached to a closed sentence (containing singular terms), then no additional explanation is required for quantification into the context created by that operator.[10]

Although this is not the place to argue the matter, I do not think that the existence of the Fregean alternative is of merely technical interest. It is true that the Fregean theory with its direct recursion on truth is very much simpler and smoother than the Tarskian alternative, whose mechanism of infinite sequences differing in at most this or that place is dispensed with. But its interest does not stem from this, but rather from examination at a more philosophical level. It seems to me that serious exception can be taken to the Tarskian theory on the ground that it loses sight of, or takes no account of, the centrality of sentences (and of truth) in the theory of meaning; Tarski's assimilation of sentences to a certain kind of complex predicate is open to objection along just the same lines as the later Frege's assimilation of sentences to a certain kind of complex name.[11] Further, in the case of some expressions which double as both sentence- and predicate-formers, a direction of explanation which takes their sentence-forming role as basic seems to be the only possible one,[12] while in all cases it is more natural.[13] This greater naturalness has a lot to do with the fact that the interpretation of these operators is empirically more determinate in their sentence-forming roles.

Important though these points are for the general theory of quantification, they are not of immediate importance for us.[14] For us, all that matters is that the Fregean theory of meaning for quantified sentences should at least be deemed to be a coherent theory. Certainly Geach's opposition to the position on pronouns which I wish to defend as coherent does not rest upon doubt about this point, for he himself is prone, in his writings, to give truth conditions for quantified sentences along Fregean lines.[15]

Let us turn directly to the bearing these matters have upon the proper treatment of pronouns.

III   Bound pronouns and pronouns with singular antecedents

What function do the pronouns have in the sentences

(2) John loves his mother
(3) John is happy when he is in love?

In addressing myself to this question, I am going to assume that there exists no compelling syntactic reason for supposing that sentences containing pronouns are derived transformationally from underlying structures in which there are repeated occurrences of singular terms. I do not make this assumption because I have been persuaded by the arguments against the existence of such a transformation, but because it seems to me that, if such were the origin of pronouns in singular sentences, the dispute between Geach and myself would have an easy resolution in my favour.

One pretty obvious answer to the question is this: the pronouns are singular terms referring to whatever their antecedents refer to. Let me try to expand this answer a bit.

Let us suppose that the base component of a grammar for English generates what I shall call *sentence-frames* of the form

(   ) loves (   )
(   ) is happy when (   ) is in love.

In addition, we are permitted to form sentence-frames from sentence-frames by linking together two or more singular term positions in any sentence-frame. Any device for this linking will do. We could use repeated occurrences of the same letter to link a number of singular term positions together, and then our sentence-frames would look like this:

(x) is happy when (x) is in love.

263

Gareth Evans

Alternatively, we could use a brace notation suggested by Quine,[16] and then they would look like this:

$$(\overline{})\text{ is happy when }(\overline{})\text{ is in love.}$$

We can call a series of singular term positions linked together in this way a *chain* of singular term positions, and for convenience we regard a single position as a 1-link chain. We can form sentences from sentence frames by the insertion of singular terms into singular term positions in such a way that there is one and only one term in every chain. Thus

$$(\overline{\text{John}})\text{ loves }(\overline{})$$

$$(\overline{\text{John}})\text{ loves }(\overline{})\text{ and }(\text{Mary})\text{ loves }(\overline{})$$

are sentences. Chained, but empty singular term positions will be realized in surface structure as pronouns of the appropriate number and gender.[17]

A semantic theory which issues the simple answer which I have just given to the question 'What are these pronouns doing here?' would be one which contained the following principle as an exhaustive account of the significance of the pronoun + brace device:

> (F) If σ is a sentence containing the singular term positions p_i and p_j which are chained together, and p_i contains the singular term τ and p_j contains the pronoun κ, then the denotation of κ in σ is the same as the denotation of τ.

By the application of such a principle, the truth-conditions of sentences (2) and (3) would be given in the (slightly non-homophonic) theorems:

'John loves his mother' is true iff John loves John's mother

'John is happy when he is in love' is true iff John is happy when John is in love.[18]

Let us call the treatment which rests upon a principle like (F) the *co-referential treatment of pronouns*. I should say right away that I regard this as a proposal quite different from the proposal that pronouns with singular antecedents are 'pronouns of laziness'. When we say that an expression 'goes proxy for' some chunk of text, we evaluate the sentence containing it just as if the expression was replaced by what it goes proxy for.[19] In many cases, the two treatments will have the same results, but they nevertheless invoke different mechanisms which produce divergent results in some examples.

Now, it has been widely thought that the co-referential treatment of pronouns is simply inadequate to deal with pronouns whose antecedents are not singular terms but quantifier expressions, like those in (4) and (5). But this criticism is ill-informed. For, if a Fregean statement of the truth conditions of quantified sentences is adopted, nothing

more needs to be said about the pronouns with quantifier antecedents
— they simply look after themselves.

Let us call expressions like 'some', 'many', 'the', 'a', 'few', 'every'
quantifiers, and a quantifier plus a common noun, like 'some man', 'a
girl', etc. a *quantifier expression.*[20] We extend the grammar to allow
that any sentence containing a singular term in a position, p_i remains
well formed when a quantifier expression is substituted for it in p_i. (Inserting the quantifier into the singular term position being generalized
upon does appear to be the way we indicate in English which quantifier
goes with which position.) Since left-right ordering is not reliably used
to indicate scope, we had better indicate with numerical subscripts the
order in which the quantifiers are inserted in the construction of a
sentence. Thus we distinguish

(Every$_1$ man) loves (a$_2$ woman) = There is a woman every man loves

from

(Every$_2$ man) loves (a$_1$ woman) = For every man, there is a woman
he loves.

The semantic account of the quantifiers will have the form with
which we are already familiar, but in which some account is taken of
the common noun restricting the quantifier. Thus, for example, we
have the following principle for the quantifier 'Every':

(G) If σ is a sentence containing in its ith singular term position the
quantifier expression 'every' $_j$ δ (where δ is a common noun
and j an index than which no other index attached to any quantifier in σ is higher) then σ is true (in L) iff on every extension
of L with respect to some singular term β which does not
already occur in σ on which the object which β denotes on that
extension satisfies δ, σ^β/p_i is true.

(I write 'σ^β/p_i' as an abbreviation for 'the sentence which results when
β is substituted for whatever occurs in the ith singular term position in
σ'.)

It should be easy to see how clauses like (F) and (G) suffice to deal
with the occurrence of pronouns with quantifier antecedents. The
grammar enables us to form sentences like:

(Some$_1$ man) loves (‾‾‾) mother

realized in surface structure as

(4) Some man loves his mother.

Certainly we would get nowhere if we attempted to apply the rule dealing with pronouns directly, for the quantifier expression 'Some man'
has no denotation. But if we apply the rule for the quantifier first, as

Gareth Evans

we should, since the order in which the sentence is constructed gives it widest scope, we find that the truth of (4) depends upon whether or not there is some true (potential) substitution instance of the form

(β) loves $(\ )$ mother.

Now the pronoun rule can apply, eventually yielding the result that such a sentence is true iff the denotation of β loves the mother of the denotation of β. By elementary manoeuvrings which can easily be imagined, we will arrive at the result that (4) is true iff there is a man such that that man loves that man's mother.

Just as a semantic theory which adopts a Fregean explanation for the truth-conditions of quantified sentences can take the truth-functional role of the connectives as basic, so such a theory can regard pronouns as devices for registering co-reference (understood strictly). Or at least, so it would appear. We shall have to consider Geach's arguments against this way of understanding pronouns, but I hope it does not appear *obviously* absurd and unpromising.

I suspect that many philosophers and linguists have meant no more by talking of the existence of variables in deep structure, and of the parallelism between pronouns of the vernacular and variables of quantification theory, than that there exists in natural language a device for marking chains of co-reference of which pronouns are the superficial manifestations.[21] But this is certainly not what Geach intends by his claim of parallelism. For Geach's claim to be correct, pronouns must be the manifestations of a device which is essentially a device for the formation of complex predicates. With the Tarskian semantics in mind, we might say: a device that registers co-assignment, not co-reference. On the semantic theory just sketched, this claim will not hold good, as we may see by considering a sentence like:

If John is here, he will be sorry.

On the one hand, the expression:

If $(\ )$ is here $(\ )$ will be sorry

receives no semantic interpretation, and is not acknowledged to constitute a semantical unit, while the expression which is realized in surface structure as 'he will be sorry' is treated as a semantical unit, and is assigned *truth*-conditions.

As I have said, Geach believes that any proposal which treats pronouns with singular antecedents as referring expressions can be shown to involve a definite mistake. We had better look at his arguments.

(i) The first argument I want to consider occurs in many places in Geach's writings. At one point, he put the argument like this:[22]

Let us consider an example:
(22) If any man owns a donkey, he beats it.

(23) If Smith owns a donkey, he beats it.

The pronoun 'he' is replaceable by 'Smith' in (23) without changing the import of the proposition; it is not thus replaceable by 'any man' in (22); so it looks as if it were a pronoun of laziness in (23), but not in (22). All the same, (23) predicates of Smith precisely what (22) predicates of any man; both contain the same unambiguous complex predicable 'If _____ owns a donkey, he beats it'. . . . On the other hand, the proposition:

(24) If Smith owns a donkey, Smith beats it

contains the completely different predicable 'if _____ owns a donkey, Smith beats it'; when attached to the quasi-subject 'any man', this gives us the proposition:

(25) If any man owns a donkey, Smith beats it

which is wholly different in force from (22). Thus the wholly different sense of the predicables 'If _____ owns a donkey, he beats it' and 'if _____ owns a donkey, Smith beats it' shows that even in (23) 'he' has a definite logical role of its own and is not a mere pronoun of laziness – not a mere device for avoiding the repetition of 'Smith'.

It is true that in this argument Geach is opposing the view that such pronouns are pronouns of laziness going proxy for their antecedents, rather than the view that they have the same reference as their antecedents. However, this does not matter since, if his argument is effective against the former view, it will be effective against the latter view also, and, on other occasions on which it is deployed, the conclusion is expressly stated as that the pronouns do not refer.[23]

Later in the same work, Geach offers an exactly parallel argument in connection with the reflexive pronoun.[24] In essence it is this:

(1) 'Everyone contradicts himself' says of everyone what 'Hegel contradicts himself' says of Hegel.
(2) 'Hegel contradicts Hegel' says of Hegel that he contradicts Hegel.
(3) If, in 'Hegel contradicts himself', the import of 'contradicts himself' were the same as that of 'contradicts Hegel', then 'Everyone contradicts himself' would say of everyone that he contradicts Hegel, which is absurd.
(4) *Therefore* in 'Hegel contradicts himself', the import of 'contradicts himself' is not the same as that of 'contradicts Hegel', and hence the pronoun 'himself' has a definite logical role of its own; it is not a mere device for referring to Hegel.

This argument is unsound; its second premise is false. Ironically, it is Geach, more than anyone else, who has been concerned to emphasize that it is false. Consider, for example, the following passage:[25]

We may in some instances recognise a common predicate in two propositions even though this predicate is not an identifiable expression that can be picked out; for example, 'John shaved John' propounds the very same thing concerning John as 'Peter shaved Peter' does concerning Peter, and thus we may regard the two as containing a common predicate but this is by no means identifiable with the mere word 'shaved' occurring in both.

The significance of Geach's observation is this: seeing the import of the proposition 'Hegel contradicts himself' as being the same as 'Hegel contradicts Hegel' does not preclude us from seeing the same predicable occurring in 'Hegel contradicts himself' as occurs in 'Geach contradicts himself' and in 'No one contradicts himself'. To maintain, as Geach's argument appears to require, that 'Hegel contradicts Hegel' contains *only* the predicable '____ contradicts Hegel' is to reject the possibility of multiple equally correct ways of breaking down a proposition into its constituents without which, as Geach has often reminded us, logic would be so hopelessly crippled.

If we follow Geach, the phrase 'What "Hegel contradicts Hegel" says of Hegel' is an expression which fails to pick out a unique predicable — there are three different candidates. Correspondingly, on the co-referential treatment of pronouns, the same would be true of the expression 'What "Hegel contradicts himself" says of Hegel'. Perhaps this is what troubles Geach; perhaps he thinks that, unlike the proposition with repeated occurrences of the proper name 'Hegel', the proposition with the reflexive pronoun admits of only one breakdown into subject and predicate. But it is difficult to see why this should be so. For while the logical relationship between 'Hegel contradicts himself' and 'No one contradicts himself' requires us to see a common predicable, a similar connection between 'Hegel contradicts himself' and 'No one contradicts Hegel' would seem equally to suggest that they share a predicable.[26]

(ii) The second argument concerns the sentence 'Only Satan pities himself'.[27]

Moreover, it is not even true that when the antecedent is a singular term, it can always take the place of a reflexive pronoun. 'Only Satan pities himself' and 'Only Satan pities Satan' are quite different in their import.

This objection may also be dealt with by taking seriously a point which Geach himself makes, namely that 'Only Satan' is not a singular term, but rather an applicational phrase in its own right.[28] Consequently, a pronoun which has the expression 'Only Satan' as its antecedent is not a pronoun to which the co-referentiality principle may be directly applied. Like the expression 'Someone other than', 'Only' is an expression which takes a name to form a quantifier. The truth-conditions of the resulting proposition are essentially those given by Geach (in Fregean style):[29]

'F(only α)' is true iff no interpretation of 'x' as a proper name makes 'F(x)' true unless 'x' names something that is named in or by 'α'.

Applying such a principle to the sentence

(Only $\overline{\text{Satan}}$) loves ($\ulcorner$ $\urcorner$)

we will be directed to consider the truth value of substitution instances of the form

(β) loves ($\ulcorner$ $\urcorner$)

to see if we can find one which is true, yet in which β does not refer to Satan. Such 'exclusive propositions' then, can present no more difficulty for the co-referential treatment of pronouns than is presented by any other quantified sentence.

It is worth taking note of the fact that certain such 'exclusive propositions' are ambiguous. For example, the sentence:

(8) Only John loves his mother

admits also of the reading on which it is equivalent to 'Only John loves John's mother'. This ambiguity can be explained quite easily.

To secure the reading on which the sentence asserts that only John is an own-mother-lover, it must be built from the sentence frame

($\ulcorner$) loves ($\urcorner$)'s mother

by the insertion of the quantifier expression 'Only John', thus:

(Only $\overline{\text{(John)}}$) loves ($\ulcorner$ $\urcorner$)'s mother.

On this reading, the quantifier has a scope wider than that of the co-referentiality brace. For the other reading, the sentence would be constructed from the sentence frame

(Only ( )) loves ( )'s mother

by the insertion of the brace and singular term 'John', yielding

(Only (John)) loves ($\ulcorner$ $\urcorner$)'s mother

in which the co-referentiality brace has a scope wider than the quantifier.

Similar ambiguities are found in a variety of sentences in which there occurs a modifier of a complex predicate containing a pronoun:

John is elderly for a man who loves his mother

John is the oldest man who loves his mother

John is too anti-semitic to love himself.

Sentences of this general character have been considered by B. H. Partee, who supposes that they constitute a difficulty for Geach's view of pronouns.[30] It is not difficult to see why this should be supposed. Capturing the reading of (8) on which it means that only John loves John's mother seems to require seeing the sentence as containing the predicable '(x) loves John's mother', which is then attached to the 'quasi-subject' 'Only John'. And so it might appear that at least *some* pronouns have to be regarded as referring to what their antecedents refer to, or at least as going proxy for their antecedents.

I do not think that the dispute between Geach's treatment and the co-referential treatment of pronouns can be settled by this kind of example. For, take that proposition which gives the truth conditions of a sentence upon the co-referential theory. Replace each occurrence of a recurrent proper name or singular term in that statement of the truth-conditions with a variable, and thus form a predicate abstract. Now, envisage a semantic theory on which truth-conditions are derived for the sentence by deriving satisfaction-conditions for that complex predicate. Such is Geach's theory. For example, Geach can represent the ambiguity in (8) as that between the results of attaching to 'John' the different complex predicates:

$$\hat{y} \ [\text{Only } y : \hat{x} \ [x \text{ loves } x\text{'s mother}]\,]$$
$$\hat{y} \ [\text{Only } y : \hat{x} \ [x \text{ loves } y\text{'s mother}]\,]$$

(iii) The third argument I want to consider is not to be found in Geach.[31] Consider the sentence:

(9) John thinks he's under suspicion.

For reasons which Castaneda has made his own,[32] this proposition is not equivalent to the proposition 'John thinks that John is under suspicion'. I have heard it suggested that here at least we should see the pronoun 'he' as being used in the construction of the complex predicate 'x thinks that x is under suspicion'.

I want to concede right away that the pronoun 'he' in (9) does not have the function of indicating co-reference. This is not because, if it did have that function, (9) would then ascribe to John the notional belief that John is under suspicion, for it would not. The ascription of such a notional belief would be the result of seeing the pronoun in (9) as a pronoun of laziness, which is a different proposal from the one we are considering. But, nevertheless, it is true that the result of applying the principle (F) can amount to no more than the ascription to John of the belief *of* John that he is under suspicion. Interpreting pronouns with singular antecedents according to (F) renders the position occupied by them referentially transparent. Beyond acknowledging that the pronoun in (9) is not to be dealt with by principle (F), I have nothing definite to say about it; perhaps we should see (9) as somehow derived from the *oratio recta* sentence: 'John thinks "I'm under suspicion" '.[33]

With that said, it is none the less true that the observation is quite irrelevant to the current dispute. For it is just as much a consequence of the suggestion that we see (9) as built up out of the complex predicate 'x thinks that x is under suspicion' and the proper name 'John', that the belief (9) ascribes to John is merely the transparent belief of John, that he is under suspicion. There is no magic in the recurrent variable 'x' that somehow ensures that we assign a 'self-conscious' belief to John. The recurrent variable merely serves to ensure that, in considering whether or not a particular sequence satisfies the predicate, we assign the same object to both occurrences of the variable as its denotation-relative-to-the-sequence. Such an explanation makes no apparent sense of the recurrence of a variable both inside and outside an opaque context. An application of a mechanism for guaranteeing co-assignment to singular term positions in a complex predicate supposes those positions to be referentially transparent in just the way an application of a method for co-reference does.

(Since confusion upon this point has occurred in the literature, I think it worth emphasizing that the relational formulation 'x believes of x that he is under suspicion' does not capture the idea of 'self-conscious' belief though, of course, if it did, so would the formulation '(John) thinks ( ) is under suspicion'. Admittedly, it is unclear *what* the relational formulation captures, for it is unclear what additional premises are required to license the inference from the notional 'x believes that a is F' to the relational 'x believes of a (that is to say b) that it is F'. But all the principles that have been suggested would appear to allow that a man could believe of someone who was in fact himself that he is F, without knowing that it was he himself. If this is so, then it is possible for a, that is to say, b, to satisfy 'x believes of x that he is under suspicion' in virtue of a's possession of the notional belief that b is under suspicion (when he does not realize that he is b).[34]

We have been able to find no reason for modifying the view that a theory which sees pronouns as devices for marking co-reference (strictly speaking) is perfectly viable, provided that it incorporates a Fregean statement of the truth-conditions of quantified sentences. In conclusion, I should like to mention a consideration which would give a decisive edge to one treatment of pronouns over its rival, *if* it applied, but which does not seem to me to apply, and some considerations which give the referential treatment a mild advantage over Geach's approach.

I come to semantic investigations with a preference for *homophonic* theories; theories which try to take serious account of the semantic and syntactic devices which actually exist in the language by deriving for each sentence of the object language a statement of truth-conditions in which the very resources employed in it occur and are not analysed

271

away in favour of resources which do not occur. To take a relatively trivial example, I would prefer a theory which was sensitive to the binary structure of the sentence 'All A's are B's' and which, being thus sensitive, was able to deduce the theorem that 'All A's are B's' is true iff all A's are B's, over a theory which is only able to deal with this sentence by 'discovering' hidden logical constants, and deducing the result that 'All A's are B's' is true iff all things are B-if-they-are-A. The objection would not be that such truth-conditions are not correct, but that, in a sense which we would all dearly love to have more exactly explained, the syntactic shape of the sentence is treated as so much misleading surface structure.[35]

Obscure though this formulation is, it is not necessary for the purposes at hand to make it any clearer. For while it must be admitted that the co-referential theory of pronouns does depart from homophony in that the truth-conditions of the sentence 'John loves his mother' are given by the sentence 'John loves John's mother', no remotely homophonic theory constructed on Geach's lines seems in prospect. The introduction of variables and the parsing of singular sentences of the kind we have been considering as involving complex predicates is as much a departure from the actual pronoun-antecedent construction which we find in English as one which eliminates pronouns altogether. Perhaps we just have to learn to live with the idea that this pronoun-antecedent construction is, in the relevant sense, just so much surface structure.[36]

I will now mention some considerations which tell against Geach's way of treating pronouns, at least in so far as it is applied quite generally to pronouns with singular antecedents.

First, Geach's treatment requires such pronouns to be bound by names, which can be regarded, for this purpose, as singulary quantifiers. He thus requires the scope of a name to include any pronoun which has that name as its antecedent. Now in extensional contexts names are scopeless, and thus no difficulties arise from this requirement since names can always be given maximum scope. But it does not appear to be true that names are scopeless in all contexts of natural language; such would be the case only if all name-containing contexts were referentially transparent. Now, take any opaque construction containing the proper name β, $O(\beta)$. If a pronoun which is outside the construction looks back to the name as antecedent, it cannot be dealt with as Geach requires. The only way of binding the pronoun would require the legitimate formation of the complex predicate

$$\hat{x}[O(x) \ldots x]$$

which as I have said, would render the context created by O transparent.

It does not appear difficult to construct sentences containing pronouns which look back to terms occurring inside opaque contexts; the following seem perfectly natural:

Oedipus thinks that Jocasta is childless, but she isn't

Giorgione was so-called because of his size, and he hated it.

Such sentences present no difficulty for the theory which treats pronouns in terms of co-reference strictly interpreted. Upon that view, all that is required is that names in opaque contexts have a referent; it is not required that their referent is all that is semantically relevant.

There is a second mild advantage to the referential treatment. Consider the following dialogue:

A: John came today.
B. Did he stay long?

It seems desirable to allow that B is using the same device of cross-reference to ask his question as we have seen used in the construction of a single sentence. (This seems particularly desirable when we observe that B may not have the epistemological resources to make a reference to John on his own account.[37]) It requires only a trivial modification of the grammar to allow the chaining of singular term positions to singular terms which occur in other sentences. No modification of the referential semantics is required at all, once we allow the units processed by our semantic theory to be chunks of dialogue, not just single sentences.

It does appear rather difficult to deal with such pronouns on Geach's view, since we would somehow have to see A and B engaged in the co-operative construction of a complex predicate in a way which appears inconsistent with assigning a truth value to either of their remarks taken independently. Do we not want to allow that B *contradicts* A when he continues

B: No he didn't ?[38]

Finally, I think that the suggestion that pronouns make a contribution which is to be explained by principle (F) can claim to be somewhat more explanatory of the morphological shape which expressions that are used in this way actually have. First of all, we should realize that many expressions other than pronouns, strictly so called, may be used exactly as pronouns are used. For example, 'that logician' is functioning like a bound pronoun in the sentence

Every logician was walking with a boy near that logician's house.

In fact, almost any singular term can be used to make a back-reference provided it is reduced in stress.[39] Thus consider the sentence

Amin was widely disliked, but the Ugandan president did not seem to mind.

Gareth Evans

We can see this sentence as resulting from the sentence frame:

(Amin) was widely disliked, but ( ) did not seem to mind;

reduced stress being the superficial manifestation of the brace.

If we collect together all the devices that can occur in a singular term position chained to some other referring expression, we discover that they are all capable of being used, in other contexts, to make independent references. This little generalization will surely come as no surprise to one who holds a theory according to which expressions occupying such positions do refer (albeit with the aid of a co-referring device). But upon Geach's theory, this generalization must remain quite unexplained. For Geach, pronouns are part of a device for complex-predicate formation. Now, as I shall argue later, there are devices in English which have precisely the function which Geach assigns to pronouns — namely the relative pronouns 'who', 'which'. In the expression 'who loves Mary and whom everyone despises', the relative pronoun is being used to keep track of which position goes with which in the formation of a complex predicate. But if such is the function of pronouns, and of expressions which function like them, there would be no more reason to expect them to be capable of being used to make independent references than there is to expect 'who' and 'which' etc., to be capable of being used in this way.

IV 'E-type pronouns'

A Introduction

In this section, I wish to defend the view that some pronouns with quantifier antecedents are quite unlike bound variables; in particular they may be assigned a reference and their immediate sentential contexts can be evaluated independently for truth and falsehood. Such pronouns are not genuine singular terms in the sense in which ordinary proper names and demonstrative expressions are; rather they are singular terms whose reference is fixed by description.[40] How exactly we are to secure the right semantical results is a matter of detail which I will discuss later;[41] to begin with I will be mainly concerned to establish the limited conclusion that such pronouns cannot be regarded as analogous to bound variables.

Consider the sentence

(10) John owns some sheep and Harry vaccinates them.

For all we have said up to now, we can see this sentence as built up in the following way:

274

( ) owns ( ) and ( ) vaccinates ( )

( ) owns (⌐) and ( ) vaccinates (⌐)

(John) owns (⌐) and (Harry) vaccinates (⌐)

(John) owns (some sheep) and (Harry) vaccinates (them).

To see (10) as built up in this way is to see the quantifier 'some sheep' as having the whole sentence as its scope, and (10) as equivalent to

> John owns some sheep which are such that Harry vaccinates them

or

> Some sheep are such that John owns them and Harry vaccinates them.

Now, although it *may* be possible to construe the sentence in this way, it is not open to dispute that this is neither the only, nor the most natural, interpretation. Upon the most natural interpretation, the sentence would not be true unless Harry vaccinates *all* the sheep which John owns. A paraphrase of (10) upon that interpretation would be

> John owns some sheep and Harry vaccinates the sheep that John owns.

In the same way, the sentence

> (11) Few MPs came to the party, but they had a marvellous time

is not equivalent to

> It holds good of few MPs that they both went to the party and had a marvellous time

both because (11) entails, while its supposed paraphrase does not, that few MPs went to the party, and also that *all* the MPs that came had a marvellous time. Similarly:

> (12) Mary danced with many boys and they found her interesting

is not equivalent to

> Mary danced with many boys who found her interesting.

What this strongly suggests is that we must see (10), (11) and (12) as the conjunction of two sentences with the scope of the quantifier going only to the end of the first conjunct.

So, the first piece of evidence that pronouns like those in (10), (11) and (12) are not functioning like bound pronouns is that, if we interpret them as bound pronouns, we do not give the sentences the meaning they are most naturally interpreted as having. There is another piece of evidence. In none of the sentences can we substitute a quantifier of the form 'No' + common noun *salva congruitate*:

*John owns no sheep and Harry vaccinated them

*No MPs came to the party but they had a marvellous time

*Mary danced with no boys and they found her interesting.

Now, upon the view that these pronouns are bound pronouns, this fact is inexplicable. For upon that view, if we remove the quantifier from these sentences, we are left with a complex predicate, which was affirmed to be satisfied in the case of some sheep, few MPs, or many boys, and which we ought to be able to affirm to be satisfied in the case of no sheep, no MP, or no boy. If the pronoun 'them' in (10) was genuinely within the scope of the quantifier 'some sheep', as it is in the sentence

John owns some sheep such that Harry vaccinates them,

then the ungrammatical sentence ought to have just the interpretation of

John owns no sheep such that Harry vaccinates them.

Essentially the same point can be made with the quantifier expression 'every' + common noun, once we move to singular sentences of the same syntactic structure. If the sentence

(13) Socrates owns a dog and it bit Socrates

was the result of attaching the complex predicate 'Socrates owns x and x bit Socrates' to the quantifier 'a dog', as is the sentence

A dog is such that Socrates owns it and it bit Socrates,

then the sentence

*Socrates owns every dog and it bit Socrates

ought to be well formed and have the same meaning as

Every dog is such that Socrates owns it and it bit Socrates.

What appears to be going on is this. The most important determinant of the scope of a quantifier is its syntactic position in the sentence. Roughly, and not inflexibly, the scope of a quantifier is naturally interpreted as constituting the smallest sentence which includes all the constituents which are *in construction with it*. (Klima defines the notion 'in construction with' so that a constituent is in construction with another iff the former is dominated by the first branching node which dominates the latter.) In (10), for example, the scope of 'some sheep' extends only to the end of the first clause. If we wish to say that some man is both bald and tall, we must not insert the 'some man' quantifier into the sentence frame:

$(\ulcorner\ \urcorner)$ is bald and $(\ulcorner\ \urcorner)$ is tall in which its scope will reach only to the end of the first clause, but we must transform the tree so that the singular term position into which we propose to insert the quantifier *governs* 'tall'.[42] For example, we may use the conjunction reduction transformation, to produce

    ( ) is bald and tall

or the 'such that' construction

    (⌐) is such that (⌐) is bald and (⌐) is tall.[43]

We must suppose a prohibition to be in force against the insertion of a quantifier expression into a singular term position to which another singular term position which it does not govern is chained — the result would be an unbound pronoun.

Let us consider a few examples:

The man who owns Fido vaccinates him ('Fido' does not govern 'him').

Fido loves his master ('Fido' governs 'his').

Fido loves Mary and also loves his master ('Fido' governs 'his').

Fido loves Mary and he also loves his master ('Fido' does not govern 'he', nor 'his').

'Mary owns Fido and beats him with her broom ('Mary' governs 'her', 'Fido' does not govern 'him').[44]

Fido barks when he is happy ('Fido' governs 'he').

If Fido barks then he is happy ('Fido' does not govern 'he').

Either Fido is unhappy or he barks ('Fido' does not govern 'he').

I think it will be discovered that when an existential quantifier 'some dogs' is substituted for 'Fido' (and 'he', 'his' are changed to 'they', 'them' etc.) then the pronouns are naturally interpreted as bound pronouns, and the quantifier as having wide scope if and only if the quantifier expression governs the pronoun. Similarly with 'many dogs', 'few dogs', 'most dogs', etc. Equally, a well formed sentence results when 'no dogs' is substituted for 'Fido' (and appropriate changes are made to the pronouns) only when the quantifier governs the pronoun.

I said 'roughly and not inflexibly' for two reasons. First of all, we can often just about hear quantifiers which are not in a governing position as having wide scope. For example, it is just about possible to hear the sentence

If a friend of mine comes, we are done for

as being equivalent to

A friend of mine is such that if he comes we are done for.

Second, there are quantifiers which we almost always interpret as having maximum scope; 'any' is one, and 'a certain' is another. Thus:

Gareth Evans

If any dog is happy he barks

If a certain friend of mine comes, we are done for

are both naturally interpreted in a way which gives the quantifier wide scope.

As far as the present topic is concerned, these points do not matter. What matters is simply the fact that there are sentences containing pronouns, whose antecedents are quantifiers, but which are not naturally interpreted in the way that would result if the pronouns were bound by those quantifiers. For the semantic role of these pronouns, another account must be provided. It really does not matter that those sentences should also be capable of another interpretation, or that other sentences, of the same grammatical pattern but with different quantifiers, should not be capable of the troublesome interpretation. Nevertheless, I think that if we exclude the wide-scope-seeking quantifiers 'any' and 'a certain', the generalization I have offered, as to which pronouns will *naturally* be interpreted as being bound by a quantifier, is substantially correct.

I should say that I have adopted the less radical and possibly the less interesting explanation of the phenomenon of E-type pronouns. According to the explanation I have adopted, sentence frames of the form

$$(\quad) \text{ loves } (\quad) \text{ and } (\quad) \text{ loves } (\quad),$$

in which 'pronominalization' takes place across co-ordinate structures, can be generated, and underlie sentences of the form

(14)   Mary loves John and he loves her.

But, on my account, we are prevented from inserting quantifiers into the chained singular term positions because their scope will not be interpreted as reaching across the co-ordinate structure to bind the pronouns. A more radical explanation would be one which supposed 'pronominalization' − or the drawing of braces between two singular term positions − to be restricted to those structures in which the singular term position to be occupied by the pronoun is governed by the singular term position to be occupied by the singular term. We would then see the pronouns in singular sentences, like (14), to be E-type pronouns, but we will so account for the semantic contribution of the E-type pronouns that when their antecedents are singular terms, the net effect is simply that of co-reference.

The attraction of this position is a measure of harmony it offers between the conditions on forward and backward 'pronominalization'. This *rapprochement* is particularly appealing since it turns out that Klima's notion of 'in construction with', which seems to account for the distribution of bound and E-type pronouns, has been called upon by those who are looking for constraints upon backward 'pronominal-ization'.[45] Unfortunately, I do not have sufficient competence in linguistics to be able to assess the plausibility of this more radical sugges-tion, for surely, if two fundamentally different processes are at work in the range of data which have hitherto been collected together as examples of 'forward pronominalization', then this fact should have countless ramifications and consequences of a purely syntactic character.

Nothing that I say of any importance hinges upon the truth of the more conservative explanation which I have offered. Nor, in fact, does it depend upon whether, in Klima's notion of 'in construction with', I have correctly identified the relevant syntactic relation. The semantic and syntactic properties of E-type pronouns are sufficiently well defined for the type to be recognized independently of its final location in the theory of syntax. It *is* important to my account that there be a syntactic distinction between bound and E-type pronouns; it is not essential that should be the distinction between pronouns which are, and pronouns which are not, governed by their antecedents. However I shall proceed upon the assumption that 'in construction with' is the relevant relation.

The view that pronouns which are not governed by their quantifier antecedents are not functioning as bound pronouns rests, so far, upon two pieces of evidence. The first is purely semantic: interpreting the pronouns as being bound by the quantifiers does not enable us to cap-ture the most natural interpretation which these sentences have. The second piece of evidence is the ill-formedness of sentences like

*John owns no sheep and Harry vaccinates them

*Every Londoner was there and he had a wonderful time.

Both pieces of evidence seem to me to point in the direction of treating these pronouns (E-type pronouns) as singular terms whose denotation is fixed by a description recoverable from the clause containing the quanti-fier antecedent. Thus the denotation of the pronoun in (10) is fixed by the description 'the sheep that John owns', in (11) by the description 'the MPs that came to the party', in (12) by the description 'the boys who danced with Mary' and in (13) by 'the dog that Socrates owns'. Roughly, the pronoun denotes those objects which *verify* (or that object which verifies) the sentence containing the quantifier antecedent. (This idea is made considerably more precise in section VI.) The first piece of evidence points in this direction simply because such appears to be the interpretation we put upon these sentences. The second piece of evidence points this way because if it is the role of such pronouns to denote the verifier(s) of the sentence containing its quantifier antecedent, then we can explain why E-type pronouns cannot follow sentences whose quantifier is 'No' + common noun, and why *singular* E-type pronouns cannot follow sentences whose quantifier is 'Every' + common noun.

Gareth Evans

I do not believe that anyone has identified the class of E-type pronouns in just the way that I am suggesting, but philosophers have often suggested treating this or that pronoun in what amounts to an E-type way. In so doing, they have drawn upon themselves the vituperation of Professor Geach, who believes that any such proposal can be shown to involve a definite mistake. For example, Geach maintains that any analysis of the sentence

(13) Socrates owns a dog and it bit Socrates

as a conjunction of two propositions with a truth-value would be 'inept'.[46] Elsewhere the proposal is described as 'quite absurd', 'a prejudice or a blunder'.[47] It is therefore with some trepidation that I confess to thinking that a conjunction of two propositions is precisely what (13) amounts to. Before we consider Geach's arguments and satisfy ourselves that there is nothing in them, let us fortify our spirits by looking at one or two additional advantages which an E-type treatment has over its bound pronoun rival.

B   Some advantages of the proposed account over its bound-pronoun rival

1 It is a feature of the account I am suggesting that the quantifiers which are the antecedents of E-type pronouns do not have to be given wide scope in order to bind them. There are several contexts in which giving these quantifiers narrow scope allows a simpler semantical treatment of those contexts, and there are others in which it appears absolutely inescapable. I shall deal with several such contexts in turn.

(a) Conditionals
Consider the sentences:

If Mary has a son, she will spoil him
If someone comes in this room he will trip the switch.

These sentences appear to contain existential quantifiers, yet do not have a sense which would result from giving that quantifier wide scope; we are not saying that there is some boy such that if Mary had *him* as a son she would spoil him, nor that there is someone such that if *he* comes he will trip the switch.

The natural way to understand these sentences is as being built out of two propositions joined by a conditional; the antecedent being, for example, that some man comes, the consequent, said to be conditional upon the truth of an antecedent, being that the man who comes will trip the switch. (Obviously, if a paraphrase is to be given which uses descriptions explicitly, they must be understood as having a scope

280

narrower than the connective.) To see the sentence in this way requires seeing the pronouns in the consequent as E-type pronouns, as would anyway be suggested by the grammatical relation in which they stand to their antecedent.

The problem presented by these sentences is familiar to students and teachers of logic — and it is normally got around by supposing in an *ad hoc* fashion that, in the antecedents of conditionals, the words 'some' and 'a man' are surface forms of the universal quantifier 'any'. This suggestion is adopted as a solution to the problem by Harman who writes: 'One plausible solution is to suppose that the deep structure quantifier in (77) [the sentence "If some arrows are green they will hit the target"] is not *some arrows* but rather *any arrows*.'[48] But as Harman points out, it is very difficult to characterize the contexts where the change from 'any' to 'some' takes place. Furthermore, as Harman also points out in the same place, a similar problem arises when any quantifier which is existential in force[49] occurs in the antecedent of a conditional such as in

If several/few/many/two/three . . . /men come they will be disappointed.

Can it be seriously proposed that 'any men' can turn into each of these? If not, how is the 'solution' to be generalized?

(b) 'Just one' sentences
Consider the sentence

Just one man drank champagne and he was ill.

If we did not have to worry about such an occurrence of the pronoun 'he', easily the most simple treatment of the expression 'just one man' is to see it as a quantifier which, when attached to a predicate A, yields a truth just in case just one man satisfies A. To use such a treatment in the sentence above, we would have to suppose the scope of 'just one man' ends at the conjunction; to let it extend beyond the conjunction would be to generate the different proposition

Just one man drank champagne and was ill.

Treating the pronoun 'he' in the second clause as an E-type pronoun enables us to adopt this simple treatment of the expression 'just one man'.

If, on the other hand, we are to treat it as a pronoun bound by the quantifier, the best we can do is to adopt the suggestion Geach has recently made[50] that 'just one man' is a binary quantifier taking two open sentences, or predicates, to make a sentence.

The trouble is, there is absolutely no evidence that 'just one man' is, in this way, a binary quantifier; we seem to have no difficulty in

281

Gareth Evans

forming a complete sentence by attaching the 'just one man' quantifier to a single open sentence, as in

Just one man opened the box.

Geach suggests that we can see that sentence as 'got by deletion' from

Just one man opened the box and he opened the box.

That Geach could make such a proposal suggests to me that he and I are engaged on different enterprises. I am interested in the quantifiers and pronouns that occur in the English natural language (and in a good many others, I bet). I am not interested in the quantifiers and devices of back reference which exist in logically possible languages which we might speak but do not.

(c) Relative scope difficulties

An abstract description of a type of sentence that will present *relative scope difficulties* for Geach's view of pronouns is this: it contains some operator O within whose scope a quantifier expression must fall, and outside whose scope a pronoun looking back to that quantifier must fall. Schematically:

... O (... Quantifier + CN ...) ... it/he/etc., ...

I shall present two examples of this kind of sentence, though no doubt many others can be found.

Consider the sentence

Just one man owns a donkey and he beats it.

I am not now concerned with the pronoun 'he' which we have just been considering, but with the nexus: 'a donkey' ... 'it', for taking 'Just one man' as our operator O, we have here an example of the kind described. Whether or not the sentence admits of a reading on which it is equivalent to

A certain donkey is such that just one man owns it and he beats it

(which I doubt), it also admits of another interpretation, on which the property said to be uniquely exemplified is that of being a donkey-owner. For this latter reading, the 'a donkey' quantifier has to have a scope narrower than that of 'just one man', which would then leave the pronoun 'it' unbound, if it were a bound pronoun. However, it is open to us to give 'a donkey' narrow scope if we treat the pronoun 'it' as an E-type pronoun — a treatment which is anyway suggested by the grammatical relation in which it stands to its antecedent.

Geach's reaction to this kind of sentence can be gauged from a discussion he offered of a sentence which presents a very similar problem; namely:

The only man who owns a donkey beats it.[51]

He wrote:[52]

> We still have not an acceptable analysis of (1) [the sentence 'The only man who ever stole a book from Snead made a lot of money by selling it']; for the use of 'The only man who ever ...' precludes our taking the initial ten word phrase in (1) to mean the same as 'The man who stole a (certain) book from Snead' ... I think the right account of the initial ten word phrase in (1) is that it neither simply means the same as 'The only man who ever stole *any* book from Snead' as it does in (2) nor simply means what 'The man who stole a (certain) book from Snead' means ... , but rather corresponds in force to a combination of the two: 'The man who stole a (certain) book from Snead, in fact the only man who ever stole any book from Snead.'

On Geach's analysis, then, we find *two* quantifiers 'a book'; one which is given wide scope, and which is therefore conveniently there to bind the troublesome pronoun, and one with narrow scope to give the intended uniqueness condition upon the description. It must be acknowledged to be desperately *ad hoc* to suggest that two quite different quantifiers, with different scopes, collapse into one in surface structure. Is there any kind of sentence which exhibits this kind of collapsing? Are we not interested in how someone might understand such a sentence upon the basis of its structure?[53]

Other examples conforming to the schematic description offered above can be constructed with the use of adverbial modifiers. Consider:

> John stupidly touched some snakes and they bit him

when it is being used to assert that it was stupid of John to touch some snakes — any snakes — not that there were some particular snakes that it was stupid of him to touch. Equally:

> John slowly kissed all the guests and they hated it

can mean that John was a slow all-the-guest-kisser, not that he slowly kissed each of the guests. But plainly, in neither of these two sentences can the pronoun fall within the scope of the adverb.

(d) Quantifiers in clauses restricting quantifiers with higher scope
Sentences which have the form of

> Most men who own a car wash it on Sundays
> Every man who owns a donkey beats it

appear to conform to our schematic description of sentences which provide relative scope difficulties for Geach's approach to pronouns.

Gareth Evans

If the sentence is to express the intended restriction upon the major quantifier — that of being a car- or donkey-owner — it would appear that the second quantifier must be given a scope which does not extend beyond the relative clause, and this rules out a bound variable interpretation of the later pronouns. Further, with sentences such as these, Geach's 'two-quantifier' proposal does not even get off the ground, since they do not entail the sentence which results when the existential quantifier is given wide scope. This provides yet another reason against adopting his proposal in the case of a sentence like

The only man who owns a donkey beats it

which should be seen as sharing a form with the initial pair of sentences. It entails a wide-scope sentence

A donkey is such that the only man who owns it beats it,

not in virtue of its form, but in virtue of particular semantic properties of the quantifier 'The'.

That the pronouns in these sentences are not functioning like bound variables is exactly what we should expect, since their quantifier antecedents most certainly do not govern them.[54] However, though it may be clear that they are not bound pronouns, what should *not* yet be clear is how they can be regarded as E-type pronouns. For on the account of E-type pronouns I have suggested, they are referring expressions; yet surely it is as silly to inquire after the reference of 'it' in our examples as it is in the case of a bound pronoun.

I cannot provide a complete answer to this objection until section V, in which relative clauses restricting quantifiers are studied in some detail. But I can indicate the main lines on which the answer will run by considering simpler sentences.

I am putting forward the view that, in the sentence

John owns a donkey and beats it,

the pronoun 'it' has the function of designating the object (if any) that verifies the antecedent clause containing the existential quantifier. However, the process of substituting quantifiers into singular term position can be indefinitely iterated: by substituting a quantifier for the remaining singular term, we may construct the well-formed sentence:

Every man owns a donkey and beats it.

Once the singular term 'John' is supplanted by the quantifier, the E-type pronoun can no longer be regarded as having a reference. But *no new explanation of its role in the resulting sentence is called for.* For, once again, provided the derivation of truth-conditions for the quantified sentence runs through a stage at which the truth-conditions of singular substitution instances are considered, the existing explanation of the role of E-type pronouns — that which assigns them a denotation determined by certain conditions — can be drawn upon. Since the 'every man' quantifier has a scope wider than that of the E-type pronoun, we do not begin evaluating the sentence by inquiring into the denotation of the E-type pronoun.

The situation is exactly the same as we found with pronouns that *were* governed by their antecedents. There, we discovered that not being able to assign 'himself' a denotation in the sentence

Every man loves himself,

neither meant that we could not say that 'himself' refers to John in

John loves himself

nor that we need say anything more.

In a parallel way, I shall argue that the pronouns in the initial pair of sentences are E-type pronouns, but that they have a scope less than that of the main quantifier, and can (and need) only be interpreted relative to some substitution instance of the main quantifier. And, when we are considering such substitution instances, it is clear that we put an E-type interpretation on the pronoun. Once again, this comes out most clearly with plural quantifiers. The evaluation of the sentence

Every man who owns some sheep vaccinates them in the spring

directs us to consider the relative truth-values of pairs of sentences

John owns some sheep; John vaccinates them in the spring

when the latter sentence is true only if John vaccinates all the sheep he owns.[55]

2 We have seen how Geach treats 'There is just one man who F's and he G's' as involving a binary quantifier. Since all the numerical quantifiers give rise to the problem to which this purports to be a solution, it is reasonable to suppose that Geach will adopt a similar account of the sentence:

Exactly two men got off their bicycles and then they fainted.

But now consider the sentence

Exactly three men got off their bicycles and they pushed the Volkswagen up the hill.

Now, perhaps this sentence does have a reading on which it entails that each of the men who got off their bicycles separately pushed the Volkswagen up the hill — the reading which would result if 'Exactly two men' was a binary quantifier whose second open sentence is 'x pushed the Volkswagen up the hill'. But there is clearly another reading which is, in the circumstances, more likely, and according to which the men are said to have together pushed the Volkswagen up the hill. This reading cannot be captured along Geach's lines. In order to capture it, the scope of 'Three men' has to be closed off at the end of the first conjunct, and 'they' must involve a plural reference.

3 Consider the sentence

Socrates owned a dog and it bit Socrates.

On the bound variable view, which Geach favours, the whole sentence is strictly equivalent to a sentence of the form

(For some dog x) (Fx & Gx)

with its logicians' paraphrase,

Some dog is such that Socrates owned it and it bit Socrates.

If this is indeed what our original sentence means, what could explain our unwillingness to express the thought:

Some finger is such that it is Socrates' and it hurts Socrates

by uttering

Socrates has a finger and it hurts Socrates ?

What can explain our reluctance to report the existence of at least one woman doctor in Manchester by uttering

There is a doctor in Manchester and she is a woman,

or the existence of a number with an even successor by uttering

A number has a successor and it is even ?

Suppose someone deduces that at least one and possibly several of the people at the meeting smoked, upon the basis of the fact that the room was filled with smoke. If Geach's 'wide-scope' rendering of these sentences was accurate, what could explain the oddness in reporting the result of this deduction in the sentence

Someone came to the meeting and he smoked ?

It is a quite clearly marked feature of the use of pronouns that are not governed by their quantifier antecedents that one does not utter a clause containing such a pronoun unless one is in a position to answer the question: 'He? Who?' or 'It? Which?'.[56] Perhaps this fact is not so striking to one who makes no distinction between pronouns that are, and those that are not, governed by their antecedents, for of course, no such requirement is made upon the use of a bound pronoun. But even so, it remains a pretty striking fact about the use of certain pronouns, not less striking for being at odds with the bound variable treatment of them. It is therefore surprising that nowhere in any of Geach's quite extensive writings on the subject of pronouns is it ever mentioned. This omission cannot be explained by Geach's professed lack of interest in the nuances of idiom; the fact I have just mentioned is no more a matter of nuance than is a blow from a sledge-hammer.

C   *The arguments against*

It cannot be over-emphasized that the proposal that I am making concerns a limited, and syntactically identified, class of pronouns. I acknowledge that many pronouns whose antecedents are quantifier expressions do correspond to bound variables at least in the sense that it does not make sense to inquire into their denotation, but I doubt that all do. The possibility of a principled, syntactic demarcation of E-type pronouns from bound pronouns is really the strongest weapon in our defensive armoury. For I am sure that the consideration that has most influenced philosophers to falter in their defence of the view that this or that pronoun with quantifier antecedent has a reference, has been an incapacity to see how to differentiate such pronouns from genuine bound pronouns, in regard to which such a view is absurd. 'So I suppose you are going to say that "his" refers to some man, in "Some man beats his dog" ', thunders the opponent, and, aghast at the prospect, one is shamed into silence. Well, that move can no longer be made. Let us see what other moves can be made.

Against my proposal, appeal has sometimes been made to an *intuition* that pronouns in the two syntactic positions are functioning in the same way. Harman, for example, considers the sentence

> If some arrows are such that those arrows are green, those arrows
> will hit the target,

and observes that the second occurrence of 'those arrows' may be replaced by the phrase 'those arrows that are green' (as we would expect, if it is an E-type pronoun) and the first occurrence cannot be.[57] But against this he appeals to the fact that 'the phrase "those arrows" seems to have the same function in both its occurrences'. But, instead of using the observation to undermine the intuition, he uses the intuition to undermine the observation, concluding that, contrary to first appearances, there is no special connection between the second occurrence of the phrase 'those arrows' and the description 'those arrows that are green' after all. One wonders how the intuition of similarity of functioning would respond to the observation that the substitution of the quantifier 'No arrows' has a different effect upon the two occurrences:

If no arrows are such that those arrows are green, those arrows will hit the target.[58]

1   'A man' does not refer

Geach tends to assume that anyone who holds that the pronoun 'it' in the sentence

John owns a donkey and he beats it

has the role of referring to some particular donkey, must hold that its job is that of 'picking up the reference made by the expression "a donkey" '. And Geach has no trouble in showing that the expression 'a donkey' *never* refers.[59]

The position which Geach refutes so decisively is a position which fails to make any discrimination between my two classes of pronouns and crudely extends the explanation in terms of co-reference which is appropriate for members of one class, to members of the other.

Such is not my position — and I wish to emphasize that *one is in no way committed, by saying that E-type pronouns have a referential role, to the view that their quantifier antecedents refer.* (In general the pronouns denote the items (if any) that *verify* the quantified sentence.)

2   'Buridan's Law'

Geach considers the sentence

(15)   Just one man broke the bank at Monte Carlo, and he has recently died a pauper

and writes the following:[60]

Supposing the first half of (15) were true, it seems plausible to take 'he' as referring to the man who broke the bank at Monte Carlo; and then the second half of (15) would be true — and thus (15) as a whole would be true — iff it were true of that man that he had (at the time of the statement) recently died a pauper. But if the first half of (15) is false, there is no plausible way of specifying a reference for 'he'; yet (15) does not then cease to be a proposition with a truth value because an ostensibly referring expression in it fails to refer — (15) is then simply false.

It is a plausible principle that no proposition whatever is expressed by purportedly genuine singular terms which lack a referent. But the same does not hold for singular terms whose reference is fixed by description. Precisely because the term has its reference fixed by description, its reference may be specified, and therefore the truth conditions of any sentence containing it may be specified, whether or not it has a referent. Of course, we cannot specify the reference in the simple form

In the second clause of (15) 'he' refers to the man who broke the
bank at Monte Carlo,

for such a specification might reasonably be taken to commit *us* to
there being such a man. The specification must rather take the form

For any x, the denotation of 'he' in the second clause of (15) is x
iff x is the only man who broke the bank at Monte Carlo.

Thus Geach's claim that, if the first conjunct of (15) is false, there is no
plausible way so to specify the reference for the pronoun, is just
wrong.[61]

Whether we say that the smallest sentence containing an empty
singular term whose reference is fixed by description is false or that it
has a third but non-designated truth value is a matter which need not
concern us here, for there will anyway be no difficulty in securing the
result that (15), which is a conjunction of a false proposition with a
proposition, is false.

What of 'Buridan's Law'? Geach states the law in various ways. On
one occasion he stated it like this:[62]

But as Buridan pointed out long since, the reference of an expression can never depend upon whether the proposition it occurs in is
true or false.

If 'the reference of an expression' is interpreted as 'whether or not an
expression has a referent', this principle can indeed be used against an
E-type analysis of the pronoun in (15) but, upon that interpretation, it
is wholly unacceptable, for it is then simply equivalent to a denial that
there can be expressions whose reference is fixed by description. For,
if an expression, α, has its reference fixed by the description ϕ, then
whether or not α has a referent depends upon the truth-value of the
proposition 'There is something uniquely ϕ', and then the conjunction
'There is something ϕ and $F(\alpha)$' would infringe the 'Law'. The 'Law'
remains unacceptable even when it is restricted to atomic sentences, for
under the same conditions, the perfectly acceptable proposition '$\phi(\alpha)$'
would infringe it.

If there is an acceptable version of the principle, it concerns the
specification of the reference of an expression. We might put the principle like this:

It is unacceptable for the specification of the reference of an expression occurring in any sentence to explicitly mention the truth-value
of that sentence; so that the only way of determining whether or
not some object x is the referent of that expression would explicitly
require a prior determination of the truth value of that sentence.

The word 'explicitly' in the principle is doing some work. There can be no objection to so fixing the reference of an expression that a determination of whether or not some object is its referent should *as a matter of fact* involve a determination of the truth value of the sentence in which it occurs; such would be the case for any sentence $\phi(\alpha)$ when α has its reference fixed by the description ϕ. In such a situation, a clear way has been laid down for determining the referent of the expression and thus the truth-value of the sentence; there just happens to be an overlap between the different stages of the operation of discovering its truth-value. We find a genuine infringement of the principle in the paralogism of a kind which, according to Geach, prompted Buridan to state the principle: In 'Is A a donkey?' 'A' shall stand for you if the right answer is 'yes' and for Brownie, the donkey on the village green, if the right answer is 'no'. Here the *specification* of the reference of an expression *explicitly* involves the truth-value of the very sentence in which it occurs, and Buridan is right to object to it. It is difficult to see what connexion a principle concerned with such a case could have with the proposal that the pronoun in (15) refers. On that proposal, a clear route has been laid down for the determination of whether or not something is the referent of the pronoun, a route which does not *explicitly* involve the truth-value of the first conjunct, let alone the truth-value of the sentence in which it immediately occurs.

3   Treating E-type pronouns as referring expressions involves assigning the wrong truth-conditions to sentences containing them

Considering the sentence

(16) Socrates owned a dog and it bit Socrates

Geach writes:[63]

> A medieval would treat this as a conjunctive proposition and enquire after the reference (*suppositio*) of the pronoun 'it': I have seen modern discussion that made the same mistake. For mistake it is. If we may legitimately symbolize (16) as '$p \wedge q$' then a contradictory of (16), correspondingly symbolizable as '$\neg p \vee (p \wedge \neg q)$', would
>
> be (17) Socrates did not own a dog, or else: Socrates owned a dog, and it did not bite Socrates.
>
> But (16) and (17) are not contradictories; a moment's thought shows that they could both be true. So '$p \wedge q$' is an inept schema to represent (16).

Presumably Geach's idea is that (16) and (17) can both be true when Socrates owns at least two dogs. But, if Socrates owned two dogs, on the proposal which I am defending (16) is not true; the second conjunct would not be true for failure of reference of 'it'. So this is really not an argument at all, but a counter-assertion. Geach claims that the sentence like (16) means no more and no less than

Socrates owns a dog which (such that it) bit Socrates.

Should we be moved by this?

I have already given strong *prima facie* evidence against this claim of equivalence in meaning. It is easy to envisage circumstances in which someone might accept as true the sentence

John has a finger which hurts him,

while rejecting its supposed paraphrase

John has a finger and it hurts him.

We can easily envisage circumstances in which someone might accept as true the sentence

John owns some sheep which he vaccinates,

while rejecting its supposed paraphrase

John owns some sheep and he vaccinates them.

Now of course it is always open to philosophers or linguists to reject such *prima facie* evidence as to the meaning of sentences in the light of a systematic theory, when that theory not only works more smoothly by assigning a meaning to those sentences other than that suggested by the evidence, but also explains why we react to the sentences in the way that we do (by showing how independently well-attested conversational factors deform and modify the sentences' strict and literal meanings). But such considerations of system and theory there are seem not to tell against, but rather to reinforce, the *prima facie* evidence of non-equivalence; in the preceding sections I have presented a mass of interlocking evidence that suggests that the pronoun in (16) is functioning in a way which is quite unlike the pronoun in its supposed paraphrase. And how can 'conversational factors' be invoked to account for the divergence sentences containing E-type pronouns have from their Geachian paraphrases, when the divergence depends crucially upon quite specific *grammatical relations* in which the pronoun stands to its antecedent?

In the light of all that has gone before, one who presses *this* argument of Geach's resembles, not so much someone executing an aggressive manoeuvre, but rather someone burying his head in the sand.

4   We are obliged to introduce psychologizing

Suppose someone says

(18)   A Cambridge philosopher smoked a pipe and he drank a lot of whisky.

Suppose further that there were two pipe-smoking Cambridge philosophers, X and Y, one of whom did, and the other of whom did not, drink a lot of whisky. Now, given that there was a Cambridge philosopher who smoked a pipe, the truth-value of (18) will be that of the second conjunct. And if we treat 'he' in the second conjunct as a referring expression, then the truth-value of the entire remark will be determined by whether or not it is X or Y we fix on as the referent of 'he'.[64]

> And so we might find ourselves trying to determine the truth value of (18) by asking who a man would have in mind when he uttered or wrote down the sentence (18) . . . Such psychologizing is really not necessary. . . .

The first point to observe is this: on the view of E-type pronouns I have so far outlined there is equally no license to engage in 'psychologizing'. On that view, the second conjunct, being equivalent to the sentence:

> The Cambridge philosopher who smoked a pipe drank a lot of whisky

will not be true, because the pronoun lacks a referent. Though, as we shall see, this position involves a certain divergence from idiom precisely because it contains no psychologizing, if psychologizing is indeed to be deplored, it still represents a much better position than any that results from an attempt to read the pronoun in (18) as a bound variable. A conviction that the bound variable approach is superior can only come from a conviction that, in the circumstances outlined above, (18) would be true. And this, in its turn, must rest upon the view that sentences of the structure of (18) are equivalent to sentences of the form

> A Cambridge philosopher both smoked a pipe and drank a lot of whisky.

And as we have seen, this view simply cannot stand up.

However, although this seems to me a perfectly adequate fall-back position, there does not seem to be any great harm in liberalizing the account we give of the truth-conditions of sentences containing E-type pronouns with a dash of psychologizing, in the interests of a greater realism. For, when the speaker is manifestly *talking about* something,[65] for example, in narrating an episode, it is acceptable to continue with the use of an E-type pronoun even when the antecedent containing sentence or clause has not provided the basis for a unique specification. One might begin a story:

> One day, a man and a boy were walking along a road, and the man said to the boy: 'Would you like to be King?'

One does not want to be committed, by this way of telling the story, to the existence of a day on which just one man and boy walked along a road. It was with this position in mind that I stated the requirement for the appropriate use of an E-type pronoun in terms of having answered, *or being prepared to answer upon demand*, the question 'He? Who?' or 'It? Which?'

In order to effect this liberalization we should allow the reference of the E-type pronoun to be fixed not only by predicative material explicitly in the antecedent clause, but also by material which the speaker supplies upon demand. This ruling has the effect of making the truth conditions of such remarks somewhat indeterminate; a determinate proposition will have been put forward only when the demand has been made and the material supplied.

Actually, this way of 'fixing the reference' of an E-type pronoun can involve cancellation of explicit predicative material in the antecedent. Consider the exchange:

A: A man jumped out of the crowd and fell in front of the horses.
B: He didn't jump, he was pushed.

It is tempting to see, in B's remark, an application of the same use of E-type pronouns as we have been considering, especially since it is quite difficult to make sense of it while construing 'he' as a bound pronoun.

If this liberalization is made, it is important to see that such psychologizing as it involves infects merely the truth-conditions of the sentences containing the E-type pronouns. The truth-condition of the simple, unquantified sentence

A man jumped out of the crowd

can and should remain as given before; the undeniable fact that we may have particular individuals in mind in uttering such sentences must not be used to tamper with their truth-conditions, which can obtain in virtue of the condition of some individual the speaker did not have in mind.[66]

In attempting to formalize the treatment of E-type pronouns in the succeeding section, I shall ignore the wrinkle introduced by this liberalization. I hope it is obvious how it can be incorporated into the final product.

D   *Are E-type pronouns 'pronouns of laziness'?*

It appears that any treatment of E-type pronouns that does justice to all the considerations we have mentioned will involve recovering a description from the sentence containing its antecedent. The ease and uniformity with which native speakers supply descriptions in answer to the questions 'He? Who?', 'It? Which?' etc., when they are raised in connection with E-type pronouns, is certainly indicative of a rule-governed process. But should we see the E-type pronoun as 'going proxy for' this recoverable description, or as a semantic element whose reference is fixed by it? This question encapsulates a summary formulation of two different anaphoric processes. If an E-type pronoun is going proxy for the description, this would mean that the semantic evaluation of the sentence containing it proceeds exactly as if the description stood in its place. Now, there certainly are sentences in English for which we appear to need to invoke such a mechanism; the sentence (1), with which we started, is a good example, as are sentences which result from verb-phrase deletion, like

John listened to music and so did Harry.

However, there seem to me to be at least two arguments against regarding E-type pronouns as going proxy for descriptions.

The first is purely semantic; the sentence which results when the description takes the place of the E-type pronoun (the 'prolix sentence') is often ambiguous in a way in which the original sentence is not. The trouble arises because definite descriptions give rise to scope ambiguities when interacting with almost all operators. As a consequence, prolix sentences have interpretations, not possessed by the original sentences, which result when the description is not given maximum scope (in its clause). Examples illustrating this point can be found with each of the familiar operators that give rise to scope ambiguities with descriptions.

Negation

John owns a donkey but it is not the case that it is male

is unambiguous, while

John owns a donkey but it is not the case that the donkey John owns is male

is ambiguous and might be asserted on the ground that there is no such thing as *the* donkey John owns, i.e. giving wide scope to the negation sign.[67]

Modality

John owns a donkey and it likes carrots though it might not have been the case that it liked carrots

seems to me to be unambiguous, with just the referentially rigid reading, while its prolix version is ambiguous:

John owns a donkey and the donkey John owns likes carrots although it might not have been the case that the donkey John owns likes carrots.

Time

> Boston has a Mayor and he used to be a Democrat

is unambiguous, while its prolix version is ambiguous:

> Boston has a Mayor and the Mayor of Boston used to be a Democrat.

Psychological attitudes

> A man murdered Smith, but John does not believe that he murdered Smith

attributes to John merely a non-contradictory belief *of* the murderer that he is not the murderer, while:

> A man murdered Smith, but John does not believe that the man who murdered Smith murdered Smith

is ambiguous, with one (unlikely) reading on which John is attributed the self-contradictory belief that the man who murdered Smith did not murder Smith.

There is another kind of argument against treating E-type pronouns as pronouns of laziness. It appears that those anaphoric devices which are evaluated as proxies actually originate transformationally; a deletion transformation being triggered by relatively superficial syntactic identity between the antecedent segment and the segment that is either deleted entirely, or replaced with a pro-form. Now, it is difficult to see how E-type pronouns could have had such a transformational origin. For the descriptions for which they are supposed to be going proxy do not correspond to any syntactically coherent unit in the antecedent sentence. The relevant description is 'reconstructible out of' the antecedent sentence but does not occur in it.[68] For example, in the sentence

> John owns some sheep which bite their tails and they are on the mountain

the pronoun 'they' would have to stand for the description

> the *sheep which John owns which bite their tails*

the italicized portion of which certainly does not correspond to any syntactic unit in the antecedent sentence.

Syntactic theory is currently in too great a state of flux for much weight to be placed upon this argument. Nevertheless, I think we may claim that, when both these arguments are taken together, at least a *prima facie* case has been established against treating E-type pronouns as pronouns of laziness. More conclusive considerations can only be forthcoming in the context of a general theory of anaphora in English.[69]

Gareth Evans

V   Quantifiers with relative clauses

A   Relative clauses introduced

We are now in a position to set about constructing a theory which incorporates a rather more rigorous treatment of E-type pronouns than
exists in the informal remarks and hints I have offered so far. To do so,
we must offer some account of the main devices with which E-type pronouns interact; this means that we must extend both the syntax and
semantics of quantified sentences to allow quantifiers to be restricted
by relative clauses. Once the extension is made we will have a fragment
of language rich enough to allow pronouns to get up to all their distinctive tricks, and a theory rich enough to deal with most of the sentences
which philosophers and linguists studying pronouns have found troublesome.

The main lines of the treatment are these. I regard all natural language quantifiers as binary, taking two predicates, or open sentences, to
make a sentence. This is partly because of my desire to construct a
homophonic theory of meaning – a theory which stays as close as
possible to the grammatical structures that are actually found in the
language. Therefore, I look with a rather jaundiced eye at the reduction
of the apparently binary structures of 'Some A's are B's' and 'All A's
are B's' into unary structures – using connectives to join the two
general terms A and B to form a single predicate. But, also, since some
quantifiers, like 'Most', appear to *need* a binary analysis, considerations
of simplicity strongly suggest adopting it for all.[70]

Intuitively, the first predicate of the binary structure has the role of
identifying the objects whose satisfaction of the second is relevant to
the sentence's truth or falsity, or, in Fregean language, the role of identifying the *relevant* (potential) substitution instances. (The relevant
singular terms are those which, when coupled to the first predicate,
yield a truth.) Hitherto, this first predicate has always been a single
common noun. We are now to allow it to be complex. Whereas before
the relevant range was restricted by expressions like 'man', 'donkey',
now it may be restricted by 'man who owns a donkey', 'donkey that
can bray', and so on.

To understand the role of the common noun + relative clause in this
way requires that the restricting clause on the quantifier with maximum
scope should yield, when attached to a singular term, a complete sentence assessable as true or false. This is just a matter of sensible logical
procedure; if we did not follow it, no start could be made upon the
assessment of the whole sentence as true or false. It is also true that to
understand the role of the expression common noun + relative clause in
a quantified sentence along these lines brings me once again into

headlong collision with Geach, who argues that the phrase cannot be understood as functioning in this way, and even its apparent unity is a kind of logical mirage. There is no more in Geach's arguments on this matter than there is to any of the arguments we have scrutinized on other matters, but for those who wish to rest their view of this subject on deductive rather than inductive grounds, I have included an Appendix specifically addressed to this point.[71]

I will treat the English relative pronouns, 'who', 'which', etc., as devices of predicate abstraction, enabling us to form a predicate:

(who) loves (John)

from a sentence frame with one free singular term position:

( ) loves (John).

Such predicates are satisfied by an object iff the sentence which results from substituting a singular term designating that object for the relative pronoun is true. (I shall ignore inflection and 'WH-movement' which together yield 'whom John loves' from '(John) loves (who)'.)

On this account,[72] the use we make of the relative pronoun is very similar to the use made of variables in forming predicate abstracts — that of indicating the position in a sentence being abstracted upon. However, the relative pronouns are not used with the full generality of variables in formal languages, since chains of co-reference *within* a clause must be left to the pronominal apparatus. Thus we have:

(who) loves (his) father

rather than

(who) loves (who)'s father.

However, when the sentence frame is truth-functionally complex we find the repeated relative pronoun doing exactly the job of recurrent variables:

(who) loves (John) and (who) does not love (Harry)
(who) loves (John) and (John) loves (who)

As we would expect, we have something parallel to 'lambda elimination':

(John) A's iff John is one (who) A's.

When we had one-word general terms restricting the quantifiers, there was no reason why the quantifier expression and the main clause into which it is to be inserted should not be generated separately, but if we are to generate, and evaluate, sentences with E-type pronouns in the main clause which look back to quantifier antecedents in the relative clause, the two constituents of a binary structure have to be

Gareth Evans

simultaneously constructed. To see exactly why this is so, let us introduce E-type pronouns into the picture.

I shall indicate that a pronoun κ is being used as an E-type pronoun by prefixing it with the symbol '#'. Syntactically '#κ' is a singular term. We also need a device for indicating which quantifier expression an E-type pronoun has as its antecedent. Since each quantifier acquires a numerical index as it is inserted into the main clause, to keep track of scope, we can attach the same index to the pronoun which has it as its antecedent. Following the old procedure, we would construct the sentence 'Socrates owns a dog and it bit Socrates' as follows:

( ) owns ( )
( ) owns (a_1 [dog])
(Socrates) owns (a_1 [dog])
(Socrates) owns (a_1 [dog]) and ( ) bit ( )
(Socrates) owns (a_1 [dog]) and ( ) bit (Socrates)
(Socrates) owns (a_1 [dog]) and (#it_1) bit (Socrates)

(Several steps of the construction could have been reversed without altering the overall effect.) So far so good. But now consider a sentence like

Most men who own a car wash it on Sunday,

in which the E-type pronoun is not actually referring, since the process of substituting quantifiers into singular term position has been iterated after the stage at which the pronoun was generated. The construction of the quantifier phrase is not difficult:

( ) owns (a_1 [car])
(who) owns (a_1 [car])
Men: (who) own (a_1 [car])
Most [men: (who) own (a_1 [car])].

The main clause, into which we insert the quantifier, cannot yet contain '#it' for want of a suitable antecedent, so it must be

( ) washes ( ) on Sunday,

which after insertion yields

(Most$_2$ [men:(who) own (a_1 [car])]) wash ( ) on Sunday.

But, now, it is *too late* to insert the singular term '#it'. For to insert it at this stage would give it wider scope than 'most men' and have the consequence that the first operation in evaluating the sentence would be to inquire into the denotation of '#it'. This would be wrong, for at the first stage in the evaluation of the sentence, the pronoun cannot sensibly be assigned a denotation.

Put briefly, the problem is that the E-type pronoun in the main

298

clause must be inserted *after* the 'a car' quantifier but *before* the 'most men' quantifier. This puts paid to the separate construction of the quantifier phrase and the main clause.

Adopting the binary form, the process of the construction of the sentence looks like this:

Car ; ( ) owns ( )
A [car] ; ( ) owns ( )
( ) owns (a₁ [car])
Man: (who) owns (a₁ [car])
Man: (who) owns (a₁ [car]) ; ( ) washes ( ) on Sunday
Man: (who) owns (a₁ [car]) ; ( ) washes (#it₁) on Sunday
Most [man:(who) owns (a₁ [car])] ; ( ) washes (#it₁) on Sunday
(Most₂ [man:(who) owns (a₁ [car])]) washes (#it₁) on Sunday.

(I shall continue to substitute the quantifier expression into a singular term position in the main clause because this does appear to be the way we indicate, in English, which position in the main clause is being quantified.)

The semantic evaluation will unpick what we have just knitted; the whole sentence will be true iff for most interpretations of β on which '(β) is a man (who) owns (a₁ [car])' is true, '(β) washes (#it₁)' is true.

B   Pronouns in relative clauses restricting quantifiers

The first thing I want to establish concerns bound pronouns, namely that it is not possible on the account of bound pronouns which I have offered to generate sentences in which a pronoun in a clause which restricts a quantifier Q is bound by a quantifier Q′ with a lesser scope than Q. It is an immediate corollary of this that there can be no pair of quantifiers each of which binds a pronoun in a clause which restricts the other. This is no weakness of expressive power, but on the contrary, a matter of correct logical procedure.

On my account, a pronoun is bound by a quantifier when that quantifier is inserted into a singular term position to which the position occupied by that pronoun is chained. So, if a pronoun in a clause restricting a quantifier Q, is to be bound by another quantifier Q′, the main clause into which Q′ is to be inserted must look something like this:

(⌐) R (Q [CN:(who) R′ (⌐)]) = (⌐) hurts (a woman:(who) loves (him))

which would turn, with the insertion of a singular term into the unoccupied chain, into a sentence like 'John hurts a woman who loves him'. Now, the quantifier Q′ could also have its restrictive clause, so that, before the insertion of Q′, we might have a binary frame which looks like this:

Gareth Evans

$$[CN:(who) R'' (*)] \; ; (\overline{}) R (Q [CN:(who) R' (\overline{})]),$$

or:

$$[Man: (who) despises (*)] \; ; (\overline{}) hurts (a [woman: (who) loves (him)]).$$

But there is no way in which the empty singular term position in the clause restricting Q', which I have marked with an asterisk, could be bound by the quantifier already *in situ*. We cannot *now* connect with a brace the *-position and the singular term position occupied by the quantifier Q, for, although we are permitted to draw such braces at any stage in the construction of a sentence, we may do so only between two as yet unoccupied singular term positions. But equally, such a brace could not have been drawn between these two positions *before* the latter was occupied by the quantifier phrase containing Q, for while we are engaged in constructing the sentence frame:

$$(\overline{}) R (Q [CN: (who) R' (\overline{})])$$

we have no legitimate place for a sentence which is going to restrict a quite separate quantifier, and thus no opportunity of creating relations of co-reference between positions like * in such a sentence, and positions in the sentence we are constructing.

There is thus no way of ending up with sentences which would look like this

(Every$_j$ [man:(who) despises (her)]) hurts (Some$_j$ [woman:(who) loves (him)])

($i > j$ or $j > i$); and a good thing too, for they are obviously meaningless.

Now, I do not deny that there are intelligible sentences which have the superficial form of this meaningless sentence — for example:

A boy who owned them ran down some sheep that were in his way.

But elementary logical considerations enable us to deduce that, in this sentence, *either* the relative clauses do not restrict the quantifiers, *or else* the pronouns cannot be bound-variable-type pronouns. Since we can produce some examples of the same construction in which the clauses must be understood as restricting the quantifier, such as

Every boy who asked him eventually got his father to agree,

sentences of this general type can be used in the construction of an elegant demonstration that at least some pronouns in English cannot be construed as bound-variable-type pronouns. Yet, paradoxically, these very same sentences have been triumphantly cited as examples which can be dealt with only if we adopt a bound variable treatment of

300

pronouns![73] It is easy to demonstrate that there is no way of assembling the 'deep-structures' proposed for these sentences into a sentence of quantification theory (restricted or unrestricted) in which every variable is bound.[74]

What of E-type pronouns in relative clauses? An E-type pronoun evidently cannot have as its antecedent a quantifier with wider scope. But, can an E-type pronoun, *in a clause restricting* one quantifier, have a quantifier with lesser scope as its antecedent? If we try to construct such sentences, we find them very odd:

Almost every man who loves her kills one of his sisters

Everyone who inherits it sells a house.

The reason for the oddness is not hard to discover. Attempting to evaluate the sentence for truth, we peel off the quantifier with maximum scope, and address ourselves to this question, for example: 'Are all of the interpretations of β, on which "β inherited #it" is true, interpretations on which "β sold a house" is true?' Well, which interpretations are these? Understanding the E-type pronoun in the only way possible, the relevant interpretations must be those on which 'β inherited the house which he sold' are true. And this means that the discovery of whether or not the interpretation is relevant already presupposes that the predicate in the main clause applies. There seems no point in allowing such sentences to be constructed.

Not all relative clauses appended to a quantifier expression need to be interpreted as restricting it; it is always possible to regard the relative clause appended to a simple existential quantifier as a non-restrictive clause. And it appears that we only find intelligible occurrences of E-type pronouns whose antecedents are quantifiers with lesser scope in relative clauses upon which a non-restrictive reading may be imposed. Thus, the sentence

A boy who owned them ran down some sheep that were in his way

may be interpreted as

A boy, who owned them, ran down some sheep that were in his way,

and thus as equivalent to

A boy ran down some sheep that were in his way, and he owned them.

It is easy to verify that we place an E-type interpretation upon the pronoun in the original sentence — for it to be true the boy has to own all the sheep he ran down.[75] Since they do not appear to raise any new problems of interest or importance, I shall not bother further with non-restrictive relative clauses.

Finally, there are some sentences in which the pronoun in the clause restricting a quantifier cannot be interpreted either as a bound pronoun or as an E-type pronoun, but has to be seen as a genuine pronoun of laziness. Consider the sentence

Every boy who plucked up the courage to ask him got his father to agree

or the sentence

The only pilot that shot at it hit the MiG that was chasing him.

These sentences appear to be interpreted as equivalent to their prolix versions

Every boy who plucked up the courage to ask his father, got his father to agree,

and

The only pilot that shot at the MiG that was chasing him hit the MiG that was chasing him.

There is every indication that these cannot be E-type pronouns. First, we noticed a general difficulty in interpreting sentences in which quantifiers having wide scope were restricted by clauses with E-type pronouns with quantifiers with smaller scope as antecedents. Secondly, E-type pronouns normally occur quite happily when there is no specific description in the antecedent clause; the material in the *whole* of the clause is used to fashion a description (and this is indeed why there is the general difficulty of interpretation mentioned in the first point). But we cannot construct happy sentences of this general shape unless there is a description in the main clause immediately ready for substitution. Thus the following sentence is infelicitous:

*Every pilot that shot at it hit a MiG that was chasing him.

Finally, we observed that E-type pronouns were referentially *rigid*, so that, if 'it' in the clause

The only pilot that shot at it

were an E-type pronoun, the whole clause would be equivalent to one in which an explicit description was given maximum scope,

The MiG that was chasing him is such that the only pilot that shot at *it*,

which, if it is interpretable at all, would require that there was a MiG at which only one pilot shot, rather than, what the original sentence requires, that there was only one pilot that shot at the MiG that was chasing him.

Obviously, such pronouns cannot be bound-variable-type pronouns, for the elementary logical reason which I mentioned earlier (which is, of course, not to say that whatever interpretation we decide the sentence has cannot be represented in the notation of the predicate calculus).

It therefore seems reasonable to see at work in the construction of these sentences the 'pronoun of laziness' device which secures the correct interpretation and for which we have independent evidence.

C The occurrence of E-type pronouns

As a final preliminary to formalization, we must state a principle about which an E-type pronoun can look back to a quantifier antecedent. In view of the ill-formedness of sentences like

*John doesn't own a car, and he drives it on Sunday

and

*Either John owns a car or he drives it on Sunday

it is obviously not sufficient to require that an appropriate quantifier antecedent (i.e. one with existential force) should occur as a syntactically coherent string in preceding material. But, in view of the well-formedness of sentences like

Either John does not own a donkey or he keeps it very quiet

If John owns a donkey he keeps it very quiet,

it is too stringent to insist that the sentence containing the quantifier antecedent should be embedded in the whole sentence in such a way that the truth of the whole sentence should require its truth.

The principle these last two examples suggest is this. Let $\Sigma(\sigma, \sigma')$ be some sentence embedding a sentence, σ, whose main operator is a quantifier of existential force, and a sentence, σ', containing an E-type pronoun looking back to this quantifier. For $\Sigma(\sigma, \sigma')$ to be well formed, it must be so constructed that, although there may be other ways in which it may be true, if there is a situation in which its truth or falsity turns upon the truth or falsity of σ', this will be a situation in which σ will also be true. (A conjunction of σ and σ' is just a special case of this.) So, intuitively speaking, if the truth value of σ' matters, there will be something for the E-type pronoun to refer to.

For truth-functional modes of embedding, we can define the required relation as follows. Let us say that a sentence σ is *affirmatively embedded* in Σ relative to σ' iff, on all valuations v to the constituents of

Gareth Evans

Σ on which $\nu(\sigma') = \nu(\Sigma) = T$ and which are such that, for all valuations ν' which agree with ν save that $\nu'(\sigma') = F$, $\nu'(\Sigma) = F$, then, on those valuations ν, $\nu(\sigma) = T$.

It seems natural to extend this concept of affirmative embedding to the binary structures in which quantified sentences originate, so that we can say that the sentence, B(who), which contributes to the restriction on a quantifier, is affirmatively embedded in the whole sentence relative to the sentence which becomes the main clause and into which the quantifier phrase is inserted. Let the quantified sentence, Σ, originally be of the form

Q_i[CN:B(who)] ; A(   ).

Now, although we cannot in general identify circumstances in which the truth-value of each such quantified Σ *turns upon* the truth-value of a substitution instance A(β), the truth-value of relevant substitution instances are always *germane* to the truth-value of Σ. But only *relevant* substitution instances are germane in this way. So that, whenever an inquiry into the truth-value of a quantified Σ obliges us to be interested in the truth-value of a sentence A(β) containing an E-type pronoun, the sentence B(β) will also be true, and there will therefore be something for the pronoun to refer to.[76]

So we shall allow for the insertion of an E-type pronoun into any singular term position in a sentence in relation to which some other sentence, whose main quantifier is existential in force, is affirmatively embedded. Notice that this rule of grammar must be understood as relating to the deep structures generated by the base rules; by the time the superficial form of the sentence is determined, the antecedent sentence may have been deleted or transformed. Thus, for example,

John does not own a donkey, but Harry does and he beats it every day

is well formed even though there does not appear in the surface structure an appropriate existential antecedent for the E-type pronoun. And the deep structure underlying

Either John does not own a donkey or he keeps it quiet

can also yield

Either John owns no donkey or he keeps it quiet.

Despite these examples, it seems necessary to state the well-formedness rule for E-type pronouns in terms of the occurrence of a specific kind of *syntactical* antecedent; a purely semantic criterion would not be able to explain the differing acceptabilities of:

John has a wife and she hates him

*John is married and she hates him.

304

VI   Formalization

The purpose of constructing the following mock-up of the syntax and semantics of quantified sentences in English is simply to lend plausibility and explicitness to the distinction between the two kinds of pronouns — a distinction which I hope can be incorporated into whichever particular approach to the syntax and semantics of quantified sentences seems, in the light of detailed syntactic investigation, to be the most plausible. Although I have been concerned to adopt, in this mock-up, a syntactic account of quantified sentences of English which is at least not known to be foreign to them, in the way in which it is generally agreed among linguists that the syntax of unrestricted first order quantification theory is foreign to them,[77] I have not tried to present something which may be expected to form part of that final, most plausible theory. I shall suppress almost all syntactic complexities which are not relevant to my main theme, indicating with an asterisk those points at which the most considerable divergences from English proper occur; where the asterisk is not self-explanatory, an amplification follows in parentheses. I do not include any of those transformations which, though introducing redundancy at the level of singular sentences, are indispensable for the expressive power of the quantified fragment of the language.[78] Another omission will be any attempt to deal with plural reference, made possible by E-type pronouns with plural quantifiers as antecedents. This is not the place to explain, in general, how plural reference is to be understood; when it is understood the modifications to the theory presented here will be obvious.

A   Syntax

We suppose the fragment to contain a stock of predicates, indexed as to their degree, some of which are called *common nouns*. It also contains a stock of singular terms, some of which are called *pronouns* and a stock of quantifiers, none of which is plural* and some of which are called *existential in force*. We also have a stock of numerals called *indices*.

(1) If π is a predicate of degree n, π followed by* n singular term positions (written thus: $\pi(\ )(\ )(\ )\ldots(\ )$) is a sentence frame$_n$. (The numerical subscript is a record of the number of singular term positions free in the frame; a singular term position is free in a sentence frame iff no expression has been substituted in it in the construction of the frame.)

305

(2) If σ is a sentence frame$_n$ $\ulcorner$Not$(\sigma)\urcorner$ is a sentence frame$_n$* and if σ is a sentence frame$_m$ and σ' is a sentence frame$_n$ then $\ulcorner(\sigma$ and $\sigma')\urcorner$ $\ulcorner(\sigma$ or $\sigma')\urcorner$, and $\ulcorner($If σ then $\sigma')\urcorner$ are sentence frames$_{(n+m)}$. σ and both σ and σ', are respectively said to be *constituents* of the complex sentences formed by application of these rules, and the constituent-relation is transitive.

(3) A common noun is a simple predicate expression$_0$.

(4) If σ is a sentence frame$_m$ $(m \geqslant 1)$ with position p_i free, and δ is a simple predicate expression (common noun), then $[\delta: \sigma^{WH}/p_i]$ is a predicate expression$_{(m-1)}$.* (*No differentiation of relative pronouns; no provision for more than one occurrence of a relative pronoun in a single complex predicate.) [As before we write 'σ^ϵ/p_i' for the result of substituting the expression ϵ in the position p_i in σ.] σ is said to be a constituent of the resulting predicate expression.

(5) If σ is a sentence frame$_m$ $(m \geqslant 1)$ and π is a predicate expression$_n$, then $(\pi : \sigma)$ is a binary sentence frame$_{(n+m)}$ of which π and σ are said to be constituents.

(6) If ρ is a binary sentence frame$_n$ of the form $(\pi ; \sigma)$ with p_i free in σ, and if Q is a quantifier and j an index, then $Q_j[\pi]$ is a quantifier phrase and $\rho^{Q_j[\pi]}/p_i$ is a quantified sentence frame$_{(n-1)}$ provided that no quantifier in ρ has an index higher than j, and that no singular term position to which p_i is connected by a brace is not governed by it. [Observe that π does *not* become a constituent of the resulting σ.]

(7) For any n, if σ is a sentence frame$_n$ with positions p_i and p_j free, then the result of drawing a brace connecting p_i and p_j and substituting a pronoun in one or other of p_i and p_j is a sentence frame$_{(n-1)}$.* (*No restriction on backward pronominalization, no gender agreement of pronouns, no pro-forms other than pronouns.)

(8) If σ is any complex sentence frame$_n$ with constituents σ' and σ'', where σ' is a quantified sentence frame whose quantifier is a quantifier of existential force whose index is the numeral j, and σ'' is a sentence frame in which the ith empty singular term position p_i of σ occurs, and if σ' is affirmatively embedded with respect to σ'' in σ, then if κ is a pronoun, $\sigma^{\#\kappa j}/p_i$ is a sentence frame$_{(n-1)}$.

(9) If σ is a sentence frame$_n$ with a singular term position p_i free, and τ is a singular term, then σ^τ/p_i is a sentence frame$_{(n-1)}$.

(10) All and only sentence frames$_0$ are sentences.

B Semantics

I shall only state the principles for the devices with which we have been concerned in this paper.

Quantifiers. I shall take 'Every' as an example; clauses for other quantifiers can be straightforwardly derived from this example. Though the clause is stated in a semi-formal metalanguage observe that, if formalized in the language of the mock-up, it could yield strictly homophonic theorems.

If σ is a sentence frame$_0$ containing in its ith singular term position the quantifier phrase 'Every' $_j$ $[\delta : B(WH)]$ (where δ is a common noun and j an index higher than any index attached to any other quantifier in σ, and the constituent represented by B(WH) is optional) then σ is true iff on every extension of the language with respect to some singular term β (which does not occur in σ), on which the object which β denotes on that extension satisfies δ, and on which $B^\beta/(WH)$ is true, if there is such a constituent, σ^β/p_i is true.

Co-reference. If σ is a sentence frame$_0$ containing positions p_i and p_j which are braced together, with p_i containing the singular term τ and p_j a pronoun κ, then the denotation of κ in σ is the same object as the denotation of τ.

E-type pronouns. The idea is to construct from the sentence containing the antecedent quantifier a description which is to fix the reference of the E-type pronoun. (Let us call this 'the antecedent sentence'.) In those cases where the E-type pronoun and its quantifier antecedent occur in co-ordinate clauses, the antecedent sentence is easy to identify; it is the smallest sentence which contains the quantifier and everything which it governs. But we have also allowed for the construction of sentences like

Most men who own a car wash it on Sundays

where the antecedent quantifier is in a relative clause restricting a quantifier with greater scope. In such cases, the question of evaluating the sentence containing the E-type pronoun will only arise relative to some substitution instance of that quantifier with greater scope: 'β washes it on Sundays'; and then the antecedent sentence is the smallest singular sentence containing the antecedent quantifier and everything which it governs, formed by substituting the same constant (under the same interpretation) in that relative clause ('β owns a car').

As we saw when considering a sentence like

John owns a sheep which bites its tail and he beats it,

the reference of an E-type pronoun is fixed by a description which is

307

Gareth Evans

formed from the antecedent sentence by the conjunction of (a) the main clause into which the antecedent quantifier is inserted ('John owns ( )'), (b) the common noun in the antecedent quantifier expression ('sheep'), and (c) any relative clause restricting the antecedent quantifier ('(WH)bites ( )'s tail'). In the example, the relevant description is 'the sheep John owns that bites its tail'.

These provisions are captured by the following laborious formulation.

If σ is a sentence frame$_0$ which is a constituent of a sentence frame$_0$, Σ, and which contains the term '$\#^\frown \kappa^\frown_i$' in its jth singular term position, and where σ' is the smallest sentence frame$_0$ containing the quantifier with index i which occurs in Σ, and which is of the form $A(Q[\delta : B(WH)])$ (with the constituent represented by 'B(WH)' optional), and where there is no larger sentence frame in Σ which has σ as a constituent and does not have σ' as a constituent[79]

OR

If σ is a sentence frame$_0$ which is a substitution instance with respect to the constant β of a sentence frame σ^* which is a constituent of a sentence frame$_0$, Σ, and σ contains the term '$\#^\frown \kappa^\frown_i$' in its jth singular term position, and where σ' is a substitution instance with respect to that same constant β of the sentence frame σ'^* which is the smallest sentence frame$_0$ containing the quantifier with index i which occurs in Σ, and where σ' is of the form $A(Q[\delta : B(WH)])$ (with the constituent represented by 'B(WH)' optional) and where there is no larger sentence frame in Σ which has σ^* as a constituent and which does not have σ'^* as a constituent

THEN

Any object, x, is the denotation of '$\#^\frown \kappa^\frown_i$' iff x is the unique object which satisfies $A(\ )$, δ, and $B(\ )$ (if there is such a constituent), and σ is true iff, upon any extension of the language with respect to a constant, γ, (which does not already occur in σ or σ') on which the denotation of γ is the same as the denotation of '$\#^\frown \kappa^\frown_i$', σ^γ/p_j is true.

Notes

1 P. T. Geach, *Reference and Generality* (Cornell University Press, Ithaca, 1962), p. 112.
2 For a record of the change in definition see first P. T. Geach, *Reference*

308

and Generality, pp. 124ff., then 'Referring Expressions Again', in *Logic Matters* (Blackwell, Oxford, 1972), pp. 97–8, then 'Back-Reference', *Philosophia*, vol. 5 (1975), p. 194. The change turns out to be important.

3   E. Klima, 'Negation in English', in J. Fodor and J. Katz, eds, *The Structure of Language* (Prentice Hall, Englewood Cliffs, 1964), p. 297.

4   A. Tarski, 'The Concept of Truth in Formalized Languages', in *Logic, Semantics, Metamathematics* (Clarendon, Oxford, 1956).

5   My attribution of this theory to Frege rests upon Dummett's. See M. A. E. Dummett, *Frege* (Duckworth, London, 1973) chapter 2 and pp. 516–17. I disagree with Dummett by holding that the Tarskian approach is not just a notational variant of Frege's.
    Fregean treatments of quantifiers may be found, for example, in B. Mates, *Elementary Logic* (Oxford University Press, New York, 1965), p. 54; E. L. Keenan, 'Quantifier Structures in English', *Foundations of Language*, vol. 7 (1971), p. 262 and *passim*, and throughout Geach's writings.

6   Dummett, *Frege*, p. 405.

7   β is a name assumed not to occur already in the sentence. It is convenient to define the relation of extension holding between languages so that, as a limiting case, each language extends itself. We define truth not just for English but all the members of a family of languages which extend the stock of English singular terms.

8   See e.g. R. B. Marcus, 'Interpreting Quantification', *Inquiry*, vol. 51 (1962), pp. 252–9. For an excellent discussion of substitutional quantification see S. Kripke's 'Is there a problem about Substitutional Quantification?' in G. Evans and J. H. McDowell, eds, *Truth and Meaning* (Clarendon, Oxford, 1975), pp. 325–419.

9   Now that this heuristic purpose has been discharged, I shall in later pages collapse the two principles into something along the more familiar lines of:
    A sentence of the form 'Something' $\frown$ A is true iff, upon some extension of the language, there is a substitution instance of the form $\beta \frown$ A which is true.

10 It is interesting to note that some of the delicacy of substitutional quantification into opaque contexts can be retained by Fregean quantifiers despite the ontological burden – that is to say, despite the fact that we are given licence to consider, for every object, a substitution instance involving reference to it. However, once we are dealing with opacities, we must interpret an object's satisfying a complex predicate $A(x)$ in terms of the truth of *some* (potential) singular sentence of the form $A(t)$ in which t refers to it, and not the truth of any such singular sentence.

11 For cogent statements of this criticism, see Dummett, *Frege*, pp. 3–7, 194ff.

12 I particularly have in mind operators like 'It is certain that', 'John believes that'. I disagree with J. Wallace's paper 'Belief and Satisfaction', *Noûs*, vol. 6 (1972), p. 85, in which the converse,

Tarskian, direction of explanation is defended.

13 This naturalness has certainly struck Quine; see the account in
    W. V. Quine, *The Roots of Reference* (Open Court, La Salle, Illi-
    nois, 1973), pp. 93–5, of the child's understanding the satisfaction
    by an object of a complex predicate in terms of the substitution of
    singular terms.

14 Those who are interested in the strengths and weaknesses of Fre-
    gean truth theory for quantifiers would benefit from reading
    T. Baldwin's paper, 'Quantification, Modality and Indirect Speech',
    in S. Blackburn, ed., *Meaning, Reference and Modality* (Cambridge
    University Press, 1975). Baldwin dispenses with the idea of enlarg-
    ing the singular terms of the language by exploiting the machinery
    independently needed for dealing with sentences containing demon-
    stratives.

15 See, for example, the truth conditions for the quantifiers given
    throughout Geach's *Reference and Generality*, and also the discus-
    sion in 'Quantification Theory and Objects of Reference', *Logic
    Matters*, pp. 141ff. It is true that it is not always possible to tell
    whether Geach has in mind purely substitutional or Fregean truth
    theories.

16 W. V. O. Quine, *Mathematical Logic* (Harvard University Press,
    Cambridge, Mass., 1965), p. 70.

17 In allowing unrestricted forward and backward 'pronominalization'
    this simple grammar is quite unrealistic, but the tricky syntactical
    question of demarcating where 'pronominalization' is allowed and
    where obligatory really does not affect the semantical issues I am
    dealing with.

18 I consider the significance of the departure from homophony below.

19 I discuss the merits of the 'going proxy for' idea below.

20 I do not introduce quantifier phrases with relative clauses until
    section V.

21 See, for example, the discussions in G. Lakoff, 'Linguistics and
    Natural Logic', in D. Davidson and G. H. Harman, eds, *Semantics
    of Natural Language* (D. Reidel, Dordrecht, 1972) p. 633; and
    E. Bach, 'Nouns and Noun Phrases', in E. Bach and R. T. Harms,
    eds, *Universals in Linguistic Theory* (Holt Rinehart and Winston,
    New York, 1968).

22 Geach, *Reference and Generality*, p. 128. The same argument is
    used many times; see 'Ryle on Namely-Riders', *Logic Matters*,
    pp. 89–90, 'Referring Expressions Again', *Logic Matters*, pp. 98
    and 101.

23 On the first and second occasions mentioned in note 22.

24 The argument with reflexive pronouns occurs in Geach's *Reference
    and Generality*, p. 132. I have made an alteration in my presenta-
    tion of this argument in response to an objection from Professor
    Geach.

25 A similar point is found at many places in Geach's writings. See,
    for example, 'Logical Procedures and the Identity of Expressions',
    Logic Matters, p. 112; 'Names and Identity', in S. Guttenplan, ed.,

Mind and Language (Clarendon Press, Oxford, 1975), pp. 139–40.

26 This point is made in Dummett's *Frege*, p. 14, and, with explicit reference to Geach's treatment of pronouns, by B. H. Partee, 'Opacity, Co-reference and Pronouns' in D. Davidson and G. H. Harman, eds, *Semantics of Natural Language*, p. 436.

27 Geach, *Reference and Generality*, p. 132.

28 ibid., p. 188.

29 ibid., p. 186.

30 B. H. Partee, 'Deletion and Variable Binding', in E. L. Keenan, ed., *Formal Semantics of a Natural Language* (Cambridge University Press, 1975).

31 Hints of this argument are to be found on p. 29 of Partee's paper, 'Deletion and Variable Binding'.

32 H. N. Castaneda, ' "He": a study in the logic of self-consciousness', *Ratio 8* (1966), p. 130, and many other papers.

33 This proposal is essentially made in G. E. M. Anscombe's paper 'The First Person', in S. Guttenplan, ed., *Mind and Language* (Clarendon, Oxford, 1975), p. 47. See also Susumu Kuno, 'Pronouns, Reference and Direct Discourse', *Linguistic Inquiry*, vol. 3 (1972).

34 For an example of confusion on this point see e.g. Wallace's paper 'Belief and Satisfaction'. Wallace symbolizes a teleological principle as follows:

$(x) (y) (z)$ [Wants $(x, <y>, z)$ and Can$(x, <y>, z)$ and Believes $(x, <x,y,z>, \hat{x} \, \hat{y} \, \hat{z}$ [Can $(x, <y>, z]$) then Satisfies (x, z)]

and writes:

> It is important to notice that this principle makes essential use of universal quantification into the argument place made available by the relational sense of belief. The reader may if he wishes give notional formulations . . . but I think he will find any such principles . . . distinctly implausible the reason being that it appears impossible to capture notionally the idea that Nelson believes *of himself* that he has the ability to perform the contemplated action.

35 A consideration first stated explicitly in J. Wallace, 'On the Frame of Reference', in Davidson and Harman, *Semantics of Natural Language*, p. 237. See also D. Davidson, 'In Defense of Convention T', in H. Leblanc, ed., *Truth, Syntax and Modality* (North Holland, Amsterdam, 1973), p. 83, and Kripke, 'Is There a Problem . . . ?', p. 356.

36 It would be an interesting exercise for the reader to attempt to construct a strictly homophonic theory for the simple 'brace' notation for co-referentiality introduced above, or for that fragment of English with the devices 'the former' and 'the latter'.

37 It is in this way that I would like to account for the fact, made much of by Kripke (see 'Naming and Necessity' in Davidson and

Harman, *Semantics of Natural Language*) that if A uses the proper name β with the intention to refer to whoever B was referring to when *he* used the name β, then the referent of β on A's lips will be the same as on B's. I do *not* wish to deal with it by so extending (and weakening) the concept of 'epistemological contact' that one is in such contact with an object x if one has simply come into contact with someone who uses a name to refer to x.

38 In order to accommodate this simple logical relation between A's remark and B's, we must use the apparatus of co-referentiality we have been considering, and must not suppose that B's reference is *fixed by the description* 'the item A referred to by his use of the token "John" '.

39 Not just expressions like 'the bastard' and 'the fool' as seems to be suggested by R. S. Jackendoff on p. 110 of *Semantic Interpretation in a Generative Grammar* (MIT Press, Cambridge, Mass., 1972).

40 I borrow the notion of a description's fixing the reference of a singular term from Kripke's 'Naming and Necessity'.

41 See section IV (D) and section VII.

42 I follow the example of K. Wexler, P. Culicover and H. Hamburger in calling the converse of the 'in construction with' relation, 'governs'. See *Learning Theoretic Foundations of Linguistic Universals*, Social Sciences Working Paper No. 60 (University of California at Irvine, 1974), p. 42. I am grateful to Mr. Geoffrey Pullum for the reference to this and other relevant literature in Linguistics.

43 There is a range of transformations -- passivization, conjunction reduction, Neg-placement, among them -- which are only 'meaning preserving' when they apply to singular sentences. (See, for example, B. H. Partee, 'Negation Conjunction and Quantifiers: syntax vs. semantics', *Foundations of Language*, vol. 6 (1970), pp. 153–65.) This strongly suggests to me that the best course is to restrict such transformations to singular sentences, and to allow quantifiers insertion to take place at any stage in the transformational cycle. If Fregean truth-conditions are given for the quantifiers, this will enable us to give the meaning of any sentence affected by these transformations in terms of the equivalence of meaning between transformed and untransformed singular sentences. This is simply an extension of the strategy we have adopted for singular pronouns.

44 It was this example which showed that the relevant relation is 'in construction with' rather than Langacker's notion of 'command', for 'Fido' does command 'him'. I am very grateful to Deirdre Wilson for pointing this out to me, and for suggesting that the relevant relation might be 'in construction with'.

45 See e.g. T. Reinhart, 'Syntax and Coreference', *Papers from the Fifth Annual Meeting of the North Eastern Linguistic Society* (Harvard University Press, Cambridge, Mass., 1974), p. 92, and P. W. Culicover, 'A Constraint on Coreferentiality', *Foundations of Language*, vol. 14 (1976), p. 109.

46 P. T. Geach, 'Quine's Syntactical Insights', *Logic Matters*, p. 118.

47 Geach, *Reference and Generality*, pp. 125 and 126.

48 G. H. Harman, 'Deep Structure as Logical Form', in Davidson and Harman, eds, *Semantics of Natural Language*, p. 45.
49 A quantifier is *existential in force* iff, if a sentence of the form A(Q + Common Noun + Relative Clause), in which Q is the quantifier with maximum scope, is true, then A('Some' + Common Noun + Relative Clause), with 'Some' as the quantifier with maximum scope, is also true. 'Any' and 'No' are the most important quantifiers which do not have existential force; 'many', 'few', 'most', 'all' and each of the numerical quantifiers has existential force (as used in English).
50 Geach, 'Back-Reference', p. 204.
51 This sentence certainly does present difficulties for Geach, but actually belongs with the sentences like 'Most men who own a donkey beat it,' discussed under (d) below. However, Geach's remarks, if appropriate at all, belong at this point, since his 'two-quantifier' solution obviously does not deal with the general problem presented by the sentences we shall consider under (d).
52 Geach, 'Referring Expressions Again', *Logic Matters*, p. 100. It is worth pointing out to those who might otherwise be misled that Geach's views on the treatment of pronouns in such sentences have undergone a complete change. In 1963 ('Referring Expressions Again') the suggestion made by L. Cohen ('Geach on Referring Expressions – A Rejoinder', *Analysis*, vol. 23 (1962–3), pp. 10–12) that such pronouns should be treated as pronouns of laziness was rejected with a certain amount of brusqueness. In 'Back-Reference' (1975), p. 195, without a word of acknowledgement, Geach makes the same proposal himself. The pronoun-containing sentence for which Cohen proposed a 'pronoun of laziness' account was:

The only man who ever stole a book from Snead eventually made a lot of money by selling it.

The sentence for which Geach proposes a 'pronoun of laziness' account is

The youngest man who brought a girlfriend to the party kissed her.

I do not myself favour the laziness account, but agree with Cohen that some other account than the bound-variable one must be given.
53 Geach is not alone in proposing a 'two-quantifier' solution to these and related difficulties; it is also to be found in N. W. Tennant's contribution to his joint paper with J. E. J. Altham, 'Sortal Quantification', in E. L. Keenan, ed., *Formal Semantics . . .* , pp. 46–60. (See especially examples (4) and (6) on pp. 53–4.) Tennant's claim is that adopting a 'sortal logic' (apparently a binary structure for quantified sentences of natural languages) enables him 'to provide many English sentences with more congruous logical forms than they would receive in the classical predicate calculus'. In so far as this claim concerns sentences which are problematical

Gareth Evans

because of the occurrence of E-type pronouns, it is entirely spurious. No essential use is made of the binary structures in dealing with these pronouns; the *ad hoc* introduction of an additional quantifier is a manoeuvre available to those working within the unary structures of the classical predicate calculus.

54 It should be pointed out that the difficulty presented for the 'pronouns as variables' view by sentences like these was mentioned in two important papers by Lauri Karttunen: 'Pronouns and Variables', in *Papers from the Fifth Regional Meeting of the Chicago Linguistic Society* (Department of Linguistics, University of Chicago, 1969), and 'Definite Descriptions and Crossing Co-Reference', *Foundations of Language*, vol. 7 (1971). See especially footnote 12 of the latter paper where Karttunen writes: 'Thus he [Geach] completely overlooks the fact demonstrated above that pronouns are sometimes used in a way which is not possible with variables in the more restricted syntax of the predicate calculus.'

55 The fact that I consider pairs of sentences rather than a single sentence is a reflection of the fact that I regard these quantifiers as binary in form. But the current point does not depend upon that; we could impose a unary structure in the normal way, in which case the substitution instance would be

If John owns some sheep then he vaccinates them in the spring,

a sentence of the form considered under (a) above.

56 This is implicitly conceded by Geach in the reply (19) given to B in an imaginary dialogue in 'Back-Reference', p. 199.

57 Harman, 'Deep Structure as Logical Form', p. 45.

58 Geach makes a similar appeal to intuition in 'Referring Expressions Again' (*Logic Matters*, p. 100). See the sentence: 'All the same the relation of the dangling pronoun "it" to its antecedent "a book" is pretty clearly the same in (1) as it is in (10)'.

59 See e.g. the discussion in Geach, *Reference and Generality*, pp. 6ff. and in 'Back-Reference', pp. 203–4.

60 Geach, *Reference and Generality*, p. 126. I have changed the number of the example to agree with our ordering in this and subsequent quotations.

61 For denotation clauses of this character see e.g. M. A. E. Dummett, 'What is a Theory of Meaning?', in Guttenplan, ed., *Mind and Language*, pp. 110–11, and T. Burge, 'Truth and Singular Terms', *Noûs*, vol. 8 (1974), pp. 309–25 (reprinted above as ch. 9).

62 Geach, *Reference and Generality*, p. 52.

63 'Quine's Syntactical Insights', in *Logic Matters*, p. 118.

64 'Logical Procedures and the Identity of Expressions', in *Logic Matters*, p. 11.

65 I use the concept 'talking about' in a way quite different from the concept 'referring to'. One talks about an item x in uttering a sentence S which contains the predicate F in such a way that S entails that something is F, iff, in uttering S, one is *expressing* a belief about x to the effect that it is F. Thus one may be talking about

something even though one manifestly refuses to let one's audience know which item it is that one is talking about, and this is inconsistent with my, and I think any decent, concept of (speaker's) reference.

66 This is ignored by C. Chastain ('Reference and Context', in K. Gunderson (ed.), *Minnesota Studies in the Philosophy of Science*, vol. 7 (Minnesota University Press, 1975), pp. 194–269), who invokes the concept of reference to give the truth-conditions of sentences containing expressions like 'A man', at least partly because of the possibility of subsequent E-type pronouns. For reasons mentioned in note 65, I would also reject Kripke's suggestion (made in the John Locke Lectures for 1973) that succeeding pronouns should be dealt with by invoking the concept of speaker's reference in connexion with sentences containing expressions like 'A man'; Kripke quite rightly insists upon leaving their truth-conditions unchanged. Neither proposal seems necessary.

67 Incidentally, this shows that Geach's two sentences (16) and (17) are not contradictories because they can both be false; it is not possible to use a sentence containing an E-type pronoun to form the full contradictory of another sentence containing an E-type pronoun, because the mere use of an E-type pronoun carries with it a commitment to the existence of a referent. E-type pronouns are like definite descriptions which insist upon widest scope.

68 This is why the change Geach has made in the concept of 'pronoun of laziness' does matter. The original idea – of an expression 'eliminable in paraphrase by a repetition of its antecedent' – might correspond to some underlying syntactic reality, whereas with the later addition 'or by a repetitious phrase somehow reconstructible out of its antecedent', the possibility of such a correspondence seems to be ruled out.

69 It was comforting to read the recent paper by Jorge Hankamer and Ivan Sag, 'Deep and Surface Anaphora', in *Linguistic Inquiry*, vol. 7 (1976), pp. 391–428. In it, they propose as generally applicable a distinction between anaphoric processes which correspond to the distinction I have made in the case of pronouns. In their terminology I am proposing that E-type pronouns are deep anaphors, and pronouns of laziness are surface anaphors. By their tests, which include an ambiguity test similar to that used in the text, deep anaphors are certainly what E-type pronouns turn out to be. See also O. Dahl, 'On So-Called Sloppy Identity', *Synthèse*, vol. 26 (1973), pp. 81–112.

70 To guard against confusion it is worth distinguishing the binary structure here adopted from the binary structure suggested by Geach for the 'just one man' quantifier, and criticized above. The break in Geach's binary structure was to come at the point marked by 'and' in the sentence

Just one man opened the box and he went home

and there is no evidence whatever that 'Just one' sentences are ill-formed unless they have two such constituents. The binary structure I am suggesting for all quantifiers would discern in the initial conjunct the two constituent general terms 'man' and 'opened the box', and there is evidence that we need both of *these* constituents to have a well-formed sentence, though when we wish, in English, to approximate the effect of unrestricted quantification, the first constituent is the universal predicate 'thing' or 'object'.

71 The Appendix was published in the following issue of the *Canadian Journal of Philosophy* (vol. VII, no. 4).

72 This is essentially the account given by W. V. Quine in *Word and Object* (MIT Press, Cambridge, 1960), pp. 110–14, and *Roots of Reference*, pp. 89–92.

73 By J. D. McCawley, in 'Where Do Noun Phrases Come From?', in R. A. Jacobs and P. S. Rosenbaum, eds, *Readings in English Transformational Grammar* (Ginn, Waltham, Mass., 1970), pp. 176–7.

74 That such sentences pose a *problem* for the 'pronouns as variables' position was clearly indicated by Harman ('Deep Structure as Logical Form', pp. 41–3).

75 Harman considers a sentence of this kind, namely: 'A boy who was fooling them kissed many girls that loved him', and claims that it seems 'roughly equivalent to'

> A boy who was fooling many girls that loved him kissed and was fooling many girls that loved him.

(Harman, 'Deep Structure as Logical Form', pp. 42–3). Notice here the lengths to which one must go to produce a reading which depends upon the occurrence of E-type pronouns without actually acknowledging them. Essentially Harman treats the pronoun 'them' in the original sentence as a pronoun of laziness, but this yields only

> A boy who was fooling many girls that loved him kissed many girls that loved him,

which does not entail that he was fooling all the girls he kissed (nor, in fact, that he was fooling any of them). So, mysteriously, instead of 'kissed', the sentence's predicate somehow becomes 'kissed *and was fooling*'. It is no wonder Harman ruefully observes that 'it is not at all obvious what transformations would be used' to get away from his deep structure to the original sentence. Anyway, Harman's ruse does not work generally, as can be seen from the non-equivalence of:

> A boy who was fooling them kissed exactly two girls that loved him

> A boy who was fooling exactly two girls that loved him kissed and was fooling exactly two girls that loved him.

76 Truth and well-formedness cannot be simultaneously and interdependently defined, on pain of ill-formed sentences being presented to the semantic theory for evaluation. In order to avoid

this objection, presented to me by Barry Taylor, we should regard the notion of affirmative embedding being defined over a fragment of English that does not contain E-type pronouns, and for which truth and well-formedness are independently defined. Then the grammatical rule extending the fragment to allow for E-type pronouns will be understood as relating to contexts certified *in the smaller fragment* as being of a type in which one sentence is affirmatively embedded in relation to another. The semantical theory for the larger language will differ from that for the smaller only in containing a single additional clause for the evaluation of E-type pronouns.

77 See, for example, J. D. McCawley, 'A Program for Logic', in Davidson and Harman, *Semantics of Natural Language*, especially p. 530, and E. Keenan, 'On Semantically Based Grammar', *Linguistic Inquiry*, vol. 3 (1972).

78 See Dummett, *Frege*, pp. 12–14.

79 The point of the clause 'and there is no larger sentence frame in Σ which has σ as a constituent and which does not have σ' as a constituent' is to ensure that the description which fixes the reference of the E-type pronoun has as wide a scope as does not include the sentence containing its quantifier antecedent. This will secure the referential rigidity which we observed these pronouns to display. At the same time, the scope of the description is not the whole sentence; so we do not end up with the inaccurate result that a sentence like

Either John does not own a donkey or he keeps it very quiet

is true iff

The donkey which John owns is such that either John owns no donkey or he keeps it very quiet

(and thus false if John owns no donkey).

15 'Most' and 'all': some comments on a familiar programme, and on the logical form of quantified sentences

David Wiggins

I

What follows is an attempt to extend the understanding of quantifiers that we have from the writings of Frege and his successors, proceeding by means of the experimental application of this understanding to the relatively neglected quantifier 'most'.

The problems that natural language quantifiers like 'most' present to the theorist are so urgent and so general that it is hard to envisage any semantical theory of natural language which was insensitive to them. But for simplicity and definiteness, and also for the sake of the detailed commentary it will suggest upon certain formulations of what still seems the right general programme, my attempt will be mounted within a framework that is shaped or informed by two particular ideas. The first is the idea that some adaptation of Tarski's semantic conception of truth like that which Donald Davidson has proposed will serve well to elaborate the insight of Frege in *Grundgesetze* 1.32, that to give the meaning of a sentence is to specify the conditions under which it has the truth-value True.[1] The second is the idea that the logical form of a sentence corresponds to the parsing or articulation imposed upon it by the exigencies of giving a truth definition for the language to which the sentence belongs.

There is something durable and lasting about both of these ideas of Davidson; but the attempt to augment with the quantifier 'most' the fragment of English for which we can envisage defining truth will suggest that there is a need for at least one emendation or qualification of his view of the relations of meaning and truth.[2] It may also help to redress among philosophers whom he has influenced a damaging underestimation of the importance for the theory of meaning of the notion of truth in an interpretation. (If I insist somewhat here, it is only because the issue touches on one of a nexus of questions that still sustain faction and prolong mutual incomprehension; and because this faction and incomprehension is eminently unworthy of a subject that aspires to describe what is involved in one man's understanding another.) But these thoughts about meaning will supervene upon my principal theme, which is the truth-theoretic management of an improvement (itself neither novel nor yet fully appreciated) of the treatment usually accorded to sentences involving 'some' and 'all'. As a bonus, there will also be some occasion, not only for some valedictory speculations about the proper shape and organization of a total theory of meaning for a natural language, but also for one modification of some working philosophers' and logicians' impressions of the history of the logic of generality. A certain continuity will be restored between modern logic and what was best in the pre-quantifier-and-variable tradition.

II

According to the conception from which I begin, a truth-theoretical treatment of 'most', or of any other expression deserving to be articulated as a word of a language L, is to be achieved by an axiom belonging to an axiomatic theory with the following overall properties:

(1) [the theory] account[s] for the meaning (or conditions of truth) of every sentence of L by analysing it as composed in truth-relevant ways of elements drawn from a finite stock;[3]

(2) [it] provides a method for deciding, given an arbitrary L sentence, what its meaning is. (By satisfying these two conditions a theory may be said to show the language it describes is learnable and scrutable);

(3) A third condition is that the statements of truth conditions . . . entailed by the theory should, in some sense yet to be made precise, draw upon the same concepts as the sentences whose truth conditions they state.

Later in the essay from which these are quoted, Davidson rolls up these first three conditions and makes the composite suggestion that

(4) To see the structure of a sentence through the eyes of a theory of truth is to see it as built by devices a finite number of which suffice for every sentence; the structure of the sentence thus determines its relation to other sentences. And indeed there is no giving the truth conditions of all sentences *without showing that some sentences are logical consequences of others*; if we regard the structure revealed by a theory of truth as deep grammar, *then grammar and logic must go hand in hand.*[4]

These are cautiously drafted sentences, but it is instructive to gloss them with others that Davidson published in the same decade.[5]

David Wiggins

(4′) Armed with the theory [of truth] we can always answer the question 'what are these familiar words doing here?' by saying how they contribute to the truth-conditions of the sentence.

The study of the logical form of sentences is often seen in the light of another interest, that of expediting inference. . . . Obviously the two approaches to logical form cannot yield independent results, for logical consequence is defined in terms of truth. To say a second sentence is a logical consequence of a first is to say, roughly, that the second is true if the first is no matter how the non-logical constants are interpreted. Since what we count as a logical consequence can vary independently of the set of truths, it is clear that the two versions of logical form, though related, need not be identical. The relation, in brief, seems this. Any theory of truth that satisfies Tarski's criteria must take account of all truth-affecting devices in the language. In the familiar languages for which we know how to define truth the basic iterative devices are reducible to the sentential connectives, the apparatus of quantification, and the description operator, if it is primitive. *Where one sentence is a logical consequence of another on the basis of quantificational structure alone, a theory of truth will therefore entail that if the first sentence is true, the second is*. . . . Adding to the list of logical constants will increase the inventory of logical truths and consequence relations beyond anything a truth-definition demands, *and will therefore yield richer versions of logical form.* For purposes of the present, however, we can cleave to the most austere interpretations of logical consequence and logical form, *those that are forced on us when we give a theory of truth.*

Finally, for the sake of even greater determinacy, we may make a guess at the minimal amendment that it is intended to make to Tarski's criterion of adequacy, as it applies to a finitely axiomatized recursive theory of truth designed to specify — even as it determines the extension of 'true in L' — the *meaning* of each of the sentences of a natural language fragment L.[6]

CONVENTION T ADAPTED: A formally correct definition of the symbol 'True', formulated in the metalanguage, will be called an adequate definition of truth if it has as consequences all sentences that are obtained from the expression 'x is true if and only if p' by substituting for the symbol 'x' a structural descriptive name (or other appropriate designation) of any sentence of the language in question and for the symbol 'p' the expression that forms the translation of this sentence into the metalanguage.'[7]

III

Citations (4) and (4') strongly suggest that Davidson would expect an adequate truth-theory for a language that included the quantificatory devices 'some', 'all' and 'most' to entail all the valid sentences of L in which validity turns on the presence of these quantifiers and/or the properties of truth-functions, just as the truth theory for a language containing 'some' and 'all' will (when presented in a standard logic) entail all the quantificationally valid sentences whose validity is owed to the presence of 'some', 'all', and truth-functions. The citations suggest this *if* indeed 'most' is a logical constant, or *if* 'most' is a quantificational device whose addition to a language can add to the stock of quantificational truths. But surely nobody will respond to an attempt to make an investigation of 'most' the occasion to test the purport or soundness of (4) and (4') and to build up a plea for the mutual relevance of meaning and truth relativized to interpretation, by maintaining that 'most' *could not* be accounted a logical constant of an extended quantificational logic. If this were the defence offered against the attempt I shall make towards the end to liberalize the framework defined by (1) (2) (3) (4) (4'), it would have little new to offer to someone who open-mindedly and genuinely needed to be persuaded of (4) and (4') in particular.

IV

What has to be achieved by a theory of the meaning of the English quantifier 'most', then, is the discovery and correct statement of an axiom which, in conjunction with all the axioms for other expressions belonging in the fragment of English under consideration, will entail an English equivalence ⌜True x if and only if p⌝ for every sentence x of the fragment containing the expression 'most'. Such an axiom should use on the right hand side, as well as mention on the left hand side, the word 'most' or some synonym (cf. citation (3)); and, in using 'most', it should state the contribution (*Beitrag* as Frege says) of this particular device to the meaning or truth conditions of the sentence in which it occurs. This requirement is independent of anything that may be controversial in citations (4) and (4').

If it is supposed that it is already known how to achieve a finitely axiomatized theory of truth for an arbitrary first-order fragment of English containing the quantifiers 'some' and 'all', then the problem may be thought to reduce to that of enriching some such going fragment with the extra quantifier 'most' and then enriching the theory of truth and logical consequence to accommodate this one extra truth-value affecting device. But, as will appear, it seems certain that, even for a natural fragment of English containing 'all' and 'some', there is one defect — by the standards that ought to be set — in the usual resolution of the problem. *Pro tempore* then, and pending a correction that will make it easier to engage with a more natural fragment of ordinary English, I suggest that at first it will be better to see our problem as that of adding 'most' to a kind of English (logician's *stylized* or *textbook object-language* English) that has *already* replaced such natural locutions as 'all kings are wise' with something like 'everything is if a king then wise' (or supplanted the natural locution 'some king is wise' by 'something is a king and (a) wise (king)'). This is still English of a sort. To begin with at least, it is all that we are concerned with. Thus the problem of the more natural locutions is postponed.

V

The restriction to such forms for the expression of generality in natural language is an artificiality that can and must be relaxed. (See below, section X, where the expressive resources of the language we begin with are significantly enlarged.) But there is a second and less damaging artificiality that will not be relaxed. The complexity of defining truth directly even for the natural language fragment just indicated (or for the larger liberalized fragment of English in which we shall readmit in due course such forms as 'all men are not immortal' or 'all immortals are not men') would obscure both needlessly and (for our purposes) trivially the workings of the definition of truth. So, regardless of whether this feature would in the end be carried over to a finished theory, truth will be defined here for syntactically even simpler languages than logician's English. These proxy languages will lack the article and copula, and will employ indexed variables in lieu of pronouns. But the very restricted proxy language and the slightly less restricted proxy language which will become available after section XII (like any other language that could play the role I here envisage for proxy languages) will bear the following relation to the corresponding fragments of English:

(a) proxy sentences are transformable by syntactic rules (specifiable but not here specified) into sentences of the intended English fragment, and vice versa;
(b) the proxy language is learnable, and intelligible in its own right;

and the rules of transformation between proxy and English are such
that, relative to the said correct understanding of the proxy language,
no proxy sentence will differ in truth-value or meaning from its
natural counterpart (i.e. they will always match by *standards of radical interpretation*);
(c) in an intuitive sense that must be gradually improved in the light
of developing theory, every proxy sentence has the same semantic
multiplicity as its counterpart.[8]

VI

Let the quantificational proxy language that is to be proxy for logic
textbook English, and is to be enriched with the 'most' quantifier, have
denumerably many variables of quantification x_1, x_2, x_3, . . . , four
sample predicates '=' (short for 'is the same as'), 'H' (short for 'man'),
'I' (short for 'immortal') and 'R' (short for 'loves'), the connectives
'not' and 'if', and the quantifier 'for all x_i', abbreviated as '(all x_i)'. The
formation rules are the habitual ones for languages of first-order logic.

The theory of truth for this language will be given in a metalanguage
that has as a proper part the language itself. To arrive at this metalanguage
we augment the object-language with the metalinguistic variables 'A'
and 'B', ranging over well-formed expressions of the object-language,
and with a device for quotation. For our elementary purposes, this can
be an unrigorous overlining convention governed by the convention
that the effect of juxtaposing metalinguistic designations and/or metalinguistic variables is to make a designation of the concatenation of the
designata. We must also augment the metalanguage with the few expressions of elementary set-theory required to state the standard Tarskian
theory of truth for the language. A new class of variables $\sigma, \sigma', \sigma''$ may
also be introduced, for the sake of convenience, to range over sequences
of objects.[9] (Greek capital sigma Σ is here a dummy sequence-name.)
Ordinary classical logic is assumed to apply for both object- and metalanguage.[10] (But importance will attach at section XVI below to the
fact that the logic can be weakened appreciably without endangering
the claims of the truth theory to meet Convention T.[11])

Framing the metalanguage in this way, we have a language of the
same delimited or proxy character as the object language whose truth
predicate we frame in this metalanguage. (The same conditions (a), (b),
(c) of section V above will therefore apply; and in so far as these conditions are all workable and satisfied here, (b) licenses us in the use of
unofficial equivalents.) A diagrammatic representation of the situation
is then as follows:

David Wiggins

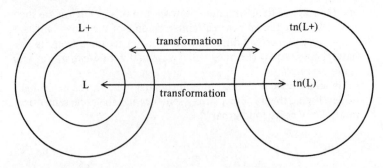

KEY

    L   =   proxy language (with indexed variables, etc.) for which truth is to be
                  directly defined − proxy for tn(L), which is a sort of English.

    L+ =   L augmented = proxy metalanguage for L = a proxy for tn(L+).

 tn(L) =   the result of transforming the sentences of L by the transformations
                  described in section V (these being constrained by (a), (b), (c)) =
                  restricted proper English with pronouns replacing variables, etc.

tn(L+) =   ditto for L+ = restricted proper English with the word 'true'.

If we think of successive efforts to redraw the boundaries in this
diagram, so that in the end what falls inside the inner right hand circle
coincides with the vast extent of object-language English, then it
illustrates well enough the general position of English speakers attempting to characterize in English the resources of English itself. Their task
will be for all practical purposes complete when (apart from boredom)
no difficulty of principle obstructs the theorist from approaching
arbitrarily close to the almost transcendental objective of stating within English a systematic theory to mate with every English sentence a
statement of the conditions under which it is true. But of course the
purpose of the present essay is one modest extension of a modest quantificational language, not the assessment of the limitation that Tarski's
theorem, or the Liar paradox or anything else may have been held to
place upon the larger aspiration.

VII

The theory of truth for the language that is to be extended is the standard or familiar one:

    (1) *The σ* (or interpretation) function*, from sequences and expres-
           sions (indexed variables) to things is defined first: for any σ,
           $\sigma^*(\bar{x}_i)$ = the ith member of σ.[12]

324

(2) *Axioms for satisfaction*

    2.11 For any sequence σ, σ satisfies $\overline{Hx_i}$ if and only if $\sigma^*(\bar{x}_i)$ is a man.[13]

    2.12 For any sequence σ, σ satisfies $\overline{Ix_i}$ if and only if $\sigma^*(\bar{x}_i)$ is immortal.

    2.13 For any sequence σ, σ satisfies $\overline{Rx_i,x_j}$ if and only if $\sigma^*(\bar{x}_i)$ loves $\sigma^*(\bar{x}_j)$.

    2.14 For any sequence σ, σ satisfies $\overline{x_i = x_j}$ if and only if $\sigma^*(\bar{x}_i)$ is the same as $\sigma^*(\bar{x}_j)$.

    2.2   For any sequence σ, σ satisfies $\overline{\text{not } A}$ if and only if σ does not satisfy A.[14]

    2.3   For any sequence σ, σ satisfies $\overline{\text{if } A, \text{ then } B}$ if and only if, if σ satisfies A, then σ satisfies B.

In order to write down the axiom by which it will be assumed in this paper that the semantic effect of 'all' has been characterized, it is necessary to introduce one more piece of notation. For each sequence σ, and for each integer j, let $\sigma(j/z)$ be the sequence that is got from σ by supplanting whatever stands in the jth place with the object z. Then

    2.4   For any sequence σ, σ satisfies $\overline{(\text{all } x_i)A}$ if and only if for all z, $\sigma(i/z)$ satisfies A.

Finally we stipulate:

(3) *Truth*

A closed sentence is true if and only if it is satisfied by all sequences.

I have preferred a satisfaction based theory using sequences etc. to a recursion on truth itself, and have made the minimum number of changes here to the original theory of Tarski in *Wahrheitsbegriff*, not so much from conservatism or the passionate conviction that this is the best mode of presentation for the sort of theory of truth we want for natural languages (probably it is not), but from the desire to focus all conservative objections upon my plea for a liberalization of the four conditions quoted from Davidson in section II. But one alteration has been imperative. Following Tarski's original axiom for 'all', we should have had:

For any sequence σ, σ satisfies $\overline{(\text{all } x_i)A}$ if and only if σ satisfies A and all sequences that differ from σ at most in the ith place satisfy A.

Not only is this needlessly complicated, and exceedingly unnatural (explaining what it is for all *objects* to have a property in terms of all *sequences* fulfilling a certain condition − refer again here to citation (2) of section (II)); it is simply unmanageable so soon as we come to quantifiers like 'most'. Sequences being non-denumerably many, we may have trouble making sense of any condition that speaks of 'most sequences' fulfilling a condition.

VIII

To extend our language to embrace 'most', the most natural first proposal is to let truth continue to be satisfaction by all sequences, and write

2.5 For any sequence σ, σ satisfies $\overline{(\text{most } x_i)}\text{A}$ if and only if, for most z, $\sigma(i/z)$ satisfies A.

And in a sense there is nothing wrong with this axiom. It delivers a correct truth-definition for 'Most things are men', or '(most x_4) (Hx_4)', for instance. But the question now arises how seemingly more complex sentences like 'Most men are immortal' or 'Most men who love all men love themselves' are to be treated. For the quantifier 'all' the corresponding problem is solved by treating 'All men are immortal' as replaceable *salva veritate* by 'Anything is if a man then immortal', and then defining the truth of the replacement by reference to a proxy of the form (x_i)A, where A is a conditional whose antecedent and consequent are open sentences. Similarly, if we were interested in introducing 'some' and 'and' into L we could solve the corresponding problem for 'some man is immortal' by a proxy sentence of the form $(\exists x_i)$A where A was a *conjunction* of open sentences. But then, if we resolve to try to treat 'most men are immortal' by the open-sentence method, we shall have to find an English replacement of 'Most men are immortal' and a proxy sentence in the form '(most x_i)A' that will be true if and only if most men are immortal. And the formula A will have to represent some complex of open sentences. Suppose δ were its connective. Obviously δ could not be 'and'. Almost equally obviously δ could not be 'if . . . then . . .'. (Almost everything is if-man-then-immortal, because almost everything is not-a-man. If δ were 'if' that would force the value *true* on 'Most men are immortal'.) And experimentation will quickly show that, so conceived, the problem is insoluble.[15] No binary truth-functional connective can play the role of δ, if a sentence of the form '(most x_i) ((Hx_i)δ(Ix_i))' is to mean what 'most men are immortal' means.

IX

Finding the complex open-sentence representation impossible for the 'most' quantifier (and having previously found it so unnatural for the 'all' quantifier that, rather than attempt 'All Fs are Gs', we preferred to describe the semantics of 'All things are if F then G' – a version of 'All Fs are Gs' that logic students resist, when it is presented as a translation, with the same determination as earlier generations, asking always where the 'if' comes from – compare section V, constraint (c)), one proper course is to return to the point where the complex open-sentence treatment was first institutionalized in logic.

X

It is well known that the strategy of treating 'All Fs are Gs' as expressing the same thought as 'Everything is if F then G' was first systematized in logic by Frege, and that in pursuit of the complex predicate strategy, Frege saw this judgment as having a form one may describe from a modern point of view as the form of a predication of a second-level concept (the concept which the phrase 'everything is such that . . .' stands for) upon the complex first-level concept that is stood for by the open sentence 'if it is a man then it is immortal'. According to the Fregean doctrine, what the sentence 'All men are immortal' then says is that everything is such that it is if-a-man-then-immortal. It is also well known that this proposal was one part of the grand strategy by which Frege solved at one stroke the outstanding problems of first-order logic that neither Boole nor Schroeder nor any of Frege's predecessors had clearly formulated. What is less often noticed is that, conformably with a certain general principle of his,[16] Frege had another way of seeing judgments of the universally quantified form.

At §47 of the *Foundations of Arithmetic* Frege elucidates 'all whales are mammals' not in the way just expounded but as expressing the *subordination* of the simple concept of whale to the simple concept of mammal. Applying this variant anaysis to 'All men are immortal', we find not a monadic second-level attribution to a complex first-level concept but the attribution of the dyadic second level 'subordination' relation to a pair of first-level concepts, the first being the simple concept *Man* (≠ any particular man – otherwise we should have to be taken as speaking even of Chief Akpanya of whom perhaps we have never heard[17]) and the second being the simple concept *Immortal*.[18] According to this variant elucidation, *Man* is subordinate to *Immortal*, or determines a subset of the set that *Immortal* determines.

David Wiggins

Now obviously it makes no logical difference which of these kinds of parsing or description you prefer wherever (as with the universal quantifier and its dual) both are available. But what we have discovered of course is that in the case of the 'most' quantifier the complex predicate elucidation is not available. The short-lived expectation of its general availability was created by the success of Frege's logic, and was sustained by the fortunate accident that all the two-concept sentences like

The concept *Man* is subordinate to the concept *Immortal*

that corresponded to the sentences that interested logicians turned out to be equivalent to sentences about one complex concept, like

Everything falls under the concept *If man then immortal.*

But now, after brief and unsuccessful experimentation, we must abandon the expectation that, for every quantifier, there will always be some suitable complex open sentence. Perhaps the illusion that such would always exist once protected formal logic from some untimely complications. But it has distracted semantics from fidelity to natural language and postponed the day when 'most', 'many', 'few', 'a few' would become tractable to formal semantical treatment. There is also a prospect that, by relaxing the fixation upon the case where there is a truth-functional complex to serve a quantifier in the way in which 'Fx & Gx' or 'Fx ⊃ Gx' serve ∃ and ∀, we shall be able to look both backward to what was virtuous in an earlier tradition, whose principal disadvantage was only its lacking Frege's invention of the quantifier and variable notation, and forward to a generalization that has been proposed recently in logic (see section XIII below).

XI

Following Frege's variant analysis of 'All whales are mammals' let us now advance to the quantifier 'most' and see 'men' and 'immortal' in 'most men are immortal' as standing for the simple concepts *Men* and *Immortal*, and 'most' as standing for a certain second-level relation between them. Then the logical form of 'most men are immortal' is

(Most x_i) (Hx_i, Ix_i).

The comma here simply separates and orders the two subjects of second-level relational 'verbs' like *all* and *most*. (Compare the way it orders the two subjects 'Shem' and 'Shaun' in the first-level predication 'Kicks (Shem, Shaun)'.) And the intuitive content of the quantifier 'most x_i' may be given in Fregean terms by the idea that it stands for some relation of 'preponderant subordination' between two first-level concepts, i.e. the 'subordination for the most part' of the concept *Man* to the concept *Immortal*.

These explanations are at once informal, ontologically expensive and technical sounding. But if it is the office of the theorist of natural language to improve upon the 'subordination' and 'preponderant subordination' accounts and use 'most' to frame an axiom stating more sparely and economically what 'most' means, then we may extend the syntax of L and L+ to allow a quantifier '(most x_i)' or '(all x_i)' to bind two open sentences simultaneously (provided that x_i is free in each) and then proceed straight to the proposal

2.51   For any sequence σ, σ satisfies $\overline{(\text{most } x_i)(A,B)}$ if and only if, for most z such that $\sigma(i/z)$ satisfies A, $\sigma(i/z)$ satisfies B.

A comparable stipulation for 'all' (designed to accord better than the conditional view of 'all' with constraint (c) of section V) will then read:

2.41   For any sequence σ, σ satisfies $\overline{(\text{all } x_i)(A,B)}$ iff (all z) ($\sigma(i/z)$ sat A, $\sigma(i/z)$ sat B).[19]

XII

Because these stipulations demote the locution 'everything is F' and 'most things are F' in favour of a conception of quantifiers as two-place second-level functors with first-level concepts as arguments, '(all x_i)(Hx_i)' and '(most x_i)(Hx_i)' will then be ill-formed. But this will not matter provided we find a two-concept equivalent for all the English sentences (such as they are) that we might have wished to represent as '(all x_i)(Hx_i)' or '(most x_i)(Hx_i)'. To render these English sentences we can introduce the universal predicate U, defined by '(all z)(Uz ≡ (Hz ⊃ Hz))' and abbreviating the English common noun 'thing', and then supply 'U' to the argument place that would otherwise have been empty. Thus 'everything is a man', if anyone ever wanted to say that, is rendered by, say, '(all x_4)(Ux_4, Hx_4)'.

XIII

It may be asked why Frege did not prefer this approach to the conditional approach for the case of 'all Fs are Gs'. The answer has to do

David Wiggins

with the greater apparent ease or directness with which propositional
logic can be brought to bear in Frege's system on the proof of such
sentences as 'If all men are mortal and Napoleon is a man then Napoleon is mortal'.[20] But, so soon as one reached the state of constructing
a model theory for the alternative system, it would be easy to justify
making sentences of the form

$$(\text{all } x_i)(Fx_i, Gx_i) \equiv (\text{all } x_i)(Ux_i, Fx_i \supset Gx_i)$$

into axioms or theorems of the logic of 'all' treated as a two-place
functor. And in that case nothing in Frege's logic of quantification has
been irrecoverably lost or abandoned. The proposal is true both to
Frege's informal method in semantics, and to what was best in the
method of Leibniz that he improved upon:

> When in a universal affirmative proposition I say 'every man is an
> animal' I wish to say that the concept of animal is involved with the
> concept of man. (For the concept *man* is the concept *rational ani-*
> *mal*.) And when I say 'every pious person is happy' I mean that any-
> one who understands what it is to be pious will understand that in
> this concept true happiness is included.[21]

> When I say that every man is an animal I mean that men are to be
> sought among the animals, or that whatsoever be not animal is not
> man either.[22]

Prescinding from all the ins and outs of Leibniz's special notion of con-
tainment, and from the details of his various ways of characterizing (in
what we should call second level terms) the relations of the concept of
the subject and the concept of the predicate in the Aristotelian A E I
and O forms (and putting aside as irrelevant all the problems of propositions with individuals for subject, also seen by Leibniz as relating a pair
of first-level concepts of subject and predicate), what should matter for
the history of the logic of generality is that, as in Frege, the terms of a
quantified sentence are always concepts, that the sentence itself is relational, and that there is a real continuity between these pre-quantifica-
tional Leibnizian analyses and the Fregean formulation:

> The word 'some' states a relation that holds in our example [viz.
> 'some numbers are primes'] between the concepts of number and of
> prime. Similarly 'all' in ['all bodies are heavy'] states a relation be-
> tween the concepts *body* and *heavy*.[23]

What is more, by viewing the quantified sentence in the fashion (albeit
ontologically sparer) of section XI, perhaps we may discern a fine con-
tinuous thread running through Leibniz's logical researches and Frege's
informal expositions to the *generalized quantifiers* that I understand
logicians are now investigating, making it possible for the domain of a

variable to be explicitly restricted by an arbitrary propositional function written into the quantified formula itself.[24]

XIV

It is manifest that the very last characterization, however familiar it may sound to one versed in modern logical practice, is alien to Frege (and alien also to our explanation of 2.41) because Frege was apt to insist that individual variables should always range over all objects, and that first-level functions should be defined for *all* objects as arguments, an insistence some have wished to implicate in the contradictions that ruined his logistical system. But doubting as I do (for reasons that this is not the place to try to substantiate) that Frege's insistence on unrestricted quantification is inextricably entangled with that which made him victim of the antinomy of the set of all sets that are not members of themselves (which we may say Russell's paradox simply shows not to be among the entities that are there to figure in the range of an unrestricted quantifier[25]), and having myself preferred in 2.41 and 2.51 to proceed in Fregean fashion and see the quantifiers '(most x_i)' and '(all x_i)' as *unrestricted* quantifiers operating on two open sentences that are coordinate[26] — rather than as quantifiers restricted by the first open sentence, I probably ought to pause here to justify the Fregean preference.

If I am right in the claims I am about to make on Frege's behalf, then I think this will suggest that, for certain semantical purposes which are Davidson's purposes (see section II, citations (1) (2) (3)), there is much to be said in favour of a thought that persons of a model-theoretic formation will regard as all of a piece with what they find system-bound or archaic in Russell's or Frege's thinking about logic.[27] The thought is indeed system bound. But it does not count against the thought that certain *other* semantical purposes will suggest that we should attempt an external standpoint, outside the 'logocentric predicament' that Russell, Frege and others accepted as inevitable.[28] No doubt these other purposes will prompt us to consider how a sentence can be 'disinterpreted' in order that we may inquire how it would be evaluated as true or false under all possible assignments of extensions to its predicates. We shall come shortly to this would-be external standpoint. What must in a certain sense precede it, however, and is surely presupposed to such disinterpretations and reinterpretations, is a different and more modest exercise which is Davidson's project, an exercise that is important precisely because it *is* modest. This is the reckoning up and enumeration of the expressive resources of the object language, describing them in the very same terms as their users. If we cannot even do that, how can we do harder things? Compare citation (3) of section II above. Taking off from that citation, consider the case in which the object language is a fragment of our own natural language, the metalanguage is also our own natural language, and we aim to define truth. If the metalanguage used an expressive device to characterize the contribution of that very same device, then surely there should be nothing in the metalinguistic use of the device which outruns the expressive power that the metalinguistic stipulation *attributes* to the device. Otherwise, *ex hypothesi*, we shall not have reckoned fully what we ought to have reckoned fully – the expressive resources of the natural language in which we think and speak.

Unless I am mistaken, this simple thought will vindicate the Fregean explanation I have preferred for the binary quantifiers of 2.41 and 2.51 over explanations that invoke restricted quantification. Suppose that we elucidate '(most z) (Man z, Immortal z)' not as 2.51 did but by seeing 'man' as defining a universe of discourse or range of entities to which the quantifier 'most z' is restricted. Then we must be involved in some stipulation to the effect that an entity is only within the domain of the variable 'z' as that occurs in our sentence if it is a man. But the statement that an entity only counts as part of the range of the quantifier if it is a man is itself an instance of quantification; and it is a quantification either *un*restricted or *less* restricted than the quantifier that it elucidates. (We need to say that the range of 'z' comprises men *and nothing else*.) But then it seems that, however we limit our quantifiers at any point, we always need to be possessed of a less restricted device of quantification. For the less restricted will be needed to express the required restriction on the more restricted quantification. I conclude that it would be a great pity for us to talk ourselves out of the *un*restricted natural language quantifier (which is surely precisely that by the understanding of which we understand the explanation of restricted quantification), and far better to describe a natural language quantifier like 'most' or 'all' as starting from a pre-existing unspecified and unrestricted mass of entities (a mass it does not even need to treat as a set or determinate totality of any kind), and then delimiting for itself some definite portion of this, which is what the sentence is *about*. (That is how the quantifiers should be taken, I mean, in the absence of contrary indications.) And we may distinguish in principle between what a sentence of the form (quantifier) (open sentence A, open sentence B) is *about* on the one hand – which depends on A, and on the other hand the class of entities that are *relevant* to the truth-value of the sentence – which depends on the understanding of the quantifier. (As regards the last, some special stipulation may or may not be in force. And context may – or may not – have some impact.[29]).

If we make this distinction (which is none the worse for its being possible to make some trade off sometimes between what a sentence is about and what entities are counted as relevant to its truth), then we shall align such quantifiers as 'all' and 'most' with quantifiers such as 'the', where the distinction between relevance and aboutness is actually indispensable. Consider the sentence, which nobody knows yet how to evaluate, 'The largest twinned prime is greater than 10^{1000}', when that is understood in the Russellian non-referential or non-entity-involving fashion, and analysed using a two-place iota quantifier as $(\imath x)([x$ is a prime and twinned and larger than all other twinned primes], $[x$ is greater than $10^{1000}])$.

As matters stand − when we do not even know whether there is a largest twinned prime − we have to regard *all* natural numbers however large as relevant to the question whether this sentence is true. But what the sentence is *about* is (what it is to be) the largest twinned prime.

XV

So much for the best reading of the binary quantifiers, and so much for the virtues of the project of discovering for a fragment of natural language a theory of truth that answers to Convention T Adapted. We are forced first into a discovery about logical form (see section VIII) or rather a Fregean rediscovery (see section X); and then forced again into the recovery of another Fregean insight (see section XIV) concerning a difference between relevance and aboutness. Here is surely some real vindication of Davidson's methodological proposals (1) (2) (3). What we now come to is Davidson's adjunction of (4) and (4′) to the enterprise that (1) (2) (3) define, his thought that (4) and (4′) belong with (1) (2) (3), and the idea − if this is really Davidson's idea − that the reckoning up of semantic and compositional resources with which citations (1) (2) (3) are concerned will *exhaust* the proper province of a theory of strict meaning. In pursuance of these questions, I shall now mention three matters which fall outside the ambit of citations (1) (2) (3) but must, I think, fall within a theory of meaning − on any reasonable acceptation whatever of 'meaning'. These points will occupy sections XVI and XVII, and motivate certain distinctions to be presented in section XVIII. Then, in the place of a conclusion, I shall pose certain questions about the proper shape and organization of a theory of meaning.

333

David Wiggins

XVI

Consider the following 'paradox'. However you segment the number series from 2 onwards into stretches of equal length most stretches contain more composite than prime numbers. But, if most equal-sized subsets of a set contain more Fs than Gs, then (a) the set contains more Fs than Gs, and (b), if everything in the set is either an F or a G, then most things in the set are Fs. So most natural numbers greater than two are composite. (Throwing in the number one makes no difference, obviously.) So on the one hand most natural numbers greater than two are composite. But by Cantor's argument, on the other hand, there are the *same* number of prime and composite numbers.

This is a trifling paradox, no doubt. But surely its resolution depends on our attaining a different kind of understanding of 'most' from that which we shall seek out under the influence of Davidson's excellent question 'What is this familiar word doing here?'. Reflection will suggest a diagnosis that our analysis at section XVII below will help to confirm. The diagnosis is that it is a necessary condition of its being true that most Hs are Fs that either the cardinal number of the concept H *or* the cardinal number of the complement of the concept F should be finite — and this is a condition that is failed by any premiss of the form 'most stretches (of any given length) of the natural number series comprise more composite than prime numbers'.

At this point we may be tempted to add some such condition to the truth condition of sentences of the form '(most x_i) (A, B)'. But this would violate Davidson's stipulation (2). And there is one sensible and legitimate enterprise for which Davidson's stipulation is eminently reasonable, viz. reckoning up the semantical and compositional resources of the language. Talk of the finitude of certain extensions is alien to that project. It would be absurd to try to introduce some such stipulation into 2.51. Someone who says that most men are bad-tempered does not *say* (say among other things) that either the cardinal number of *Men* is finite or the number of the complement of *Bad-tempered* is finite. He does not speak of cardinal numbers at all. To forget this — or to have mistaken the Fregean formulation in terms of a relation of concepts for a report of what is strictly *said* by 'All bodies are heavy' — would be to lose hold of the very feature of Davidson's conception of saying that is delicate and sensitive to all those questions of ontology and of nuance that are worthy to excite the interest of a competent linguistic philosopher. (No matter how many of the other concerns of linguistic philosophers fall outside Davidson's conception, and no matter what Davidson's own attitude may have been to the miscellaneous anecdotal materials out of which we have so garrulously attempted to construct a philosophy of language.) The theorist's subjects do not

334

say this sort of thing. That is one point. But nor yet – moving now to a second thing that must concern a complete theory of meaning – do they make explicit (even if in some way the context fixes) *how many* more H and G things there are than H and not-G things. There is vagueness here, and it is the business of *some* department of semantics to say what such issues of vagueness turn upon, and say how context impinges upon their determination. This is not within the capability or ambit of truth-conditional semantics; but, provided that truth-conditional semantics is not presented as an exhaustive account of meaning, that is no criticism of the project of elucidating meaning by truth-conditions.

XVII

The same conclusion, viz. that truth-theoretical semantics cannot be a complete theory of meaning, may be made to appear a more pressing criticism of the pure truth-conditional programme if we attend to what Davidson appears to have intended by the methodological requirements (4) and (4').

Equating together the logical form of a sentence in the sense with which we began (see section I) and logical form in the sense of what remains after non-logical vocabulary is replaced by schematic letters, (4') directs us to expect that any new quantificational truths that accrue to the language by the addition of 'most' will be derivable from the theory of truth for the language as augmented by the new axiom 2.51. For, on the supposition that we have here a well-made unitary conception of form, it would seem that, if there were formally valid truths that were not derivable, then something central to structure or composition would have eluded or escaped from the theory of truth that was to have served as the theory of meaning. But now I think that we must take stock of all our expectations.

The addition of 'most' to a language and the corresponding augmentation of what is counted as logical vocabulary will not in fact enrich very greatly the store of logical truths. There are not very many new sentences to prove. But, unluckily for the unitary conception of logical form, 2.51 will not suffice to prove even the first interesting logical truth that is imported by the arrival of 'most':

† If $(\text{most } x_4) (Fx_4, Gx_4)$, then $(\text{some } x_4) (Fx_4, Gx_4)$.
  If most Fs are Gs, then some F is G.

And surely (†) is true in virtue of the meanings of 'most' and 'all' or 'some'. Nevertheless 2.51 satisfies all the requirements of Convention T Adapted.

David Wiggins

We could enrich the deductive apparatus of the theory of truth to embrace (†). Indeed we shall show in due course why (†) *must* be true. But this is not the same as to say that its proof belongs in the theory of truth. And no interesting defence of (4′) would result from the plea that (†) should always have been an axiom of the metalanguage. For this will only arouse our interest in the question whether, before 'most' was added and the meaning of the simpler quantificational language was being characterized, Convention T Adapted could have been fulfilled for that familiar language on the basis of a weaker logic than was required to deduce all the quantificationally valid sentences in which 'all' occurs. And the answer to the question is positive.[30] Not very much logic is *forced* on us by Convention T Adapted.

XVIII

Now my own reaction to this and to the fact that, in some central way, (†) is true in virtue of meaning, is not to relinquish Davidson's methodological principle (3). Surely (3) has something right about it (embodies indeed that which makes interesting the so-called 'homophonic' theories of truth that obey conditions (a) (b) (c) of section V). Still less would my reaction be to regard Convention T Adapted as irrelevant to all serious semantical purposes simply because it fails to demand everything that ought to be demanded for these. Rather I think we should make certain distinctions.

First we may distinguish the question whether (†) is a logical truth – it surely is – from the question whether, in the sense we ought to give to 'structure', it is true in virtue of its formal structure. (See below Section XXI on Evans.) This ought not to be a new question. Long before we got to 'most', we should have asked: in the sense we *ought* to give to 'structure', is the theorem

$$*((z)(Fz) \,\&\, (z)(Gz)) \supset (z)(Fz \,\&\, Gz)$$

true in virtue of structure? The question was always worth asking because it may be that there is some serious and grammatically justified sense of 'structure' such that we should cherish this sense and use it to frame a reasonable requirement to the effect that a theory of truth should entail all the truths true in virtue of structure (in that *grammatical* sense). And perhaps neither (†) nor (*) qualifies as valid in virtue of structure in that compositional or grammatical sense of 'structure'. Perhaps neither then is a sentence that a theory of truth unrelativized has to validate on pain of counting as an inadequate theory of truth.

Second, I think we should distinguish between the interest of effecting a full reckoning in essentially the same terms as speakers themselves employ of the semantic and compositional resources of the language ('What are these familiar words doing here?' etc.) and a new interest. This new interest is the answer to the question 'What, *in virtue of* their linguistic practices and over and above what they say, do speakers *commit* themselves to think true? If a speaker utters sentence *s* in the sense that the theory of truth ascribes to *s*, then what *else* is he thereby committed to agree to?' Here the theorist has to predict and describe not merely the meaning that linguistic practice confers upon the sentence, but also what follows in virtue of these linguistic practices.

XIX

Let us look at (†) again in this light. Manifestly, the necessity of this conditional follows from the use that speakers make of the quantifier 'most'. That use not only justifies the truth-theorist's rendering of the word; it also justifies the semantic theorist in remarking that 'most As are Bs' is true in L if and only if the number of the concept that $\overline{A \& B}$ stands for is larger than the concept that $\overline{A \& \text{not-B}}$ stands for. This is not the theorist's truth-conditional rendering of the antecedent of (†). (That would violate condition (3) and could not qualify as an account of what speakers say by means of ⌜most As are Bs⌝.) But nevertheless it is an absolutely stable feature of their use of the sentence to make a true statement. And now, if so much is allowed, the theorist can argue as follows: No matter what subsets of a non-empty set are assigned to A and to B in the sentence ⌜most As are Bs⌝, if the sentence is true then the cardinal number of the product of these sets is more than the product of the first set with the complement of the second. But then the first cardinal number is unity at least, and there must be something which satisfies both A and B. But that suffices for the consequent to be true. So there is no interpretation of (†) that makes the antecedent true without making the consequent true. So (†) is valid, or true under all assignments from no matter what non-empty domain of entities.

XX

There is a fall-back position that some followers of Davidson may now consider retreating to, rather than make the room I am urging them to

make within the theory of meaning for the notion of truth in an interpretation. They may say that it is no new discovery that there can be
rival theories of truth that meet the formal requirement of adequacy.
(This was already implicit in the possibility of interpretation or translation being indeterminate.) What the theorist of natural language has to
do, it may be suggested, is always to prefer the theory that answers to
the requirements (1) (2) (3) in the most explanatory and enlightening
fashion. These requirements were what first prompted the theorist to
look for a theory of truth modelled on the pattern of Tarski's. And in
so far as a materially adequate theory of truth failed to validate a seemingly valid sentence belonging to the object-language for which it
defined truth, the theory would be inferior considered as a theory of
truth to any rival theory that *did* validate this conditional. (Either that,
it may be said, or the alleged formal validity is illusory.)

This is not what (1) (2) (3) (4) (4') seem to claim. But never mind
that (someone may say), it is what ought to have been claimed. And it
may be added here that, if the theorist proceeds in this way, then there
is nothing to prevent the best theory of meaning and truth taking the
form of a theory of *non*-relative truth expressly contrived to imply all
sentences with a claim to be true no matter how the non-logical expressions are supplanted by other expressions of the same type.

There would be a point in a prolonged examination of the notion of
explanatoriness this reply invokes, except that there are two intract-
able difficulties. First, in his anxiety to gather everything that counts
as meaning into conditions of non-relative truth, the defender seems to
be forced into Quine's special account of what it is for a sentence to be
valid. Instead of counting a sentence valid if it is true under all assignments to non-logical words of subsets of all non-empty domains —
which involves the idea of truth in an interpretation —, he has to count a
sentence as valid if and only if it is both true and insensitive in respect
of truth-value to all grammatical uniform replacements of non-logical
vocabulary. But these requirements need not amount to the same thing,
and the former is the more faithful general account.[31] (For instance,
unless '=' is simply stipulated to be a non-logical word, $(\exists x)(\exists y)$
$(y \neq x)$ will be valid in the one sense without being valid in the other,
viz. true with respect to all non-empty domains.)

XXI

Someone who was determined to establish a fundamental affinity between the purport of citations (4) and (4') of section 2 and the requirements (1), (2), (3) might not care very greatly about this last point. But

it will combine with another which is due to Evans[32] and was touched upon in section XVIII. What reason is there to suppose that the distinctive intuition that some valid conditionals are valid in virtue of exemplifying a distinctive grammatical or syntactical structure, e.g. [(term (verb (adverb of class K)))] ⊃ (term (verb))], can only be brought within the reach of theory by means of an assimilation of structural (or grammatically induced) validity to the formal validity of logical truths that depend upon the meaning of certain logical words like quantifiers? Indeed in the case of the logical truths themselves, we may well ask why the presence in a sentence of this or that particular logical constant, as endowed with a particular lexical meaning that is exploited by the theory of truth in an interpretation, is so often descriptively assimilated, by received accounts of logical grammar and valid inference patterns, to a compositional or structural feature of the sentence that it occurs in?

It is true that, as Wittgenstein may be held to have shown in the *Tractatus*, the lexical and the structural can be traded off against one another at the expense of the lexical. But that hardly shows that in English, as we at present have it and characterize it, the lexical and the logical can be for all purposes amalgamated in some unitary idea of the logical structure or skeleton of a sentence. Nor does it demonstrate that Davidson is well advised to see himself as *forced* to view the structural validity of 'If he ϕ-d in the bathroom, he ϕ-d' in the same sort of way as we see the logico-semantical validity of a quantificational sentence like (†) or $(x) (\phi x \supset \psi x) \supset ((\exists x) (\phi x) \supset (\exists x) (\psi x))$, whose validity depends not on composition but on the meanings of particular quantifiers and connectives.[33]

XXII

The moral I draw from the failure of 2.51 to satisfy us under any of the headings rehearsed in sections XVII and XVIII, and from the clear failure of truth theories naturally conceived to measure up to the task of accounting for such facts as the fact that (†) is true *in virtue of its meaning*, is not that there is something special or lax about the particular sort of meaning in virtue of which (†) is true, or that there is something strict and special about those aspects of strict meaning that a truth-theory will enumerate and describe. Rather, having first distinguished the theorist's enumeration and characterization of the expressive resources of a language from the further exploration by other means of what speakers commit themselves to when they make this, that or the other judgment (i.e. employ the enumerated resources in conformity

339

with the practices that sustain these particular meanings); and then having limited to the first enterprise the operation of Davidson's condition (3); I think the next step will be to attempt to say how logical form in the truth theorist's sense can seem as an *input* to the theory of truth in an interpretation (and to prepare to ask what the theory of truth in an interpretation must feed into if we are to engage with further questions of vagueness, context, etc.). Or alternatively should we rather see the simple theory of truth as a by-product of a theory of truth in an interpretation, as Evans does? Whichever of these conceptions we adopt we shall face questions that are not easy and involve much more than extrapolation from previous success. How exactly is the transition to be made back and forth between the truth-theoretic and the model theoretic representations of a sentence? Not only do these differ in ontology — we are already prepared for that — they may also differ, as they do in the 'most' case, in the *form* that they project upon the sentence. (See again the informal proof in section XIX, which requires drastic redeployment, involving both conjunction and negation, of the open sentences A and B.) This is a complication that advocates of 'meaning postulates' did not so far as I know either anticipate or provide for. How then, in the light of fresh thoughts about the provinces of the structural, the formal and the lexical, are we to reapportion all the tasks that these advocates subsumed together under one heading? When we come to face these questions, the only enemies will be our haste, our incompetence in the face of the complexity of the natural languages we actually speak, and our passion to arrive quickly at claims of the form 'All there is to strict meaning is . . .', 'Every feature of meaning can be represented by a theory having the property . . .'.

Notes

It will serve both to explain and to emphasize the scant novelty and aspirations of this essay if I record that it has resulted from the attempt to improve, expand and update the text of two lectures that I have given once a year since Autumn 1973 in London as a contribution to an intercollegiate lecture course on the philosophy of language for undergraduate students. Even after abbreviation and revision, there is much more remorseless reiteration of the obvious than chastity of taste or austerity of logic could tolerate in a research paper in semantics or in philosophy. But this is neither of these things.

1 In the first instance at least, we are concerned with Tarski's original conception of truth; that is unrelativized truth, not truth in an interpretation (which Davidson himself holds to be of less relevance to the description of meaning). See 'The Concept of Truth in

Formalized Languages' in A. Tarski, trans. J. H. Woodger, *Logic, Semantics and Metamathematics*, Oxford, 1956.

Davidson's first published article about the relation of truth and meaning was 'Truth and Meaning', *Synthèse*, 1967. He stressed the importance (which it is the purpose of this paper not to question but only to qualify) of non-relativized truth in 'In Defence of Convention T' in H. Leblanc (ed.), *Truth, Syntax and Modality*, Amsterdam, 1973.

2 The case for the emendation in question can be made out in general terms, and has been stated quite independently of the argument of the present essay. See Richard Grandy, 'Some Remarks About Logical Form' in *Noûs*, 1974; Gareth Evans, 'Semantic Structure and Logical Form' in Gareth Evans and John McDowell, *Truth and Meaning: Essays in Semantics*, Oxford, 1976. On the problem of natural language quantifiers, see also Gareth Evans, 'Pronouns, Quantifiers and Relative Clauses (II)', *Canadian Journal of Philosophy* 7, 4, 1977.

3 Donald Davidson, 'Semantics for Natural Languages' in Bruno Visenti (ed.), *Linguaggi nella Società nella Tecnica*, Milan, 1970, p. 178.

4 ibid., p. 184, my italics.

5 Donald Davidson, 'On Saying That', in D. Davidson and J. Hintikka (eds), *Words and Objections*, Holland, 1969, p. 160; my italics. And compare here Donald Davidson, 'The Logical Form of Action Sentences' in N. Rescher (ed.), *Logic and Decision*, Pittsburgh, 1967, p. 83, where Davidson speaks of the logical relation holding between 'Jones buttered the toast in the bathroom' and 'Jones buttered the toast', and embarks on the project of reflecting this logical relation by a theory of truth. (Cf. also the further explanation offered in 'Action and Reaction', *Inquiry*, 1970, especially pp. 143–4.) Whether or not we sympathize with this particular project will finally depend not so much on whether we accept Davidson's view of the proper role of a theory of truth as on whether we share his intuition that this particular entailment is in some usable sense *structural*. For the distinction of structural and formal, see Evans, 'Semantic Structure and Logical Form'.

6 'Translation' occurs essentially in Convention T Adapted and for purposes of the theory of meaning, seemingly question-beggingly. We may supplant it by amending Convention T a second time to require that the set of replacements for 'p' in 'x is true iff p' should have the following overall properties: (a) every T-sentence biconditional entailed by the theory is true, (b) the biconditionals so entailed both contribute and contribute better than any rival set — by means of the interpretation that each equivalence will put upon uses of the sentences x in assertings, commandings, questionings, etc. — to the project of attributing an intelligible collection of propositional attitudes (beliefs, desires, projects, concerns, etc.) to speakers of the language. See J. H. McDowell, 'On the Sense and Reference of a Proper Name', *Mind*, 1977 (this volume ch. 8), Davidson, 'Semantics for Natural Languages', p. 186; Evans and McDowell, op. cit.,

Editorial Introduction; and section 1 of McDowell's article, 'Truth Conditions, Bivalence, and Verificationism'. The new requirement is as controversial as the idea of the rational intelligibility of the speakers' total conduct is controversial. It is fully vague, holistic and controversial enough to replace the equally vague and controversial notion of 'translation' in Tarski's statement of Convention T. And by replacing 'translation' there, we finally clear the truth-conditions account of meaning of the charge of circularity.

7   For 'formally correct' and 'structural descriptive names' see Tarski, 'The Concept of Truth', sections 1–2 and p. 156 respectively.

8   Conditions (a) and (b), which represent an attempt to tighten up certain matters of transformation rules, homophony, etc. that have been left in a condition of mixed obscurity and laxity, are intended to exclude certain transformation-based trivializations of the programme of characterizing meaning by a truth-definition, and to expose certain speciously homophonic theories.

Caution is required in the interpretation of the constraint that requirement (b) places upon transformations. These transformations, from semantically interpretable sentences to semantically interpretable sentences, must be such that (on any reasonable pre-theoretical conception of meaning that a semantical theory should aim to articulate) the total effect of applying them to any sentence leaves its meaning unchanged. (Cf. note 6 above, if circularity is suspected.) But this does not entail that out of a set of transformations one can deduce straightforwardly any unproblematic fully generalizable principles of synonymy.

Condition (c), however vague it may be, is in practice a valuable safeguard against gratuitously indirect or *ad hoc* rules of transformation. It is also possible to imagine a future state of the study of language at which some sort of neuroscientist who requested a linguist to provide him with a compact complete description of the syntax and semantics of English might be greatly relieved if the condition had been respected.

By 'radical interpretation' I mean, in the statement of condition (b), more or less what Davidson means, e.g. in 'Radical Interpretation', *Dialectica*, 1973.

9   A sequence, say $\langle$Caesar, Augustus, Aetna . . .$\rangle$ is determined by associating with each natural number that numbers a place in the sequence, an object. Thus each place in the sequence is indexed. If σ is a sequence, then $\sigma(n)$ is the entity in the nth place of the sequence. The axioms for sequence existence are as follows:

    (i) there is at least one denumerable sequence

    (ii) for every sequence σ, for every natural number i, and for every individual y, there is a sequence σ' which differs from σ in at most the ith place, and whose i^{th} member is y.

It will sometimes serve the purpose of clarity to use in the metalanguage, in addition to sigma variables and indexed x variables, 'y' 'z' 'w'. But to arrive at the official version of any such formula supplant these by unused indexed variables 'x_1' 'x_2' . . . which are common to object and metalanguage. Even the sigma variables are thus dispensable as soon as the predicate 'sequence' becomes available in the metalanguage. Read '(for all σ) (. . .)' as e.g. '(all x_2) (if x_2 is a sequence then . . .)'.

10 Augmented in the metalanguage by the postulates of sequence theory (see foregoing note), which presuppose elementary arithmetic.

11 See Grandy, 'Some Remarks', pp. 162–3 and Evans, in Evans and McDowell, op. cit.

12 Thus, where Σ is the particular sequence ⟨Caesar, Augustus, Aetna, Aetna, Aetna . . .⟩ with Aetna filling every subsequent place, for ever, and the second member of Σ, $\Sigma(2)$, is Augustus, $\Sigma^*(\overline{x_2}) =$ Augustus. Read this as follows:
  The interpretation for the particular sequence ⟨Caesar, Augustus, Aetna, Aetna, Aetna, . . .⟩ of the variable 'x_2' is Augustus.

13 Thus our sample sequence Σ satisfies $\overline{Hx_2}$ if and only if $\Sigma^*(\overline{x_2})$, which is Augustus, is H. Remembering what 'H' abbreviates, we shall find that Σ does in fact satisfy $\overline{Hx_2}$. It does not satisfy $\overline{Hx_4}$, however, for Aetna is not a man.

14 Thus our particular sequence satisfies $\overline{\text{not } (Hx_4)}$ if and only if Σ does not satisfy $\overline{H(x_4)}$. Σ will not satisfy $\overline{H(x_4)}$ if and only if it is *not* the case that $\Sigma^*(\overline{x_4})$, which is Aetna, is a man. But Aetna is not a man. So Σ does satisfy $\overline{\text{not } H(x_4)}$.

15 See Nicholas Rescher, 'Plurality Quantification', *Journal of Symbolic Logic*, 27, 3, 1962, pp. 373–4; and compare also J. E. J. Altham and Neil W. Tennant, 'Sortal Quantification' in E. L. Keenan (ed.), *Formal Semantics of Natural Language*, Cambridge, 1975, p. 51.

16 We must not fail to recognize that the same sense, the same thought, may be variously expressed . . . it is possible for one sentence to give no more and no less information than another . . . if all transformations of the expression were forbidden on the plea that this would alter the content as well, logic would simply be crippled; for the task of logic can hardly be performed without trying to recognize the thought in its manifold guises.
(Frege, 'Concept and Object', in Geach and Black, *Translations from The Philosophical Writings of Gottlob Frege*, Oxford, 1952, p. 46n.)

17 Cf. 'Review of Husserl's *Philosophie der Arithmetik*' in Geach and Black, *Translations*, op. cit., §IV, p. 83.

18 Cf. 'On the Foundation of Geometry' as translated by Eike-Henner W. Kluge in *On the Foundations of Geometry and Formal Theories of Arithmetic*, Cambridge, Mass., 1971, p. 70:
  [In] 'whatever is greater than 1 is a positive number', the first grammatical proposition actually takes the place of the subject and the second contains the predicate belonging to it. Here we have . . . the relation of subordination of the concept *greater than 1* under the concept *positive number*.

David Wiggins

19 Such axioms should really be written in our official metalanguage.
Recasting them so as to make object-language and metalanguage
part and whole and align simultaneously the treatment of 'most'
and 'all', we should have for 2.51 (say) the following official
version:

(all x_2){ [sequence x_2], [x_2 satisfies $\overline{(\text{most } x_\text{i}) (A, B)}$ ≡
(most x_3) ($x_2(\text{i}/x_3)$ satisfies A), ($x_2(\text{i}/x_3)$ satisfies B)]}.

Here the two concepts which are arguments for the 'all' whose
scope is marked with curly brackets {. . .} are placed, each of them,
in square brackets. And the two arguments for the 'most' quantifier which is used within the complex open sentence standing for
the second argument of the 'all' are marked by round brackets.
Here as in the text overlining extends sloppily over metalogical
variables like 'A' and 'B'. It is to be treated there as inert.

To derive T-sentences as required by Convention T Amended,
the following principle of extensionality will be needed in conjunction with axioms 2.41 and 2.51:

From any object language sentence (Ωx_i) (_____ A _____)
together with any object language sentence (all x_j) (A ≡ B), to
derive the object language sentence (Ωx_i) (_____ B _____)
where A and B are well formed formulas, where Ω is either
'all' or 'most' and '(_____ A _____)' is any context of our object
language in which the formula A is embedded.

Suppose we have to prove that 'Most men are immortal' is true if
and only if most men are immortal.

Underlying this surface form we find, say,

True $\overline{(\text{most } x_4) (Hx_4, Ix_4)}$ ≡ (most x_4) (Hx_4, Ix_4)

Equivalent to the left hand side we have

a. All sequences satisfy $\overline{(\text{most } x_4) (Hx_4, Ix_4)}$

Consider an arbitrary sequence Σ

b. Σ satisfies $\overline{(\text{most } x_4) (Hx_4, Ix_4)}$

Therefore, by 2.51 of section VII,

c. (Most x_4) ($\Sigma(4/x_4)$ sats $\overline{Hx_4}$, $\Sigma(4/x_4)$ sats $\overline{Ix_4}$)

But by 2.11

d. $\Sigma(4/x_4)$ sats $\overline{Hx_4}$ ≡ $\Sigma(4/x_4)^*(\overline{x_4})$ is H

And by the definitions of $\sigma(\text{i}/z)$ and σ

e. $\Sigma(4/x_4)^*(\bar{x}_4) = x_4'$

Therefore

f. $\Sigma(4/x_4)$ sats $\overline{Hx_4}$ ≡ Hx_4.

2.12 yields a similar equivalence (g) for $\overline{Ix_4}$. Thus, using the extensionality rule to intersubstitute equivalents within the scope of
'most', we get from (c), using (f) and (g):

h. (Most x_4) (Hx_4, Ix_4).

20 Cf. 'Logische Allgemenheit' in Hermes, Kambartel, Kaulbach (eds.), *Gottlob Frege: Nachgelassene Schriften*, Hamburg, 1969, p. 280.

21 Leibniz, 'Calculus Consequentiarum' in Louis Couturat (ed.), *Opuscules et fragments inedits de Leibniz*, Paris, 1903, p. 85. This article of Leibniz was first published in volume V of C. J. Gerhardt's *Die Philosophischen Schriften von G. W. Leibniz*, Berlin, 1875-90.

22 Couturat, op. cit., p. 235.

23 Geach and Black, on Frege's review of Schroeder's *Vorlesungen über die Algebra der Logik*, p. 93n.

24 See J. Barwise, 'Axioms for abstract model theory', *Annals of Mathematical Logic*, 7, 1974, pp. 221-65, cf. pp. 239-41. I owe the reference to Wilfrid Hodges, who has also shown me that the theory of Mostowski referred to by Tennant, in 'Sortal Quantification' (see note 15 above), involving quantifiers that say how many elements of a domain satisfy an open sentence and how many elements of the domain do not satisfy it, cannot yield the generalization required to embrace natural language quantifiers like 'most'. For the theory Tennant refers to, see A. Mostowski, 'On a Generalization of Quantifiers', *Fundamenta Mathematicae*, 44, 1957, pp. 12-36.

For the comparable idea of 'sortally relativized' quantifiers see John Wallace, *Journal of Philosophy*, 72, 1965 (also his Ph.D. thesis *Philosophical Grammar*, Stanford, 1967); and Altham and Tennant, 'Sortal Quantification'. For some criticism of the last article see Evans, 'Pronouns, Quantifiers and Relative Clauses', *Canadian Journal of Philosophy*, 7, 4 (1977). Altham and Tennant would call the first of our pair of open sentences a 'sortalizer', but it is worth notice that there is in fact no genuine restriction to sortal predicates here. Consider 'All blue things are extended', for instance.

25 Cf. A. N. Prior, 'Entities', *Australasian Journal of Philosophy*, 32, 1954. Against the thought that the paradoxes of set theory have resulted from taking a universe of discourse that is 'too big', it is surely worth asking whether the thought itself admits of coherent expression. If the thought is true then it is expressible. But by what it says about how big a universe of discourse can be it surely implies that it, the very same thought, is inexpressible, and that the standpoint from which it judges is an impossible one.

It is worth noting perhaps that Boole, who is normally credited with the idea of a universe of discourse (and so with the germ at least of the idea of the range of a quantifier), explicitly allows the mode of thinking and talking that Frege insists upon. Cf. *Laws of Thought*, ch. Three, Proposition I, section 4: 'The most unfettered discourse is that in which the words we use are understood in the widest possible application, and for them the limits of discourse are coextensive with those of the universe itself.'

26 Cf. again Evans, 'Pronouns, Quantifiers and Relative Clauses (II)'.

David Wiggins

27 For a sympathetic account of the contrast see for instance
    Warren D. Goldfarb, 'Logic in the Twenties: the Nature of the
    Quantifier', *Journal of Symbolic Logic*, 44, 2, 1979.
28 For the 'logocentric predicament' see Goldfarb, op. cit., with
    references to Sheffer's review of Russell and Whitehead, *Isis* 8, pp.
    226–31; Russell, *Principles of Mathematics*, 1903, p. 15; Frege,
    'Foundations of Geometry', Part III.
29 For contextual restriction, see W. A. Hodges, *Logic*, Harmonds-
    worth, 1977, pp. 194–5.
30 See Grandy, 'Some Remarks', and Evans, 'Semantic Structure and
    Logical Form'.
31 For the variant account of quantificational validity see W. V.
    Quine, *Mathematical Logic*, Cambridge, Mass., 1940. Cf. Donald
    Davidson and Gilbert Harman in *The Logic of Grammar*, Encino,
    Calif., 1975, p. 2. For the difficulties see e.g. C. A. B. Peacocke,
    'What is a Logical Constant?', *Journal of Philosophy*, LXXIII,
    1976, pp. 222–3; cf. B. A. W. Russell, *Introduction to Mathemati-
    cal Philosophy*, ch. 18; A. M. Quinton, 'The A Priori and the Ana-
    lytic', *Proceedings of the Aristotelian Society*, 1963.
32 Evans, 'Semantic Structure and Logical Form'.
33 Cf. 'The Logical Form of Action Sentences', p. 83 and 'Action and
    Reaction', *Inquiry*, xiii, 1970, p. 144. The remark in the text is
    not to be construed as an expression of contentment with the
    predicate modifier theory of adverbs, against which Davidson's
    objections seem to me persuasive. Nor is it an objection to David-
    son's event ontology. It is a remark about Davidson's construal of
    the task that such structures present to the theorist.

Index

Index